The Yale Library of Military History

Donald Kagan and Frederick Kagan, Series Editors

A QUESTION OF COMMAND

Counterinsurgency from
the Civil War to Iraq

Mark Moyar
Foreword by Donald Kagan
and Frederick Kagan

Yale University Press New Haven & London

Published with assistance from the Kingsley Trust Association Publication Fund
established by the Scroll and Key Society of Yale College.

Set in Minion type by Tseng Information Systems, Inc.

Library of Congress Cataloging-in-Publication Data
Moyar, Mark, 1971–
A question of command : counterinsurgency from the Civil War to Iraq /
Mark Moyar ; foreword by Donald Kagan and Frederick Kagan.
p. cm. — (Yale library of military history)
Includes bibliographical references and index.
ISBN 978-0-300-15276-0 (alk. paper)
1. Counterinsurgency—History. 2. Counterinsurgency—United States—History.
3. Command of troops. I. Title.
U241.M69 2009
355.02'180973—dc22
2009013368

A catalogue record for this book is available from the British Library.

This paper meets the requirements of ANSI/NISO Z39.48–1992 (Permanence of Paper).

To the armed forces of the United States,
sentinels on the parapets of freedom

Contents

Foreword by Donald Kagan and Frederick Kagan   ix

Preface   xiii

Acknowledgments   xv

1. Leader-Centric Warfare   1
2. The Civil War   15
3. Reconstruction in the South   33
4. The Philippine Insurrection   63
5. The Huk Rebellion   89
6. The Malayan Emergency   109
7. The Vietnam War   133
8. The Salvadoran Insurgency   169
9. The War in Afghanistan   191
10. The Iraq War   213
11. How to Win   259

Appendix: Counterinsurgency Leadership Survey   287

Notes   303

Select Bibliography   333

Index   339

Illustrations follow page 124

Foreword

War has been a subject of intense interest across the ages. Very early literary works like Homer's *Iliad* and the Rigvedic hymns of ancient India talk of war. Few can fail to be stirred by such questions: How and why do wars come about? How and why do they end? Why did the winners win and the losers lose? How do leaders make life-and-death decisions? Why do combatants follow orders that put their lives at risk? How do individuals and societies behave in war, and how are they affected by it? Recent events have raised the study of war from one of intellectual interest to a matter of vital importance to America and the world. Ordinary citizens must understand war in order to choose their leaders wisely, and leaders must understand it if they are to prevent wars where possible and win them when necessary.

This series, therefore, seeks to present the keenest analyses of war in its different aspects, the sharpest evaluations of political and military decision-making, and descriptive accounts of military activity that illuminate its human elements. It will do so drawing on the full range of military history from ancient times to the present and in every part of the globe in order to make available to the general public readable and accurate scholarly accounts of this most fascinating and dangerous of human activities.

Events of the twenty-first century have turned the attention of military historians and their readers from the more conventional conflicts between great armies in the field to the modes of fighting employed by irregulars, terrorists, and insurgents. Wars in Afghanistan, Iraq, and elsewhere have posed difficult problems for those nations that need to engage and defeat unconventional forces that threaten their national interests and security. In this up-to-date study, *A Question of Command,* Mark Moyar brings a new focus to the problem of counterinsurgency warfare: leadership.

Some have argued that modern counterinsurgents win by creating superior human "networks" or by sustaining the popular will to endure the onerous costs of counterinsurgency. Other views center on the belief that the best way to defeat insurgents is to destroy them with force. The most popular view, embraced by the highly influential *U.S. Army/Marine Corps Counterinsurgency Field Manual* and most other recent texts, holds that defeating insurgency hinges on understanding the nature of the insurgency and selecting methods that will win the people's hearts and minds.

Mark Moyar challenges all of this conventional wisdom, asserting that the key to counterinsurgency success is selecting commanders who are rich in certain leadership attributes. He rejects the view of the hearts-and-minds school that economic, social, and political reforms deserve high priority in resource allocation, and instead recommends focusing resources on security, civil administration, and leadership development. In addition, he calls for a new calculus in determining whether to intervene in future insurgent conflicts, arguing that cost projections should be based primarily on evaluation of the elites that will provide the leaders for the insurgents and the counterinsurgents.

Through a series of case studies stretching from Ulysses S. Grant to General David Petraeus, Moyar identifies the ten critical attributes of counterinsurgency leadership and shows why some governments have fared much better than others in developing and selecting counterinsurgency leaders. From the history of these conflicts, he draws out lessons that can be applied now and in the future. His analysis of today's U.S. military and its allied partners in Afghanistan and Iraq offers compelling guidance for a dramatic revamping of personnel systems.

The events of the past decade foretell American engagement in counterinsurgency for years to come, making it imperative that we educate our policymakers, military leaders, and citizens on this crucial subject. *A Question of Command* should shake up the study of counterinsurgency and take a place among the standard readings on irregular warfare. Wholly original, this book makes a thoughtful and well-supported case that "counterinsurgency is 'leader-centric' warfare, a contest between elites in which the elite with superiority in certain leadership attributes usually wins."

Donald Kagan and Frederick Kagan

Preface

The inspiration for this book germinated in the early 1990s with interviews of American and South Vietnamese veterans of the Phoenix program, a counterinsurgency initiative aimed at destroying the Viet Cong's leadership during the later stages of the Vietnam War. Having read the standard Vietnam War histories before conducting the interviews, I asked these veterans why the South Vietnamese forces were ineffective at counterinsurgency. To my surprise, the interviewees almost invariably responded that the premise of the question was incorrect, as some of the South Vietnamese forces were very effective. Having read many of the standard counterinsurgency texts, I asked whether those forces were effective because of good training, favorable social and economic conditions, use of sound counterinsurgency methods, or U.S. advisory and financial support. It was none of those things, they said. The effectiveness of South Vietnamese units, the interviewees explained, was determined by the quality of their commanders. If the unit's leader was good, then the unit obtained intelligence and other forms of cooperation from the villagers, aggressively hunted down insurgents, and captured or killed large numbers of enemy personnel. If the unit's leader was poor, then the unit alienated the population, shunned contact with the enemy, and endured heavy losses when attacked. Over the next fifteen years, my research for two books on the Vietnam War turned up overwhelming evidence that leadership was the key to success at all times and in all aspects of countering the Viet Cong insurgents.

In the spring of 2005, as a recently arrived professor at the U.S. Marine

Corps Command and Staff College, I was directed to create a new course to prepare mid-level military officers for Iraq, Afghanistan, and other conflicts that demanded recourse to forms of power other than conventional military force. It was part of a broader Marine Corps effort to increase education in subjects related to counterinsurgency. Perusing the huge list of counterinsurgencies past and present, I chose for the course those that seemed most capable of yielding lessons applicable in the twenty-first century. Teaching the course in the ensuing years revealed that leadership was as crucial, and as underappreciated, in those conflicts as in the Vietnam War. In the middle of 2007, with the streets of Baghdad running red with American and Iraqi blood, with Americans at home engaging in bitter recrimination, I decided to postpone the second volume of a two-volume history of the Vietnam War to write this book on counterinsurgency leadership, using as case studies many of the counterinsurgencies covered in the Marine Corps Command and Staff College course.

This book is intended to assist counterinsurgents in Iraq, where the situation has greatly improved in the year that passed during its completion; in Afghanistan, where the situation has not improved so much; and wherever else tyrannical insurgents threaten. Its conclusions are not to be found in the counterinsurgency books currently in use at our service academies, military graduate schools, counterinsurgency training facilities, or civilian national security institutions. Nor are they found in *The U.S. Army/Marine Corps Counterinsurgency Field Manual* that was published in December 2006 and widely acclaimed as the new gospel on counterinsurgency. Although the manual's list of best counterinsurgency practices includes "Embed quality advisors and special forces with host-nation forces," it makes no mention of empowering quality American or host-nation commanders. That practice, I shall argue, is the most important one of all.

Acknowledgments

Few places in the world afford such a favorable setting for the study of counterinsurgency and leadership as the U.S. Marine Corps University, where I have been privileged to teach for the past five years. Veterans of the present wars in Iraq and Afghanistan and other recent counterinsurgencies, like those in Somalia and Colombia, fill the halls and classrooms, carrying with them knowledge and memories that are rarely found in so concentrated a form. They have a staggering range of perspectives and experiences, coming from all of the U.S. armed services, a variety of civilian agencies, and dozens of foreign countries. I would like to thank all of the students and faculty who have graciously and patiently shared their thoughts and recollections with me. This book is much the better for their assistance.

It would be impossible to name all of the military officers in the United States, Iraq, and Afghanistan who provided insights and served as sounding boards for ideas, but I will mention those whom I interviewed formally or with whom I spoke at great length. During 2007 and 2008, I had the good fortune to discuss counterinsurgency leadership with General George W. Casey, Jr., General Charles C. Krulak, General James N. Mattis, General David Petraeus, Lieutenant General David W. Barno, Lieutenant General John Cooper, Major General George J. Flynn, Major General John F. Kelly, Major General Douglas M. Stone, Brigadier General H. R. McMaster, and Brigadier General John A. Toolan. I have also enjoyed the privilege of speaking with Colonel Anthony Abati, Colonel Dale Alford, Captain Aaron D. Anderberg, Colonel Allen Batschelet, Lieutenant Colonel Jason A. Beaudoin, Brigadier General Manuel Martins Branco, Colonel Willy Buhl, Lieutenant Colonel Frederick E. Cale, Major Patrick J. Cashman, Major Brian S. Christmas, Major Mark H. Clingan, Major Carl E. Cooper, Colonel Frank Corte, Colonel Lewis Craparotta, Colonel Stephen W. Davis, Major J. R. Deimel, Major Oliver H. Dunham, Colonel Todd Ebel, Major Keith A. Forkin, Lieutenant Colonel Mark Grdovic, Colonel Timothy A. Green, Major Robert M. Hancock, Colonel Jeff M. Haynes, Major Brendan Heatherman, Colonel Bill Hix, Colonel Michael L. Howard, Major Kevin Hutchison, Lieutenant Colonel Darin S. Morris, Lieutenant Colonel Jason L. Morris, Colonel Michael F. Morris, Colonel Nicholas F. Nanna, Major Edward T. Nevgloski, Major Michael B. Prosser, Lieutenant Colonel Larry Redmon, Colonel Patrick Redmon, Colonel Shawn M. Reinwald, Colonel Ritch Rodebaugh, Lieutenant Colonel Michael V. Samarov, Colonel Jeffrey A. Schaf, Lieutenant Colonel Wayne A. Sinclair, Major Adam Strickland, Major Jeffrey J. Stower, Major Robb A. Sucher, Lieutenant Colonel Alex Vohr, Lieutenant Colonel Richard R. Warmbold, Colonel James L. Welsh, and Colonel Billy West.

The U.S. Marine Corps and CENTCOM made possible a visit to Iraq and Afghanistan in the spring of 2008 that enabled me to see contemporary counterinsurgency firsthand. Colonel Thomas C. Greenwood and Lieutenant Colonel William H. Vivian set me on the right track, and Lieutenant Colonel Shawn Keefe and Colonel Patrick Kanewske pushed me along it. Once I reached the CENTCOM area of operations, I was able to visit the right people and places with help from Colonel Steve Boylan, Lieutenant Colonel John K. Carroll, Master Sergeant Marcial Flores, Lieutenant Colonel Claudia Foss, Captain Rebecca Garcia, Colonel Robin Gentry, Major Chris Gillette, Lieutenant Colonel Mark S. Harrington, Colonel Thomas R. Kelly, Master Sergeant Richard A. Krause, Chief Warrant Officer 2 Michael M. Osilla, Major Corinna Robinson, Lieutenant Colonel Joseph Yoswa, and the staff of the 201st Corps advisory group.

I am grateful to the veterans of the wars in Iraq and Afghanistan who filled out the survey on counterinsurgency leadership that is located at the back of this book. These respondents, most them holding ranks from captain to colonel, provided hard data on subjects for which the evidence had previously been thin. Their written comments, too lengthy to include in this volume in their entirety, influenced my thinking on a variety of leadership issues.

Lieutenant Colonel John Nagl at Fort Riley and Dr. James Willbanks at Fort Leavenworth went beyond the call of duty in helping me find suitable veterans for the survey.

I was also most fortunate that drafts of the historical chapters were reviewed by some of the world's leading experts on the counterinsurgencies in question—Andrew Birtle, John Coates, Anthony James Joes, Brian M. Linn, and Kalev Sepp. These individuals were invaluable in helping to sort facts from the fictions that appear in some accounts of these wars, and their critiques helped me refine my interpretations, even if we did not always agree entirely. Anonymous readers commissioned by Yale University Press and the Smith Richardson Foundation also offered useful comments. Bert Moyar and Susan Vohr read the entire manuscript and corrected errors and infelicities. In addition, I benefited from correspondence with other experts on these conflicts, including Sarah Chayes, Sandy Cochran, Conrad Crane, Ali Jalali, Peter Mansoor, Sultana Parvanta, Lewis Sorley, and Amin Tarzi. Responsibility for any errors or omissions is, of course, mine alone.

While working on this book, I had opportunities to discuss some of my preliminary findings with a number of senior government officials and military officers. I hope that they gained from our interaction; I know I did, and for that I owe them an extra dose of appreciation.

Special thanks go to Kim T. Adamson, the U.S. Marine Corps University Foundation, and the Smith Richardson Foundation for providing funding for this project. Brigadier General Thomas Draude and Lieutenant Colonel John Hales of the Marine Corps University Foundation and Nadia Schadlow and Marin Strmecki of the Smith Richardson Foundation were generous of their time and energy. Major General Donald R. Gardner, the president of the Marine Corps University, was also instrumental in advancing this project. Susan Vohr and Carol-Anne Parker accelerated its completion through their help with a broad array of tasks, bringing to bear their extraordinary attention to detail and putting in extra hours at crunch time.

I enjoyed the services of an indefatigable agent, Alexander Hoyt. At Yale University Press, Chris Rogers was quick to see the potential of this project and bring it to fruition, and Mary Pasti took the book through the editorial process with exceptional vigilance and diligence. Don Larson and Mary Swab of Mapping Specialists promptly and efficiently produced the maps that appear at the beginning of the chapters. Frank Smith of Cambridge University

Press gave me a reprieve from my other publishing commitments to get this book done. As always, my parents, Bert and Marjorie Moyar, were a constant source of support.

My largest debt of gratitude goes to my wife, Kelli, and our children, Greta, Trent, and Luke. Hours that I would have liked to have spent with them were spent instead completing this study. I devoted those extra hours in order to publish the book as rapidly as possible, in the hope that it will benefit the American troops serving in Iraq and Afghanistan and their allies, for whose toils all Americans should be thankful.

A Question of Command

CHAPTER 1

Leader-Centric Warfare

Had someone predicted ten years ago that counterinsurgency would be a leading topic in the White House in 2009, or that popular television shows would run features on counterinsurgency doctrine, or that the U.S. government would be spending billions of dollars on counterinsurgency research, the prophecy would have been relegated to the company of Al Capone's vaults and the Jupiter Effect. In 1999, Americans viewed counterinsurgency as passé, of interest only to antiquarians, for Vietnam had taught us to steer clear of insurgencies. On the rare occasion when a conference on counterinsurgency was held, it was attended by a few grizzled Vietnam veterans and an even smaller number of scholars who had haplessly devoted years to such an unfashionable subject.

The National Security Strategy that the United States published in 1999 made no mention of counterinsurgency; it deemed America's principal national security challenges to be negotiating international peace agreements, reforming international commerce, and curbing proliferation of weapons of mass destruction. It discussed the U.S. military mainly in terms of how it could deter aggression and promote cooperation with other nations.[1] Most elements of the American military were themselves focused on either conventional warfare or peacekeeping. Even within the military educational system, where the study of warfare was exalted, counterinsurgency specialists were generally viewed as purveyors of eight-track tapes in an age of digital music.

Tragically, the outbreaks of insurgency in Afghanistan and Iraq turned counterinsurgency into the most important problem confronting the United States in the early twenty-first century. They also made counterinsurgency a high-growth industry, attracting attention and money from defense contractors, military research institutes, and private think tanks. The result has been a deluge of counterinsurgency studies. The most valuable ones have focused on individual cases of counterinsurgency or on specialized topics across multiple subjects, such as disarmament, doctrine, or advisory duty.[2] Considerably less progress has been made in identifying how to achieve success in counterinsurgency. The trees have been seen better than the forest.

The forest has not been misperceived for want of effort. Theorizing about success in counterinsurgency has surged since 2001, with most of it emanating from political scientists and military officers trained in political science.[3] The "network-centric warfare" concept of the 1990s, which held that future wars would be won by technologically driven networks, was seemingly vindicated by the initial successes in Afghanistan and Iraq in 2001 and 2003, respectively, but the bubble of technological omnipotence was soon burst by the failure of high technology to defeat Afghan and Iraqi insurgents. New theorizing about network-centric warfare has emerged, however, according to which modern counterinsurgencies are to be won by human-driven networks that employ all types of power with little hierarchical direction.[4] Another novel theory maintains that success in counterinsurgency is determined by a country's willingness to tolerate the horrible brutality and heavy casualties supposedly inherent in effective counterinsurgency.[5]

Most of the recent theorists have written works supporting a somewhat older theory of counterinsurgency, the "population-centric" or "hearts-and-minds" theory, and as a consequence, this theory suffuses the new *U.S. Army/Marine Corps Counterinsurgency Field Manual* and most other texts assigned to military officers today. According to the theory's adherents, success in defeating insurgents lies in understanding the nature of the insurgency and devising sound methods, both military and nonmilitary, to deprive the insurgents of the support of the people, whose opinions are the primary determinant of the war's outcome.[6] Social, political, and economic reforms must be implemented, say the theorists, to redress the grievances that cause people to support the insurgents. Examples of these reforms include promoting public participation in government, providing jobs or services to the poor, and recruiting people into self-defense organizations. Counterinsurgents should use as little force as possible because the use of force tends to alienate the population. Security forces should not be used to seek out and destroy insurgent armed forces but only to protect the population from exploitation and harm by the insurgents. While some of these theorists acknowledge that leadership can be a factor in the outcome of an insurgent conflict, they treat it as one of many factors of relatively similar weight, such as training, logistics, foreign support, morale, and economic conditions.

The most well-known school of thought after the population-centric school is the "enemy-centric" school, which contends that the best way to defeat insurgents is to destroy their will and capabilities with coercion and armed force.[7] One group within this school advocates using violence against the insurgency's civilian supporters as well as its armed forces, a position with few advocates in the West today because of Western sensitivity to civilian casualties.[8] A larger group maintains that counterinsurgent violence need only focus on the armed insurgents, for the rest of the population can be sufficiently cowed through threats, nonviolent punishments, and the annihilation of insurgent armed forces.[9]

This book holds that counterinsurgency is "leader-centric" warfare, a contest between elites in which the elite with superiority in certain leadership attributes usually wins. The better elite gains the assistance of more people and uses them to subdue or destroy the enemy elite and its supporters. Elements of this view of counterinsurgency have been articulated by counterinsurgency practitioners and a small number of historians and contemporary commentators, and some are contained in such classic counterinsurgency treatises as the *Small Wars Manual* of the U.S. Marine Corps and *Counterinsurgency Warfare: Theory and Practice* by David Galula.[10] But no previous attempt has been made to present this interpretation comprehensively or to find supporting evidence from a wide range of cases. Nor, indeed, has any previous book focused on counterinsurgency leadership, despite the proliferation of books analyzing either counterinsurgency or leadership.

Whereas the population-centric theory considers the people's social, political, and economic grievances to be the foremost cause of popular insurgencies, the leader-centric theory maintains that a talented insurgent elite, which may or may not be motivated by such grievances, is the principal cause. The masses, however aggrieved, do not turn into insurgents on their own; they become insurgents only by following an elite that has decided to lead an insurgency, and only if that elite appears to be more virtuous and capable than the governmental elite. Consequently, insurgencies tend to be strongest where the insurgents enjoy the greatest advantage over the counterinsurgents in leadership quality, not where the people live in the most objectionable conditions.

The insurgent elite almost always has higher levels of education than most of its followers, and different motives, although elites and followers may share some of the same grievances. The elite tends to be more ideologically driven, and it seldom relents when the government acts to redress grievances, dismissing such efforts as devious counterinsurgent tricks. Only the threat or use of force can stop the hard-core insurgent leaders from attacking the counterinsurgents. To wield force in that manner with adequate consistency, the counterinsurgents must establish security in and around the populace by means of military domination. The establishment of security also prevents uncommitted elites and the uncommitted masses from abetting the insurgent elite because it denies the insurgents the access required to persuade and coerce civilians and because civilians of all cultures are inclined to favor the militarily dominant side, as it is more likely to protect them from harm.

The foregoing realities confirm the assertion of enemy-centric theorists that security is paramount in all counterinsurgencies. The enemy-centrists, however, do not appreciate the importance of leadership in attaining security. Nor do they recognize that talented leaders have won people to their side through more than just force, principally through charisma, sociability, and good governance, while poor leaders have driven people toward the opposing side by their deficiencies in these three areas. In assessing a government during an insurgency, elites and masses put a premium on persuasive communications, impartial law enforcement, incorruptibility, and respect for personal property, all of which depend on the character of the leaders. Major social, economic, or political changes, to which population-centric theorists attach great weight, have historically had much less impact. Such changes have, in certain instances, gained the counterinsurgents some supporters among the masses and uncommitted elites, but they have rarely turned a losing war into a winning one, and they have never done so in the absence of good leadership and armed force.

If, as the population-centric school of thought maintains, counterinsurgency were primarily a question of finding the right methods—or tactics, techniques, and procedures, as they are known in military parlance—then victory would be won easily once the proper methods were identified. History, however, does not record such outcomes. Sound counterinsurgency methods dictated from on high, in the form of orders or doctrine, have consistently failed when good leaders were lacking. The installation of good leaders, by contrast, has most often produced success even if those individuals were not told in detail how to do their job.[11]

Some broad principles do apply to every, or almost every, counterinsurgency. They have been understood for centuries, and they have been inscribed in countless publications. Examples are:

- Obtaining intelligence on the insurgents is essential to success.
- Civil and military authorities should work closely together in countering the insurgents.
- Counterinsurgents should strive to gain the assistance of the population.
- Local self-defense forces are an effective means of obstructing insurgent activities.
- Counterinsurgent security forces should maintain a permanent presence in populous areas.

Aside from basic administrative and military methods, however, the specific tactics, techniques, and procedures for putting these principles into practice— for instance, methods for obtaining intelligence or organizing self-defense units—apply only in certain circumstances. Counterinsurgency requires different methods from one place to another because of differences in the local population, the insurgent forces, the counterinsurgent forces, and the terrain. It requires different methods from one moment in time to another because the insurgents change their behavior frequently, often in response to the actions of the counterinsurgents. Studying counterinsurgency methods that have worked elsewhere is valuable in providing the commander with ideas, but the effective commander must be able to determine which ideas are transferable and which are not, and to adapt methods and create new ones, abilities in which not all commanders are equal. Then the commander must be able to implement the methods effectively, usually the most difficult part of all.[12]

Decentralized command has been the hallmark of effective counterinsurgency since ancient times, except in those cases where insurgents and counterinsurgents clashed with large conventional forces. National leaders and intermediate leaders—those between the national leaders and the local leaders—typically communicate the mission and a list of restrictions to local commanders and then let the local commanders decide how to accomplish the mission. Neither today nor at any time in the past has decentralization involved eliminating hierarchy entirely and replacing it with self-sustaining "networks" that cooperate without leadership. Counterinsurgency command remains hierarchical at the local level, with leaders—typically company or battalion commanders or civil officials with equivalent authority—providing crucial direction to subordinates. Efforts to produce networks without strong leadership have consistently failed because the various entities became inert or unruly or because they went off in their own directions.

At the local level, successful counterinsurgency commanders select methods and adjust them repeatedly to capitalize on changes in the insurgent environment before the enemy does. National and intermediate leaders have usually been most successful not when they have identified appropriate methods, although some have helped in this regard, but when they have installed able subordinate commanders, monitored their performance, and coached them. Regardless of how brilliant or dynamic the national and intermediate leaders are, they do not achieve success in counterinsurgency when their local commanders are devoid of leadership abilities. Good local commanders, on the other hand, can succeed under poor senior commanders, provided that the latter do not micromanage or impose undue constraints.

The talented local commander can also be thwarted if forced to comply with poor counterinsurgency doctrine, poor strategy, or poor national policy. A doctrine or strategy that dictates in detail how to defeat the insurgents will compel at least some local commanders to adopt methods that are ill suited to local conditions. Strategy or policy may permit hostile foreign forces to intrude into the counterinsurgency theater and wreak havoc on the counterinsurgents, nullifying the achievements of good local leadership. At times, strategy or policy allocates fewer personnel or material resources to local counterinsurgents than even the best counterinsurgency commander needs in order to succeed.

More often, strategy or policy inhibits success by neglecting or undermining the process of appointing counterinsurgency commanders. Time and again, when choosing which elites should lead the organizations prosecuting the war, counterinsurgent strategists and policymakers have selected elites without the proper leadership capabilities or, by accident or design, excluded elites who did not take kindly to being excluded. Such decisions have resulted in countless deaths and maimings and in the destruction of governments and societies. For reasons of both humanity and national security, therefore, strategists and policymakers must learn the dynamics of counterinsurgency leadership before issuing any decrees that confer or strip authority.

Counterinsurgency experts who acknowledge the importance of leadership in counterinsurgency often treat it as a factor that is fixed and thus not worthy of much attention. Many a senior leader, adhering to this view, has made no effort to upgrade counterinsurgency commanders. Yet, as the cases in this book illustrate, numerous senior leaders have been able to effect major changes in the quality of leadership at lower levels. They have done so by replacing weak commanders with strong ones or, over an extended period of time, by developing new leaders.

The tasks of finding and developing the right leaders and getting them into key command positions are far more complex and daunting than is generally recognized. Counterinsurgents vary widely in their ability to accomplish these tasks, which results in massive differences in overall effectiveness. The surest way to test an individual's suitability for counterinsurgency leadership is to put that person in command of a unit engaged in counterinsurgency operations. But determining how well a commander is performing can consume much precious time, and the price of failure is tallied in blood, so every effort must be made to estimate aptitude before handing authority to an officer untested in the cauldron of experience. The best way to predict the suitability of inexperienced candidates for counterinsurgency command or counterinsurgency leadership development programs is to screen them for the characteristics common to effective counterinsurgency commanders.[13]

Only a very few attempts have been made to identify those characteristics, and they have been incomplete.[14] As a consequence, one of the principal objectives of this book is to identify the critical attributes of effective counterinsurgency leaders. Analysis of the seven past counterinsurgencies and two present-day counterinsurgencies covered here reveals that ten attributes have consistently been the most important. The most valuable attributes did not vary from case to case despite wide variations in the nature of the insurgents and the counterinsurgents, although the relative importance of each attribute did vary according to the dynamics of the insurgency and the level of the counterinsurgency commander in the counterinsurgency hierarchy.

In some of the cases, the insurgents operated primarily in rural areas; in others, they were almost exclusively in the cities. Insurgents operated in small, loosely connected groups that seldom mustered more than a few dozen men for battle, or they had strong hierarchical organizations that fielded conventionally outfitted soldiers in battalion strength. Whereas some insurgent groups sought radical political and social change, others were fighting simply to displace a governing elite that they considered alien or unjust. Established elites, newly empowered elites, foreign elites, and transnational elites played varying roles on both the insurgent and the counterinsurgent sides, and foreign militaries operated independently as counterinsurgents, under the control of indigenous authorities, or as advisers to indigenous forces. The states on whose behalf the counterinsurgents fought included both democracies and autocracies, both independent nations and colonial possessions. Some of the states were scions of Western or Latin American civilizations, others of Middle Eastern or Far Eastern civilizations. The same leadership attributes produced success in these diverse circumstances because all of the insurgent environments shared two essential characteristics: they all hosted contests between human elites, and they all presented variations and changes that demanded frequent adaptation.

The Ten Attributes of Effective Counterinsurgency Leaders

1. Initiative

This attribute has two parts, both of which are critical for success. The first is the ability to act without specific guidance from above, which is of obvious importance in an enterprise like counterinsurgency where authority is usually decentralized. The second is the propensity to act energetically and aggressively, which enables counterinsurgents to preempt the insurgents, fight them on favorable terms, and invigorate all counterinsurgent programs, military as well as nonmilitary. When commanders lack initiative or when their initiative is stifled by others through excessive demands and restrictions, their troops lack enthusiasm and vigor, their enemies organize the population and prepare for battle without hindrance, and counterinsurgency assets suffer attacks at the time and place of the enemy's choosing.

2. Flexibility

Counterinsurgency's changing circumstances and numerous activities demand the flexibility to switch rapidly from one type of thought or action to another. No matter how much training and education the counterinsurgent leaders have received and no matter what doctrinal publications they hold in their hands, they will encounter unfamiliar challenges that require divergence from established practices. Individuals lacking flexibility, of whom there are many, will rely on standard tactics, techniques, and procedures rather than accept new ones of greater utility. Flexibility also helps leaders deal effectively with the moral and political ambiguities endemic to counterinsurgency warfare.

3. Creativity

With counterinsurgency leaders, as with anyone, creativity comes in many varieties. Officers at higher levels may generate new counterinsurgency methods that have broad applicability across the theater of operations. More often, creativity occurs at the local level, where counterinsurgents regularly encounter new problems of such diversity and unpredictability as to render them immune to textbook solutions. Creative thinkers who prefer abstraction often come up with new methods that solve recurring problems across a given area, while more practical creative thinkers excel at improvising solutions to immediate problems. Recent pronouncements about "adaptive leadership" sometimes give the impression that creativity and flexibility are the same, but in fact one quality is often present without the other. Flexible officers who are not very creative do not develop new methods well but are adept at implementing new methods created by others. Creativity without flexibility entails a reluctance to challenge constraints, which limits the space in which creativity can operate.

4. Judgment

Judgment, the use of logic and intuition to evaluate information and make sound decisions, enables commanders to discern which methods and actions will work against the particular insurgents they face. Weighing the multitude of complex, competing, and changing factors that shape, and are shaped by, counterinsurgency actions challenges the most powerful of human intellects. A decision on whether to shoot back at insurgents firing from a village, for instance, necessitates an estimate of the insurgent casualties that the return fire would inflict, the damage it would cause to the village's economy, the influence it would exert on the minds of the villagers and village officials, the reaction it would generate through national and international media, and the impact it would have upon the morale of the counterinsurgents who are under fire. At higher levels of command, judgment is also required to determine how well subordinate commanders are performing and to decide whether underperforming commanders should be reprimanded or relieved.

5. Empathy

Empathy enables leaders to appreciate the thoughts and feelings of others, thereby boosting their ability to anticipate the consequences of actions. This asset is of obvious value in influencing the civilian populace in an insurgent conflict. It also permits commanders to inspire their subordinates effectively and to gain cooperation from other commanders. Empathetic commanders are also better than others at forecasting the enemy's next moves.

6. Charisma

Acting partly through the subconscious and the irrational, the charisma of counterinsurgency commanders makes people more willing to follow their lead and more vigorous and resolute in their actions. Charisma in a commander acts not only on subordinates but also on every other friendly or neutral person the commander touches. Although charismatic leaders wield influence in all cultures, some of the characteristics that make for a charismatic leader vary from one culture to another.

7. Sociability

Through one-on-one interaction, sociable leaders impress and influence others in the insurgent environment. Sociability and charisma do not necessarily go together—more than a few leaders with the charisma to inspire groups during speeches or in the heat of combat are unable to move an individual during a conversation, and vice versa. Counterinsurgency commanders must talk with leaders of other organizations and other nationalities to obtain their cooperation in all manner of endeavors, and they speak regularly with citizens who can provide invaluable assistance. Cultivating relations with the media, a crucial task in nations with a free press, likewise requires extensive personal interaction. In addition, sociable commanders tend to spend more time than unsocial commanders visiting those under their command, which enhances their capacity for influencing and monitoring subordinates.

8. Dedication

Effective counterinsurgency leadership involves grueling labor, frequent movement through insecure areas, long workdays, and the danger of assassination. Individuals of modest dedication will avoid these costs by neglecting important tasks, staying inside headquarters, or minimizing operations. They may quit altogether. Dedicated officers will work twenty-hour days and lead patrols into insurgent-infested territory even as men collapse or die around them. In the vicious Darwinian world of counterinsurgency, victory is sometimes decided by perseverance.

9. Integrity

Counterinsurgency commanders are vested with considerable authority and resources so that they can act swiftly and forcefully against fierce, cunning adversaries. Because they often operate with little supervision and few rules, possibilities for abuse of power are endless. Among the abuses most tempting to counterinsurgency leaders are corruption, extortion, favoritism in law enforcement, unwarranted use of force against civilians, and mistreatment of prisoners. Leaders of integrity, whose conscience tells them that such acts are wrong, resist these temptations and, through example and discipline, prevent those under their command from perpetrating abuses of power. Absent integrity, counterinsurgency leaders are prone to commit every imaginable infraction and to permit subordinates to do the same, which fuels domestic and international hatred of the counterinsurgents.

10. Organization

Counterinsurgency commanders must excel at organizing people and actions if they are to prevent the derailment or collision of the numerous complex activities which it is their duty to direct. Well-organized commanders maintain discipline and regularly check on subordinates to ensure that they are carrying out their assigned tasks effectively and staying out of mischief. They keep civilians involved in valuable projects, preventing them from siding with the insurgents. Organizational ability also comes in handy when commanders restructure organizations or build new ones, as they often do in counterinsurgency.

Extremely few leaders rate high in all ten of the key attributes, but excellent performance requires superiority in only a substantial number of them. The nine cases reviewed here, as well as voluminous psychological research, show that an individual's levels of most of these ten attributes are partially determined by heredity.[15] They are shaped, moreover, by the cultures in which individuals have been immersed and the families in which individuals have been reared, which further impede attempts to enhance those attributes, because cultures and their effects have shown themselves very resistant to deliberate change. But most of the attributes can be boosted through self-improvement and practice, and senior leaders can enhance them further in their subordinate commanders by coaching and inspiring them, setting the proper command climate, and providing the right types of training and education. The case studies show which attributes can be increased, and how.

Two other important aspects of effective counterinsurgency leadership will be explored at length in this book. The first is the advantage of shared identity. People the world over are more willing to follow a leader who belongs to their own group or groups than a leader who does not, whether the group is ethnic, tribal, religious, political, socioeconomic, or cultural, so it is advantageous to assign leaders to followers with the same group affiliations. There have been, however, many instances where people enthusiastically followed strong leaders who did not belong to their groups.

The second is the advantage of experience. Experience can augment leadership attributes, provide valuable knowledge about leadership and counterinsurgency, and command the respect of others. In general, commanders at the lowest levels fare considerably better if they have at least a few years of leadership experience under their belts, and the top local commanders usually do better with ten or more years of experience. It does not have to be experience in counterinsurgency, and very often it is not; leadership experience in high-intensity war, in peacetime armed forces, or in other types of organizations usually suffices. Experienced leaders who lack counterinsurgency experience will, however, benefit from introduction to basic principles. The experience factor rises to special prominence when commanders are created or replaced in great numbers, as will be seen in several of the cases.

Counterinsurgents seeking to put the most suitable officers into the most important command positions often encounter enormous impediments, such as internal politics, rigid personnel policies, and nepotism. The case studies in this book reveal the methods that counterinsurgents have employed to overcome the obstacles and put excellent leaders into critical commands. As with other counterinsurgency methods, most are not universally applicable, so their implementation itself requires good leadership.

For all of the nine cases, only a small fraction of what transpired in the leadership realm was recorded by contemporary observers or historians. For the two present wars, moreover, much of the recorded information is not yet available to outside researchers. Consequently, it is not possible to cover every important aspect of counterinsurgency leadership in each chapter. But these aspects surface in enough of the chapters to permit valid conclusions. Those conclusions are summarized in the final chapter.

Studying a variety of historical insurgencies imparts a familiarity with counterinsurgency leadership and methods that theories alone cannot provide. It also illuminates the importance of political, social, cultural, and military contexts. With few exceptions, crafting remedies to leadership problems and the other problems of counterinsurgency requires keen analysis of local contexts and their relevance to counterinsurgency warfare.

Books on counterinsurgency can actually undermine counterinsurgents by revealing counterinsurgency methods or principles to which the insurgents can then develop countermeasures. This book does not fit into that category. The insurgents in Afghanistan and Iraq recognize the importance of leadership in counterinsurgency—which is why they are killing counterinsurgent leaders in regrettably large numbers. It is mainly the West, with its cerebral assumptions about the nature of human affairs, that does not recognize the leader-centric nature of counterinsurgency and will profit to learn it.

BRITISH TERRITORY

Minnesota

Dakota
Territory

Michigan

VT

New
York

Wisconsin

Nebraska
Territory

Iowa

Ohio

PA

NJ

MD DE

Illinois

IN

Kansas
Territory

Missouri

Kentucky

W. Va.

Virginia
Apr. 17, 1861

North Carolina
May 20, 1861

Unorganized
Territory

Arkansas
May 6,
1861

Tennessee
May 7, 1861

South
Carolina
Dec. 20,
1860

Alabama
Jan. 11,
1861

Georgia
Jan. 19,
1861

Miss.
Jan. 9,
1861

ATLANTIC
OCEAN

Texas
Feb. 1, 1861

Louisiana
Jan. 26, 1861

Florida
Jan. 10,
1861

Gulf of Mexico

MEXICO

SECESSION, 1860–1861

States seceding before Fort Sumter's surrender

States seceding after Fort Sumter's surrender

Slave states adhering to the Union

Free states and territories adhering to the Union

CHAPTER 2

The Civil War

For most Americans, the Civil War is Stonewall Jackson's Virginia infantry gathering at Henry Hill and mowing down onrushing federals to seize victory at the First Battle of Bull Run. It is two days of metal tearing through 23,746 men at Shiloh. It is George Pickett's division charging into devastating canister fire on the third day of Gettysburg. It is, in short, grand conventional warfare.

Outside the circles of Civil War historians and dedicated buffs, it is little known that insurgent warfare composed a large proportion of the fighting in the Civil War. Insurgency of one sort or another sprang up in most of the Southern and border states as Northern forces progressively intruded into their territory. Not all of the insurgents were the civilian-clad guerrillas most commonly associated with insurgencies—some wore uniforms and reported to the Confederate States Army. But most were farmers waging guerrilla warfare in civilian garb and were not under the control of the Confederate States Army or the Confederate government in Richmond, which generally viewed their manner of fighting as dishonorable. They raided lightly defended Union positions, attacked supply lines, and assassinated federal officials and soldiers. They intimidated and, on occasion, murdered pro-Union civilians. From their numerous supporters among the civilian populace they received forewarning of approaching Union forces, allowing them to disperse and resume civilian activities.

For many of the Union's conventional army divisions, the insurgents were not merely annoying gnats but stinging hornets. By destroying bridges, tearing up railroad tracks, and ambushing wagons, they wreaked havoc on Union logistics, seriously impeding large conventional operations and requiring the diversion of troops to guard against further ravages. At times, Southern irregulars tied down as much as one-third of the total Union army in static defense of logistical lines and bases. Even with so many troops assigned to countering the irregulars, Union commanders incessantly griped that they had far too few troops to contend with them.

Early in the war, President Abraham Lincoln and most other Union leaders tried a policy of conciliation in the occupied regions. The great majority of white Southerners, they believed, did not really favor secession; they had merely been duped into supporting the Confederacy by a small number of wily agitators. Thus, they could be won back to the cause through kindness and blandishments. The armed guerillas, having likewise been tricked, needed only to be imprisoned, not put to death.

Like man in Thomas Hobbes's state of nature, the Union policy of conciliation had a difficult and short life. In much of the territory under occupation, Union commanders did not possess the attributes required for thwarting insurgency by nonmilitary means. Ill-led Union troops spoiled conciliation by stealing from the citizenry and committing other petty crimes, in the process converting pro-Union or neutral citizens into Confederate sympathizers. But even good Union leaders seldom won over Southern whites through beneficence, because in most of the Confederacy the white population was steadfastly opposed to federal rule and steadfastly loyal to the local elites who had led the South to secession and, in the occupied areas, to insurgency. The Southern elites enjoyed this loyalty because of superior leadership abilities, a common heritage, and a shared belief that Southern civilization was under attack from a tyrannical federal government. The Union could not have ended the state of insurgency by nonviolent means short of abandoning the fundamental objectives for which it was fighting. As a consequence, the Union counterinsurgents usually had to operate amid populations that strongly supported the elite leadership of the insurgency, and, most important, they could not recruit locals to help them combat the insurgents.

The difficulty of operating in and around such a populace emerges with special clarity from the experiences of Captain Richard Blazer in Virginia's Loudon County. A native of what would become West Virginia and a very talented leader, Blazer had so impressed his seniors in the U.S. Army that they assigned him one hundred crack cavalrymen and the task of fighting some of the Confederacy's most formidable guerrillas, the Rangers of John Singleton Mosby. Blazer's talents matched the task. Seizing the initiative, Blazer took small detachments of cavalrymen into areas of Loudon County where other Union officers had not dared tread with less than a brigade or a division. Even though he hailed from a place that Virginians considered backward and traitorous, Blazer became one of the few Union counterinsurgency officers who gained the admiration of secessionist whites, owing to his sociable nature and his respect for the citizenry and their property. "His kindness to citizens was proverbial," remarked one Virginian, "and everywhere within the range of his activities the citizens were ready to bear honorable testimony to his character." Yet even Blazer could not stop the citizenry from supporting Mosby's insurgents. After a short period in which Blazer disrupted Mosby's activities in Loudon County, Mosby, with the help of local informants and scouts, decimated Blazer's elite unit and took Blazer captive.[1]

In the face of armed resistance from guerrillas who enjoyed popular backing, Lincoln and most local Union commanders eventually abandoned the idea of conciliating every Southerner and moved over to the view that a minority of pro-Union or neutral whites were friends to be protected, while the other whites were enemies to be punished or destroyed. Union leaders responded to guerrilla activities by fining, imprisoning, forcibly relocating, or burning the crops or houses of individuals suspected of aiding the guerrillas. Executing captured guerrillas on the spot became standard practice.[2]

To forestall or deflect guerrilla attacks, Union forces across the occupied states adopted similar tactics. Typically, some troops were dedicated to guarding railroads, bridges, depots, and other critical installations. In major towns, the federals set up posts from which small troop detachments patrolled the countryside in search of guerrillas, and at county seats, they stationed mobile reserves. To keep some control over the populace and prevent further deterioration of the Union's prestige, the federal government took charge of local civil administration. Because no civilian federal agencies provided personnel for local Southern posts and because local Unionists were usually too scarce or too frightened to fill the jobs, the Union army's officers carried out just about every function. They collected taxes and ran sanitation departments. They served as legislators and judges and policemen.

Similar military tactics did not, however, produce similar military outcomes. Success hinged on the abilities of the local Union commanders to employ these tactics aggressively and creatively. With respect to counterguerrilla operations, which ranged in size from patrols of a few men to sweeps with an entire division, the counterinsurgency historian Andrew J. Birtle concludes, "What usually determined the success or failure of these operations was not their size, but the amount of drive and ingenuity exhibited by the commanders."[3]

In combating insurgents, the Union high command relied on decentralized command, leaving local commanders to decide how to fight the war in their areas. Colonel George Crook, one of the best Union counterinsurgency commanders, crushed the guerrillas in a portion of West Virginia by picking good officers and setting them loose in the countryside with no specific instructions on how to accomplish the mission of defeating the insurgents. "I selected some of the most apt officers," Crook recounted, "and scattered them through the country to learn it and all the people in it, and particularly the bushwhackers, their haunts, etc." Crook's officers ended the state of insurgency in some areas by capturing or killing large numbers of guerrillas, although in one county the insurgency was so strong that they resorted to burning the whole area.[4]

Insurgency assumed its largest and most gruesome form in Missouri. At the outbreak of the war, the governor and the legislature of the state had favored the Confederacy, but Captain Nathaniel Lyon of Connecticut, the commander at the federal arsenal in St. Louis, drove them out of Missouri by force of arms. Federal military authorities organized a new Unionist government and spread troops thinly across the state to enforce its writ. The Missouri government-in-exile, meanwhile, officially joined the Confederacy, which recognized Missouri as the twelfth Confederate state.

The overthrow of the elected government, along with popular support for slavery and states' rights, propelled much of Missouri into rebellion. Guerrillas blossomed in household after household. Unbeholden to the nearest Confederate military command, which was hundreds of miles away, local insurgent leaders waged war as they saw fit. Because large swaths of the populace supported them, the insurgents had excellent intelligence and could evade Union troops with minimal difficulty.

In the middle of 1861, Major General John C. Frémont arrived in St. Louis to take command of the federal Department of the West, which encompassed Missouri and the other western states. Frémont was among the most prominent of the "political generals." In the first months of 1861, with many of the U.S. Army's best officers having departed for the Confederacy and with the federal armed forces slated for rapid expansion, the Union had been in serious need of additional general officers. Rather than promote from within the ranks, Lincoln gave generalships to popular politicians in the hope that they would help raise troops, rally the public, and ensure the support of various other Northern political figures. Many had little, if any, military experience or knowledge, a fact that the army's West Point graduates never tired of bemoaning. Frémont, remembered then and today mostly for his daring expeditions into the western territories, had some military experience, but he was not highly esteemed as a military officer and, indeed, had once been convicted of mutiny. He received the lofty command in the West because he was a popular former senator and had been championed by Radical Republicans in Congress.[5]

Frémont ranks high on the list of men who gave the political generals a bad name. For his staff, Frémont brought in Hungarian and German immigrants and other political allies who draped themselves in fancy uniforms that only made their ineptitude more pathetic. Corruption flourished. Huge amounts of supplies went missing, leaving Union troops without uniforms or weapons.[6] Frémont holed up in a St. Louis mansion surrounded by a magnificent walled garden, at an expense to the army of a staggering $6,000 per annum rent, and his splendidly attired bodyguard corps compelled visiting officers to wait for as long as three days to see him. Ulysses S. Grant, at the time a brigadier general, described his encounters with Frémont at St. Louis: "He sat in a room in full uniform with his maps before him. When you went in he would point out one line or another in a mysterious manner, never asking you to take a seat. You left without the least idea of what he meant or what he wanted you to do."[7]

The Union commanders whom Frémont charged with ruling Missouri's counties were incompetent, politically partisan, and corrupt. Under the exhortation of Radical Republicans, these commanders unleashed violence indiscriminately on the civilian populace, sometimes with the help of pro-Union guerrillas, which caused more than a few pro-Union and neutral civilians to turn against the occupiers.[8] Frémont allowed General James Lane, Charles Jennison, and other "Jayhawkers" from Kansas to enter Missouri to hunt down rebels, which they and their followers did in the manner of hooligans. In addition to liberating slaves, the Jayhawkers "liberated" property for their own use and burned houses, driving many more citizens of Missouri into the rebel camp.[9] A leader with good judgment and empathy would have recognized the damage that such actions inflicted on the Union cause. A leader with organizational talent and deep devotion to the cause would have stopped them.

In the fall of 1861, after a mixed force of Confederate militiamen and regulars vanquished the federal army at Wilson's Creek and advanced into southwestern Missouri, Frémont imposed martial law over the entire state and ordered draconian measures, including the destruction of rebels' property and the shooting of anyone bearing arms behind Union lines. Frémont and his subordinates lacked the vigorous initiative, sound judgment, and empathy that might have made these measures effective. President Lincoln frowned over Frémont's failure to bring the rebels under control and his poor administration, but not until Frémont made an unauthorized decision to emancipate the slaves of Missouri secessionists did Lincoln give Frémont the boot.[10]

Major General Henry W. Halleck, a professional soldier of fame and distinction, took Frémont's place in November 1861. Halleck had graduated third in the West Point class of 1839 and had, in 1846, published a book entitled *Elements of Military Art and Science* with the prestigious D. Appleton and Company of New York. Based largely on the writings of the Swiss military theorist Baron Henri Jomini, the book became required reading for U.S. military officers, and it profoundly shaped the decisions of American military leaders on both sides of the Mason-Dixon line during the Civil War. Theorists of Halleck's ilk are often poorly fit to run large organizations, but Halleck proved an exception. As an army officer in California in the late 1840s and as a businessman after his retirement from the army in 1854, Halleck displayed outstanding organizational abilities. The secession of the southern states in 1861 made him sad rather than angry, and it was with some reluctance that he accepted a request from General Winfield Scott to rejoin the Union army in the summer of 1861.[11]

General George B. McClellan, Halleck's superior, informed Halleck in advance of his arrival in Missouri, "I have intrusted to you a duty which requires the utmost tact and decision. You have not merely the ordinary duties of a military commander to perform, but the far more difficult task of reducing chaos to order, of changing probably the majority of the personnel of the staff of the department, and of reducing to a point of economy, consistent with the interests and necessities of the State, a system of reckless expenditure and fraud, perhaps unheard-of before in the history of the world. You will find in your department many general and staff officers holding illegal commissions and appointments not recognized or approved by the President or Secretary of War. You will please at once inform these gentlemen of the nullity of their appointment, and see that no pay or allowances are issued to them until such time as commissions may be authorized by the President or Secretary of War."[12]

The replacement of Frémont with Halleck illustrates wonderfully the importance of leadership and the difference that one man could make in countering an insurgency. Acting swiftly and decisively, Halleck cashiered not only most of Frémont's staff but also many of the commanders whom Frémont had sent to the counties of Missouri. Into their billets he brought professional officers with West Point training and a penchant for aggressive action. With his superior skills of organization, Halleck fixed weaknesses in the bureaucracy that had permitted corruption and inactivity. He prohibited his troops from confiscating or destroying civilian property, which he viewed as "an outrageous abuse of power and a violation of the rules of war," and compelled Kansas Jayhawkers to leave Missouri.[13]

As Halleck watched the Missouri rebels continue to displace and rob Missouri Unionists, however, he became less respectful of property rights and civil liberties. In response to guerrilla strikes, Halleck began exacting fines from Missouri's high-society secessionists.[14] After fruitless efforts to catch guerrillas in the counties where they enjoyed widespread support, his commanders carried out mass arrests of civilians in those areas. Other means of inspiring trepidation in would-be insurgents included mandatory loyalty oaths, although no rebels proved averse to breaking them, and the posting of bonds, which had some deterrent effect via the pocketbook. Halleck even decreed that people who provided guerrillas with militarily useful information were to be put to death. Insurgents caught bearing arms were summarily shot.[15]

For the most part, the counterguerrilla forces in Missouri fought in small detachments with wide latitude. Poor leadership and lack of pay remained serious problems, even after Halleck took over. Officers often permitted their men to carry out brutal and wanton acts of revenge against the civilian populace because they shared the view of their men that guerrilla excesses justified counter excesses and because they failed to appreciate the negative impact of counter excesses on civilians who had not previously opposed the Union. Integrity was in very short supply. When Union troops were accused of wrongdoing, including murder of suspected guerrilla sympathizers, junior officers usually spared them from punishment by assuring the higher-ups that nothing criminal had been done. Once in a while, an officer was sacked for the flagrant plundering of innocent civilians or for corruption, but the replacement was seldom an improvement.[16]

Halleck was able to replace fewer commanders in Kansas than in Missouri. In contrast to Missouri's governing elites, the power brokers of Kansas were Unionists who remained in place after the war started and kept control over appointments by means of influence in Washington. Kansas politicians engaged in all manner of intrigues and backstabbing, of the sort that twenty-first-century Iraqis would be hard pressed to outdo. Foremost among the conspirators was James Lane, a Radical Senator and abolitionist. When Halleck assigned General James W. Denver to Kansas, Lane protested directly to Lincoln, for Lane despised Denver and feared that the appointment would frustrate his ambitions to control military affairs in Kansas. Lincoln suspended the appointment. Lane then tried to get a relative of his, Brigadier General Thomas A. Davies, into the job. Secretary of War Edwin M. Stanton declared that he would resign if Davies received the appointment, after which the position went to Brigadier General James G. Blunt, another Lane favorite.

Blunt, whose nickname was Fat Boy, had done little militarily to justify his generalship and had Lane to thank for getting promoted ahead of many officers of greater worth. Although a man of some courage and aggressiveness, he lacked many of the key counterinsurgency leadership traits, above all integrity and dedication. A drunkard and a womanizer, Blunt took "female servants" with him into the field. He did the partisan bidding of Lane, and together they made their own fortunes by taking bribes from businessmen who were supplying the army.

Eventually, Lane used his influence with Radical Republicans in Washington and the army to gain control over other military appointments in Kansas, appointments that should have been the responsibility of Governor Charles Robinson. Some of this influence derived from his success in raising several regiments of troops for the Union cause. That achievement was, however, tarnished by Lane's decision to put one of these regiments under the command of his son-in-law and another under a political crony.[17]

In May 1863, Lincoln put Major General John M. Schofield in command of Missouri and Kansas, prompting an outcry from Lane and his friends in the Radical press. Their protestations failed to undo the appointment, but Schofield gave Lane's faction something of a concession by putting "Fat Boy" Blunt in charge of portions of Kansas and Missouri. Lane erupted in fury again when Schofield assigned key sections of those two states to Thomas Ewing, Jr., a commander whom Lane disdained, but Lane's efforts to have Ewing removed were fruitless.[18]

Ewing had great trouble dealing with the Bushwhackers, as the insurgents in Missouri were called, because the junior officers in Missouri at this time consisted mainly of the dregs of the Union officer corps, and the number of troops under their command was meager. Becoming frustrated with the inability of his forces to find and neutralize the guerrillas, Ewing turned to a counterinsurgency method that could be done without large numbers of troops or talented officers: depopulation. In August 1863, Ewing began compelling relatives and supporters of the Bushwhackers to leave Missouri for points south. He served eviction notices to all the residents of several Missouri counties that the Bushwhackers had used as bases for raids into Kansas towns. Without decent leaders to control them, the troops who enforced the evacuation engaged in plunder and other crimes. Despite its injustices, forced resettlement achieved its objectives, reducing Bushwhacker activity and ending Bushwhacker raids into Kansas.[19]

Ewing's success in uprooting Missouri citizens failed to placate Lane, who continued to denounce Ewing and even accused him of showing too much restraint when he forbade Kansas vigilantes to enter Missouri. A spellbinding orator, Lane exhorted a large gathering in Leavenworth to give several Missouri counties "extermination for revenge, desolation for security." On September 30, Lane and other Kansas Radicals went to the White House to beseech Lincoln to remove Schofield. John Hay, Lincoln's private secretary, recorded that these Radicals were more noteworthy "for sincere earnestness and stubborn determination than for either high average intelligence or adroitness." Lincoln had the good sense to keep Schofield in place. In October, Schofield improved matters for humanity, if not for Lane, by firing Blunt. Fortunes changed again in 1864, however, when Schofield went to Tennessee to work for Grant and a Lane favorite took his place.[20]

In parts of Tennessee could be witnessed more scenes of major insurgency. In early 1862, Ulysses S. Grant overran the Confederate defenses at Fort Donelson and Fort Henry, two critical bulwarks in the Confederate defensive line across northern Tennessee, and knifed down the Tennessee River to the state's southern frontier. The audacious Confederate attack at Shiloh in April bloodied and shook the federal army but failed to pry it out of southwestern Tennessee. During the summer the principal threat to Grant's forces came from insurgents, who struck Union troops and the Union supply arteries running from north to south. Grant and Major General William T. Sherman took on the job of combating these rebels, and like so many Union officers before them, they began by attempting to win over the populace through conciliatory measures. When that approach failed to stem guerrilla attacks, Grant and Sherman replaced the olive branch with the torch. In response to guerrilla marauding, they exacted property from active rebel sympathizers or burned their houses or even entire towns. At times they deported families to Confederate territory, even if they could not tell whether the families had any connection to the insurgents. Although they tried to secure the support of the local Unionist minority by protecting it from the insurgents, the Unionists themselves were alienated by the destruction and displacement wrought by the federal troops. The levels of guerrilla activity did not recede.[21]

Grant and Sherman were endowed with some of the key counterinsurgency leadership attributes, such as initiative, dedication, and organizational skill. Those attributes made distinguished conventional commanders of them. But they were deficient in others, particularly empathy, creativity, and flexibility, which explains why their counterinsurgency records are much less impressive. They preferred the straightforward, certain business of war to the twisty ambiguity and conniving of politics, a serious handicap in trying to defeat insurgents. Later in the war, Sherman told his brother, Senator John Sherman, "If you ever hear anybody use my name in connection with a political office, tell them you know me well enough to assure them that I would be offended by such association. I would rather be an engineer of a railroad, than President of the United States, or any political officer."[22] Grant later became president, but he was as unsuccessful in politics as he was successful in conventional war, becoming one of the worst presidents in American history.

Counterinsurgency in the state of Tennessee later came under the command of Andrew Johnson, former U.S. senator from Tennessee and future president of the United States, whom President Lincoln had appointed the state's military governor following Union military advances into the state. Having failed to learn from the experiences of Grant and Sherman, Johnson initially sought to win the people over through outstretched hands, and then in frustration decided to employ the fist. He was especially tough in western and middle Tennessee, where the insurgents continued to enjoy great support among the populace, but he also used force liberally in eastern Tennessee, one of the few areas in the South that was crawling with Unionists. Johnson allowed federal troops to respond to guerrilla depredations by forcing nearby civilians to pay fines, incinerating their farms, or deporting them. His military government fined and imprisoned members of the upper class suspected of abetting the insurgents.[23]

Johnson, however, demonstrated more flexibility and imagination than Grant, Sherman, and other Union counterinsurgency leaders, as evidenced by his decision to arm Tennessee natives and send them on counterinsurgency missions. The task was admittedly easier in Tennessee than in other zones of occupation because of eastern Tennessee's large pro-Union population. The effectiveness of these units varied according to their leadership; some captured or killed numerous guerrillas, but others were either passive or prone to indiscriminate destruction.[24] Two leaders of the passive type were Colonel John Brownlow of the First Tennessee Cavalry and Colonel William B. Stokes of the Fifth Tennessee Cavalry, who were charged with rooting out secessionist guerrillas in White County. Both were political colonels—Brownlow was the son of one of Tennessee's most prominent Unionist politicians, and Stokes was a former Tennessee state legislator of the Unionist persuasion. Neither was an accomplished military officer, and Stokes was positively awful. The guerrillas of White County flourished during their successive tenures. Another documented case was that of Lieutenant William Estrada, who was berated by the provost marshal general, Brigadier General Samuel P. Carter, for his lack of initiative. Rather than chasing the guerrillas, Estrada kept his men at the base to which they had been dispatched. Carter scolded, "This was not the design of sending you into that section. You are expected to scour the country. . . . The General expects you to be vigilant and active, and do everything in your power to bring the villains . . . to justice."[25]

Preventing abuse of Tennessee's civilian populace required leaders of considerable integrity and organizational talent. Provost Marshal General Carter was a politically savvy man and a fair one, but he did not keep a close eye on the thirty-two deputy provost marshals who were charged with civil governance in the counties. Many of them were assigned to their home counties, which had the advantage of empowering people with great local knowledge but also gave them the ability to settle old scores by official means. Some of the provost marshals took advantage of their position to avenge wrongs suffered earlier in the war, when the Confederates occupied most of the state, oftentimes by punishing all Confederate sympathizers, not merely those who had perpetrated deeds against them. In addition, they tolerated theft and violence against civilians by their subordinates, which created enormous resentment among the civilian populace, including Unionists. These provost marshals were a major reason why the Union failed to restore order in most of Tennessee.[26]

Another reason for Unionist woes in Tennessee was the shortage of supplies among the counterinsurgency forces, the result of resource constraints and poor judgment and corruption at higher levels of command. Union troops sometimes received no more than a few crackers or an ear of corn per day, producing hunger so intense that they pilfered from the citizenry despite all threats of punishment and the actual harsh punishments meted out by higher commands. One Union general who tried unsuccessfully to stop the foraging asserted that "hungry men are difficult to control after fasting for five months on half and quarter rations." Another said, "No laws, nor orders, nor regulations, nor activity on the part of a commander, can prevent the demoralization . . . of an Army compelled, by the necessity of the case, to subsist on the country in which it may be operating."[27]

Insurgency developed in the Confederate state of Arkansas after the Union victory at Pea Ridge in March 1862. Capitalizing on the triumph, Union invasion forces drove toward the heart of the state, the capital city of Little Rock. News of their progress compounded the disarray into which the Arkansas state government had already fallen. Governor Henry M. Rector had become enraged when the Confederate government in Richmond sent huge numbers of native Arkansans to fight in Tennessee and Mississippi, which had denuded Arkansas of regulars and left it vulnerable to Union invaders. No more Arkansans would leave, he vowed publicly, until the Confederates sent an army capable of protecting the state. Jefferson Davis dispatched Major General Thomas C. Hindman to rescue the situation. Imposing martial law, Hindman conscripted young Arkansas men into a new conventional army and ordered the state's citizens to form guerrilla companies. Hindman wanted these guerrillas to harass Union forces as they pressed further into the state, in imitation of the Spanish guerrillas who had bled Napoléon's armies from 1808 to 1813.

Commencing the guerrilla war in June 1862, Hindman ordered the guerrilla companies to concentrate their wrath on Union supply lines.[28] During their first year in action, the Arkansas insurgents repeatedly broke the Union's supply lines, an achievement of strategic importance because it prevented Union forces from reaching Little Rock. In the winter of 1862–1863, however, the insurgency began to unravel. Although Hindman intended to exert control over the guerrilla companies, he was unable to do so, leaving responsibility for discipline to the company commanders, many of whom were not men of strong conscience. The guerrilla companies acquired a knack for pillaging. When the Confederate regular army learned of their misdeeds and told them to desist, they began fighting the Confederate army as well as the Union one. Until the war's end, guerrillas plundered and terrorized Arkansans of all political persuasions, reserving special harshness for Unionists, and their crimes severely weakened support for the Confederate cause in the state. Guerrillas with virtuous leaders, on the other hand, ably defended their counties against Union forces and retained the approval of the public.[29]

As elsewhere, the federal forces in Arkansas received little guidance from above but did gravitate toward common tactics. They responded to guerrilla ambushes by burning homes, farms, and towns, and they executed guerrillas for not wearing uniforms. Poor judgment and lack of integrity and empathy characterized many of the federal counterinsurgency leaders in Arkansas, and citizens of all loyalties suffered. Brigadier General Cyrus Bussey reported that several thousand Unionist families in his area had been "robbed of everything they had by the troops of this command, and are now left destitute and compelled to leave their homes to avoid starvation." When expropriating forage, horses, cattle, and other property, some soldiers had provided receipts, but Bussey noted that the receipts could not be settled. "Many good loyal people have been shamefully treated by our army," Bussey lamented. "In most instances everything has been taken and no receipts given, the people turned out to starve, and their effects loaded into trains and sent to Kansas."[30]

Even with so blunt an instrument as the incineration of property belonging to guerrilla sympathizers, the traits of the commander often made the difference between success and failure. When determining whose property to set afire, good commanders tried hard to separate friendly civilians from hostile civilians and weighed all of the consequences, such as the impact of crop destruction on the food available to federal troops in the future. Other commanders discriminated little, if at all.[31]

The ability of local commanders in Arkansas to devise innovative counterinsurgency methods led to major Union counterinsurgency advances in the war's final years. Marcus La Rue Harrison, an Indiana native who was one of the most creative Union commanders in Arkansas, developed fortified Unionist colonies in which residents were required to serve in home guard units. Depriving the insurgents of easy access to their supporters, the program seriously weakened the insurgency and freed up federal troops for action elsewhere. The colonies also provided sources of food for federal soldiers and way stations for cavalry on patrol.

The most effective commanders were those who both possessed the right attributes and were native to Arkansas, for they knew the land, could distinguish guerrillas from other civilians, and, unlike officers from the North, shared the people's regional and cultural identities. Large numbers of white Arkansans supported the Union, especially in the Ozark region of northwestern Arkansas, and were willing to lead or serve in Unionist armed forces. With respect to the Arkansas Unionist forces, the leading historian of the Arkansas guerrilla war writes, "When backed by firm leadership and a well-developed counterinsurgency plan, they proved the worst nemesis of the Confederate guerillas in Arkansas." Hailing from Arkansas did not mean that they were softer on the rebels; even Arkansan Unionist leaders often set alight the property of suspected insurgent sympathizers and the gristmills where rebels met, on the grounds that the counterinsurgents had too few horses to combat the guerrillas with patrols and ambushes.[32]

Yet another interesting site of conflict, from the perspective of counterinsurgency leadership, was Louisiana. On the night of April 24, 1862, a Union fleet under the command of David Glasgow Farragut steamed up the Mississippi River toward Fort Jackson and Fort St. Philip, the two Confederate river forts guarding New Orleans. When the warships reached the forts, Confederate batteries opened fire and Confederate gunboats rushed out to engage them in battle. The fighting raged for three hours, with the Union giving better than it took. After sinking most of the Confederate gunboats, the Union fleet outflanked the forts and compelled them to surrender. Then it sailed into New Orleans, the largest city of the Confederacy, to deposit an invasion force. Though expecting a fierce fight, the Yankee troops were not greeted by organized violence, just howls from city mobs and the billowing smoke of burning cotton. The Confederate army, spread thin by fighting on many fronts, had been unable to assign large numbers of troops to the city's defense, and the city's small garrison had fled upon learning of the approach of the Union navy.

Arriving with the first federal troops was the new military governor, Benjamin Butler. Before the war, Butler had been a popular legislator in the Democratic Party. He had very little military experience, but in 1861, Lincoln made him a major general and put him in command of an army, viewing the appointment as a means of gaining the support of the opposition party and recruiting Massachusetts men into the army. Eventually, whispers would be heard that Lincoln kept Butler in the military to prevent him from running for president. Butler, who possessed an inflated estimation of his own talents, constantly demanded promotions, even after his limitations had become manifest. Although he fared poorly in early military engagements, he was highly successful in getting young men in New England to join the army, so the promotions kept coming.[33]

Once ensconced in New Orleans, Butler took on the tasks of a military commander, state governor, and city mayor. While the political generals had a long record as poor commanders of both regular forces and counterguerrilla forces, a record that Butler lengthened further during his time in New Orleans, they did have an advantage over professional military officers in one area, governance of occupied territories, since they had years of experience in government. In much of the occupied South, professional military commanders turned civil affairs over to such individuals, so that the military men could stick to what they knew best, the use of force.[34] Because of Butler's political experience and his considerable organizational talents, he served well in the roles of governor and mayor, taking the initiative with preventive measures that kept a major insurgency from arising. Some historians have questioned the wisdom of his early attempts to cow the thoroughly pro-Confederate population with a few drastic punishments, the closure of hostile newspapers, and an order that women who insulted federal soldiers be treated as prostitutes, for these measures made him a despised figure throughout the South. Yet his actions did help deter would-be insurgents in New Orleans and elsewhere in Louisiana. In addition, Butler succeeded in recruiting large numbers of Louisiana blacks into the Union armed forces.[35]

Butler's successor as military governor was a man of very similar specifications, Nathaniel Prentiss Banks. Prior to the war, Banks had served as the Speaker of the U.S. House of Representatives and the governor of Massachusetts. His only knowledge of the military came from his service on the House Military Affairs Committee, a position he had used primarily to steer contracts to an armory in his district. Because of Banks's political clout, Lincoln bestowed on him the rank of major general in June 1861, bypassing every regular officer except General Winfield Scott and all volunteer officers except George B. McClellan and John C. Frémont. Banks continued to receive important field commands even after he had exposed himself as a third-rate general.[36]

In governing New Orleans, Banks put his prior gubernatorial experience to good use, although his efforts to conciliate all parties sometimes made him popular with no one. No significant insurgency percolated in the city. In the military sphere, his actions were much less sound, and they became a major concern to the Union high command. Most infamously, Banks led an expedition into the Red River area of northern Louisiana, where the Confederate state government had set up temporary quarters, and suffered a resounding defeat.

Top military officers were also upset that Banks devoted more of his energies and resources to administrative control and policy enforcement than to military operations. When Halleck urged Banks to send troops to fight Confederate forces in the hinterlands, Banks refused. This controversy was emblematic of a larger problem: the political generals thought that the key to the war was controlling the Southern population, whereas the professional generals believed that the key was defeating the Confederate armies.[37] When this dispute arose, determining which tack to take often proved very difficult, because controlling the population and destroying Confederate regulars were both vital tasks. Dividing resources between them required judgments based on incomplete knowledge of the enemy and speculation about the results of various actions.

By Palm Sunday, 1865, the day that Robert E. Lee surrendered to Ulysses S. Grant at Appomattox Court House, the Union had extinguished the insurgents in just a few parts of the Confederacy. Only in Arkansas could the successes be said to have been statewide, and even there pockets of insurgency persisted until the bitter end. The Union's biggest counterinsurgency successes occurred, by no coincidence, in areas where local Unionists served in leadership positions, particularly Arkansas and eastern Tennessee. Union leaders may be excused for their inability to recruit local civilians in solidly pro-Confederate locales, because staunch loyalty to local secessionist elites and resistance to the Union's policy objectives made it a nearly impossible task. Secessionist civilians refused to switch sides even when outstanding Union leaders like Captain Richard Blazer were in charge and even when Union commanders began destroying the property of Confederate sympathizers. Less excusable was the Union's alienation of whites in Southern and border states who had started out the war pro-Union or neutral. By condoning gross misconduct and otherwise displaying a lack of virtue, the counterinsurgency's leaders turned many people into insurgents or insurgent supporters. Union leaders could have won them over had they prevented subordinates from misbehaving, governed with sense and foresight, exercised their charisma, and spent time meeting and talking with the people.

Obtaining such leaders would have required much more careful attention to command selection. Only a small number of senior Union leaders consistently selected the most suitable officers for command. The difference that this capability made for senior leaders can be seen clearly in the transition from Frémont to Halleck in Missouri. Whereas Frémont put political hacks into leadership jobs, Halleck fired them and installed good professional officers in their stead. Better officers could also have been obtained by taking officers from conventional units, but that would have degraded the forces that had to fight the war's decisive battles.

Although the counterinsurgents employed similar tactics, techniques, and procedures for the most part, the more creative and flexible commanders made adjustments to the standard methods based on local circumstances, usually with beneficial results. Effectiveness also varied widely based on the presence of the leadership characteristics necessary for keeping violent force under control. On account of poor leadership, Union troops frequently fell into habits of wanton destruction, violence, and criminality against the civilian populace in many Southern locales, at great detriment to the Union cause. Those leaders who maintained authority over their troops and punished only full-fledged insurgents had considerably more success in obtaining cooperation from locals, especially those of neutral or pro-Union disposition. Even draconian instruments, such as the burning of possessions belonging to suspected enemy sympathizers, worked far better when implemented by officers who had the judgment, empathy, and integrity to manipulate those instruments properly.

Initiative and dedication often differentiated effective leaders from ineffective ones, in conventional warfare as well as in counterinsurgency. Both traits were essential to success, but by themselves they were sufficient for success only in conventional war, for counterinsurgency leadership required a broader range of talents than conventional leadership. Some fine conventional commanders with superior initiative and dedication, like Grant and Sherman, had great trouble using destruction and violence in a suitably discriminating way. Only with the crudest of implements, depopulation, could leaders get by on initiative and dedication alone.

Few wars can provide as much insight as the Civil War into the interference of domestic politics in leadership selection. Although some of Lincoln's political generals turned out to be good military leaders, many others undermined the Union military effort and wasted men's lives with their amateurish performances. On the other hand, some of them served ably as civil administrators in occupied territory, outdoing most of the professional military officers in that regard, and through their political influence they bolstered support for war in the North. To his credit, Lincoln sometimes did remove truly awful political generals, such as Frémont, and at times he resisted calls from Northern politicians to put their good-for-nothing cronies into positions of military authority, as with many of Senator Lane's demands in Kansas.

Poor cousins to the armies of George B. McClellan and Ulysses S. Grant, Union counterinsurgency forces regularly suffered from want of resources, principally troops, food, and pay. If severe in extent, these shortages presented problems that no strength of leadership could overcome. With the conventional war absorbing most of the North's military manpower, the Union high command seldom could assign large numbers of soldiers to mobile counterguerrilla operations, a severe handicap in any war against guerrillas. Lack of food and pay caused troops to steal from the populace, and even fine leaders could not stop them if they were starving.

Nearly all of the insurgents laid down their arms in 1865 when the Confederate government capitulated. Many never returned to their insurgent ways, and a few, most famously John Singleton Mosby, became enthusiastic proponents of the federal government. For others, however, the insurgency did not truly end in 1865.

CHAPTER 3

Reconstruction in the South

As the Union army mowed through the South in 1864 and the first months of 1865, the land suffered the ravages of hard-bitten generals like William T. Sherman and Philip H. Sheridan, wreckers of Georgia and South Carolina and Virginia, men whose names would be etched on the minds of generations of Southerners to come. Federal soldiers turned cities into ashes, stripped factories to the beams, and peeled mile after mile of railroad track off the earth. Once the Union military machine had passed through a plantation, every object of value had been eaten, burned, or taken away. Union officers also overturned existing civil authorities and freed slaves as they went, ushering in violent anarchy in places.

When at last the Confederate armies laid down their weapons, vast numbers of Southerners had no food, livestock, or shelter. Personal savings, having been put into Confederate bonds, were gone. Farmers and business owners could not pay workers, resulting in massive unemployment for both whites and blacks. Northern blacks wearing Union uniforms and carrying Union rifles arrived to occupy sections of the former Confederacy, and newly liberated slaves were recruited to do the same—further humiliation for the white South.

Although most Confederates, including Confederate guerrillas, stopped fighting after General Lee's surrender at Appomattox, violence persisted in some of the Southern and border regions populated by mixtures of secessionists and Unionists. In east Tennessee, secessionist guerrillas continued to clash with federal regulars and with roaming bands of armed Unionists who beat and killed civilians who had supported the Confederacy. Local authorities in towns like Knoxville, Athens, and Morristown allowed Unionist ruffians to engage in murder, horsewhipping, lynching, and larceny, viewing such deeds as just punishment for Confederate outrages against Unionists during the war, and neither the federal government nor the new Unionist state government did much to interfere. The state legislature, dominated by east Tennessee Unionists, instructed the populace to shoot insurgents on sight.[1] After discharged federal soldiers murdered a former Confederate in front of the Knox County courthouse, William G. Brownlow, a Methodist minister of Unionist persuasion who had become Tennessee's governor in April 1865, commented that "injured, insulted and oppressed Union men will redress their own wrongs — and for the life of us, we are not able to see that they are in error."[2] Had Unionist excesses been limited in number and severity, they might have sustained the secessionist insurgents, but they were so widespread and cruel that instead they caused a mass exodus of former secessionists from east Tennessee, sucking the breath out of the insurgency.

In Missouri, Unionists attacked civilians who had supported the Confederate cause, and secessionist guerrillas who tried to surrender were executed by federal troops or Unionist civilians, all of which caused the remaining armed secessionists to continue the fight into the summer of 1865. Where the guerrillas receded, Radical Republicans took control of local governments and used their powers to punish citizens, officials, and clergy who did not share their views. Missouri residents who had sided with the Confederacy were, however, more plentiful and resilient than their counterparts in east Tennessee. Meeting violence with violence, they were not dislodged from their homes in massive numbers.[3]

As far as counterinsurgency leadership is concerned, the most instructive episode from post–Civil War Missouri was the deployment of state troops to Lexington in November 1866. The Radical Republican state governor sent a militia company to the town after Conservatives — men who accepted Unionism but opposed major social and political change — compelled the townspeople to vote for Conservative candidates at gunpoint. The militia company commander, Major Bacon Montgomery, proved to be exactly the type of man one would not want for this delicate assignment. Forgoing any semblance of fairness, Montgomery refused to hold a new election and instead simply installed Radicals in office. When a local newspaper editor criticized the militia, Major Montgomery destroyed the paper's printing press and threatened to hang the editor as a "God-damned traitor, rebel liar . . . and Son of a Bitch." Not yet done, Montgomery allowed the militiamen to rampage through town like frontier bandits. Conservatives appealed to the federal military for help, an ironic request coming as it did from men who had renounced the federal government in 1861 for intruding into states' affairs.

This appeal induced the army to send a Major James R. Kelly to the town for the purposes of observation. During his first two days in town, Kelly witnessed a murder, three armed robberies, a stagecoach robbery, and a barroom brawl involving gunfire that struck a passerby, all instigated by the militia. The militiamen, he reported, were "the most condemned set of ruffians I ever saw, while it is strange but true, that nearly all the Conservative men of this place . . . are apparently gentlemen, and men of good standing and wealth." Major General Winfield S. Hancock rectified the situation by sending three companies of federal infantry to Lexington. The federal troops placed Montgomery under arrest, compelled his militia to disperse, and let Conservatives occupy the offices for which they had been elected.[4]

In most other parts of the former Confederacy, the end of the conventional war meant a halt to all bloodshed, at least among whites, and occupation by federal troops. Although Andrew Johnson had resorted to tough tactics as governor of occupied Tennessee during the war, as president he adopted Lincoln's positions on the postwar South: the defeated white Southerners should be treated gently, and blacks should not be made the political equals of whites. Like Lincoln, Johnson criticized Radical Republicans for seeking to deal with the South as a conquered territory and impose racial equality, for in his view that approach would perpetuate hatred and require an indefinite federal presence in the South. Johnson allowed the Southern states to maintain existing state laws, except those concerning slavery, and to keep existing officeholders in place, save for governors and legislators.[5]

Many in the North, having just fought a bitter and bloody war against the armies of Lee and Bragg, were disconcerted when the Southern state governments formed after the war were filled with men who had been wearing Confederate uniforms only months earlier. They were troubled, too, by news that Southern states were denying the vote to blacks, tolerating white violence against blacks, and passing paternalistic legislation, known as the Black Codes, that limited the freedoms of blacks. Moderate Republicans soon became disillusioned with Johnson's version of Reconstruction and began supporting the Reconstruction platform of the Radical Republicans. Moderates joined the

Radicals in supporting the Union League, which sent representatives to the South to register black voters and protect Unionists, as well as the Freedmen's Bureau, which performed a wide range of services for freed slaves, such as obtaining land, supervising labor contracts, providing health services, and establishing schools. The Republicans passed legislation authorizing the federal government to protect blacks by imposing punishments on white civilians and carrying out trials by military tribunals. President Johnson attempted to halt the deluge of Republican laws with his veto power, but the congressional Republicans assembled enough votes to override the vetoes.

As in most environments where the soil is fertile for an insurgency, the government had early opportunities to either ease or worsen the conditions needed for an insurgency to germinate. What was made of these opportunities depended to a great extent on the leaders responsible for extending federal power into the states, principally the local commanders of the army, the Freedmen's Bureau, and the Union League. The army had both a military presence and a civil presence in the South, for it was regularly called upon to perform functions that local governments and the federal government lacked the people or resources to perform, such as law enforcement, railroad repair, and sanitation. President Johnson and General Ulysses S. Grant, the commanding general of the federal army, set a few constraints on local commanders but delegated most decision-making power down to the local level, on the grounds that the man on the spot was the one best qualified to reach decisions.[6]

In the last months of the war, Grant and Secretary of War Stanton had purged many of the political generals for want of military proficiency, a purge that helped the Union army in its final fights with Robert E. Lee's stubborn Army of Northern Virginia but also kept the political generals from receiving top commands in the postwar South, jobs for which they were highly qualified. The professional military officers charged with occupying the South after the war were certainly better leaders on average than most of the officers who had been relegated to counterinsurgency duties during the war, but they were ill prepared and, more important, often ill suited to reconstruction work.[7] Their shortcomings frustrated preventive counterinsurgency in many Southern counties.

From the very beginning, certain Union officers demonstrated an uncanny ability to bungle nonmilitary tasks and poison relations with the Southern population. On April 29, 1865, General Henry W. Halleck reported to Grant on the incompetence and crimes of the 25th Corps in its occupation of Virginia, stating that "want of discipline and good officers in the Twenty-fifth Corps renders it a very improper force for the preservation of order in this department. A number of cases of atrocious rape by these men have already occurred." Halleck recommended transferring the entire corps someplace else, where it could not cause more damage. Taking its place, said Halleck, should be a corps more skilled and more respectful of the population, which would require "officers and men of more intelligence and character than we have in the 25th Corps."[8] Grant promptly moved the 25th Corps to a training camp and brought in a better-led unit.[9]

Brigadier General J. S. Fullerton, assistant commissioner of the Freedmen's Bureau in Louisiana, wrote in December 1865 that the people's reaction to the bureau ranged from very positive to very negative, based purely upon the characteristics of local agents. "On the part of some agents there has been a want of tact, conciliation, and sound judgment," Fullerton observed. "The acts of a few local agents of the bureau were such as to destroy the confidence that should exist between these planters who were endeavoring to give free labor an impartial trial, and the freedmen who worked in their fields." For instance, such agents "would listen to the story or complaint of the black man alone, refusing to hear his white neighbor on the same subject, or if they did listen, with the determination not to believe."[10]

Brigadier General John Tarbell, who saw the Freedmen's Bureau at work in several Southern states, rejected the view of many Northern Radicals that white Southerners uniformly despised the Freedmen's Bureau because of blind hatred of Reconstruction. Rather, he said, the whites hated it only in districts where its officers were incompetent or corrupt, of which he had seen a considerable number. "In districts where they had upright, intelligent, and impartial officers of the bureau, the people expressed entire satisfaction," Tarbell noted. "They stated to me that where they had such officers, and where they had soldiers who were under good discipline, they were entirely welcome, and indeed they were glad to have their presence — in some cases approving the action of the bureau officers in punishing white men for the ill treatment of colored people, saying that the officers were perfectly right."[11]

At the state level, where the responsibilities of leadership consisted primarily of supervising local leaders and providing general guidance, one of the best Freedmen's Bureau leaders was Major General Charles H. Smith of the Arkansas bureau. A recipient of the Congressional Medal of Honor for heroism at the Battle of St. Mary's Church in June 1864, Smith had commanded the

28th U.S. Colored Infantry before going to Arkansas, during which time he had demonstrated the ability to empathize with both blacks and whites. That ability served him well in Arkansas. Smith kept close watch over the Freedmen's Bureau agents through frequent visits, and he removed those who performed poorly. Through his creativity, flexibility, and evenhandedness, he calmed the black and the white populations alike. Convinced that drastic change would cause dangerous social and political turmoil, he sought to keep the freedmen working on plantations and strove at the same time for gradual improvement in their economic and political conditions.[12]

In the early days of Reconstruction, the federal government committed some of its most flagrant violations of personal liberty and welfare in Texas, the result of both the general defiance of white Texans and the presence of Union leaders who were not fit for taming this bronco of a state. Outside observers usually ascribed Texan defiance to the state's good fortune, during the last years of the war, in escaping the devastation visited upon most other Confederate states.[13] The ultimate source of the Union leadership problems in the Lone Star State, Major General Philip Sheridan, had caused a goodly share of said devastation, having turned the fertile farms of the Shenandoah Valley into a long black smoldering streak in 1864. Following his rampage through the Shenandoah, during the twilight of the Confederacy, Sheridan had become the most celebrated Union general after Grant and Sherman, owing to his tactical skill, his ability to motivate troops, and the praise of Grant. At the Battle of Cedar Creek, he had, through force of personality, single-handedly turned around a retreating and dispirited army of 30,000 men and crushed the Confederate army that had attacked it. "As a soldier, as a commander of troops, as a man capable of doing all that is possible with any number of men, there is no man living greater than Sheridan," Grant pronounced. "I rank Sheridan with Napoleon and Frederick and the great commanders of history."[14]

In the middle of May 1865, Grant dispatched Sheridan to Texas to vanquish the last organized Confederate armed forces, which were commanded by General Edmund Kirby Smith. But while Sheridan was in transit, Smith surrendered his little army, leaving Sheridan to take control of Texas unopposed. Reporting to Grant three days after Smith's capitulation, Sheridan wrote, "Texas has not yet suffered from the war and will require some intimidation."[15] The behavior of white Texans in the first months of the occupation convinced Sheridan that almost every white man in the state was given to cruelty and insolence and that only force could fix this problem. Showing more brazenness than whites in most other parts of the occupied South, the Texans repeatedly beat and murdered blacks, along with whites who tried to help blacks find jobs beyond the plantations where they had been slaves. When federal troops tried to compel planters to honor labor contracts arranged by the Freedmen's Bureau, whites murdered the troops. When the Freedmen's Bureau built schools for blacks, whites chased away the teachers who were willing to flee, killed the rest, and burned down the schools. Attempts to prosecute the perpetrators of these various crimes in local courts typically came to naught, for the white juries would not issue guilty verdicts. The newly elected state government, though avowedly pro-Union, opposed racial equality and tolerated the mistreatment of blacks.[16]

Texan resistance to change persuaded some of Sheridan's subordinate commanders that strict imposition of Reconstruction policies would alienate whites to such a degree that they would oppose all collaboration with federal authorities and refuse to provide the assistance the federal authorities needed to rein in vigilantes and terrorists. Major General Horatio Wright and Major General Samuel P. Heintzelman, two of the top Union commanders in Texas, moderated federal Reconstruction policies and thereby gained the cooperation of Governor James W. Throckmorton and other elected officials.[17]

Sheridan, on the other hand, believed that Reconstruction ought to be rigidly enforced, and the objections of white Texans discounted. By nature a man who preferred absolutes to compromise, he looked with abhorrence on the idea of diluting Reconstruction policies to appease white Southerners. And he refused to delve into the tangle of local politics or speak persuasively to whites, actions that might have enabled a stricter adherence to federal Reconstruction policies to yield some lasting gains. On one occasion, Sheridan frankly confessed to a confidant that he simply would not set foot in the muddy realm of politics: "If I am disliked," said Sheridan, "it is because I cannot and will not cater to rebel sentiment and be an instrument to advance the merits of political parties or particular reconstruction schemes. I do not permit anyone to approach me on politics, but go on minding my own business and my legitimate military duties as though I did not care whether the Southern States were readmitted tomorrow or kept out for twenty years."[18]

To compound matters, the crimes of a minority of whites produced in Sheridan an abiding contempt for the entire white Southern population, which exacerbated his aversion to interaction with local elites. Sheridan wrote to F. C. Newhall, a close friend of his, "The more I see of this people the less I see to admire."[19] Sheridan told a newspaperman, "If I owned hell and Texas, I would rent out Texas and live in hell!"[20]

Sheridan's differences of opinion with Wright and Heintzelman over the strictness of Reconstruction led him to remove both men in 1866. He shuffled Wright off to Washington, D.C., and replaced him with Major General George W. Getty, who had served with Sheridan in the Shenandoah Valley. Still hobbled by an injury sustained in the Wilderness campaign of 1864, Getty lacked the stamina necessary for the job. After he took charge, the federal army's mistreatment of Texas civilians increased considerably.[21]

To take Heintzelman's place, Sheridan appointed Charles Griffin, a stern disciplinarian who had performed splendidly as an artillery officer and division commander during the war. Griffin's severity helped curb the disciplinary problems among federal soldiers and officials in the state, but it also carried with it inflexibility and callousness. Like Sheridan, Griffin believed that his mission was to enforce Reconstruction policies in their entirety and that the opinions of white Texans should not be permitted to cause any deviation from that course or any slowing of the pace. His personality inclined him even more in this direction than Sheridan's inclined him. Griffin was one of those Radical Republicans who cared a good deal more for humanity in the abstract than for the people he met in person, especially Southerners. "Bluff, bellicose, outspoken, and quick to take offense" was how one observer described him.[22] Griffin had few friends, and no Southern friends.

At first, Griffin was able to work harmoniously with Governor Throckmorton, although that achievement probably had more to do with Griffin's initial cautiousness and the relationship with the governor established by his predecessor than with any talents of his own. Griffin used army troops to protect settlers on the frontier, and in return Throckmorton allowed Griffin to use army forces to punish whites who mistreated blacks or federal troops.[23] But the romance between Griffin and the state government soon turned sour. By insisting on radical changes and forcing them on the state with little tact, Griffin gained the hatred of Throckmorton and most other white Texans. Throckmorton later called Griffin "a dog, mangy and full of fleas, and as mean as the meanest radical in Texas."[24]

Contempt for white Texans led men like Sheridan and Griffin to show inordinate lenience toward federal troops and Unionist civilians who harmed them, whether in retaliation for particular transgressions or not. Throughout Sheridan's stint as viceroy of Texas, the whites of the state endured a multitude of cruelties, greater and lesser, at the hands of Union soldiers whose officers could not, or did not try to, keep them under tight discipline. Perhaps the worst case was that of the rowdy drunken federal troops who one night set the town of Brenham ablaze and roughed up its inhabitants. Sheridan made a medium-sized problem into a big one by blaming the destruction of Brenham on the civilian population and refusing to punish the two federal officers who should have brought the soldiers under control. Toleration of bad behavior in this instance proved costly again in the future, for the two officers who should have been sacked were later charged with other crimes—destruction of court records in one case and embezzlement from the Freedmen's Bureau in the other. The unruly and indiscriminate character of the violence ensured that it would not stop the white Texan wrongdoers and that it would inflame many who had not favored insurgency.[25]

In March 1867, Radical and moderate Republicans in the U.S. Congress transformed Reconstruction throughout the South by passing, and overriding President Johnson's veto of, the First Reconstruction Act. Appalled by the resistance of the elected Southern governments to equal rights for blacks, the Republicans declared the governments of ten Southern states illegal and divided the South into five military districts. Each district commander was to use federal troops to protect blacks, maintain order, and punish wrongdoers, by military court if necessary. The First Reconstruction Act was followed by legislation authorizing the district commanders to register voters, remove state officials, and pass laws. The Radicals barred from governmental service most former Confederate leaders, which meant most of the Southern white male elites.

During the next twelve months, the Radical legislation completely changed the political landscape in the South. The military registered millions of black voters and protected other organizations that helped register blacks while excluding ex-Confederates from casting votes or holding office. Republicans of both races were voted into office in great numbers, and Republicans gained the dominant position in the state governments. The new Republican governments gave legal rights to blacks for the first time and ran courts that were likely to treat blacks favorably. The state governments and the army also organized new militias and police forces that enforced Republican policies.[26]

A certain number of Southern whites were intent on resisting Radical Reconstruction simply because of their inveterate opposition to black advancement. The majority of whites in the South, however, found it objectionable less because of the goal of black advancement than because of the means and speed with which it tried to achieve that goal. In the first years of Reconstruction, they had resigned themselves to cooperation with the federal government and to greater, though far from complete, rights for blacks. As much as 30 percent of the Southern white population had voted for Republicans, and influential planters, merchants, bankers, and even former Confederate officers had taken on leading roles in the Republican Party. White Democratic elites had, for the most part, been willing to tolerate the federal authorities and their programs to advance the conditions of blacks, even if they tried to slow the rate of change.[27] The treatment of blacks under the Black Codes that the white South accepted in 1865 and 1866 was a dramatic improvement over their treatment in the days of slavery and, except for the unwillingness of some state governments to protect blacks from white violence, was not very different from what President Lincoln had envisioned. It was, indeed, better than what blacks would endure under the Jim Crow laws that were passed in the South after Radical Reconstruction had destroyed the faith of most Northerners and all white Southerners in federal guidance of the South's political affairs.[28]

Within a few years of its birth, Radical Reconstruction would turn nearly all Southern whites, including most who had previously voted for Republicans, into fervent opponents of Reconstruction. One reason was that the Radical program sought to advance the political and legal rights of blacks more rapidly than most whites found acceptable. The other, and more important, reason was the wholesale replacement of elites. Prohibiting former Confederates from voting or holding office guaranteed the hostility of most of the elites of Southern white society. Even if deprived of power legally, these individuals retained great influence over the rest of the white population. General John Schofield, in objecting vainly to the policies of the Radicals, had warned presciently that barring former Confederates from government service "excludes from office, both State and federal, nearly every man in the South whose social position, intellectual attainments and known moral character entitle him to the confidence of the people."[29]

The fact that many of the new elites were Northerners or blacks was a major handicap in gaining the allegiance of Southern whites who harbored prejudices against both groups. The new elites, nevertheless, almost certainly could have gained the grudging respect and cooperation of a dejected populace, for whom group prejudices did not preclude personal affections, if they had provided virtuous leadership. Instead, they provided the very opposite type of leadership. Most Southern whites soon equated Radical Reconstruction with misrule and oppression by "Carpetbaggers" (Northern Republicans, who often arrived in the South with cheap carpetbag luggage), "Scalawags" (Southern white Republicans), and blacks. Many of the Scalawags eventually came to the same conclusion about Carpetbaggers and blacks, both of whom tried to push prominent Scalawags out of the government in the later years of Reconstruction.[30] The Democratic press, which did much to shape Southern white perceptions, exaggerated the misdeeds of the Reconstruction authorities with regularity, but there were plenty of real misdeeds, most of which could be traced to bad leadership at the state and local levels.

Although the Radical governments of the South contained persons of talent, commitment, and fairmindedness, most of the leaders ranged from mediocre to abysmal. Marshall Jewell, a leading figure in the Republican Party establishment, was exaggerating only slightly when he lamented that the Carpetbaggers did not have "among them one really first class man." Some of the least able elements of Northern society joined the ranks of the Carpetbaggers. Owing to the conditions of slavery, the Southern blacks in the Radical governments frequently lacked the requisite education, experience, and initiative.[31]

State and local militia and police forces of both races frequently engaged in disorderly and damaging behavior. Blacks composed the bulk of the state militia in many Southern states, either because Southern whites did not want to serve Radical state governments or because Republicans deliberately tried to keep white Democrats out of the units.[32] Otis A. Singletary, author of a history of the black militias that was generally sympathetic to the black militiamen, commented that much of the white hatred of Reconstruction "resulted directly from deeds involving Negro militia forces." Singletary concluded, "Militiamen were not nearly so vicious as they were painted by their enemies but they did from time to time become involved in activities that contributed to the deterioration of relations and led almost inevitably to outbreaks of violence." Singletary put much of the blame for the poor morale and conduct of black troops on their officers, who were a mixture of Carpetbaggers, Scalawags, and blacks. "Although some of the officers were both competent and conscientious," he observed, "the over-all level was very low indeed, resulting from the fact that most of them either were political appointees or had been elected by the men, usually without regard for ability or for past experience." Numerous officers were court-martialed for "drunkenness and conduct unbecoming an officer and a gentleman." One lieutenant in Tennessee had to stand before a court-martial on charges of "habitual drunkenness and utter worthlessness."[33]

The Republican governments also outraged the white population through innumerable transgressions of a less direct sort. Dawdling security forces and partisan courts permitted lawlessness to take hold in some areas, leading to crimes against whites that the white population then attributed to Republican incompetence or neglect.[34] The leaders of the Republican governments committed countless acts of corruption of every imaginable type, a reality that not even their most sympathetic defenders tried to deny.[35] On repeated occasions, the state governments and militias and the Freedmen's Bureau tampered with elections and obtained the votes of blacks through pressure or monetary compensation. And often the government simply failed to perform normal administrative duties.[36]

Whether from the Democratic press, from friends and neighbors, or from personal experience, white Democrats were regularly informed of the government's failings. Unable to influence the government by legal means, many turned to insurgency, with the traditional elites assuming leadership positions and all other elements of white society represented in the ranks.[37] The earliest and most famous of the white insurgent groups was the Ku Klux Klan, which rose to power in middle Tennessee during 1867 with the avowed aim of protecting whites from the oppression and chaos caused by Governor William G. Brownlow, the same William G. Brownlow who had previously tolerated and encouraged brutality against former Confederates in east Tennessee. Brownlow was trying to run middle and west Tennessee with officials and militiamen who were either white Republicans from east Tennessee or blacks from across the state, making no effort to court the Democrats who composed most of the white population in the middle and west. The individuals whom he installed in leadership posts were generally a sorry lot, appointed in some cases purely because they were friends or supporters of Brownlow. As one prominent Radical Republican lamented, "The great impediment of the Republican party of this state is the incompetence of its leaders."[38]

Because of spotty leadership, Tennessee militiamen behaved badly with locals, hurling insults and threats at them and acquiring a reputation for public inebriation. They overreacted to defiant and obnoxious white Democrats, becoming reckless in their punishments and excessive in their use of force. Brownlow promised to arrest and try one officer whose troops had killed an ex-Confederate under dubious circumstances and committed various other crimes known to the public, but Brownlow did not make good on the promise. Whatever good work some officers performed was overshadowed by the highly publicized, and sometimes exaggerated, misconduct of troops under officers without integrity, empathy, or the ability to maintain discipline.[39]

Brownlow's officials and militiamen further alienated the white populations of middle and west Tennessee by failing to maintain order among the populace. Drunkards, thieves, and other miscreants of both races perpetrated countless acts of violence and theft that went unpunished. Those who did get charged with crimes were likely to receive pardons from the Brownlow government if they were Republicans. The Ku Klux Klan rose to prominence by holding out the promise of law and order. Using the whip and the hangman's noose, they punished blacks who were accused of committing crimes, which led to a sharp reduction in criminal activity and consequently a sharp rise in white support for the Klansmen. At first, the Klan punished only blacks accused of crimes; not until its later phases did elements of the Klan target all blacks and their white allies.[40]

In late 1867 and early 1868, the Ku Klux Klan spread into every former Confederate state plus Kentucky, with considerable help from the Democratic press and the exertions of the Klan's Grand Wizard, Nathan Bedford Forrest. A former Confederate general, Forrest had caused endless trouble for the Union during the Civil War with his magnificent cavalry raids. Sherman said that "Forrest was the most remarkable man our Civil War produced on either side." Forrest "had a genius for strategy which was original, and to me incomprehensible. . . . He seemed always to know what I was doing or intended to do, while I am free to confess I could never tell or form any satisfactory idea of what he was trying to accomplish."[41]

At the end of the war, Forrest told his troops to "cultivate friendly feelings toward those with whom we have so long contended" and to "obey the laws" of the federal government.[42] In the next two years, however, Forrest came to believe that Brownlow and other white Radicals were tyrannizing the white South by arming black militiamen, disfranchising former Confederates, and failing to maintain order. He told a reporter from the *Cincinnati Commercial* that he did not hate the federal government, only the "radical revolutionists who are trying to destroy it." The Radical Republicans, especially in Tennessee, were, in his opinion, "the worst men on God's earth — men who would hesitate at no crime."[43]

Although Forrest did much to encourage the creation of new Klan dens, neither he nor anyone else ever held authority over most of the dens; how each den operated was up to its own leaders. Independent organizations similar to the Klan also sprang up across the South, with names like the White Brotherhood, the Invisible Empire, the Swamp Fox Rangers, the Knights of the Black Cross, and the Young Men's Democratic Clubs. As time went on, the leadership of the organizations shifted from respected men of the upper classes to common criminals and other disreputable characters who were inclined to violence against any and all blacks and white Republicans. Early Klan leaders like Forrest, as well as other members of the white Democratic elite, were appalled by the later excesses of these organizations and tried, with some success, to halt them.[44]

The primary counterinsurgency armed forces were the federal army and the state militias. The army could cover little territory, for it had fewer than 20,000 soldiers in the entire South for most of Radical Reconstruction. When federal troops came to a county rife with insurgency, the insurgents almost always avoided attacking them, for army units tended to be well equipped and proficient in combat, and antagonizing them could cause the terrible swift sword to swoop down, in the form of hundreds or even thousands of additional federal troops. The damage inflicted on the South by the likes of Sherman and Sheridan had instilled in Southerners a ghastly fear of federal forces that would not go away, no matter how small their current presence in the South. White insurgents usually evaded capture by federal troops by dispersing and lying low until the troops departed. Federal soldiers, in any event, could not normally take action against suspected insurgents without a request from local authorities, some of whom were afraid of or sympathetic toward the insurgents. The large majority of suspects arrested by the army were set free because of lack of evidence or because of concern about local opinion.[45]

The state militias were not very successful at counterinsurgency either, but for different reasons. The poor leadership of black militia units ensured that they would not perform skillfully, hold together under fire, or behave professionally with the citizenry. The Republican state governments often avoided using black militiamen at all because of questions about their competence or because of fear of antagonizing whites.[46] The white state militia units generally had better officers and were more effective in counterinsurgency missions, although they too committed a goodly number of mistakes and crimes. Though not separated from the rest of the white South by the chasm of race, these militiamen were usually separated by acrid political differences—the bulk of white militiamen were staunch Unionists from Tennessee or Arkansas—and these differences encouraged misbehavior on both sides.

As Klan violence mounted in Tennessee, Governor Brownlow recognized that his militia's poor conduct was increasing popular support for the insurgents, so he endeavored to make more selective use of the militia in 1868, relying mainly on threats to deploy militia units rather than actual deployment, a sensible way of using badly led militiamen. During the summer of 1868, the Tennessee state legislature authorized Brownlow to send state militia units to any county where ten Union men attested that they were needed, and permitted him to impose severe fines and prison terms on anyone who joined or encouraged any secret organization "that shall prowl through the country or towns of this state, by day or by night, disguised or otherwise, for the purpose of disturbing the peace." Alarmed by Brownlow's new powers, conservative leaders in middle and west Tennessee prevailed upon the Klan to halt the violence, and they cut a deal with Brownlow whereby the people of middle and west Tennessee would support the laws in return for the withholding of the state militia. Despite some subsequent tensions, this deal held for the remainder of Republican rule.[47]

The Klan spread across Arkansas as 1868 unfolded, to the point that it rivaled the state government as the principal authority. In the middle of the year, Arkansas governor Powell Clayton resolved to suppress the Klan by arresting and trying its members by military commission. With the state legislature's permission, he declared martial law in the ten counties most beset by Klan depredations and deployed 2,000 militiamen, mainly white Unionists from northern and western counties and blacks from other sections of the state. These troops came under the command of three district commanders—Robert F. Catterson, Samuel W. Mallory, and D. P. Upham, all former Union military officers who were serving in the state legislature. The militiamen were told to procure food and other supplies from the local population and to offer citizens vouchers as compensation. As it turned out, the state government often honored only those vouchers held by Republicans.[48]

On November 13, 1868, Catterson assembled 360 mounted militiamen at Murfreesboro, and proceeded to demonstrate the importance of intelligence collection, preemption, and the decisive use of force. Upon learning that the enemy had gathered munitions and horses at the town of Center Point, his deputy, Major J. H. Demby, sent 100 militiamen to the town to seize the stores.

After accomplishing that mission handily, they obtained intelligence indicating that 500 men from neighboring counties were gathering against them, so they pulled back to Murfreesboro.

The next morning, Catterson sent Demby back to Center Point with a larger detachment. At the town, the lead elements of Demby's forces ran into 400 insurgents, who fired at them from the windows and balconies of houses. Evidently the insurgents had not expected or prepared for a large militia force, for as Catterson's columns swung in from the flanks, the 400 retreated and reassembled behind a church in disorderly fashion. When the state militiamen charged the church, the insurgents scattered and ran for the nearest hiding places. Searching the town for trap doors and hidden attics, the militiamen caught sixty suspected Klansmen, whom they placed under arrest and tried by military commission.

The Arkansas militia suffered a total of just one killed and five wounded during the Battle of Center Point. Clayton commented afterward, "Had it not been for the quickness of perception and promptness of action that characterized General Catterson's operations and his immediate and vigorous attack upon the enemy without parley or delay, the assembling of this very considerable insurgent force might have turned the tide against the State Government and led to the most serious results." The battle and the ensuing roundup of insurgents ended armed resistance in this section of Arkansas.[49]

Catterson next took his militia west into Sevier County, then headed southward into Little River County before bobbing back east through four counties abutting the Louisiana border. Along the way, his troops arrested suspected Klan leaders and hanged a few Klansmen for horrendous crimes. But they also reportedly tortured a number of prisoners to extract confessions and other information, and Catterson did not punish those responsible for the torture. Catterson was, in addition, less than vigilant in preventing his militiamen from confiscating more civilian property than was absolutely necessary. He did, however, respond sternly to reports that his men were raping local women, which were the greatest source of public outrage, and ordered the execution by firing squad of at least one militiaman for such a crime.[50]

Mallory, in command of the southeastern district, proved to be a far less effective counterinsurgency leader than Catterson. For one thing, he failed to instill discipline in the three companies of black militiamen under his authority. One Saturday night, soon after the establishment of a base at the town of Monticello, some of the militiamen got out of hand and fired their weapons wildly for several minutes. No one was reported injured, but the next day whites from both political parties traveled to Little Rock and beseeched Clayton to disband Mallory's companies, offering to put two companies of nonpartisan white militias in charge of the area. Governor Clayton agreed to the proposal. Mallory's troops were discharged without supervision, which led to more trouble, for they pillaged extensively on their way home.[51]

Catterson's militia was called on to complete the tasks that Mallory's men had barely managed to start. Arriving at Monticello in December, Catterson and his troops arrested several important Klansmen and executed one for the murder of a deputy sheriff and a black man. Most of the remaining trouble-makers disappeared as fast as their horses or feet could carry them. This part of the state, long a hotbed of violence, suddenly became a model of peace and quietude. Catterson's militia returned to Little Rock in January to an official parade hosted by the governor, and marched to the state house to the tunes of a military band. They were soon mustered out.[52]

Upham, who arrived with his troops in the northeastern district in early December, proved to be as adept as Catterson in acquiring information on enemy plans and preempting them. Learning that 200 insurgents led by Colonel A. C. Pickett were massing for an assault near the town of Augusta, Upham took fifteen Klan sympathizers hostage and vowed that he would kill them and raze the town if the insurgents attacked. Upham also released a delegation of town citizens to beseech Pickett to call off the assault. Sufficiently intimidated, Pickett sent his men home. A short time later, another insurgent force assembled near Augusta, and Upham again drew his saber before the enemy did, dispatching troops who quickly found, engaged, and defeated the insurgents. Of the suspected Klansmen apprehended by Upham's men, some were tried by military commission and a few were executed.

A number of Upham's men proceeded to plunder the town of Augusta. As one federal officer said, "The men that were disposed to be wild terrorized the people of the city." Upham came under criticism for failing to discipline his troops, although he did on at least some occasions arrest plunderers and return property to its rightful owners. Upham incarcerated his own deputy, Captain John H. Rosa, for detaining residents and demanding ransom payments, a practice that had generated the handsome sum of $4,000. Upham eventually convinced Colonel Pickett and other local notables to disband the Klan, which led Governor Clayton to terminate martial law in the district.[53]

After the onset of the militia campaign, Clayton added Crittenden County, opposite Memphis, to the list of targets on account of widespread violence against blacks and white Republicans and the collusion of the sheriff with the Ku Klux Klan. Local Klansmen had been so brazen as to shoot a captain of the Freedmen's Bureau in the middle of town in broad daylight. When Clayton declared martial law in Crittenden County, the white men in the county announced that they would resist the invaders. But they were caught off guard by the rapidity of the state's reaction. Just after Christmas, a cavalry squad stormed into the county and arrested key figures before any resistance could be offered.

Colonel J. L. Watson subsequently arrived with 400 militiamen, who turned the county jail into a fortress and used it as a base to hunt for Klansmen. A few of these militiamen engaged in violent crimes against civilians, which the Democratic press in Memphis publicized along with some false accusations. Watson put to death one of his militiamen after he was convicted of murder and four more who were guilty of rape. The local Klan besieged the fortress, forcing the militiamen to stay in at night, but eventually the U.S. cavalry came to the rescue and broke up the Klansmen. The most notorious Klan members left the state for Memphis and other places where the authorities did not have Klan-chasing high on their priority lists. By early February most of the militiamen had been withdrawn, and in March Clayton lifted martial law.[54]

By early 1869 the Klan had stopped functioning in Arkansas, laid low by the intimidation and force applied by strong counterinsurgent leaders. The excesses of certain militia units, however, had increased anti-Republican sentiments among whites in Arkansas and elsewhere. The Democrats of Arkansas exploited that hostility when they turned from violence to the ballot box during the succeeding years. In the state elections of 1874, they would sweep the Republicans from power.

After Ulysses S. Grant became president in March 1869, he helped Southern states combat the Klan in ways that Johnson had not, providing weapons and ammunition, for instance, to the state militias of North Carolina and South Carolina. But Grant was reluctant to employ federal troops in counterinsurgency missions because of his political inexperience and his fear of being likened to tyrants like Caesar, Cromwell, and Napoléon.[55] During Grant's first two years in the White House, Klan activity was limited enough that he was spared tough decisions on federal intervention. In early 1871, however, Grant was inundated with requests from Southern Republican governments for help against surging Klan violence, the most alarming of which came from South Carolina.

The Klan was rising in South Carolina as a result of the arming of black militias and the corruption in the state government. Whites accustomed to deferential blacks complained profusely of undisciplined black militiamen marching through the streets with their weapons and insulting whites. Militiamen committed arson against whites with considerable frequency and murdered one white man, a one-armed Confederate veteran who had refused to let passing militiamen steal the whiskey barrels from his wagon. The Klan responded with threats and whippings and, on several occasions, murder. Some of the Klan violence was inflicted on individuals who had committed crimes. As had happened elsewhere, though, vigilante justice was overtaken by racial and political terrorism against blacks and white Republicans as more and more thugs joined the Klan or disguised themselves as Klansmen to conceal their criminal activities.[56]

Because of the Klan resurgence in South Carolina and other states, Congress passed the Ku Klux Klan Act on April 20, 1871. The act made it a federal offense to "conspire together, or go in disguise upon the public highway, or upon the premises of another for the purpose . . . of depriving any person or class of persons of the equal privileges or immunities of the laws." It authorized the president to suspend the writ of habeas corpus until the end of the next congressional session and to use the armed forces to stop the violation of civil rights.[57] Still reluctant to intervene militarily, Grant hoped that the mere passage of the act would compel the Klan to back off. In early May he publicly announced his support for the act, then went to Long Branch, New Jersey, for the summer and left the problem to his subordinates, with whom he maintained communication by mail and telegraph.

A couple of weeks later, concerned by continuing reports of Klan violence, the secretary of war and the attorney general hired detectives to investigate the Klan in several states. Posing as businessmen or job seekers, the detectives quickly turned up all sorts of information about the Klan and its members and found that it remained in operation, if often in a subdued manner. In July the Justice Department issued orders to commence prosecutions of Klansmen. The U.S. attorney for northern Mississippi, G. Wiley Wells, was among the swiftest in pushing ahead, producing nearly 200 indictments by early September. In North Carolina, the federal government obtained the conviction of forty-nine offenders. Arrests were made in relatively modest numbers in other states because of Klan inactivity or the unwillingness of federal and state authorities to detain Klan suspects for fear of provoking more insurgent violence.[58]

The prosecutions of July and August failed to intimidate the insurgents in much of the South, for Klan outrages continued on a large scale, especially in South Carolina. Brigadier General Alfred Howe Terry, commander of the Department of the South, told Grant in late August that the army ought to crush the Klan decisively in one place, South Carolina, to discourage Klansmen elsewhere. Because the army's presence in the South was so small—only 8,038 regulars were on occupation duty in 1871—it was impossible to attack the insurgents in many states at once.[59]

The reports from South Carolina in late August so worried Grant that he left Long Branch and sent the U.S. attorney general, Amos T. Akerman, to visit the Carolinas to see what was going on. Akerman reported back that the president should use everything at his disposal, including suspension of habeas corpus, to strike at the Klan. On October 17, Grant suspended habeas corpus in nine South Carolina counties, the first time the writ had been suspended in peacetime, and the U.S. marshals and federal troops began mass arrests. As the federal government cracked down, the insurgents offered little armed resistance, opting instead to lie low or flee the state.

The most effective Union commander in the South Carolina campaign was Major Lewis Merrill, who was assigned to York County, in the Piedmont area bordering North Carolina. Merrill had attended West Point, where he was an unexceptional performer, graduating twentieth of the thirty-four students in the class of 1855, and a serious troublemaker, having nearly been court-martialed for threatening an instructor. A tall man of athletic build and elegant bearing, Merrill exuded charisma. In 1861 and 1862 he led Union cavalrymen in hunting down secessionist guerrillas in Missouri, showing little mercy to the enemy. After he executed twenty-two captured guerrillas by firing squad, he became so controversial a figure that President Lincoln summoned him to the White House for an explanation. Merrill described to the president the murders these men had committed, and said that he had tried unsuccessfully to obtain approval from Washington for the executions. Lincoln put his hand on Merrill's shoulder and said, "Remember, young man, there are some things which should be done which it would not do for superiors to order done." Merrill went on to participate in the capture of Little Rock in 1863. During his service in Missouri and Arkansas, he demonstrated a variety of talents, most notably the ability to adapt to changing circumstances. In the last years of the war, however, he was assigned to garrison and escort duty, involving only minor skirmishes with enemy irregulars, which prevented him from rising as high in the ranks as his peers. After the war, he served in the army as a judge advocate and inspector general, acquiring experience in legal and investigative tasks that served him well later.[60]

Merrill arrived in York County near the end of March 1871. Because of the presence of federal troops and the concern of white citizens that the Klan had gone too far in recent times, the Klan was at first quiescent. In the middle of April, however, the Klan erupted, starting with the Saturday night whipping of an elderly black man whose son had eluded Klan pursuers. Merrill decided that although Klan members were a small minority of the population, they enjoyed the sympathies of practically the entire white population, so large numbers of people ought to be held accountable. But Merrill and his ninety men could only support local law enforcement authorities, who were sympathetic to the Klan. Any major actions would have to await the dispensation of authority from above.

As Merrill bided his time, he took the initiative in collecting information about the local Klan. He and his troops spoke with everyone they could find, from local dignitaries to reputed Klansmen to blacks who had witnessed Klan violence. They hired informants, including some within the ranks of the Klan. Using the mass of facts thus obtained, Merrill compiled a detailed description of the Klan's organization and personnel and a lengthy catalog of its activities, including six murders and four hundred whippings since the previous December, both of which he forwarded up the chain of command. His reports helped convince Congress and the president to take action in South Carolina.[61]

When Grant announced the suspension of habeas corpus in the nine South Carolina counties, great numbers of white men fled York County before the arrests could begin, but a surprisingly large group of Klansmen did not. Upon receiving the authorization to act, Merrill spread out his forces and ordered them to move against the insurgents simultaneously to deny any more of them time to escape. Because of his investments in intelligence collection, Merrill was able to target the insurgents with pinpoint accuracy. Merrill's troops apprehended numerous suspects, and hundreds more turned themselves in after the arrests began. Merrill sent troops to Shelby, Rutherfordton, and other towns across the North Carolina border to snatch Klansmen who had evaded the first of the nets he had cast.[62]

On only a few occasions did Merrill's troops arrest the wrong people. Through further investigation, Merrill discovered their innocence and released them. Attorney General Akerman said that Merrill was ideally suited to the task at hand, summing up Merrill's leadership abilities by describing him as "resolute, collected, bold and prudent, with a good legal head, very discriminating between truth and falsehood, very indignant at wrong, and yet master of his indignation; the safer because incredulous at the outset, and, therefore, disposed to scrutinize reports the more keenly."[63]

Merrill apprehended close to 700 people in York County by December 31. The government did not have enough prosecutors to handle that many cases, so detainees not guilty of serious offense were released after they confessed. Even more detainees would have been released had Merrill not compiled so much evidence against the defendants, for his handiwork allowed the prosecutions to proceed expeditiously.[64] In the other South Carolina counties where arrests had been made, far fewer people were arrested, prosecuted, or convicted because federal officers had not collected evidence as energetically or carefully as Merrill.

The campaign against the Klan in South Carolina was seriously set back by the resignation of Akerman in December 1871, for his successor, George H. Williams, was much less vigorous in prosecuting Klan members. As a result, many of the accused received generous plea bargains or no sentences at all, and only a small number of the accused—those who had committed the most serious crimes and were implicated by the most solid evidence—paid serious penalties.[65] The South Carolina campaign, nevertheless, succeeded in discouraging white violence in the state and across the South. By 1872, the Klan and the other white insurgency organizations were moribund in most Southern states.

One exception was Louisiana, where from 1872 to 1874 white insurgents clashed with federal troops with some regularity. The Louisiana insurgency was fueled by poor Republican governance and disputes between Republicans and Democrats over state elections. The hotly contested gubernatorial race of 1872 between Republican William P. Kellogg and Democrat John McEnery, which was characterized by unusually widespread voter intimidation and fraud on both sides, produced a standoff that required presidential intercession. Believing that it was impossible to know who had really won the election, Grant decided after some hesitation to declare Kellogg the winner. To his own consternation and that of many other Americans, Grant had to use the army to protect Kellogg from enraged Democrats. McEnery registered his protest by setting up a shadow government, which Grant tolerated until March 1873, when one of McEnery's lieutenants formed an insurgent militia and attacked a large police station in New Orleans. Federal troops came to the rescue, causing the rebels to flee and the Democratic press to issue biting condemnations of federal tyranny. Kellogg then used the city police to break up McEnery's legislature.[66]

Kellogg controlled the state government for the rest of 1873 and 1874. His government was chock-full of incompetents and was notable even by Reconstruction standards for its surfeit of corruption and its inordinate number of pardons to Republican criminals. It failed to exert any authority in some sections of the state because the state militia suffered from the usual leadership problems and federal forces were too few in number to fill the void. Kellogg removed elected Democratic officials in certain parishes and replaced them with Republicans, to which the insurgents responded by driving away blacks and white Republicans.

The largest outbreak of violence occurred at Colfax, the seat of Grant Parish, in the middle of the state, where Kellogg had kicked out the elected sheriff, Christopher Columbus Nash, and replaced him with a Republican. The Republican sheriff added to popular resentment by fortifying the courthouse and using it as a base for several hundred militiamen. Organizing a posse of whites from nearby parishes, the ousted Nash launched an attack on the courthouse. The poor quality of the militia unit's leadership was evident in the militiamen's flight from their fortifications before they had inflicted significant casualties and in their attempt to regroup in a building that could easily be surrounded. The insurgents ended the militia's resistance by setting the building on fire. Thirty-seven black militiamen who survived the fire were taken prisoner and shot that night. The total number of black militia casualties was never determined, but a deputy U.S. marshal subsequently found sixty-nine of the unit's men in a shallow grave. The army and Kellogg's government responded vigorously in this case, sending troops to Colfax and arresting as many of the insurgents as they could find. Nash escaped under fire, swimming his horse across the Red River, but nine others were apprehended and put on trial in federal court, although they received little to no prison time.[67]

The White League, an insurgent organization that supported McEnery and the Democratic Party, expanded rapidly in 1874 in response to the proliferating reports of misrule by the Carpetbaggers and blacks in the state government. In

July, the White League published a manifesto stating its intention of "restoring an honest and intelligent government to the State of Louisiana" by replacing blacks with Southern whites. "Where the white rules," it asserted, "the negro is peaceful and happy; where the black rules, the negro is starved and oppressed."[68] With a large presence in eighteen parishes, the White League held approximately 14,000 men in its ranks by the end of August. During the summer, the White League lynched several blacks and forced numerous Republican officials to relinquish their positions.[69]

On the afternoon of September 14, the former Confederate colonel David B. Penn, who was McEnery's "lieutenant governor," urged a crowd of White Leaguers in New Orleans to "arm and assemble for the purpose of driving the usurpers from power."[70] After Kellogg rejected a demand from the group to resign, 8,400 insurgents fetched their weapons and seized the city hall. Later in the afternoon, they clashed with 3,600 members of the state militia and police in what became known as the Battle of Liberty Place. The insurgents overpowered the militia and police forces, who broke rank and fled. The White League proceeded to occupy all of the public buildings except those held by federal forces—the latter including the Custom House, where Kellogg had gone for protection.

Hoping to avoid further armed conflict, Grant issued a presidential proclamation in which he ordered all "turbulent and disorderly persons [who] have combined together with force and arms to overthrow the State government of Louisiana . . . to disperse and retire peaceably to their respective abodes within five days." If they did not obey this command, Grant warned, the federal military would deal with them. Grant gave the White League five days because it would take five days for the reinforcements he had summoned from Alabama, Tennessee, Georgia, and South Carolina to arrive in New Orleans. The threat worked. McEnery decided that political competition and guerrilla warfare were preferable to a conventional war that would most likely have an unhappy ending, so he convinced the White Leaguers to go home and let Kellogg retake power.[71]

Although the attempted coup had failed in New Orleans, it emboldened White Leaguers elsewhere in the state to force Republicans out of office. The reach of the Kellogg government, never very long, was reduced such that it barely extended beyond the outskirts of New Orleans. As General William H. Emory, commander of the Department of the Gulf, reported, "Nearly every parish in the State, following the example of New Orleans, is more or less in a

State of insurrection." Emory asked for and received more federal troops and cavalry to fight rebels in the parishes.[72]

The federal infantry and cavalry concentrated in northern Louisiana, the most insubordinate and lawless part of the state. At the head of these forces stood the Union's premier counterinsurgency commander, Lewis Merrill. As soon as Merrill arrived in Shreveport, he took active measures to subdue the "fools and unreasoning hot heads," as he called the insurgents. He sent troops to arrest James H. Cosgrove, editor of the *Natchitoches People's Vindicator*, which was sympathetic to the White League, and arrested other prominent persons who had participated in violence or otherwise violated Reconstruction laws. At the same time, he reinstated most of the Republicans whom the insurgents had compelled to resign. Merrill, however, was unable to bring insurgents to justice as effectively as he had in South Carolina because the U.S. attorney general's office lacked interest in pursuing the matter.[73]

The Democratic press denounced Merrill even more harshly than it had in South Carolina. He took it stoically, commenting, "So long as freedom of the press means license to lie and slander at pleasure every officer whose discharge of duty offends one or frequently both political parties, there would seem to be no remedy for the officer, and nothing for him to do but possess his soul in patience, and wait for a change of station to some frontier post, where the savages, whose feelings he must hurt, have no newspapers through which to assail him."[74]

During the elections for the Louisiana state legislature in 1874, the Republican-dominated state elections board declared that the two parties had won an equal number of seats, but the Democrats had good reason to believe that they had won more. With another crisis looming, Grant ordered Philip Sheridan to Louisiana with instructions to "ascertain the true condition of affairs" and to provide "such suggestions . . . as you may deem advisable and judicious."[75] Having come to doubt the abilities of Emory, Grant told Sheridan that he could take command of the Division of the South if necessary. Grant believed that Sheridan was the best man for the job because of his brilliance and his ability to act quickly and decisively on his own initiative, which would be critical in a fast-moving situation that probably could not be guided from Washington. But the choice of Sheridan was ill advised, given Sheridan's stumbles in Texas during the early years of Reconstruction and his reputation for cruelty among white Southerners. When word got out that Sheridan was heading to New Orleans, Democratic journalists started firing broadsides.

"We know him for the man who desolated the valley of the Shenandoah, and brought fire and the sword and famine among its people," pronounced the *New Orleans Picayune*. "He has been sent here by the President in order to add this crowning outrage to the outrages which have already been heaped upon us."[76]

At noon on January 4, 1875, the new state legislature met for the first time. Democrats in the audience pulled out pistols and knives, and Democratic representatives put themselves in charge. Kellogg called on the army to oust the Democrats, at which point Sheridan ordered federal troops to kick out the Democrats and give the Republicans control over the legislature, which they promptly and efficiently did.[77] That evening, Sheridan took over command of the federal forces from Emory, whom he described as "a very weak old man, entirely unfitted for this place."[78]

An outcry against Sheridan's use of the army spilled forth from prominent Northerners as well as from white Southerners. A man of greater political shrewdness, flexibility, and impartiality would have attempted diplomacy before using force, they argued. Sheridan dug himself, and the whole cause of Reconstruction, into additional trouble with his next actions. In telegrams that soon found their way into newspapers, Sheridan recommended using military courts to try the leaders of the White League, provoking a new chorus of accusations that he had sunk into tyranny. The *New York Times* likened Sheridan to Oliver Cromwell during the Protectorate and declared that the federal troops in Louisiana "should be placed under a commander who is able to keep his head and his temper under control."[79] James A. Garfield, a Republican congressman who was a few years away from becoming president, lamented, "This is the darkest day for the future of the Republican party I have ever seen. The Louisiana question now appears to be the mill stone that threatens to sink our party out of sight. That question is difficult when handled with the utmost wisdom, but it has been so terribly botched by the President and General Sheridan during the last four days as to place the great burden of the trouble upon us."[80] The state legislatures of New York, Pennsylvania, Ohio, Illinois, Missouri, and several Southern states issued condemnations of Sheridan.[81]

The besieged Grant publicly expressed confidence in Sheridan and denounced the White League but said that he would not follow Sheridan's recommendation to circumvent the civil courts. The U.S. House of Representatives sent a committee to Louisiana for three weeks to investigate the calamity, which provided Sheridan with yet more opportunities to trip and fall. Sheridan gave the committee long lists of political murders committed by the White League in Louisiana, but his statistics were self-contradictory and came from disreputable sources, which cast new doubts on his integrity. The House committee concluded that Sheridan, as well as the state elections board, had deliberately undercounted Democratic votes. The Democrats actually deserved sixteen more seats in the legislature than the Republicans. In a stark demonstration of Sheridan's inability to maneuver politically, it was the committee members themselves who forged a compromise between the two political parties of Louisiana: the Democrats let Kellogg continue in office unmolested, and the Republicans gave the Democrats a majority of seats in the legislature.[82]

From the late 1860s to the mid-1870s, news of corruption and election tampering by Carpetbaggers, Scalawags, and blacks across the South caused the majority of Northern whites to turn against Radical Reconstruction. Northern politicians chose not to intervene in the early 1870s when Southern whites, becoming unified in their opposition to Reconstruction, began voting Democratic state governments into power, even when those whites used violence and intimidation to prevent blacks from voting. Ultimately, the shortcomings of Radical Reconstruction, supplemented by the general corruption and ineptitude of the Grant administration, led to Reconstruction's inglorious demise. To end the dispute over the 1876 presidential election between Democrat Samuel J. Tilden and Republican Rutherford Hayes, the Democrats, desperate in their hatred of Radical Reconstruction, agreed to let Hayes have the presidency in return for the withdrawal of federal troops from the South. The removal of those troops precipitated the collapse of Republican power in the Southern states as white Democrats took over the state governments that had not turned Democratic already. Across the South, Democrats stripped blacks of many of the protections and privileges they had received during Reconstruction.

Over the course of its history, Radical Reconstruction had, despite a great deal of incompetence, suppressed most of the armed insurgents who had challenged federal authority. They did so more by the threat of force than by the use of force, and with much help from the insurgents, who hurt themselves in the eyes of Southern white society by moving from vigilantism to political and racial terrorism. Yet, in the end, Radical Reconstruction failed to prevent its opponents in the South from achieving their political objective of restoring white political and economic dominance, because it alienated nearly all Southern whites and broke the will of Northern whites to impose egalitarian racial policies.

Northern Republicans could have made Reconstruction more palatable to Southern whites by introducing political and social change more gradually, although it is not certain that Northern public opinion would have accepted such gradualism in the late 1860s. Their worst mistake was supplanting the existing Southern elites with Carpetbaggers, Scalawags, and blacks. The Radical Republicans did more than enough to alienate the traditional elites but not enough to destroy or even seriously reduce their influence over the population. Taking away the elites' rights to vote and hold office did not prevent them from mounting resistance through insurgency and, later, through democratic elections. Given the strong traditional loyalties of Southern whites, permanent neutralization of the native white elites would have required the barbarity of the French, Russian, and Chinese revolutions, which the American people would never have accepted and which, in any case, would have been as disastrous in America as it was in France, Russia, and China.

The Northern Radicals failed to introduce new elites who could have wrested influence away from the old elites. Committing a common and often fatal error in counterinsurgency, they did not properly gauge the merits of the elites whom they were empowering. Some overestimated the quality of the newly created elites, while others fell victim to the fallacy that leadership quality varies little from one group to the next. Nor was much effort made to balance considerations of merit against considerations of politics in leadership appointments; the scales almost always tipped too heavily toward politics. The Carpetbaggers, Scalawags, and blacks lacked the initiative, integrity, and dedication necessary to gain and maintain the support of the South's white population. They failed to build militia and police forces capable of safeguarding the people's security and instead jeopardized the people's security by fielding unruly militiamen. Rather than inspiring the people with moral rectitude, they alienated them with rigged elections, biased justice, and pilferage from the public coffers.

If the South's traditional leaders had been adamantly opposed to any advancement for blacks, the Republicans could perhaps have been excused for trying to circumvent them. But that was not the case. Many of these leaders had supported the Republican Party in the pre-Radical phase of Reconstruction, and most others were willing to accept a moderate form of Reconstruction. Although the white elites objected to the drastic nature and rapid pace of change envisioned by Northerners, the federal government almost certainly could have done more for blacks by gradually nudging these whites along and forging an enduring partnership than by undertaking the Radical program and losing practically everything. Had it not been for the imposition of the new, ineffective elites during Radical Reconstruction, Southern and Northern whites would not have been so receptive in 1877 to the idea of eliminating federal oversight of the South or to the idea of rescinding most of the political rights gained by blacks since the Civil War.

In contrast to the state governments of Radical Reconstruction, the U.S. Army could boast that its leaders in the South included hundreds of accomplished men. But commanders who had vanquished their Confederate foes in the big conventional battles of the Civil War often proved less effective in combating insurgents. Some, including Grant and Sheridan, failed to cope with the ambiguities and compromises of the political side of counterinsurgency because they were, by temperament, much less comfortable with counterinsurgency than with conventional warfare. Some lacked the empathy, integrity, or organizational talent to keep their troops from harming the civilian population. Those who shared Sheridan's contempt for the entire white South could hardly work effectively with the local whites.

At the same time, the army did have some commanders who were cut out perfectly for counterinsurgency duty. Officers like Major General Charles H. Smith and Major Lewis Merrill possessed the right attributes and brought much grief to the insurgents, whether by cultivating white elites, gathering information with skill and vigor, or insisting on impartial treatment of the local population. But top authorities in the army and the federal government did not try very hard to promote such men or bring more of them into the army. For the U.S. Army, this problem would recur in future wars of insurgency. In fact, it is still present today.

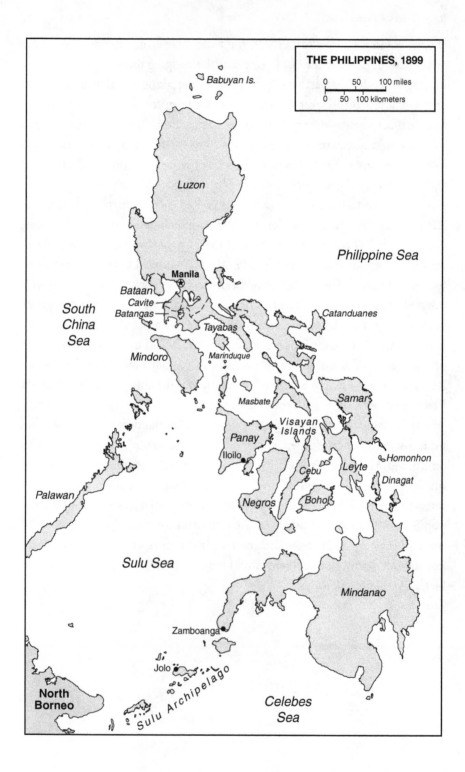

THE PHILIPPINES, 1899

0   50   100 miles

0   50   100 kilometers

Babuyan Is.

Luzon

Philippine Sea

Manila

Bataan

Cavite

Batangas

South China Sea

Catanduanes

Tayabas

Mindoro

Marinduque

Masbate

Samar

Visayan Islands

Panay

Iloilo

Homonhon

Cebu

Leyte

Dinagat

Palawan

Negros

Bohol

Sulu Sea

Mindanao

Zamboanga

Jolo

North Borneo

Sulu Archipelago

Celebes Sea

CHAPTER 4

The Philippine Insurrection

As the sun rose over Manila Bay, seven American warships chugged forward from the southwest. The flagship, the USS *Olympia*, sported four 8-inch guns and steel deck plates, and the squadron also had a "baby battleship" with four 6-inch guns and various other cruisers of 1880s vintage, members of the last generation of warships propelled by both sail and steam. The huge Spanish shore guns hurled projectiles at the intruders to no avail, their rounds plopping harmlessly into the water.

The American ships intended to destroy those guns, but only as a secondary objective. What had enticed them to Manila Bay were the seven Spanish warships moored at the Cavite navy yard. Though equal in number to the American ships, the Spanish ships were older, slower, smaller, less heavily armed, and less thickly armored. Some were made of wood or had enough wood on board to make excellent tinder. The Spanish ships fired first, at 5:15 a.m., before the American ships were in range. Commodore George Dewey, commanding the U.S. squadron from the bridge of the *Olympia*, waited until the distance had closed to 5,500 yards before ordering his ships to fire. At 5:22 a.m., as ship bands played "The Star-Spangled Banner," 250-pound shells began vaulting from the turrets of the American cruisers.

The U.S. squadron concentrated its fire on the Spanish flagship, the *Reina Cristina*, and scored one direct hit after another. Shells took down the mizzenmast and the national flag, smashed into the sick bay, the after magazine, and the fire room, and created a gaping wound in the hull, which spewed steam from the superheater. When more than half of the 352 Spanish crewmen lay dead or wounded and the magazines stood in danger of exploding, the ship's commander ordered the ship to be sunk. The American turrets then swiveled toward the remaining Spanish ships.

To the astonishment of both sides, rounds from the Spanish ships and shore batteries dropped all around the American ships but scored very few hits, and most of the hits caused only superficial damage to decks or rigging. Only one Spanish round penetrated the hull of an American ship, the *Baltimore*, putting a gun out of action and exploding ammunition, but it inflicted only eight minor wounds. Remarkably, no American was killed during the entire battle.

By 7:30 a.m. all of the Spanish ships were ablaze from the Americans' methodical salvos, and the Spanish guns were incapable of firing. But the Americans did not move in for the kill. Commodore Dewey pulled the flotilla back out of range because of a report—erroneous, it turned out—that some of his ships were running low on ammunition and needed to restock. As the ships regrouped, Dewey let all the crewmen have breakfast. They ate a leisurely meal of sardines, corned beef, and hardtack and then smoked cigarettes, strolling the decks as if enjoying a pleasure cruise. The break lasted for nearly three hours.

Once the battle resumed, the Spaniards endured another couple of hours of bombardment before deciding to scuttle their fleet and run up a white flag at the shore arsenal. The American squadron landed a party of seven men to finish the destruction of the vessels in the navy yard, then steamed the short distance up the coast to Manila, where it took up a menacing position near the city. That night they could still see the hulls of the Spanish ships burning at Cavite. Magazines periodically exploded and shot fiery debris up hundreds of feet.

Dewey sent word to the Spanish that if the shore batteries at Manila fired on his squadron, he would pulverize the city with his mighty guns. The Spanish agreed not to fire. Occupying the city was not an option for the United States at this point, however, for Dewey did not have enough men for the task. Instead, the American fleet undertook a blockade of Manila and awaited troops and further orders from Washington.[1]

Commander Dewey had, in a few hours, made what would be the first step in America's march to European-style imperialism. That truth was not, however, readily visible. President William McKinley had ordered the Manila Bay attack of May 1, 1898, to hurt the Spanish in the early moments of the Spanish-

American War and increase his leverage in future negotiations, not to take permanent control of the Philippines. He had gone to war with Spain over Cuba, and then only after overcoming his own doubts about the wisdom of such a course. Averse to bloodshed and beholden to businessmen who opposed war for economic reasons, McKinley had resisted the clamors for war from the "yellow journalists" of Hearst and Pulitzer and other jingoists like Assistant Secretary of the Navy Theodore Roosevelt. Even after an official American inquiry into the explosion of the USS *Maine* in Havana harbor attributed the event to a Spanish mine, McKinley had hesitated, eliciting from Roosevelt the remark that "McKinley has no more backbone than a chocolate éclair."[2] What ultimately led McKinley to declare war remains a point of contention; it may have been disgust with Spain's harsh repression of Cuban rebels, deference to overwhelming American public opinion, or some other consideration.[3]

Soon after the stunning victory at Manila Bay, McKinley ordered the organization of an American expedition to take Manila and hold it as a bargaining chip. In the interim, to undermine the Spaniards in the rest of the archipelago, an American steamer brought ashore an exiled Filipino nationalist named Emilio Aguinaldo, who in 1896 had started a revolt against Spanish rule. The Americans gave him a supply of rifles, a decision they rued later, when those rifles were turned on the Americans. In June, Aguinaldo declared the Philippines independent and appointed himself ruler. Few Americans, however, were paying attention to Aguinaldo at this time, focused as they were on Cuba, where a clumsy U.S. Army was battling an even clumsier Spanish force.

Manila came back into America's view in August, following the capitulation of the Spanish forces in Cuba. On August 13, newly arrived American forces initiated a ground assault on Manila and overwhelmed a tepid Spanish defense. Aguinaldo and his rebel armed forces sought to enter the city with the American victors but were kept out, for the Americans feared that the rebels would, among other things, kill priests and other civilians, as they had done elsewhere in recent weeks. Aguinaldo responded by cutting off the city's water supply and demanding that he be treated as the independent leader of the Philippines.

In the United States, American public sentiment for annexing the Philippines was on the rise. Many reasons were given. The Philippines could not be left to Spain, which by now had assumed devilish proportions in American eyes, nor to the other European imperial powers, which were only marginally better than Spain, nor to Aguinaldo and other Filipinos, who had demonstrated a mixture of incompetence and tyranny in their early attempts at governance. Annexation, said its supporters, would enable the United States to extend its military and economic power and spread its superior civilization. On October 28, for reasons that remain obscure, McKinley ordered the annexation of the Philippines, and the Senate, after contentious debate, ratified it by a vote of fifty-seven to twenty-seven.

McKinley instructed the expeditionary commander, General Elwell S. Otis, to extend American control across the Philippine archipelago, a diverse array of islands extending over 500,000 square miles, home to approximately seven million people. McKinley instructed the army to remember that "we come, not as invaders or conquerors, but as friends," and decreed that "it should be the earnest and paramount aim of the military administration to win the confidence, respect, and affection of the inhabitants of the Philippines by assuring them in every possible way that full measure of individual rights and liberties which is the heritage of a free people, and by proving to them that the mission of the United States is one of benevolent assimilation, substituting the mild sway of justice and right for arbitrary rule."[4]

Aguinaldo continued to insist on Philippine independence, and he built up a military presence outside Manila that did not go unnoticed in General Otis's headquarters. Tensions mounted between Aguinaldo's forces and the American soldiers. On the night of February 4, 1899, a small number of men from each side got into a gunfight in Manila, which each side accused the other of starting, and combat exploded across the outskirts of the city like a chain of firecrackers. The next morning American artillery opened up on Aguinaldo's main line of defense, on the Santa Mesa Ridge, while American infantrymen dashed ahead under the artillery smoke. The Filipinos fought back with varying degrees of intensity and skill and generally little organization. Within a few hours, the Americans took the blockhouses on the ridge, and during the afternoon they overran Aguinaldo's main strong points on the ridge. Most of Aguinaldo's forces in Manila were defeated in a single day.

Attacking outward from Manila, the Americans battled Aguinaldo's Army of Liberation of the Philippines for the next several months. Aguinaldo had tried to model his army after European armies, but the final product was merely a patchwork of local volunteer militia units, with neither the leadership nor the training that enabled European and American armies to operate coherently in large groups. Even when defending fortified positions in terrain ideally suited for defense, Aguinaldo's rebel forces consistently lost to the

Americans. But Aguinaldo was able to prolong the war by retreating across jungles and rivers, where the absence of roads compelled the Americans to advance at a slog. American operations came to a halt in the summer, when monsoon rains turned the islands into mud. In the fall, however, the Americans returned to the offensive and wiped out most of Aguinaldo's army before the season was out. Narrowly evading capture, Aguinaldo ordered his commanders to switch from a conventional war to a guerrilla insurgency.

Aguinaldo's provincial commands retained small groups of regular troops, armed with rifles, who conducted hit-and-run attacks on the Americans and intimidated or killed Filipino collaborators. Operating out of the archipelago's dense jungles, high cogon grass, and mountains, they proved a very difficult target for the counterinsurgents. More numerous were militiamen who lived as ordinary civilians. Typically armed with only bolo knives or spears, these insurgents largely avoided combat and instead concentrated on such as tasks as moving supplies, setting booby traps, gathering information, and spreading rumors that the Americans were intent on raping all women.[5] Local rebels with no ties to Aguinaldo controlled most militia forces, and they also operated shadow governments that collected taxes, recruited civilians into the rebellion, and enforced law and order.

In most regions of the Philippines, the insurgent leaders consisted exclusively of men from the *principalia,* the Filipino upper class, who had taken to arms to gain independence from foreign control. Redistributing wealth and altering relations between the upper and lower classes were not on the agenda. The less affluent Filipinos usually supported the rebellion because of longstanding loyalty to the principalia, although in select provinces they participated for a variety of other reasons, such as religion, compulsion by the insurgents, or local power struggles. As in times past, the peasants obeyed the dictates of the principalia and gave them a large fraction of their crops, while the principalia provided land, security, religious ceremonies, and insurance against poor harvests. Many peasants served in insurgent units commanded by their own landlords.[6]

In early 1900, General Otis spread the American occupation forces across the islands of the archipelago. An officer in the 140th New York Infantry during the Civil War, Otis had distinguished himself in the pivotal fighting on Little Round Top during the Battle of Gettysburg. In the ensuing decades he had published articles on military law and American Indians and directed a long series of administrative and logistical tasks, most recently the transportation of American forces to the Philippines, the swiftness of which stood in stark contrast to the appallingly sluggish deployment of American troops to Cuba. In addition to his considerable intelligence and administrative skills, Otis had a knack for designing conventional military campaigns.

Otis broke down the conventional forces in the Philippines into small occupation units and divided command by geographic region. His dispatch in reorganizing the forces and reorienting them toward civil affairs was impressive. But he had serious flaws as a counterinsurgency leader. Through his overbearing, self-righteous, and sarcastic comportment, he managed to alienate American officers of every rank. His leadership was made even less inspiring by his dullness and his unappealing appearance—he was often compared to a beagle with muttonchop whiskers. His abrasive and boring personality also guaranteed failure in dealing with the American press, whose reports from the Philippines had much power to undermine American popular and congressional support for the war. Relying on a leadership style that had served him well in managing the movement of troops and the acquisition of supplies, Otis seldom left Manila, which prevented him from staying adequately informed about the status of the war or the performance of his subordinates. For most of his long workdays, Otis sat in his office reviewing the mounds of papers that covered his desk and the tables he had ordered brought in to hold more mounds. Details consumed him. When he left his palatial residence and went into the city, he talked only to the wealthiest segment of Manila society, who conveyed to him the misleading impression that most Filipino elites favored American annexation and detested Aguinaldo.[7]

Otis issued all U.S. commanders some detailed guidance on the methods they should use and those they could not use, but, being far removed from most of the fighting, he could not compel commanders to adhere to that guidance. Some of the departmental and district commanders, occupying positions on the organizational chart between Otis and the local commanders, attempted to control the conduct of local counterinsurgency efforts, unwisely taking decisions away from local commanders who possessed superior comprehension of conditions on the ground. Commanders at the departmental and district levels were typically appointed based on seniority rather than suitability for the job, a bureaucratic policy more appropriate for a peacetime army than one at war. In only a few cases did the army rapidly promote young officers and propel them into departmental or district commands, most famously the cases of Frederick Funston and J. Franklin Bell, both of whom had led brilliantly during the conventional war at home and won Congressional Medals of Honor. The advisability of supplanting seniority with merit was amply demonstrated when men like Funston and Bell excelled as counterinsurgency commanders, while officers selected based on seniority often fizzled.

A prime case of fizzling was Major General John C. Bates. A decent but undistinguished field officer in the regular army, he was appointed commander of the department of southern Luzon on the basis of seniority. He spent nearly all his time in Manila and on his rare visits outside the capital went only to nearby provinces. His inability to familiarize himself with the realities in the areas under his command did not stop him from rejecting innovative proposals from the provincial commanders, to the general detriment of the war effort. Because of his isolation and inattentiveness, he could not identify which of his subordinates were underperforming, a critical task for an officer at that level.[8]

Intermediate commanders who attempted to micromanage the war from their perches, especially those with no tact or charisma, drained initiative and dedication from their subordinates. The best departmental and district commanders left most decisions in the hands of local commanders while monitoring them and correcting or replacing the poor performers. Brigadier General Samuel B. M. Young, commander of the first district in northern Luzon, epitomized this type of leadership. By refusing to force specific actions on his subordinates and by shielding them from the demands of the central authorities in Manila, Young promoted creativity and initiative. A fine judge of talent, he relieved subordinate commanders who were unfit for their jobs. Not by coincidence, his district was among the most innovative and successful in combating the insurgents.[9] One other function that intermediate commanders could and sometimes did perform was the persuasion of Filipino elites to support the United States.[10]

Local commanders, even those serving under officers who sought to micromanage, enjoyed a great deal of autonomy because distance and terrain limited the frequency of communications and supervisory visits. Commanders in the provinces found ways to disregard or only partially comply with orders that they considered foolish, which dampened the impact of leadership weaknesses at higher levels. Consequently, the success or failure of counterinsurgency depended largely on the overall quality of the pool of junior officers and the ability of senior officers to put the best of the junior officers into provincial and post commands. The American leadership did not always place junior officers wisely, but this handicap was overcome by the richness of talent in the junior officer pool.

During the critical period of the insurgency, most of the American company-grade and field-grade officers serving in the Philippines belonged to the U.S. Volunteers, a newly formed entity with an exceptionally gifted officer corps. Created by the Army Act of 1899, the U.S. Volunteers replaced the State Volunteers and U.S. Army Regulars, who had fought the conventional war, and were much superior to both because of the War Department's rigorous screening of officers. The colonels, lieutenant colonels, and majors in the U.S. Volunteers were picked from highly experienced officers who had distinguished themselves in the Regulars in 1899. The majors alone had an average of twenty-seven years in the army, and only two were under the age of fifty. The principal sources of captains and lieutenants were top State Volunteer officers, experienced noncommissioned officers who had fought well in the Philippines or Cuba, and, in the case of the lieutenants, recent West Point graduates. Nearly all of the captains were men over forty with at least twenty years in the army. Governors, congressmen, former officers, and even a few mothers sent telegrams or made personal visits to McKinley and War Department administrators to advocate for candidates. During the rush to raise forces in 1898, such entreaties had brought commissions in the Regulars to more than a few men whose political significance far exceeded their leadership talents. After learning of the problems caused by such men, McKinley and the War Department resolved to avoid repeating the mistake this time around, and therefore the selection of the officers of the U.S. Volunteers was almost always based on merit.[11]

The enlisted men in the U.S. Volunteers were also very high in quality, having been handpicked from a huge mass of men who, in the spirit of patriotism or adventure, had volunteered for service. Physically and mentally fit men in their twenties, they possessed experience in a wide variety of civilian occupations relevant to running a country.[12] Yet having such fine men in the ranks did not much reduce the importance of fine officers. Counterinsurgency thrived under good officers and drooped under bad ones. Henry T. Allen, who as chief of the Philippine Constabulary witnessed the counterinsurgency efforts on most of the islands, commented, "It is a fact that the disposition of nearly every town in the archipelago depends upon the officer or officers who have been commanding in that town."[13]

The extreme decentralization of authority made initiative, dedication, and integrity paramount requirements for American commanders. Combating guerrillas, influencing the population, and gathering intelligence required active measures, pursued unstintingly. As Colonel William E. Birkhimer, commander of the second district of southern Luzon, explained to a subordinate, leaders who constantly sent troops to hound the enemy generally fared better than those who did not. "You must seek these malefactors and assassins," Birkhimer said, "not wait for them to commit crimes and then follow at [a] distance as they retreat. Send out small parties under energetic officers. Let evil doers have no rest. . . . Do not let officers or men get the idea that they are in garrison life, but rather that no species of warfare the American troops ever engaged in required such persistent activity as that now confronting them here."[14]

With conditions varying widely from town to town, theories and standardized methods gave way to the inventiveness of local commanders. Creative and flexible officers excelled at formulating new counterinsurgency methods or modifying old ones. After sizing up local conditions, they took conventional tactics learned for use on European battlefields and adapted them to the counterinsurgency environment. Some innovations worked well and were retained; others failed and were discarded. Through trial and error, American commanders developed new and effective methods for marches, ambushes, and night operations and modified their supply systems to make use of Filipino porters and such native animals as water buffaloes.[15] Brian Linn, the preeminent historian of the Philippine Insurrection, observes that the "key to the Army's success was its lack of adherence to rigid doctrines or theories and the willingness of its officers to experiment with novel pacification schemes."[16]

Success in recruiting and leading Filipinos depended heavily on American officers' charisma, integrity, and social skills, the last especially important for the few officers who had the good fortune to speak Spanish. It also depended on the desire of officers to help the Filipinos. For the most part, U.S. officers displayed a strong commitment to advancing the welfare of the Filipino people, a commitment commonly attributed to their faith in America's form of government and to their belief that American civilization ought to be exported to backward countries.[17] Although they shared the attitude of U.S. Army officers in Reconstruction—that they were spreading a morally superior way of life—they often differed from them in their attitudes toward the local people. Whereas many American officers in Reconstruction had loved the American people in the abstract but could not stand Southerners in the flesh, officers in the Philippines looked down upon the Filipinos in the abstract as members of an inferior race but got along with them splendidly in practice. They understood the people's grievances and acted with enthusiasm, skill, and honesty to advance their lot in life. "Many soldiers saw no contradiction between detesting the Filipinos as a people and liking them as individuals," states Linn. The Americans' views of Filipinos as inferiors "did not prevent soldiers from doing a great deal of good."[18]

During the first months of 1900, General Otis ordered U.S. commanders to concentrate on civic action—the activities of civil government, broadly conceived—rather than military action. Otis and a good many other Americans predicted that Filipinos would support the United States once they saw all the benefits of American rule, and believed that the use of armed force and other stern measures would alienate them.[19] Americans in the field generally adhered to Otis's approach initially; it seemed the sensible thing to do given the infrequent insurgent military activity in early 1900. American troops built schools, markets, roads, and bridges. They set up health clinics and pharmacies that doled out prescriptions free of charge, and went house to house on health inspections to administer vaccinations and implement smallpox quarantines. Dramatic improvements in medical care and public sanitation caused rapid drops in mortality rates. U.S. officials, in addition, rewrote the legal code and reformed the convoluted tax system.[20]

In highly detailed directives to his officers, Otis specified how indigenous governments were to be organized in the towns, mixing elements of American government and the preexisting governments. In keeping with Spanish precedent, as well as Aguinaldo's precedent, Otis limited suffrage to the wealthier and better-educated Filipinos, but he reduced the qualifications needed to vote in order to involve more Filipinos in the political process. Filipinos were to assume leadership roles, from the position of mayor on down.

In many a town, however, American officers found that Otis's model was poorly suited to political realities. The more adaptive of these officers came up with alternative ways to organize the town governments. One alternative, common in the plentiful areas where fear of insurgent violence kept citizens from voting, was appointment of the local officials by American officers. In much of Luzon, commanders opposed creating any local governments at all until the insurgency had been squelched, because of the scarcity of anti-insurgent Filipinos or the likelihood of death for those who agreed to serve. Other American commanders formed local governments even though they knew Filipino officials would secretly work for the insurgents, believing that such governments could still do more good than harm.[21]

In April 1900, Otis requested that he be relieved, having concluded that civic action had erased any organized insurgency that might have existed. Scanning the islands, one could see all sorts of signs that the Philippines had been pacified. American civic-action projects and virtuous American soldiers had caused Filipinos to admire and, to a lesser extent, cooperate with Americans. Large numbers of Filipinos were serving in municipal governments organized by the Americans. In some areas, Filipinos petitioned the Americans to keep their garrisons in place or to bring new garrisons to their towns. One leading official in Bulacan province reported that the insurgents had placed a 300-peso reward on the head of the American provost marshal in San Miguel de Mayumo, but "no one is willing to kill him, as he is beloved by all."[22]

Otis had fundamentally misjudged the situation. By holing himself up with piles of papers instead of talking with officers in the field or seeking other knowledgeable sources, he had missed information indicating deep problems. Municipal governments were infiltrated by insurgents, and shadow governments held sway over numerous towns. In seemingly peaceful neighborhoods, the insurgents were making ready for armed attacks on the occupation troops. The insurgents had already begun fighting in some areas, and American provincial and post commanders were taking countermeasures, many of which diverged from Otis's original guidance. Having become convinced that benevolent civic action would not foil the insurgents, these commanders had, by the spring, begun intensive military operations and punitive actions.[23]

Colonel Arthur Murray, the commanding officer in Leyte, had at first tried to win over the locals by providing free health care, raising the pay of schoolteachers, and eliminating duties on hemp. But in the early spring of 1900, in the face of heavy insurgent violence, Murray concluded that unalloyed benevolence was a recipe for defeat. Murray remarked, "Kindness and consideration I regret to say appear to me largely if not wholly unappreciated by these people, who seem to regard our lenient and humane treatment as an evidence of weakness on our part." Military operations henceforth became the primary component of counterinsurgency on Leyte.[24] On Samar, after 600 insurgents overran a thirty-one-man garrison at the town of Catubig, the Americans destroyed thousands of bushels of rice and set the town on fire. The American commander proclaimed that Samar's residents had to fight against the insurgents or suffer dire punishments.[25]

General Arthur MacArthur replaced Otis as supreme commander in the Philippines in May 1900. He was, like his son Douglas, a man with fervent admirers and equally fervent detractors. His admirers thought him a brilliant commander who deserved credit for the defeat of the Philippine Insurrection. The detractors derided his self-righteousness and self-promotion and considered his role in the victory to have been a good deal smaller than he claimed. MacArthur had become a lieutenant during the Civil War at the precocious age of seventeen by claiming to be nineteen, and at the age of eighteen he had performed an act of heroism in the 24th Wisconsin Volunteer Regiment that would earn him the Congressional Medal of Honor. In the middle of his regiment's assault up Missionary Ridge, on the fringes of Chattanooga, the regimental color sergeant collapsed of exhaustion, so MacArthur took the regimental battle flag from his hands and rushed to the front of the Union line. Braving withering Confederate rifle fire and the explosions of canister rounds rolled down by Confederate artillerymen, MacArthur and his flag carried the troops forward. He led the regiment all the way to the top of the 600-foot ridge, where they drove the Confederates from what had been considered an impregnable position. A captain who witnessed the event said, "Arthur was magnificent. He seems to be afraid of nothing. He'd fight a pack of tigers in a jungle." After the Civil War, MacArthur's career advancement was slowed to a crawl by the dramatic downsizing of the army. He languished at the rank of captain for twenty-three years. When war broke out with Spain, he was just a lieutenant colonel, but he managed to obtain command of a brigade and then a division in the Philippines, thoroughly impressing his superiors in both capacities.[26]

In personality and management style, MacArthur was much like Otis. His pomposity, egocentricity, and aloofness ensured that he remained without admirers among younger officers. MacArthur worked hard, but he spent almost all of his time in Manila and rarely met with any of his commanders. Unlike Otis, however, MacArthur did not immerse himself in minutiae or send detailed directives to commanders many levels below him. Rather than become obsessed with official papers, MacArthur read broadly on Asian colonial administration and history, ordering a Hong Kong bookseller to send him every book available on the Far East. He grasped the military and political problems across the islands better than Otis had.[27]

Just as MacArthur was taking over, insurgent attacks intensified. American weekly casualty rates rose above the figures for the period of conventional war, and assassinations of Filipino citizens who assisted the Americans soared. With the U.S. Army spread too thinly to protect many of its would-be friends, Filipinos shunned American requests for help.[28] Lacking information on the enemy's whereabouts and identity and frustrated by American casualties, a growing number of American commanders authorized their troops to set fire to crops, houses, and towns in response to guerrilla attacks. The Americans declared martial law in some provinces, imposing severe restrictions on the movement of adult males and requiring Filipino mayors to participate in enforcement.[29]

In September guerrillas launched a string of large attacks, with the goal of swaying the upcoming American presidential election in favor of William Jennings Bryan, who was promising to grant independence to the Philippines. Although the guerrillas suffered numerous setbacks, they did inflict significant defeats on two American units, both led by incompetent officers.[30] The September onslaught prompted the press and MacArthur's own subordinates to accuse him of softness toward the insurgents. It was time for the type of drastic measures that had been used against the American Indians, they said. "You can't put down a rebellion by throwing confetti and sprinkling perfumery," General Loyd Wheaton fumed. The time had come for "swift methods of destruction," for it was "no use going with a sword in one hand, a pacifist pamphlet in the other hand, and trailing the model of a schoolhouse after."[31]

MacArthur now arrived at the conclusion that numerous officers in the field had already reached: that no quantity or quality of benevolent civic action would suffice to end the insurgency. Compulsion and violence would be required in conjunction with continued civic action. In orders to lower echelons, MacArthur declared that all prominent Filipino families unwilling to commit themselves publicly to the American side, by either word or deed, should be considered accomplices of the insurgents. Prisoners of war would no longer be released, as had been the case until now, but would be kept in prison, and part-time guerrillas posing as civilians would no longer be accorded the privileges of prisoners of war but would be tried for crimes punishable by death. In actions against the insurgents, said MacArthur, "the more drastic the application the better," although he also forbade "unnecessary hardships and personal indignities" and violations of the laws of war in handling detainees.[32] MacArthur's pronouncements convinced some of his subordinates to adopt severe tactics or caused them to take actions for which they had eagerly awaited permission, but the extent of his influence was more limited than he and his admirers later asserted, for many local commanders had already made the transition of their own accord in previous months.[33]

American counterinsurgency operations intensified in November as reinforcements arrived and the weather improved. Wherever American commanders caught a whiff of guerrilla warfare, they put primary emphasis on military action and punishment of insurgents and insurgent supporters. American troops and Filipino auxiliaries marched into the mountains and swamps and patrolled day and night, nabbing some guerrillas and keeping the others on the run. Guerrilla leaders who surrendered almost invariably spoke of aggressive pursuit by American forces as a leading cause of their failure and capitulation. Insurgents who surrendered or were captured provided information on how to find yet more insurgents, and the Americans were vigorous in collecting information from the townspeople, enabling them to apprehend members of the shadow governments, insurgent agents within the real governments, and insurgent sympathizers among the populace. Even Filipino officials who simply did nothing, hoping to antagonize neither side, were sometimes arrested for failing to report on guerrillas. Tried by U.S. Army provost courts, detained officials faced heavy fines or imprisonment with hard labor if convicted. These courts produced a sharp increase in the cooperativeness of local officials.[34]

To deny food and shelter to the guerillas and discourage the landowning principalia from leading or helping them, American troops systematically confiscated or destroyed the food and property of all who abetted the insurgency. In the areas most thoroughly infested with insurgents, they burned huge swaths of farmland to the ground. These measures compelled the insurgents to spend most of their time looking for food or hiding instead of milking the population or attacking the occupiers. Thanks in part to MacArthur's orders, American commanders stopped releasing prisoners of war and did away with some legal niceties in the processing of prisoners. In a few provinces they hanged insurgents who had masqueraded as civilians. American officers forced the population to concentrate in select areas where they could be controlled, and treated everyone outside those areas as insurgents, punishing them with property destruction, arrest, or death.[35]

Here as in the Civil War, most of the brutish instruments of counterinsurgency warfare still depended for their efficacy upon how leaders used them. In Abra province, Major William C. H. Bowen routinely destroyed property and conducted mass roundups, but unlike some of his peers, he largely avoided antagonizing the local populace because he acted with tremendous care and tact. The insurgent general in command of Abra noted that the "meritorious and prudent conduct" of Bowen had "brought the capitulation of the guerrilla soldiers of Abra." The province's citizens later petitioned, successfully, to have Bowen serve as the province's first civil governor.[36]

The high overall quality of American leadership ensured that American troops seldom perpetrated murder, rape, or other serious crimes against civilians despite the increasing severity of the war and the strains of hardship and enemy atrocities. Officers maintained discipline, repeatedly explained what would not be tolerated, and made clear the consequences of bad behavior by issuing stiff penalties for the occasional American wrongdoer. With prisoners, on the other hand, American lieutenants and captains tolerated torture, and majors and colonels and generals seldom reprimanded them. Although gruesome tortures were rare, American troops regularly beat prisoners or administered the "water cure," pouring large volumes of filthy water down a prisoner's throat. To justify these measures, American soldiers and their officers argued that the facts thus extracted saved American lives. The benefits came at a high cost to the war effort, however, for the press learned of acts of torture and publicized them, along with much else that was half true or worse, generating outrage in the United States. Courts-martial ensued against perpetrators fingered by the press, although many were acquitted or given light sentences.[37]

The insurgents' military defeats and the destruction of property belonging to insurgent supporters rapidly diminished ardor for the insurgency among most Filipinos, leaders as well as followers. To save themselves and their property, principalia started working for the Americans or providing them with information, and the masses followed their lead. Insurgent terrorism, which in the past had prevented such defections, no longer worked, either because military operations had rendered terrorism unfeasible or because the citizenry had been emboldened to strike back at the insurgents with help from the Americans.[38]

Although force was essential in eliciting cooperation from the Filipinos, the cooperation was given more willingly, and hence was more valuable, when American officers employed the art of persuasion at the same time. By developing strong personal relationships with the local people and governing virtuously, local American commanders frequently gained the support of the principalia and the clergy. The benefits of American schools and health-care and economic programs also encouraged some Filipino elites to side with the

Americans, but even American leaders who gave little attention to civic action programs, like Frederick Funston, were able to convince Filipinos to switch sides by employing charisma, social graces, and the good behavior of their troops in conjunction with robust military action.[39] The Americans recruited prominent Filipinos into the Federal Party, which organized pro-American rallies in the towns and provided individuals for service in municipal government, taking on a serious risk of assassination. Whether the Federal Party played a major part in pacification hinged on the quality of its leaders and the willingness of American commanders to promote the party's activities. In recruiting members of the principalia into the party, savvy American officers watched for signs of competence, dedication, and incorruptibility, for these characteristics were in short supply among this class.[40]

At the end of 1900, MacArthur encouraged American officers to recruit Filipinos into police and scout forces, and, more important, he provided resources for that purpose. MacArthur had heretofore resisted arming the Filipinos, for fear that they would beat up unarmed citizens or become insurgents, but with the approaching departure of the U.S. Volunteers, he decided that he needed the extra manpower. Filipino forces did not play a significant counterinsurgency role in every province, because some American commanders could not find enough trustworthy volunteers or did not trust organized Filipino units enough to bestow on them more than the simplest of responsibilities. Elsewhere, however, native security forces constituted a key component of pacification. With their knowledge of the language, the culture, and the terrain, they could find insurgents whom the Americans never would have found. By the end of 1900, Filipino policemen were taking over security duties from the Americans in provinces where the guerrillas had been sufficiently beaten down, thereby freeing American soldiers for operations in other provinces. Much of the credit for the success of these indigenous units belonged to the high caliber of their officers, who, for the most part, were Americans. One senior American officer, who had the duty of selecting U.S. officers for Filipino units, explained: "The Filipinos, like all people, will fight when properly paid, fed, and disciplined, but above all when properly led. This is the keynote to an entirely successful use of Filipinos as soldiers. . . . It is therefore of the utmost importance that high-grade officers, thoroughly courageous, upright, sober, intelligent, and energetic, be placed over them. It is folly to assign as officers men unfit for duty with American soldiers."[41]

From December 1900 to July 1901 the counterinsurgents decimated most of

the remaining insurgent armed forces by killing them, arresting them, or causing them to defect, and put Aguinaldo and a host of other insurgent leaders
out of action. By the middle of 1901 the insurgents were capable of continuing the armed struggle only on the islands of Samar, Cebu, and Bohol and in
the southwestern Luzon province of Batangas.[42] Although later theorists have
contended that counterinsurgents need ten or twenty times as many troops as
the insurgents have in order to succeed, the Americans plus the Filipinos who
fought on the American side frequently vanquished insurgents who outnumbered them.

The American forces and their Filipino allies had major advantages in
weaponry, and they were permitted to destroy the food sources upon which
the insurgents relied, something that governments in other wars have forbid-
den their counterinsurgent forces from doing. Their greatest advantage, however, was in command. The insurgent leaders were, on the whole, considerably less talented than the American leaders. Because of superior leadership,
the counterinsurgents fought much more cohesively and adjusted their tactics
much more rapidly than the insurgents did. They more often took the initiative and persisted in the face of hardship and were far less prone to internal
strife and corruption.

Four principal factors account for the large disparity in quality between the
insurgent and the counterinsurgent commanders. First, the insurgent leaders
came from one narrow segment of small island societies—their status was
based on birth and wealth—whereas the American leaders had been selected
from multiple segments of a huge society. Second, nationalism was weaker
among Filipinos than among Americans, so the insurgent leaders were less
dedicated to their cause, Philippine independence, and less willing to follow
directives from above. Third, and related to the second, Aguinaldo's control
over his movement was so tenuous that he did not discipline bad officers, as
they would have been disciplined in the American army, out of fear that they
would cease supporting him. And fourth, American officers had extensive
training and experience in military operations and leadership, whereas the insurgent leaders not only had to learn everything on the job but typically had
less experience relevant to this line of work.[43]

On July 4, MacArthur turned over his military command to Major General
Adna R. Chaffee. His civil-military governorship was transferred to William
Howard Taft, the future president and the future chief justice of the Supreme
Court, but Chaffee would be the man most responsible for counterinsur-

gency. Chaffee had served under Sheridan in 1864 during the devastation of the Shenandoah Valley, and after the Civil War he had spent decades fighting the Kiowas, Comanches, Cheyennes, and Apaches, giving him intimate familiarity with the harsh forms of counterinsurgency that he soon employed in the Philippines. A tough man who always put the mission ahead of compassion, Chaffee did not hesitate to remove officers who were reluctant to use harsh measures.[44]

The two big insurgent strongholds that remained to be subdued after Chaffee's assumption of power were Samar and Batangas. Samar, an eastern island, had never been completely controlled by the Spanish. The 5,000-square-mile interior was filled with swamps, mountains, jungles, and disease-ridden animals, ranking it among the least inviting areas in the archipelago. The persistence of insurgent activity on Samar could be traced not only to terrain but also to the quality of the insurgent commanders, who were among the best the insurgents had to offer.[45] The American troop presence on the island, moreover, had been small in 1900 and most of 1901. Samar did not attract much attention from Manila until a series of assaults in the autumn of 1901, culminating with an attack at Balangiga on September 28.

Of the seventy-four Americans performing garrison duty in the town of Balangiga, nearly all were having breakfast at an outdoor kitchen when the insurgents struck. The town mayor, an insurgent agent, had previously obtained American consent to let 100 covert insurgents into the town on the pretext of employing them in public works projects. The Balangiga police chief, another covert insurgent, began the sneak attack, leading a handful of men in silently killing the three unsuspecting American sentries, the only Americans who were carrying rifles. The rest of the 100 insurgents then stormed out of tents and the parish church, clutching bolos and axes, and descended on the kitchen. Most of the Americans were eating at tables when the attackers set upon them, and many were cut to death before they knew what was happening. The company sergeant's head was split apart by an axe. Another man's head was severed with a bolo and fell into his breakfast plate. The company commander, Captain Thomas W. Connell, was standing in his pajamas in the officer quarters, a former convent, when the onslaught commenced. Jumping down from his second-story window, he ran toward his troops but was cut down by a bolo before he reached them.

Those who survived the insurgents' first slashes grabbed meat cleavers, cookpots, baseball bats, rocks, and whatever else they could find and met the attacking horde in desperate and vicious battle. The slaughter might have been total had it not been for one enormous American, Sergeant George F. Markley, who brawled his way to the enlisted barracks where the weapons were stacked, grabbed a rifle, and started shooting down insurgents. The survivors rallied around Markley and fought their way to a beach, where they escaped by boat. When the bloodbath was over, forty-eight Americans were dead and twenty-two wounded. The insurgents mutilated the American corpses, in one case gouging out a lieutenant's eyes and spreading jam on his face to attract insects.[46]

Chaffee concluded that the American soldiers had been attacked because of Captain Connell's excessive kindness to the natives, but Connell had been far from kind to the people of Balangiga. His poor conduct and that of his men may, in fact, have triggered the attack. Connell had infuriated the townspeople by forcing them to work without pay and live in conditions so overcrowded and squalid that they appalled some of the American soldiers. Troops under Connell's command had reportedly committed numerous acts of violence and theft against the populace, another clear indication of a deficit in leadership.[47]

Chaffee would have replied vigorously to such a slaughter in any case, but his misperception of its causes ensured that the retribution was extreme. The navy's gunboats and the army's forces on Samar received orders to "make a desert of Balangiga." Vengeful sailors and soldiers flattened everything in the town save for the stone walls of the church. Next, Chaffee increased the army's troop strength on Samar to 4,000 soldiers and assigned a new commander, Brigadier General Jacob "Hell Roaring Jake" Smith, a diminutive man named for his booming war cries.

As a rule, Chaffee liked to replace a new commander when a job was not getting done, and he usually found a new commander who was more effective than his predecessor, but in this instance Chaffee erred badly in choosing the replacement. Having served previously with Smith, Chaffee should have heeded the indications that Smith deserved to be kept away from such a job at all costs. After performing without distinction in the Civil War, Smith had spent three decades at the rank of captain. He had been court-martialed three times, twice for insubordination and once for the illegal sale of alcohol. In the Philippines, Smith had improved his reputation by performing competently as a regimental commander and district commander, but he owed his appointment at Samar more to his success in schmoozing MacArthur and Taft than to worthy service. If giving command to an erratic man like Smith was unavoidable, he should have been kept on a short leash, yet Chaffee not only instructed Smith to impose draconian measures but set no limits on what he could do on Samar.[48]

To halt the shipment of contraband to Samar, Smith ordered tight restrictions on the movements of commercial boats—a good first step. But Smith thereafter neglected to issue sound orders or to supervise, critical failures in so trying an environment. Smith was "wholly lacking in tact, judgement and administrative capacity," observed Taft's deputy. Smith informed American gunboat crews and infantry companies that they could destroy any village that was abetting the insurgents, which, in conjunction with his lack of oversight, made him culpable for several atrocities committed by his subordinates.[49]

The greatest notoriety accrued to Major Littleton W. T. Waller, commander of a Marine battalion that had been shipped to Samar after the Balangiga disaster. Smith told Waller, "I want no prisoners. I wish you to burn and kill; the more you burn and kill, the better it will please me."[50] Every male over the age of ten should be killed, Smith said, and the interior of the island should be turned into a "howling wilderness." Waller did not systematically slaughter males over the age of ten, but he did orchestrate much burning and killing. During an eleven-day stretch in October and November, Waller's Marines burned down 255 houses, destroyed one ton of hemp and half a ton of rice, killed thirty-nine men, and captured another eighteen. In December, Waller took fifty Marines, two Filipino scouts, and thirty-three Filipino porters on a hasty and senseless expedition to Basey, ignoring warnings from more experienced army officers about the perilous terrain and the difficulties of resupply. Waller and his followers met thick jungle that had to be hacked away at a snail's pace. Within six days, the men were near exhaustion, and so were their supplies, so Waller and his followers turned back. At one point, Waller and some of the other officers split off into small groups to fend for themselves, leaving other Marines and the porters behind, stranded until relief parties reached them on January 18. Eleven Marines perished during the debacle.

Some of the surviving Marines reported that three Filipino porters had hidden food or disobeyed orders during the expedition, so Waller and his adjutant, Lieutenant John H. A. Day, summarily executed these three—plus nine others in order to put the number of dead porters above the number of dead Marines. Waller and Day were subsequently court-martialed for murder. Day evaded punishment by saying that he was under orders from Waller, and Waller evaded punishment by claiming that he was under orders from Smith.[51]

In January 1902, following barrages of complaints about Smith's conduct from every conceivable direction, Chaffee ordered Smith to abandon the harshest measures and get food to famished Filipino civilians. Smith said that he would do so. Before these changes made their way to the field, however, the American forces and their Filipino allies finished off the insurgents, who by now had been driven close to starvation by the ruination of the island's farmland. The top guerrilla commander on the island was captured on February 18, and the last guerrillas surrendered on April 27.[52]

Justice caught up with Smith in April, when he was relieved of command, sent to Manila, and put under investigation. By this time, word of the misdeeds on Samar had spread across the Philippines and the United States, stirring up outraged condemnation in both countries. Smith was found guilty of "conduct to the prejudice of good order and military discipline" for the orders he had issued on Samar. His only punishment, however, was forced retirement, leniency being granted in recognition of his "long career distinguished for gallantry and on the whole for good conduct."[53]

In the province of Batangas, the counterinsurgents faced a situation no less daunting than the one in Samar. Well-led guerrilla troops ran rampant, aided by a civilian populace that freely gave them food and forewarned them of American operations. Such was the military strength of the guerillas that the Americans needed thirty to forty soldiers to go anywhere and had to keep troops so concentrated that they could garrison only a few of the towns. In October 1901, Chaffee decided that the commander responsible for Batangas was not good enough and replaced him with J. Franklin Bell. This time, Chaffee chose well. Just about everyone in the Philippines viewed Bell as the best American officer of the war. Even the American reporters who hated the military liked him. The army, to its credit, had kept Bell and some other fine American officers in the Philippines for the duration of the war, now under way for more than three years, rather than rotating them to the United States or other countries.

Bell spent the first week of his new job meeting with Filipino elites across Batangas, probing for information on present conditions and options. Once he had taken in the dynamics of the insurgent environment to his satisfaction, he decided that victory could best be reached by punishing into submission the principalia who were guiding and underwriting the insurgency. Possessed of a bluntness that would have necessitated unceasing apologies and early retirement had he lived a century later, Bell remarked that punishing one member of the principalia was more valuable than punishing 100 commoners, for "the common people amount to nothing. They are merely densely ignorant tools, who blindly follow the lead of the *principalia*."[54] Bell told his men to be "considerate and courteous in manner" and to refrain from cruelty toward Filipinos, including prisoners; he refused to tolerate the flagrant atrocities that Smith had countenanced in Samar. Such differences help account for the widely differing impressions that Bell and Smith made on their military colleagues during these campaigns, with Bell adding to his fame and Smith becoming an embarrassment.[55]

Bell, nevertheless, fully appreciated the shortcomings of benevolent pacification and was convinced that the stern application of armed force and population control measures was the most effective, and hence also the most humane, way to win. "A short and severe war," he said, "creates in the aggregate less loss and suffering than benevolent war indefinitely prolonged."[56] In public proclamations, Bell warned that Filipinos who did not actively participate in counterinsurgency activities would be classified as enemies and penalized with fines, property destruction, imprisonment, or perhaps even death. Bell delivered this threat in the most dispassionate tone possible, and he otherwise avoided issuing threats at all, for he was convinced that threats from the counterinsurgents generally conveyed weakness to the population, particularly when made in anger or exasperation. "Say little, and let acts, not words, convey your meaning," he instructed his subordinates. "Words count for nothing. The more an officer talks, the less they think he is going to do. The more he does and the less he says, the more apprehensive they become while waiting for what is to happen next."[57]

Bell employed some of the best U.S. counterinsurgency officers as provost marshals and granted them authority to make mass arrests and impose hefty fines. Swiftly carrying out interrogations and investigations, the provost marshals unearthed and broke apart the shadow governments. Bell's officers confiscated the weapons of Filipino policemen and cut their pay, then told them that to regain their weapons and their pay they would have to help the U.S. Army defeat the insurgents, a policy that had a salutary effect on the police. At Bell's command, American officers took their troops into insurgent hotbeds to eliminate every form of animal and plant life fit for human consumption.[58] In all of these endeavors, Bell gave his subordinate commanders much freedom of action, assuring them that "it is not necessary to seek or wait for authority from these headquarters to do anything or take any action which will contribute to the end in view."[59]

On December 8, Bell told his commanders that they had twenty days to transplant all civilians and their possessions into protected areas. After the twenty days had elapsed, anything outside these areas was subject to destruction, and any male caught beyond the boundaries would be arrested or, if he resisted arrest, shot. Bell gave his post commanders latitude in enforcing this order, permitting them to exempt civilians in areas of minimal guerrilla activity and to use the threat of concentration, not necessarily its implementation, to coerce local Filipino leaders.

Once the people had been relocated, they were compelled to participate in support tasks for the U.S. armed forces without compensation. They could harvest crops only under the watch of American troops. Bell ordered post commanders to ensure that the relocated Filipinos had adequate food, health care, and sanitation, and commanders generally did their best to comply, although in a few instances they did not provide enough food or failed to maintain adequate public sanitation. Unfortunately, the concentration of the civilian population facilitated the spread of diseases, especially malaria. Approximately 11,000 people died during the first months of 1902 in Batangas, almost all from disease.[60]

With Bell preaching relentless action, the American lieutenants and captains in Batangas searched unflaggingly for the insurgents and their strongholds. Filipinos served alongside them as guides and informants, in some cases willingly, in other cases not. As with everything else he put in his sights, Bell greatly improved the collection and dissemination of intelligence, especially that pertaining to the principalia. Although he had approximately the same number of troops as the insurgents, he devastated the insurgents militarily in a few months, thanks to the removal of civilians and food from the countryside, effective intelligence gathering, and well-executed military operations. Counterinsurgent military victories and the Americans' punitive measures caused numerous principalia to switch their allegiance to the Americans, with some signing up for work as counterinsurgent leaders. A number of guerrillas killed their officers and surrendered, and others deserted. The insurgency was thoroughly gutted by the time Miguel Malvar, the top insurgent leader, surrendered in April 1902.

Bell's methods and the thousands of civilian deaths in the relocation zones aroused indignation in some quarters of the United States, where it was emphatically noted that the United States had condemned the Spanish for employing similar methods in Cuba. Most American soldiers, on the other hand, believed that Bell had done a superb job, and he even gained the respect of his insurgent adversaries. Insurgent leaders subsequently attested that the war would have gone on for at least a few more years had it not been for Bell's harsh methods, lending credence to Bell's judgment that a severe war would be shorter and thus less harmful than a benevolent war.[61]

Bell's campaign in Batangas and Smith's campaign in Samar underscored one of the most important lessons of the Philippine Insurrection—that drastic measures could defeat the insurgents quickly without large-scale violence against the civilian populace, but only if the right type of leader commanded the counterinsurgents. Dedicated commanders with integrity and strong organizational skills made sure that the troops remained disciplined and did not murder and pillage. The American atrocities during the war, in Samar and elsewhere, most often occurred because commanders did not keep an eye on subordinates or gave them directions that sanctioned indiscriminate destruction. When excesses occurred on the watch of a good officer, the officer meted out stern punishments to prevent repetition, while the officer who did not punish permitted and encouraged more excesses. Good commanders, moreover, were selective in the use of the most highly destructive instruments, recognizing that in some locations a pair of scissors worked better than a saw. Of course, political considerations often deny twenty-first-century counterinsurgents the use of the saw, but the same cautions apply to less drastic measures.

The U.S. response to the Philippine Insurrection contradicts the view, held nowadays by a preponderance of highly educated Westerners, that civic action is invariably more effective than military action in defeating insurgents. For most of 1900, the United States concentrated on civic action but failed to curb the insurgency or to obtain much assistance from the civilian populace, because the citizenry either sympathized with the insurgents or submitted to them to avoid assassination by insurgent hit men. In most areas afflicted with rebellion, the Americans did not begin to weaken the insurgency until they started arresting and killing insurgents and punishing their civilian accomplices. Once the Americans resorted to force, elites began switching their allegiance—they realized that the cost of supporting the insurgents had gone up, the risk of falling victim to insurgent assassins had gone down, and the likelihood of ultimate victory had shifted to the counterinsurgent side. Civic action did help convince some Filipinos to support the Americans, both early in the war and later, by showing that American rule could better their lives, but many willingly switched sides where civic action was scarce. The optimal mix of civic action and military action depended upon local circumstances; whether the counterinsurgents achieved that mix or something approximating it depended on the ability of the local commander to comprehend those circumstances and act accordingly.

Except in a few places where the United States empowered entire tribes or sects and not rival groups that belonged to the insurgency, American commanders did not try to supplant the traditional elites with new elites, as had been tried so unsuccessfully in the United States during Reconstruction. Instead, they gained the cooperation of the traditional elites, the principalia, which ensured the cooperation of the masses, since the masses largely did as the principalia told them. Although the counterinsurgency started out principally as an American affair, in its later stages it relied heavily on the members of the principalia who took on leading roles in municipal governments, security forces, and the Federal Party. The defections of the principalia eventually enabled the United States to turn over most security duties to the Filipinos, an important consideration in light of the mounting U.S. public opposition to the war.

The repeated American command changes during the Philippine Insurrection produced an excellent database from which to glean conclusions about various leadership practices. American commanders at higher levels benefited a great deal from traveling into the field to acquire information from local officers. Upper-level leaders who micromanaged the war unfailingly impaired the counterinsurgency, since local commanders were more familiar with local conditions and most had the judgment and other traits required to make sound decisions on their own. The most effective senior leaders minimized constraints on local commanders, aside from those forbidding unlawful conduct, thereby allowing officers to improvise and adapt nearly unfettered, which was crucial in a war where the multiplicity of challenges defied textbook solutions. The ability of U.S. forces to adapt to the demands of the situation contradicts the view of most modern counterinsurgency theorists that armies trained for conventional war reflexively treat irregular wars as conventional wars. It also contradicts the conclusion, popularly derived from that view, that the preparation of counterinsurgency forces requires massive changes in training and doctrine.

Last, the Philippine Insurrection highlights the importance of command selection in defeating insurgents. Some American commanders had the power to remove subordinate commanders for inferior performance, and when they exercised this power, they usually installed replacements who were richer in the necessary leadership attributes and thus improved the output of the American forces. At the more rarefied levels of command, however, appointments were very often made and sustained based on seniority. This was an understandable policy in peacetime but a harmful policy in wartime, for it gave life-and-death decisions to older officers of sundry abilities while excluding highly capable young officers. In the few cases where junior officers were promoted upward rapidly, they outperformed most of their new peers. The War Department did demonstrate noteworthy flexibility in its personnel policies by retaining superior officers in command positions throughout the war. Counterinsurgent forces reached their maximum effectiveness when the relatively small number of key commands were occupied for long stretches by the most talented officers.

CHAPTER 5

The Huk Rebellion

After the defeat of Aguinaldo's Army of Liberation of the Philippines, Manuel Tinio returned to his 1,000-acre estate in the central Luzon barrio of San Ricardo. An upstanding member of the principalia, Tinio had served as a general under Aguinaldo, but now he put politics aside and concentrated on his piece of land, an expanse of virgin forest and meadows. Over the next two decades, he allowed peasants from other areas to clear parcels, a few acres per family, and cultivate rice; they gave him 55 percent of the crop as rent. As was customary, the tenants helped Tinio with various chores, and he accorded them a variety of benefits and privileges. Tinio allowed them to grow vegetables and raise chickens for their own consumption and to cut down trees for firewood and lumber. Becoming almost a member of their families, he paid for baptisms and weddings, became the godfather of their children, and helped in the rice fields when a family member was sick. Most important, Tinio loaned them rice or cash at no interest for months at a time, providing a critical safety net when typhoons or floods or other disruptions deprived the tenants of food for their families. These arrangements pleased both Tinio and his tenants.

When Manuel Tinio died in 1924, his son Manolo inherited the estate. A recent graduate of Cornell University, Manolo Tinio had absorbed modern business ideas in America. He viewed the tenants strictly as business clients, and the 1,000 acres as a business enterprise from which to pull out the maximum profit. Consequently, he discontinued the interest-free lending of money and rice to the tenants, which forced them to borrow at crippling interest rates from moneylenders. Other tenant benefits, such as free unhusked rice at harvest time to feed to their chickens, came to an end. Frequently absent from his lands, Manolo hired overseers to keep watch over the tenants and declined to sponsor baptisms or weddings or even give gifts on those occasions. Yet he expected the tenants to do everything for him that they had done for his father. Peasants who had loved Manuel Tinio had only contempt for his son.[1]

The Tinio family story resembles that of countless other principalia families during the first decades of the twentieth century. Once the troops of Arthur MacArthur and Adna Chaffee had extinguished the insurrection, the rural elites drifted from their estates to Manila and other cities, attracted by the modernization and urban prosperity stimulated by American rule. The United States plugged the Philippine countryside into the world economy, which enabled the principalia to sell rice and sugar from their estates on the world markets, providing cash for the purchase of imported goods. It became commonplace for landlords to give control of family estates to profit-maximizing overseers who cut the peasants' benefits and raised rental rates, and for peasants to resent their landlords for abdicating their traditional responsibilities.[2]

In some regions of Luzon, tenant farmers responded to the changes by hiding crops from the overseers, who tended to be less knowledgeable than the landlords. Others supported organizations that called for the landlords to repeal rent hikes and resume their former paternalistic activities. The tiny Philippine Communist Party—which was formed in the 1920s as the Comintern was creating Communist Parties across Asia—and a small number of other left-wing radicals took up arms against the landlords and the government. Hoping to capitalize on the breakdown of the traditional peasant-landlord relationship, the radicals sought to take the place of the landlords as authority figures.

All resistance activities came to an abrupt halt with the Japanese invasion of the Philippines in December 1941. Having neutralized American air and naval forces with surprise air attacks, the Japanese sent ashore huge numbers of amphibious forces, compelling the Philippine and American forces of General Douglas MacArthur to fall back to the fortresses of Bataan and Corregidor. Besieged by the Japanese, the American and Philippine forces held on for several months but eventually were defeated by lack of food and overwhelming Japanese force. As the end approached for the defenders at Corregidor, President Roosevelt ordered MacArthur to go to Australia, which MacArthur did, albeit burdened with the knowledge that most of the American and Philippine soldiers had to be left behind. Philippine president Manuel Quezon likewise fled the country, stopping in Australia before moving to the United States to set up a government-in-exile. The 70,000 Americans and Filipinos captured in Bataan were force-marched for six days with no food or water in 100-degree heat as Japanese soldiers beat or shot those who had trouble keeping up. Fifteen thousand perished on the "Bataan Death March."

American officers who had evaded the Japanese took to the hills and recruited Filipinos into guerrilla units called the U.S. Armed Forces Far East (USAFFE). The Philippine Communist Party set up a separate guerrilla organization called Hukbo ng Bayan Laban so Hapon, abbreviated to Hukbalahap or Huk, meaning "anti-Japanese army," which, like the USAFFE, claimed to be fighting simply for liberation from the Japanese aggressors. The Huks' public professions of nationalism masked their real intentions, which included promoting international revolution. Luis Taruc, the top Communist military commander, was an anomaly, for he possessed real nationalist sentiments and was also a religious man, heresies that the party tolerated only because of his exceptional leadership gifts.[3] In 1942 the Huks repeatedly rebuffed calls by American officers to put themselves under the complete command of the USAFFE, leading the USAFFE command to declare that all guerrillas not in its employ were enemies of the United States.

The Japanese at first raped and pillaged on a large scale, but then settled down and got Filipinos to do much of the raping and pillaging for them. As the war progressed, oppression by Filipino units often weighed more heavily on the people than Japanese oppression did. Murder, rape, and other vile acts by Philippine collaborators and Japanese troops drove many peasants to join the Huks, as did a series of early Huk military successes. In 1942, Huk strength rose from less than 300 to 3,000, and by September 1944 it had reached at least 10,000. At "Stalin University" in the Sierra Madre mountains, Huk officers received training from seasoned Huk leaders and veterans of the Chinese Red Army. Most of the guerrillas did not receive formal instruction, learning guerrilla tactics instead on the job and from experienced comrades. Their attacks on the Japanese were small in scale and duration because of their limited ammunition and the ability of the Japanese to bring reinforcements quickly. Generally, they directed more violence at Filipinos who collaborated with the Japanese than at the Japanese themselves, killing 20,000 Filipinos during the war as opposed to 5,000 Japanese.[4]

Huk forces established shadow governments in central Luzon, their prin-

cipal base of operations, an area forty miles wide and over 100 miles long be-
tween the Zambales mountain range and the Central Cordillera. In 1943 the
Huks started encroaching on territory that had been the sole domain of the
USAFFE guerrillas, on several occasions exchanging fire with USAFFE forces.
A few Huk units provided interpreters or guides to Douglas MacArthur's 8th
Army after its entry into the Philippines in October 1944, but cooperation was
the exception rather than the rule. American officers recognized that the Huks
were dangerous radicals, feigning friendship as a temporary expedient until
they were ready to expel the Americans from the Philippines. Major Robert
Lapham of the Central Luzon USAFFE wrote in January 1945 that the Hukbalahap was a "subversive" and "radical" organization, guilty of "carnage, revenge, banditry and highjacking" that was "never equalled in any page of history of the Philippines."[5]

With the coming of peace and victory over Japan, MacArthur ordered
that the Huks be disbanded. Some Huk guerrillas were disarmed at gunpoint
after refusing initial requests to turn in their weapons, and a number were
imprisoned for subversion, kidnapping, or murder. Unlike Philippine veterans
of the USAFFE, who received back pay and veterans benefits and who were
welcomed into the Philippine Military Police Corps, most Huks received no
benefits and were barred from governmental service.

Sergio Osmena assumed the presidency of the restored Philippine nation,
having replaced Manuel Quezon after the latter's death at Saranac Lake, New
York, two months before MacArthur's return to the Philippines. An inept and
uncharismatic leader, Osmena was in every respect the opposite of what was
needed in this precarious hour. Much of Manila and the other large population centers had been reduced to rubble during the last months of the fighting, and critical government departments such as sanitation and law enforcement were in chaos, with few personnel remaining and few buildings intact.
Osmena failed to step forward with energy or urgency to reassemble the governmental structure. Although the United States sent millions of tons of food
and hundreds of millions of dollars, it entrusted the distribution of the aid to
Osmena's regime in the spirit of promoting self-government, which allowed
corrupt and ineffectual officials to pocket or waste vast sums.

Wary of Communist subversion, Osmena appointed known anti-
Communists to head the local governments and security forces in central
Luzon. Aside from their opposition to Communism, however, the only other
noteworthy characteristic of many of these appointees was an aptitude for

crime. Soldiers and policemen plundered the barrios without restraint. Even worse was the behavior of the civilian guards hired by landlords at war's end to help secure property and enforce rent increases. In response, Huk veterans banded together and used whatever weapons they could find to attack government forces and the private security forces.[6]

During the spring of 1946 the government sent additional forces with armored cars to wage war in central Luzon. The Huks continued to fight back while also preparing for the national elections, which were held in April, just before the Philippines received full independence from the United States. The leaders of the Philippine Communist Party created a new political organization called the Democratic Alliance, which purported to be a party of the moderate left. The Democratic Alliance recruited huge numbers of non-Communists, most of whom did not know that Communists held all of the top leadership positions in the Democratic Alliance or that the Communists intended to use the organization to overthrow the government by 1952.[7]

In the national elections Luis Taruc and five other Democratic Alliance members from central Luzon were elected to the Congress. But Manuel Roxas, the newly elected president, and congressmen from his Liberal Party voided the election of these six because Democratic Alliance thugs had intimidated and terrorized voters in central Luzon. Roxas, a charismatic man who enraptured audiences with speeches promising heaven on earth, tried to appease the Huks by compelling landlords to let tenants keep 70 percent of their crops, but the Huks responded with impossible demands, such as the disbandment of the national armed forces. So Roxas renewed the attacks on the Huks, and some of his men apparently murdered the Democratic Alliance leader Juan Feleo in August. Both acts convinced much of the Huk leadership that violence promised better results than political action.

For the next two years, provincial Communist Party organizations and Communist front organizations like the Democratic Alliance and National Peasants' Union led a guerrilla war against the government and the landlords in central Luzon. Much of the national Communist Party leadership did not at first embrace violence, preferring to focus on trade unions and other legal political means of obtaining power, but top party officials like Luis Taruc and Casto Alejandrino were active in directing Huk military activities early on. Organized in typical Communist fashion, the Huks had a mixture of full-time fighters, part-time fighters, service supporters, and civilian sympathizers. Peasants often provided the Huks with information on government and landlord forces. After counting government trucks and armored cars as they passed and noting the types of troops, peasant scouts sent the information by runner to the nearest Huk field command. The Huks also had numerous agents among government officials and in the Philippine Police Constabulary, who warned them of government operations in advance.[8]

In response to the rise in insurgent violence, Roxas declared that the government would use an "iron fist" to destroy the insurgents within sixty days. The iron-fist campaign lasted two years and never achieved this objective. The first problem was a shortage of troops. In 1946 the government had only 37,000 men in its security forces, scattered across the entire archipelago, of whom 25,000 were in the regular armed forces. Arrayed against them were 10,000 well-led, experienced Huk regulars and many more Huk irregulars. The government's repression might nevertheless have undermined the insurgency had it been undertaken by talented and persistent leaders who deftly eliminated insurgents and convinced the citizenry that the insurgents were going to lose. Without such leadership, it merely antagonized the population.

Primary responsibility for fighting the insurgents belonged at first to the Philippine Military Police Corps, later renamed the Philippine Constabulary. After this organization flunked the test of battle, the Philippine army entered the fray, bringing with it artillery, tanks, armored cars, and aircraft, but the army did scarcely better. Many of the most successful leaders from the prewar constabulary and army had been killed fighting the Japanese or had died in Japanese prisons, and after the war new officers were chosen hastily, based on personal connections or their services to the ruling party, not ability or track record. Roxas, soaring rhetoric notwithstanding, did little to ameliorate the problem after assuming the presidency.[9] Most constabulary and military leaders lacked the initiative, dedication, and tactical judgment required for fruitful military action. They kept their forces inside their posts for much of the day and all of the night. It was commonplace for units to avoid forays into the countryside entirely, other than an occasional brief excursion during which they fired off their rifles at nothing in particular and then submitted reports that they had inflicted heavy casualties on the Huks. Government officers who were more motivated to hurt the Huks often did not know where the guerrillas were and thus flailed blindly while the insurgents jabbed at them from all sides.[10]

The inability to hit back at the guerrillas naturally made the counterinsurgents angry, and some leaders allowed their troops to give vent to this anger by ravaging villages suspected of abetting the Huks. Constabulary and army officers permitted troops to steal food, burn houses, make dubious arrests, and commit violent crimes against civilians, all of which stoked the people's desire to support the insurgency. The landlords' civilian guards committed the same offenses. And the Philippine court system did not protect peasants but instead protected the interests of government officials and the wealthy.[11]

Across central Luzon, peasants joined or assisted the insurgents primarily to avenge victimized relatives or to avoid becoming victims themselves. The Pampangans, the dominant ethnic group in central Luzon, were culturally inclined to resist oppression fiercely by organizing themselves under unusually strong leaders, which does much to explain why the insurgency flourished there and failed to sprout in other areas of the Philippines despite the Huks' repeated dispatching of armed proselytizers.[12] The Huks, who deterred their own people from committing abuses by making mistreatment of innocent civilians a capital offense, came across as protectors of law and order against the unruly government and landlord forces.

The Huks' burgeoning military strength and their battlefield successes also helped them win over the people of central Luzon. William J. Pomeroy, an American Communist who spent several years in the Huk ranks, remarked, "The people are always impressed by the arms, not out of fear but out of a feeling of strength. We get up before the people then, backed up by our arms, and give them the message of the struggle. It is never difficult after that."[13]

Factors other than government and landlord mistreatment and Huk military strength had little bearing on the peasants' political orientation. In propaganda, the Huks vowed to give sharecroppers ownership of the land they tilled, which might have seemed very appealing in a country where 90 percent of farmers did not own any land, yet interviews with Huk veterans indicate that land reform did not rank among their principal sources of motivation for joining. In practice, Huk agrarian policies were often limited in scope, aimed mainly at compelling landlords to restore interest-free loans and raise the percentage of crops kept by tenants to what it had been in the past—a return to wealth lost, not a grab for wealth never held.[14] During a 1970 interview, former Philippine Communist Party general secretary Jesus Lava recalled that "it was the party that propagandized the slogan 'Land for the Landless.' That didn't come from an outcry by the peasants. Few peasants then—or even today—were willing to fight with guns for land. Most really only wanted larger shares of the harvests."[15]

Of even less importance to the peasants was Marxist-Leninist ideology. Whereas the Communist leaders were highly educated intellectuals from cities, where the wealthy citizens drove cars and kept their food in refrigerators, most of the Huks were recruited from barrios, where the typical peasant possessed at best an elementary school education and occupied a thatched-roof bamboo hut with no running water or electricity. At first, the peasants failed to grasp Communist ideology simply because of a lack of education, and they failed to grasp it even after serving for several years in the Huks because the party misled the fighters into believing that land redistribution was an ultimate objective, not what it really was—an intermediate step that was to be followed by abolition of private ownership. One of the dedicated Communists among the Huks explained: "Since the peasants do not understand the benefits of collective ownership you have to cater to their backward thinking."[16]

In April 1948, Roxas died of a heart attack during a visit to Clark Air Base on Luzon. The presidency was transferred to Vice President Elpidio Quirino, a man who owed his high position in the Liberal Party to his lack of collaboration with the Japanese during the war, rather than to any abilities of his own. Under his administration, corruption surged. Observers disagreed over whether Quirino himself was especially corrupt, but his failure to rein in the venal individuals around him was undisputed. As a result of the siphoning of public funds, the Philippine economy stalled. The Americans, who were pouring in aid to help the Philippine government fight Communism, beseeched Quirino to halt the pilfering, but to no effect. Secretary of State Dean Acheson spoke wistfully of replacing Quirino but restrained himself with the thought that American involvement in Quirino's removal would become known publicly and damage the standing of the United States across Asia.[17]

In the 1949 presidential race between Quirino and the Nationalist Party's José Laurel, Quirino supporters used cash payments and intimidation to obtain votes. They registered children, dead people, flowers, and birds as voters and filled ballot boxes with votes for Quirino. Laurel's supporters also committed acts of fraud, but apparently of a lesser magnitude, for Quirino finished with more votes and retained the presidency. The electoral misdeeds, widely publicized by the Huks and the press, made Huk supporters out of people who were becoming disenchanted with the two largest national parties.

The fraud in the 1949 election also convinced the Philippine Communist Party to abandon its remaining hopes for gaining power through elections and to concentrate exclusively on military action. Huk military attacks of late had been crowned with victories, driving terrified government officials from the provinces to Manila. The Huk forces were approaching an armed strength of 15,000 men. In January 1950, the party resolved to accelerate the armed struggle in order to topple Quirino's government by 1952.[18]

From March to May 1950, the Huks raided towns in central Luzon, killing government forces, stealing weapons, and raising the hammer and sickle over town squares. The government responded with predictable feebleness. An American military adviser warned that the Huks were on the verge of taking complete control of sections of central Luzon. In August, 500 Huks launched two attacks on army bases, inflicting debilitating and embarrassing losses on government forces. During one of these attacks, the Huks killed the patients in the base hospital, raped the nurses prior to killing them, and released forty-seven prisoners from the provincial jail. As a result of these victories, the party leadership moved up the target date for achieving decisive victory to 1951.[19]

It was during this time of despair that a new leader arrived to pull the drowning Philippine government out of the water. Ramon Magsaysay was born in 1907 in a hut made of bamboo and cogon grass, the Philippine equivalent of Abraham Lincoln's log cabin. His father taught carpentry until he was fired for flunking the school superintendent's son, after which he opened a small store that sold retail items in very small quantities to impoverished peasants. A strict disciplinarian, the elder Magsaysay required his children to work long hours during the day and stay home after dark, and he beat them for misbehaving. Through his hard work and that of his eight children, the father eventually collected enough money to open a blacksmith shop. Ramon chopped down trees and made charcoal, which he took to the forge, where he pumped the bellows while his father hammered away on the anvil.

Ramon Magsaysay also spent much of his youth milking water buffaloes and working his family's modest plot of farmland. By doing a peasant's work and talking with peasants, he became much more knowledgeable about the peasantry than most members of the middle class to which his family was ascending, not to mention the urban elites. He sympathized with the peasants then, and also years later, when he had the power to translate sentiments into governmental action.[20]

Magsaysay attended college in Manila, then went to work at a bus company as a mechanic. With talent and hard work he became a manager, making him a full-fledged member of the expanding Philippine middle class, which included quite a few young idealists intent on making political and economic reforms that the upper class had been unwilling to make. When the Japanese invaded the Philippines in December 1941, he joined a Philippine infantry division, and after the fall of Manila he signed on to a USAFFE unit to fight as a guerrilla. He so impressed the Americans that in February 1945, MacArthur made him military governor of Zambales province.

In 1946, Ramon Magsaysay won election to the Philippine House of Representatives as a member of Roxas's Liberal Party. He served ably on the House Committee on National Defense and became its chair in 1949. While on a trip to the United States in April 1950, Magsaysay met Edward Lansdale of the Office of Policy Coordination, a covert action outfit that was later merged into the CIA. Lansdale, who had operated in the Philippines as a military intelligence officer after World War II, had recently been sketching plans for saving the Philippines from Communism. His superiors found his ideas incisive and were considering sending him to Manila. At their first meeting, Magsaysay and Lansdale discovered similarities in thought and commitment. The next day, Lansdale informed American military and civilian officials that Magsaysay could help rescue the Philippines, and he presented the dashing Philippine congressman to them in person. The Office of Policy Coordination and the State Department, which by this point were thoroughly disgusted with Quirino, concluded that Magsaysay ought to be propelled to a position of greater prominence in the Philippine government. They decided, in addition, to send Lansdale to the Philippines with a few sidekicks and a large bank account to assist Magsaysay and the Philippine government in general.[21]

George Chester of the Office of Policy Coordination and Livingston Merchant, deputy assistant secretary of state for Far Eastern affairs, flew to the Philippines to join forces with the head of the American advisory group, Major General Leland Hobbs, and the American ambassador, Myron Cowen. Converging on Quirino like a herd of salesmen, they urged him to appoint Magsaysay secretary of national defense. The appointment, they made clear, would lead to further U.S. aid, something that Quirino knew would be difficult to obtain after his failure to meet repeated American demands for reform. Some of the Philippine Liberal Party senators, alarmed by the government's inability to check the Huks' advances, also pushed hard to get Magsaysay appointed. Quirino was reluctant to make the appointment, for he viewed Magsaysay as a potential political rival. On the other hand, Magsaysay might fail, and Quirino could not, in any event, afford to forfeit the American aid. He did not hesitate long before agreeing to grant the American request. When he extended the job offer, Quirino asked Magsaysay what he would need to destroy the Huks. Magsaysay replied, "An absolutely free hand." Quirino assented.[22]

Magsaysay became secretary of national defense in September 1950. Fearing that Huk assassins would target his home, he sent his family to Bataan and moved in with Lansdale, who had just arrived under the cover of intelligence adviser to the Philippine government. Having no experience as a national executive, Magsaysay was receptive to Lansdale's offers of advice and quickly came to rely on him. During the first months, Magsaysay conducted much of his official business in Lansdale's bungalow, where Lansdale could feed him ideas as Philippine officials filed in and out. At night, Magsaysay tossed out thoughts and Lansdale sorted and critiqued and added to them. Lansdale steered Magsaysay's thinking so subtly that Magsaysay was convinced that he had created and developed the ideas all by himself, which ensured that he would act on them.[23] While Magsaysay possessed in abundance most of the characteristics of a strong counterinsurgency leader, much of the flexibility, the good judgment, and especially the creativity that he exhibited early on sprang from the mind of Edward Lansdale.

Although Lansdale was a man of ideas, he was not the sort who clings to libraries or offices. He did not trust the written reports of U.S. government officials or the articles and books by American scholars who were considered experts on the Philippines. "Maybe we should be more cautious in our listening to 'experts' and pay more heed to how they have come to know that of which they speak," Lansdale once said. "When was the 'expert' last invited to be a guest in an 'average' Filipino household to share a meal? When did he last spend a night with Filipinos in the provinces? . . . Does he honestly know whereof he speaks? Or, does he merely know Manila, the largest city, and a coterie of acquaintances?"[24]

To see the truth for himself, Lansdale traveled frequently into the countryside, at considerable risk to his person and in disregard of official U.S. regulations prohibiting Americans from venturing beyond a few safe zones. When people complained about his violations of those rules, he persuaded General Hobbs to grant him a special exemption. Although Lansdale had to rely on an interpreter to converse, he invariably succeeded in charming the local Filipinos he encountered, including some Huks. Lansdale "could make a friend of everybody except Satan," remarked one of the Americans who worked with him.[25] By talking with people and observing the situation in the countryside firsthand, Lansdale concluded that the crux of the problem was the government's harsh and unjust handling of the populace, and that this poor conduct stemmed from poor leadership.

After obtaining Magsaysay's concurrence in this assessment, Lansdale helped him find ways to fix the leadership. The solutions they formulated were not complicated but required vigor, perseverance, and moral rectitude, qualities with which Magsaysay, unlike his predecessors, was overflowing. Clad in an aloha shirt and slacks to conceal his identity, Magsaysay went to barracks and military installations without prior warning to check on his officers. On more than a few occasions, Magsaysay caught officers loafing or sleeping at their posts. After conversing with officers and enlisted personnel, he wandered over to the charcoal fires where civilians were cooking to consult them, often walking unaccompanied through dangerous areas and impressing all around him with his courage. Making maximum use of the free hand that Quirino had given him, Magsaysay fired or demoted officers wherever he found evidence of incompetence, inertia, corruption, or maltreatment of the citizenry. He also gave promotions on the spot to officers who had performed exceptionally well. Magsaysay made these inspection visits with astonishing frequency, but he also sent out trusted individuals to carry out surprise inspections at all hours. Once word had spread about the unannounced visits, many officers who had been lackadaisical perked up and began taking their jobs seriously. Those who did not became the next to feel the axe.[26]

During his first month as secretary of national defense, Magsaysay relieved thirteen high-ranking Philippine officers, including the chief of staff of the armed forces. Quirino, who was a good friend of many top officers, objected to these firings but acquiesced after Magsaysay said he would quit if Quirino revoked his authority to replace personnel. Officers who were relatives or chums of Magsaysay did not escape, either. When a committee of generals complained that all the changes were demoralizing the army, Magsaysay replied, "I don't care. If they are bad I will demoralize them some more." In the place of ousted officers, Magsaysay put men whom he and his American advisers knew to be dedicated and active. He replaced battalion commanders with young officers, ranging in age from twenty-five to thirty-two, who had a history of good performance. In addition, Magsaysay was able to make wholesale changes to the leadership of the ill-disciplined constabulary by convincing Quirino to transfer the constabulary from the Department of the Interior to the Department of National Defense. As a rule, Magsaysay avoided assigning officers to their native provinces so that they could not use their powers to act upon old grudges, and he broke up factions within the officer corps by shuffling officers around periodically.[27]

To his officers, Magsaysay emphasized winning the people over through good conduct. He insisted that officers promptly report theft and atrocities by Philippine troops and made sure that the perpetrators were duly punished. As a safeguard against officers who refused to report adequately, Magsaysay invited citizens to send him complaints of wrongdoing by government personnel. He had each complaint investigated, and disciplined the accused when they were found guilty.[28]

Because of his charisma and his manifest dedication, Magsaysay was an outstanding motivator. Napoleon Valeriano, a Philippine military officer, and Charles Bohannon, an American adviser, asserted that Magsaysay had an "outstanding ability to inspire effective action by small units, to rally to his support leaders at all echelons." They noted that Magsaysay's subordinates strove to emulate his persona, which they described thus: "new, dramatic, infinitely energetic, determined to overcome, by any means necessary, the obstacles to effective action against the Huk."[29] Magsaysay also inspired his officers to higher levels of integrity by living simply and displaying modesty in public appearances. Often he drove his own car rather than use a chauffeur. Government officials and officers became less disposed to corrupt behavior and to exhibitions of wealth that would raise suspicions of corruption.[30]

So magnetic was Magsaysay's personality that even some Huks turned into government supporters. After Magsaysay publicly offered to speak with any Filipino who wanted to help fight the insurgents, the Huks sent a young officer posing as an ordinary civilian to accept the offer and assassinate Magsaysay. When the young man showed up at his meeting with Magsaysay, he was ready to kill, but first he let Magsaysay speak. The would-be assassin was so impressed that he decided to switch to Magsaysay's side. In a stroke of remarkable good fortune for the government, the convert told Magsaysay that the top Huk leadership could be located by following a twelve-year-old girl in Manila who passed messages while selling meats and vegetables from a basket. Putting the girl under surveillance, Magsaysay speedily apprehended 150 Communist Party members, including the top twelve members of the politburo, along with the complete records of the Communist Party. For the Huks, it was a devastating blow, though not a fatal one.[31]

Magsaysay's new leaders in the military and the constabulary transformed central Luzon with the swiftness and totality of a tsunami. In stark contrast to their predecessors, battalion commanders regularly conducted patrols far from bases and roads, going deep into the jungles and swamps to look for Huks and collect information. They kept their men in the field for several days at a stretch, rather than bringing them in every night. Curtailing the use of large sweep operations, which the enemy easily evaded, they concentrated on aggressive small-unit patrolling, which not only made them less visible but also let them cover more ground and afforded more opportunities for inter-action with the population. The army did retain large mobile reserve units that sped by motorized transport to the sites of big Huk attacks and, on occasion, mounted large assaults on enemy bases and supplies.[32]

Fundamental to the success of all these operations, as recounted in a book produced by the faculty of the Philippine Infantry School, were "the initia-tive, improvisation, and aggressiveness of the commander."[33] In the hunt for information about the Huks, some commanders outdid others because they exercised greater initiative in collecting intelligence above and beyond what the intelligence organizations were already gathering, and sought information to corroborate that from single sources. The same commanders were usually the most aggressive and relentless in their military operations. The centrality of this type of leadership in bringing down the Huks is reflected in accounts from the other side. In November 1950, William Pomeroy described the new situation that he and the Huks faced: "Reports come in from all along the Sierra Madre. The enemy is becoming more aggressive. Spies are everywhere in the towns, and patrols are often in the forest now, where once they never came. Our [Field Commands] ambush them, shoot up their vehicles on the roads, make death traps of mountain paths, but the patrols do not stop."[34] Im-provisation was crucial because the counterinsurgency methods taught at the Infantry School and the Ground Combat School, which were largely derived from standard American counterinsurgency doctrines, often did not work in certain locales or worked only when adjusted to local conditions.[35]

The Infantry School study identified commanders, especially battalion commanders, as the sole determinants of troop morale and discipline. Effec-tive battalion commanders routinely visited the men and looked into the problems that adversely affected their performance and welfare, fixing those problems whenever possible. They supervised small unit operations and made effective use of their staff. When such a battalion commander was replaced with an officer who did not lead properly, the morale and discipline of the battalion sank precipitously.[36] Because of the prevalence of good command-ers and hence good discipline after Magsaysay took over, Philippine troops committed far fewer crimes against the population than before, which led to greatly increased cooperation from the civilians. The new commanders also reined in the landlords' unruly civilian guards, the other leading source of peasant discontent.[37]

The improvements in the counterinsurgency effort were facilitated by huge increases in U.S. aid to the Philippines during Magsaysay's term as secretary of national defense, the result of heightened American fears of Communist expansionism in Asia following Mao Zedong's victory in China and North Korea's invasion of South Korea. The aid, however, was secondary in importance to leadership — corrupt and inept Philippine leadership would have found ways to fritter away the aid, no matter how plentiful. Magsaysay used some of the aid to raise the pay of Philippine soldiers, which enabled them to live decently without robbing the populace. Other funds were dedicated to ensuring that troops always had food, whether by transporting it to them by vehicle or allowing them to buy food locally, so that hunger did not drive them to take chickens or rice from peasant families.[38]

With American aid and Lansdale's advice, Magsaysay established programs and enacted reforms in such areas as agricultural credit, health, roads, and irrigation. Though modest in scale, these initiatives did much to bolster Magsaysay's image and the government's image because they were well publicized. Lansdale, tapping his expertise as a former advertising executive, helped the government sell itself in print and on the airwaves, and Magsaysay held numerous press conferences in which he persuasively articulated and justified his policies.[39]

Magsaysay received the greatest propaganda value from a program that was more ambitious in nature but similarly small in size. Dubbed the Economic Development Corps (EDCOR), the program gave former insurgents title to lands on Mindanao, chosen from tracts that had been publicly owned so as not to alarm the landowning elites. In February 1951, EDCOR began clearing the land, building roads, and establishing basic public services, and three months later the first settlers arrived. Each family received a plot of roughly fifteen acres of farmland and was issued tools and farm animals on credit. Philippine troops helped the settlers build homes of nipa palm or wood and illuminated them with electrical power, a luxury that most peasants had never before experienced. The communities had new hospitals, libraries, schools, and recreational facilities. A second site was established on Mindanao late in 1951, and two more in Luzon in 1954, in areas unmolested by guerrillas. All told, the program resettled only 1,200 families, many of whom contained no former

Huks, having been selected because the government wanted enough staunchly anti-Communist families on the land to guard against subversion. Nor did it affect tenancy in the areas of high insurgent activity. Yet the program seriously undermined support for the rebellion and caused Huks to defect because government propagandists bombarded the populace with detailed reports on the program.[40]

Huk sources testified that the tide of the war turned against them between late 1951 and the first half of 1952. Aggressive and cunning government combat operations, they observed, inflicted fearsome casualties and destroyed bases. Government forces lay in ambush around towns and lived among the people, forcing the insurgents to hide in mountains or swamps or forests, where they could not obtain information or recruits or food — even the lush tropical forests contained almost no edible foliage. When the government forces went into the mountains and swamps and forests to track the guerrillas down, the Huks had to change locations constantly, depriving them of the time to recuperate and reorganize that almost every successful insurgency has had. Numerous Huks defected or surrendered because counterinsurgent military operations forced them into an existence devoid of food and rest and convinced them that the revolution was failing.[41]

Within the villages, the government's military successes eroded support for the Huk cause.[42] The other critical development that helped divest the Huks of popular support was the improved behavior of government personnel and the landlords' private security forces. Having never been converted to the radical ideology of the Communist Party, most Huks and Huk supporters were ready to abandon the cause once their original grievance — abuses of power by government personnel and the landlords — had been removed. "When Magsaysay started making reforms in the Philippine army and in the government generally," Jesus Lava recounted, "it had an impact not only on the movement's mass support but on the armed [Huk] soldiers as well. Many left because repression was ending, and they were not ideologically committed enough to stay in the movement, especially as things grew worse for the Huks."[43] Another former insurgent commented, "Once the landlords and government showed they would stop abusing us, we were ready to put aside our guns."[44] The loss of peasant support compelled the Huks to rely on intimidation and violence to get food and supplies from the peasants, which alienated the peasants further.

By the fall of 1952 the Huks had been reduced to an estimated 4,000 men, most of them on the run with few supplies and little contact with the population. At this juncture, Luis Taruc and his brother Peregrino called for a peaceful settlement of the war, which prompted the Philippine Communist Party leadership to suspend Luis and expel Peregrino. The party's leadership made another change of course a short time later, replacing plans to overthrow the government quickly with plans to conduct a protracted struggle using predominantly nonviolent and legal political means.[45]

Despite the remarkable reversal of momentum, Magsaysay was not content with the pace of progress against the Huks. Large elements of the Quirino administration, he believed, remained corrupt and indifferent to the problems confronting the common people, especially the need for land. In February 1953 his frustrations boiled over, and he resigned as secretary of national defense. Magsaysay spent the next nine months running for president, with Lansdale performing most of the functions of a campaign manager. The U.S. government provided Lansdale with a secret $1 million bank account to use for Magsaysay's campaign, although Lansdale claimed to have spent only $60,000 of it. Lansdale drummed up $250,000 in campaign contributions from American businesses that wanted good relations between the United States and the Philippines, including Coca-Cola, in violation of Philippine campaign-financing laws, and also obtained large sums from Philippine sugar producers. Ever the charmer, Lansdale persuaded American and Philippine journalists to write favorable profiles of Magsaysay and to pillory Quirino for his corruption and election tampering. In response to Lansdale's persuasive entreaties, Nationalist Party leaders José Laurel and Claro Recto agreed to back Magsaysay. The National Movement for Free Elections, a citizens' organization funded secretly by the United States, helped get people to turn out for the election, and it monitored election sites to prevent fraud.

On election day, Magsaysay defeated Quirino by a tally of 2.9 million to 1.3 million votes. In central Luzon, the home of the Huks, he won a stunning 70 percent of the vote. American help must have gained Magsaysay a considerable number of votes from people who had not previously appreciated his many virtues, but the margin of victory suggests that it did not win him the election. He had already impressed the press and the Philippine people with his charismatic personality, his dexterous mind, and his success in reforming the government, with help from Lansdale's masterful propaganda.[46]

During the ensuing weeks, Magsaysay displayed his customary diligence in selecting cabinet ministers and other high officials. He appointed most of them in an acting role, saying that their jobs would become permanent only after they had proven their worthiness. When relatives, friends, and campaign supporters lined up at his office to beseech him for jobs, he refused to give them preferential treatment. "My personal feelings and those of my friends are subordinate to the interests of the nation," he explained. "And the interests of the nation dictate that I be drastic. Otherwise, the lesson will be lost. The welfare of the Philippines is bigger than any one man."[47]

President Magsaysay opted to serve as his own secretary of national defense. He continued to travel around the country checking on officers and officials and talking with peasants. Aside from the Department of National Defense, the government's departments had heretofore contributed little to the war against the Huks because previous presidents had not pressed them, but with Magsaysay it was different. Brooking no resistance or sloth, Magsaysay quickly had these departments bringing to bear valuable capabilities in education, health, and other areas. To discourage corruption, Magsaysay ordered that all public officials publish their assets. He instructed the department heads to be accommodating to journalists and did everything else possible to woo the press, including raising money for the National Press Club building in downtown Manila and giving government jobs to journalists, their families, and their friends.[48]

As president, Magsaysay organized public works projects to improve the government's image and provide jobs. He tried to initiate large-scale social welfare programs and sweeping land reform, but the Philippine congress, which was dominated by the landlord class, blocked most of these initiatives. The problems of landlessness and poverty persisted for the remainder of President Magsaysay's time in office.[49] Yet the lack of major social and economic changes did not thwart the counterinsurgency effort, because the population still cared less about such issues than about security, good government, and charismatic leadership. During Magsaysay's first year as president, the remaining popular support for the Huks dissipated, and adroit governmental military operations battered the remnants of the guerrilla units, turning the Huks into a mere nuisance, consisting of widely scattered groups of no more than three to five men.[50]

The defeat of the Huk Rebellion illustrates splendidly how a single leadership change at the top can alter the entire complexion of a counterinsurgency. Ramon Magsaysay, with some help from Edward Lansdale, engineered the government's meteoric transition from failure to success, primarily by replacing poor field commanders and finding good officers to take their places. Because he had demanded and received a free hand to make personnel changes when he became secretary of national defense, he was able to sweep away even the president's cronies, something that few cabinet ministers have accomplished in any government. In picking replacements, Magsaysay renounced the common practice of giving jobs to family members, friends, and political supporters, which was personally painful for him but profoundly beneficial for the nation.

Magsaysay roused his officers to new heights of performance through natural charisma and exemplary conduct. Consciously or not, his officers followed his example of constant activity and perseverance in the face of adversity. In an atmosphere where corruption was rampant, Magsaysay's austerity inspired officers to keep their hands out of the public treasury. Magsaysay demonstrated every other key counterinsurgency attribute to his subordinates, and Lansdale was able to stay in the background to such a degree that no one realized his talents had augmented Magsaysay's, especially in the area of creativity.

In explaining Magsaysay's successes, external observers have often focused exclusively on improved governance or social and economic reforms. Good governance, the product of good leadership, was indeed crucial; social and economic reforms could not have been, because they were very small in effect. Well-led intelligence and military operations were also essential to overall success, and indeed to good governance. Without them, the Huks would have been able to kill government officials in the towns and barrios, and much of the populace would have stuck with the Huks in the belief that they would prevail in the end.

No case illustrates better than the Huk rebellion how a foreign power can stimulate improvement of an ally's counterinsurgency capabilities without adverse repercussions. In the elevation of Magsaysay, the first key step for the United States was identifying Magsaysay as a man of exceptional leadership faculties. Most members of the Philippine elites could not have turned the war around, no matter how much assistance the United States heaped upon them. Next, the Truman administration coaxed Philippine president Quirino, with words and the dangling of dollars, to appoint Magsaysay secretary of national defense. By sending the enormously skillful and personable Lansdale to the Philippines, the Americans boosted Magsaysay's effectiveness and ensured that he acted in accordance with American interests. Finally, the United States covertly provided money and other resources to get Magsaysay elected to the presidency. In the early twenty-first century, as the leaders of Iraq and Afghanistan are struggling to combat insurgencies, the United States should seriously consider using such techniques to promote talent within the governments of those allies.

CHAPTER 6

The Malayan Emergency

T he Malayan Communist Party, like its counterpart in the Philippines, traces its origins to the Comintern's missionary expeditions of the 1920s. Communist agents from China began the hunt for supporters in Singapore, at the tip of the Malay Peninsula, in 1924, but with only modest success. The Malayan Communist Party was not formally organized until 1930, at which time the Vietnamese Communist leader Ho Chi Minh, a French Communist leader, and some Chinese Communists presided over its official founding and placed it under the direction of the Comintern's Far Eastern Bureau in Shanghai. Japan's invasion of Manchuria in 1931 created a groundswell of anti-Japanese and pro-Chinese sentiment among Malayans of Chinese ethnicity, prompting large numbers to flock to the party. Over the next decade, British police chased the party's members and, with the help of spies within the organization, made numerous arrests, but the party was still able to organize labor strikes and recruit new members.[1]

Malaya's turn for a Japanese invasion came at the same time as the Philippines', in December 1941. The British and the Malayan Communists put aside their differences to fight the hated Japanese, and, as the fall of Malaya approached, the British even trained and equipped 200 Communist guerrillas and sent them into the jungle as members of the new Malayan People's Anti-Japanese Army. British officers who escaped the Japanese conquest fled to the jungle to serve as military advisers to the guerrillas and assist with communications and logistics. For the next few years, the Communist guerrillas conducted harassing and scout actions against the Japanese, but they refused to take part in large assaults, preferring to concentrate on recruiting civilian supporters and conserving strength for the future.

The Japanese occupiers imprisoned British officials and the Europeans who ran tin mining and rubber planting, the two industries that had employed the most people in the country. As a consequence, a large fraction of the roughly one million ethnic Chinese in rural Malaya lost their jobs, and close to half of them became squatters on the lands of jailed miners and planters in the western coastal lowlands. More than a few entered the ranks of the guerrillas after feeling the pitiless whip of the Japanese. The British forces that retook Malaya after the collapse of the Japanese empire in August 1945 lacked the administrative strength to force the squatters to relinquish their lands, which left the door open for future trouble.

The Communists were not yet ready to govern Malaya at the end of the war, so they consented to the return of the British and agreed to disband their guerrillas, with the understanding that the Communist Party would be able to participate in society as a legal political organization. The Communists handed over most of the weapons the British had given them during the war, but at secret jungle caches they retained a significant collection of small arms, most of them stolen from British depots and armories during the chaotic British defeat in 1942. All told, the Communist stores contained enough weapons to arm eight guerrilla regiments.

For the next few years, the Communists pursued political power through nonviolent means, such as infiltrating non-Communist political organizations and orchestrating strikes. The Communist Party and its front organizations recruited new Chinese members through social and family networks, capitalizing on dissatisfaction with unemployment, the abusive labor practices of European business owners, and the racism of the ethnic Malays. The Malayan Communists were drawn almost entirely from Malaya's Chinese minority, who, with two million people, made up 40 percent of Malaya's total population. Indeed, the overwhelmingly Chinese character of the Communist Party, coupled with its atheism, guaranteed the perpetual hostility of most of the ethnic Malays, who cherished both their ethnicity and their Islamic faith.

Twenty-three-year-old Chin Peng assumed leadership of the Malayan Communist Party in the spring of 1947, after the party's previous leader had absconded with most of the party's funds and received sanctuary from the British, to whom he had secretly been passing information. For his first year as party chief, Chin Peng heeded the recommendation of the Chinese Communist Party to continue the legal methods of strikes and demonstrations along with covert subversion. The seminal change in the party's strategy took place at a meeting of the party's Central Committee in March 1948. Some party leaders believed that the legal struggle was too slow in advancing the party down the path to revolution, a view that gained in popularity at the meeting thanks to the appearance of Laurence Sharkey, the secretary general of the Australian Communist Party. Sharkey told them that the Communist Party of India had just decided on armed struggle, and declared that the Malayan Communist Party never should have dissolved its guerrilla force. At this same time, the Central Committee of the Malayan Communist Party received an intelligence report that the British were preparing to terminate the party's involvement in labor unions.

After weighing these developments, the party leadership came out in favor of violence, starting with the assassination of strikebreakers. Subsequent planning called for jungle-based guerrillas to attack the remote tin and rubber estates, in coordination with ethnic Chinese sympathizers among the civilian population. If successful, these operations would force government personnel to flee or die, which eventually would permit the consolidation of insurgent base areas and the organization of larger attacks.[2]

The insurgents kicked off the armed conflict in May 1948 with tried-and-true techniques like intimidation, assassination, sabotage, and rioting. During the first half of June, the rate of armed attacks accelerated, with special emphasis on assassination of British plantation managers, leading figures of the Chinese Nationalist Party, and government officials. Each of those groups begged the central administration in Kuala Lumpur to take stern measures to protect them. But Sir Edward Gent, the British high commissioner in the Malayan capital, and the Labor government in London dismissed the attacks as mere banditry. The police offices did not change their hours, remaining open only from 8:00 a.m. to 6:30 p.m. during the week and 8:00 a.m. to noon on Saturday, with no hours at all on Sunday.[3]

Kuala Lumpur was finally stirred to action by the events of June 16, 1948. The first occurred at the office of Arthur Walker in Sungei Siput, a tin-mining township in northern Malaya. The manager of an English-owned estate, Walker had reportedly been among the most domineering of the strikebreakers. Three Communists let themselves in his door and found him completing some paperwork. "Good day, sir," they said to Walker in Malay, to which he replied, "Good morning." The visitors shot him in the head and chest, killing him instantly, then fled on bicycles. Half an hour later, ten miles away, a different group of Communists apprehended another plantation manager, also an alleged strikebreaker, along with his assistant, who was supposed to be transferred the next day to another estate as acting manager. The insurgents tied the two men to chairs and fired pistols into their skulls. For good measure, they burned a smokehouse containing 56,000 pounds of packed rubber. Later the same day, Communists executed several other hapless individuals in various stretches of the Malayan countryside.[4]

High Commissioner Gent declared a state of emergency as soon as he learned of the day's events. During the next three days, in a dragnet called Operation Frustration, the government rounded up 1,100 members of the Malayan Communist Party and its front organizations. Gent initiated a set of emergency measures that included warrantless searches, detention without trial, and the death penalty for unauthorized possession of firearms. The Communist Party's leaders had failed to anticipate so swift a response, believing that they would have several months to make an orderly withdrawal to the jungle before intensifying attacks in September. Some of the hard-core Communists were caught in the dragnet. A large number of others, however, escaped, thanks mainly to the government's lack of intelligence on the party, and took refuge in the jungle. Chin Peng had a narrower escape than most, evading British and Malayan policemen by hoisting himself up a jambu tree to surmount the stone wall surrounding the house where he had been staying.[5]

The party leadership summoned former guerrillas to jungle camps for retraining. In the midst of the squatter population, the Communists mobilized front organizations with names like the Peasants' Union, the Liberation League, and the Self-Protection Corps, which were known collectively as the Min Yuen. These organizations transferred essential assets—recruits, rice, weapons, ammunition, and medicine—from the civilian population to the guerrillas encamped in the jungle bases. Heavily influenced by displays of military strength, the squatters joined or assisted the Min Yuen much more readily when government forces were scarce or suffered defeats at the hands of the guerrillas. An estimated 60,000 rural Chinese voluntarily abetted the Communists in the early stages of the insurgency, and most of the other squatters were prodded or intimidated into supporting them.[6]

At the start of the Emergency, the Malayan police numbered only 9,000 men, which in a country of five million would have been too few to maintain a strong presence in most villages even if most of the policemen had been competent, which they were not. The police leadership had never recovered from the deaths of veteran leaders in Japanese prison camps during World War II. Most of the replacements shipped to Malaya by the British government after the war were inexperienced civilians, many of them deficient in integrity and other important qualities. Police morale was near its nadir, and internal criticism of the senior officers, for cronyism and other vices, was approaching its zenith. Almost all of the police rank and file were ethnic Malays; the scarcity of ethnic Chinese was a serious impediment to obtaining information in the Chinese sections of the country, where the Communists were concentrated.[7]

In response to the outbreak of insurgent violence, the government began a police recruitment campaign, which in six months increased the total strength of the police to 50,000, some of whom were assigned to a new police organization, the Special Constabulary, which was responsible for protecting rubber plantations and tin mines and their managers. In addition, the British formed a police intelligence organization, the Special Branch, in an attempt to fill the void of intelligence on the insurgents. London, however, failed to provide enough officers of quality to keep pace with the expansion of any of the police branches. A substantial number of police officers and sergeants were transferred to Malaya from Palestine, which the British had just handed back to the United Nations, and although some of these individuals were well suited to their new jobs, many held the opinion that every Chinese was a current or future bandit and hence ought to bashed around. While finding good police officers was far from easy, the architects of the police expansion program could have done a good deal better had they appreciated the power of leadership and given more attention to improving it. They were victims of the assumption, all too common among novices, that leadership ability does not vary all that much from one individual to the next. As one senior officer commented, "Inexperienced people often think that you have but to organise a force or service on paper, equip it with suitable weapons, and fill the establishment with men." It was "a hopeless attitude" because "it is men that count, not bodies."[8]

The civil administration, which also had a crucial part to play in controlling the civilian population and identifying insurgents, likewise suffered from serious leadership shortcomings. It, too, had been decimated during World War II and insufficiently rehabilitated thereafter. The leadership weaknesses began at the very top, with the high commissioner. Gent was relieved from that position very soon after the insurgency sprang up, and was replaced with Sir Henry Gurney. Aloof and uninspiring, Gurney spent most of his waking hours in his office, where he diligently carried out administrative duties. Seldom did he travel outside the capital, and then only to visit large towns to meet sultans or deliver speeches. His absence from the countryside restricted his comprehension of the conflict and prevented the infusion of any sense of urgency into a civil administration that seemed to be operating as if no war were in progress.[9]

Beneath Gurney, a Malay sultan ruled each of Malaya's nine states. The sultans resisted the high commissioner's efforts to involve the state administrations in the war and demanded instead that the federal government clean up the mess. The high commissioner received considerably more cooperation at the district level, one level of administration down from the state, where the leadership consisted largely of British officials. When the emergency began, experienced British civil servants were taken out of other jobs and thrown into understaffed Malayan districts, but they eventually returned to their old positions, and London provided too few civil servants to plug the holes left in the administrative structure. The civil servants dispatched to Malaya after the initial deployments, moreover, were mostly untrained young officers who could not speak Chinese or Malay, and some of them opposed Britain's Malayan policies to boot. Below the district officials were the village officials, most of whom were Malays, another handicap for the government in the Chinese villages.[10]

On account of the frailty of the police and the civil administration, the British government brought the military into the conflict, albeit under the control of civil authorities. The infantry battalions, however, had only 4,000 riflemen, and many of them were at first sent to guard rubber plantations and tin mines, which kept them from plunging into the jungle to chase the guerrillas and demolish their bases. As the police expanded and took on static guard missions, the army began moving into the jungle, but it possessed little information on the whereabouts of the insurgents and their supporters because its intelligence sections were very small and received no tips from the inept police. Consequently, most of their patrolling was based on hunches rather than hard information, and they produced only modest numbers of enemy casualties.[11]

During the war's first years, defective military leadership, like defective police leadership, resulted in frequent beatings of Chinese citizens. In some instances, the victims were known Communist supporters who possessed valuable information on the enemy, but very often the victims had little or no connection to the Communists, their only crime having been their proximity to government forces exasperated by the insurgents' elusiveness and cruelty. Gurney condoned such behavior because he thought it would terrify the Chinese into cooperating with the government. The Chinese might have been scared into cooperating if the government had been able to protect them from Communist retaliation, but because it was unable to do so, its cruelties only gained adherents for the Communists.[12]

Not every disadvantage was on the government's side, nor every advantage on the insurgency's side, in the early years. The insurgents had major leadership problems of their own, which resulted in military disorganization and repeated failures to attack the government at its weakest points. Possessing few heavy weapons, the insurgents could not tear out large chunks of the enemy's forces in a single battle. Aggressive British military officers frustrated the insurgency's initial military strategy, despite their inability to inflict heavy casualties. General Sir Neil Ritchie, commander in chief of the Far Eastern Land Forces, ordered battalion-sized operations in the early months of the insurgency to prevent the enemy from massing and gaining the initiative. The decision was based on the history of the Chinese Civil War—when the Chinese Nationalist government had dispersed small units of troops to expand its control of territory and population, it had had too few mobile forces to retain the initiative and prevent the Communists from concentrating their troops into large units. The Chinese Communists had proceeded to swallow up the small government detachments one at a time and take control of whole regions of the country, the "liberated areas" from which Mao launched the conventional attacks that won the war. That the Malayan Communist Party intended to establish such base areas and move toward bigger attacks was manifested in late 1948 by its two attempts to seize and hold towns in the state of Kelantan, both of which were thwarted by large British forces. The government's big military operations early on frustrated other insurgent plans to establish liberated areas by breaking up large guerrilla units, overrunning guerrilla bases, and keeping the guerrillas on the move.[13]

Some of the British military officers were veterans of past jungle and guerrilla wars and knew how to stalk small guerrilla units. The uninitiated, on the other hand, often began by launching clumsy large sweep operations, which the enemy spotted well in advance and dodged. Even if a large formation did manage to locate guerrillas, it had minimal advantages over a smaller one because low visibility in the jungle allowed only a small number of men, at the head of the column, to open fire in the brief moments before the guerrillas turned tail. The better battalion commanders soon realized that these sweep operations were futile, and came up with more effective tactics by experimenting or learning from army training and publications. In combating small guerrilla forces, the most productive tactics generally involved sending small groups of men on patrols and ambushes but did not necessarily entail abandoning the concentration of large numbers of troops in a small area; battalions sometimes sent out numerous small detachments simultaneously in close proximity to one another, which afforded a higher probability of catching fleeing guerrillas than did widely dispersed operations.[14]

In these jungle operations, success came down to the initiative, dedication, and integrity of junior officers, who for the most part were isolated by terrain from higher authorities. Few other types of terrain proved so grueling to the foot soldier as the steamy jungles of Malaya. By hacking their way forward with machetes, men could move through the jungle at half a mile per hour at best, with the rate falling to a few hundred yards per hour in dense sections. According to Lieutenant Bryan Wells, a platoon commander, "It was very hard physical work for the young officer. I found it was also a very lonely existence to maintain discipline throughout that period of time. . . . You needed to have that individual drive to be able to constantly motivate people to carry out their function in that environment because it was only too easy to just sit back, put up your hammock and lie there for three days and send in a patrol report that said you'd carried out these enormous activities."[15]

At the beginning of 1950, the guerrillas launched an offensive of unprecedented strength. Seeking to rectify their equipment shortfalls, they made the capture of enemy weapons the primary objective of their attacks. They flirted with the transition into conventional warfare, on occasion mustering as many as 300 troops for a single operation. The police, who bore the brunt of the guerrilla strikes since they were easier to find and to defeat, suffered 100 dead per month. The insurgents incurred significant casualties themselves but replaced all of their losses through recruiting.[16]

A few months into this new offensive, the British government decided that the senior leadership in Malaya was not up to snuff. Sir Harold Briggs was brought out of retirement and put in charge of the security forces. An army lieutenant general with many years of service in Asia, Briggs had fought with distinction in the jungle battles of World War II. Colleagues described him as creative, perceptive, and tactful. Over the course of his career, Briggs had been promoted from one command to the next because he made sound decisions quickly and achieved good results under trying circumstances.[17]

Briggs arrived in Malaya in April 1950, and within a month he formulated a comprehensive plan for action. The plan's most prominent feature was its relocation of the population into compact settlements, which would help isolate the guerrillas from their Min Yuen suppliers and force them to attack the security forces under unfavorable conditions. Security forces would clear the country of Communists, starting in the south and moving north. To improve intelligence collection, the plan called for expanding and strengthening the local civil administrations and the Special Branch. Police outposts were to be established in remote areas; the army would patrol the areas that the police could not patrol, and it would interdict guerrilla supply trails in the jungle. To remedy the lack of cooperation among the civil service, police, and military, Briggs created interagency executive committees that would run the war at the state and district levels. The district committees became the most important leadership entities in the country, and the district officers who chaired them wielded enormous power, provided that the committee members worked well together. For this reason, as one leading government official later put it, "A good District Officer is worth more than a battalion."[18] Cooperation among district leaders, however, would often be absent in the coming year and a half.[19]

On June 1, 1950, the major military operations of the Briggs plan commenced in the southern state of Johore. Concentrating forces in the state, the army crisscrossed the countryside with ambushes and patrols at a breakneck pace in order to eliminate insurgents, establish security over the population, and control food supplies. But their inability to obtain intelligence from the Chinese population, the result of the Malay dominance of the security forces, prevented the security forces from neutralizing significant numbers of guerrillas or stopping the populace from abetting them. Briggs found fault with some of the commanders of the security forces, but he lacked the authority to set them aright. The terms of his employment required that he issue guidance through the national army and police commanders, both of whom preferred to dilute or discard his directives. Furthermore, the efforts to resettle Johore's population soon fell behind schedule. The original idea of starting in the south and moving to the north consequently had to be abandoned; Johore, as it turned out, was not cleansed of insurgents until 1958.[20]

The troubles encountered during the first months of the plan's implementation led Briggs to conclude that squatter resettlement was a prerequisite for success, so he assigned relocation the highest priority across the country in 1951. Over the course of 1951, the government completed the resettlement of the bulk of the country's squatters, bringing the total number resettled to 385,000. The government pushed some of the squatters into existing villages but compelled most to move either to one of the 500 New Villages, located predominantly on sites that had just been cleared of jungle for the purpose, or to one of the 1,500 smaller regroupment areas within the estates where the squatters worked. Resettled families typically received 800 square yards within the fenced settlement perimeter, enough to grow vegetables and keep a few chickens, and another two acres of farmland within a two-mile radius. For housing, the government built frames of timber and roofs of palm leaves or corrugated iron, then supplied the residents with materials to build the walls.[21]

The mass relocations began hindering guerrilla food collection during 1951. At the end of the year, however, most of the New Villages and the other resettlement areas were nowhere near what Briggs had envisioned. The squatters remained either hostile to the government or apathetic, a problem that in many ways originated with poor leadership within the government. The resettlement officers, who were European, did not perform well except in a few cases. The assistant resettlement officers, who were Chinese, often suffered from gross incompetence. And the police, who had primary responsibility for defending the New Villages, remained in disarray throughout 1951 because of continuing leadership deficiencies.[22] A report from the state of Perak, for example, stated, "There have been an increasing number of disquieting incidents where jungle squads and special constable posts have failed to stand up against enemy action, either permitting the enemy to pass their posts unmolested or, if attacked, tamely surrendering their arms and ammunition. In addition, there have been cases of refusal of duty, incidents of the shooting of innocent people and of hysteria leading to panic firing for little or no cause. The lack of good leaders thrown up from the special constables is most marked, as indeed it is in the regular police."[23]

Briggs tried to bring Chinese personnel into the police in 1951, but few joined, for most Chinese looked down on police service as inferior in pay and social status to jobs in private business. Those Chinese who did serve in the police were considered untrustworthy. In another effort to improve village security, Briggs conscripted 79,000 adult males into a self-defense militia called the Home Guard, but failed to find suitable leaders, leaving the Home Guard in such a dubious condition that the government refused to issue weapons to many units.[24]

In 1951 guerrilla attacks on the New Villages brought the level of insurgent violence to new highs. Geography had precluded the establishment of the New Villages in locations remote from the insurgency's jungle bases, so the guerrillas could dart in for a raid and disappear back into the jungle just as quickly. With the assistance of the Min Yuen, the guerrillas killed collaborators, civil servants, and police. The number of government security forces killed in 1951 was more than 25 percent higher than in the previous year. Insurgent losses increased as well, but the insurgents, through recruiting, continued to make good all their combat losses. At the end of 1951, the Malayan Communist Party had an estimated 6,000 guerrillas, 10,000–15,000 workers, and more than 100,000 active supporters. The British Defence Co-ordination Committee was on the mark when it reported late in the year that "the Communist hold on Malaya is as strong, if not stronger, today than it ever has been."[25]

The one bright spot for the government was the jungle war. Still short on intelligence, government soldiers did not kill large numbers of insurgents, but through relentless patrolling and destruction of insurgent bases, they made it harder and harder for the enemy to operate in large groups. In October 1951 guerrilla commanders curtailed large military operations because of counter-insurgent military operations as well as the Communist leadership's desire to emphasize political action. The change had dramatic implications, for police outposts could not hold out for long against 200 insurgents, but when the enemy attacked with 20 or 30 men, the police could usually keep them at bay until relief forces arrived.[26]

October 1951 also saw several crucial changes on the British side. On the sixth, High Commissioner Gurney left Kuala Lumpur with his wife in a black Rolls-Royce for Fraser's Hill, a small resort sixty-five miles distant. He was traveling in a four-vehicle convoy, but because of an equipment problem, two of the vehicles had to stop while the Rolls-Royce and a police Land Rover continued ahead. At a sharp turn, thirty-eight guerrillas opened fire from steep, jungle-encrusted slopes. When one bullet punctured a tire on the Rolls-Royce, immobilizing it, Gurney stumbled out of the car and was shot. Relief forces eventually drove off the ambushers, but by then Gurney was dead. Psychologically, it was the government's worst setback since the start of the war.

Gurney's death was followed in short order by the departure of the rest of the top British leadership in Malaya. Briggs, afflicted with a serious illness, left at the end of November and returned to retirement in Cyprus, where he died a few months later. The director of intelligence resigned because of differences with the police commissioner, and a short time later, the police commissioner himself left.

On October 25, the Conservatives won the British parliamentary elections, returning Winston Churchill to the prime ministership. Having long maintained that the Malayan Emergency required a vigorous and forceful approach, the Conservatives now resolved to put their ideas into practice. The new secretary of state for the colonies, Oliver Lyttelton, visited Malaya in December 1951 to size up the situation and determine how exactly the war needed to be prosecuted. Lyttelton reported back that the police and the civil administration had to be upgraded, through the replacement of commanders, to halt the enemy's activities in the New Villages. Because of the inexperience of the civil servants, Lyttelton noted, the central government "finds it necessary to issue more and more directions. In this way the central authority becomes itself desk-bound, clogged with paper and remote. I was told by one man in a district which I reached from Kuala Lumpur in forty-five by Auster, that I was almost the only man from Kuala Lumpur (apart from the High Commissioner and the Director of Operations) whom he had seen since the Emergency began. A cold wind must blow some of the paper out of these Government offices. Only an experienced, forceful and ruthless administrator will succeed in creating a system equal to its task." This individual, Lyttelton concluded, should be a general who had command of both military and civil affairs, for the separation of the military and the civil had fostered disunity and prevented resolution of key problems. To the arguments from the British political opposition that the military should not control political affairs, Lyttelton paid no heed.[27]

Shortly after Lyttelton released his report, Field Marshal Bernard Montgomery sent Churchill an appraisal that built upon the report and encapsulated the situation in penetrating fashion: "The problem has been studied by the Secretary of State for the Colonies; the measures necessary to begin to put things right are clearly set out in his Report. But to determine what must be done is only half the answer, and the easiest half; that *of itself* will not achieve success. In all this welter of trouble 'the man' is what counts. The second half of the answer is to produce good men, really good men, who have the courage to issue the necessary orders, the drive to insist that those orders are carried out, and the determination and will-power to see the thing through to the end. Such men do not exist today in the Malayan Federation." Getting down to specifics, Montgomery asserted that "the first and really urgent need is to put a really high class man into the Malayan Federation as High Commissioner, and give him a first class Chief Secretary and a first class Commissioner of Police." Only one of those three posts, chief secretary, was currently occupied, and according to Montgomery, its occupant, Vincent Del Tufo, "has no power of command and gives out no inspiration" and "is, of course, quite useless as Chief Secretary."[28]

In accordance with Lyttelton's advice, Churchill decided that the next high commissioner should be a military officer with control over all civil and military operations. Lyttelton's first recommendation for the position, General Sir Brian Robertson, turned the assignment down, eliciting derision from other senior officers, who thought that he ought to retire if he was unwilling to take command in a time of war. Field Marshal Sir William Slim also declined the job, but he had better cause, since he had already retired from the army and he exceeded Robertson in age by five years. Slim, as well as Montgomery and other generals, emphatically advocated General Gerald Templer for the position. Churchill summoned Templer on January 11 for an interview. Favorably impressed, Churchill asked Templer to take the job, telling him that he could have whatever he wanted, including fine civilians and soldiers for the most important leadership positions in Malaya. Templer accepted the assignment and thanked Churchill, noting that having "the men to do the job" was "of primary importance."[29]

Born to an Irish Protestant family just before the turn of the century, Gerald Templer left high school early to join the British army in the middle of World War I. He attended the Royal Military Academy Sandhurst, where he was a poor student and might have been kicked out had the army not been so desperate for infantry officers. In August 1916, as his countrymen were dying by the hundreds of thousands at the Somme, the seventeen-year-old Templer was commissioned into the Royal Irish Fusiliers. Told that he could not join a battalion in France until he turned nineteen, he and his father tried to use personal connections with high-ranking officers to get him to France posthaste. It took over a year, however, before the young Templer got to the front lines. Arriving in France in October 1917, he had more than one year of war on the horizon, but a series of lucky escapes spared him the injuries and mortal wounds that befell most of his comrades. In March 1918, for instance, he was hospitalized for diphtheria just before his unit of 800 men suffered 763 casualties at the Battle of St. Quentin.

After the war ended, Templer had several tours in the Middle East, including a stint fighting guerrillas in Palestine during which he was twice decorated. He was evacuated from Dunkirk in 1940 along with much of the British army, which left him furious with Allied ineptitude but failed to shake his conviction that Britain would ultimately prevail. So ardent and determined was he that his seniors sent him to demonstrate British resolve to American ambassador Joseph Kennedy, who was predicting an imminent German conquest of England. When Kennedy said that Hitler was about to wring England's neck like a chicken's, Templer exploded in what he later admitted to be "the most undiplomatic language" and stomped out of the room.

In 1942, Templer became the youngest corps commander in the British army. He grew impatient, however, at the lack of combat opportunities for his corps, and eventually, in the summer of 1943, he relinquished the corps command in order to take command of a British division set to participate in the Italian campaign. His most distinguished performance occurred in February 1944 at Anzio, where his division helped foil the Wehrmacht's attempts to overrun the Anglo-American beachhead. Constantly visiting the troops at the front, Templer inspired his soldiers to hold on against ferocious German attacks that reduced the division to one quarter of its original strength. At the end of the war, Templer assumed command of the British sector of occupied Germany, where his most memorable deed was firing Konrad Adenauer, mayor of Cologne and future chancellor of West Germany, for inactivity.[30]

The situation in Malaya at the time of Templer's arrival in February 1952 was even bleaker than it had been when his predecessor was killed. Gurney's death had buoyed the spirits of the guerrillas and deflated those of the British forces and had led to a slackening of British operations.[31] In mid-February the British writer Malcolm Muggeridge observed in the *Daily Telegraph*, "Over large areas of the country law and order have, to all intents and purposes, broken down. Communications, especially by rail, are continuously interrupted; road travel is hazardous, and often requires an armoured vehicle and an armed escort to be tolerably safe."[32]

Templer began by overhauling the top level of the Malayan government. Just a few weeks after arriving, Templer fired Chief Secretary Del Tufo, for unsatisfactory performance. For senior commands that lay vacant, Templer scoured every nook and cranny of the British empire to find men of the highest caliber. For the position of director general of information services, to provide one example, Templer chose the headmaster of a grammar school in Shropshire, an outstanding organizer who had been in charge of British black propaganda operations in Malaya during World War II. To head the Special Branch, Templer appointed Guy C. Madoc, a Malayan police officer of fine judgment and superior organizational talents. The one appointee not selected by Templer was the new commissioner of police, Colonel Arthur Young, whom Lyttelton chose personally after an exhaustive search for the empire's finest senior police commander.[33]

Next came the middle and lower levels of leadership. Templer made these the object of intensive and ongoing attention, and provided much of the attention himself. Throughout his twenty-eight months as supreme commander, Templer devoted the bulk of his time to touring the country, leaving most of the administrative duties of Kuala Lumpur to two deputies. With little or no advance warning, Templer visited every place where the war was being fought, from villages and police posts to infantry battalion commands and district headquarters. By observing commanders, questioning them, and talking with others who had observed them, Templer identified weak leaders. Four lieutenant colonels on Templer's staff also traveled across the country regularly to gather information on the merits of local leaders. Having received complete authority over both the civil and military sides, Templer mercilessly fired ineffective personnel in all branches of the government. With the British officials at the top of the Malayan civil service, who had been left alone by previous high commissioners, Templer moved more gingerly, avoiding the immediate large-scale purge that seemed justified, for fear that it would do more harm than good. At first, he fired only the two worst he could find, one whom he described as "an awfully nice fellow but quite gaga," the other whom he called "absolutely burnt out and useless, though a nice chap." Templer gradually eased others out and replaced them with more vigorous and capable men.[34]

Templer and his leadership team excelled at finding replacements for the castoffs. In response to requests from Templer, Lyttelton sent high-quality British army officers to serve in Malaya in a variety of capacities. While searching for additional civil servants to send into the districts, Templer asked the Colonial Office for British administrators who spoke Chinese, but received few, so he found an energetic former missionary to track down Chinese-speaking missionaries and persuade them to work for him. Through the constant evaluation of officers serving in Malaya, Templer was able to identify those meriting advancement into positions of greater authority. He hand-picked the Malayan cadets for the new multiracial Federation Regiment and sent two dozen of Malaya's best cadets to Sandhurst for training.[35]

Intent on dramatic improvement in intelligence collection, Templer enlarged the Special Branch and raised its quality by importing first-rate British intelligence officers who had worked in India and elsewhere in the British empire. Demonstrating greater initiative and creativity than their predecessors, these officers enticed current and former members of the Min Yuen to serve as informants. Templer shrank the other elements of the police, from 71,000 to 54,000, on the grounds that funds and good officers had been stretched too thin by rapid expansion.[36]

Templer wished to enlarge the Chinese Home Guard units and entrust them with weapons, but he struggled at the outset to find adequate officers. As he saw it, the Home Guard would function better under the leadership of British and Australian officers than under officers from the Chinese population because the Chinese had shown themselves to be apathetic and unreliable. Convinced that good government deserved precedence over self-government at the present time of crisis, he had no qualms about putting white officers in charge of Chinese troops. British and Australian officers were, however, in short supply. In September 1952, Templer wrote to Lyttelton, "The Home Guard is not progressing as fast as I would wish or had hoped. This is almost entirely due to the lack of expatriate officers (about which I sent you an urgent telegram). . . . We will never get any sense into the thing until we get the British and Australian officers for whom we have been striving so long." Soon after this message left Templer's office, carefully screened British and Australian officers began to show up in Malaya for service in the Home Guard. As a direct consequence, the Home Guard experienced considerable improvement during the remainder of Templer's term. By 1954 the Home Guard received full responsibility for the defense of 150 New Villages.[37]

Templer's unremitting visits were also intended to bolster the spirits of the counterinsurgents and never failed to accomplish that mission. Templer delivered rousing speeches to civil servants and soldiers at every stop. A British official wrote that "the impact was electrifying. Templer combined high powered vitality and a slightly Machiavellian expression with ruthless determination and an infectious sense of humour. . . . I, for one, returned to Seremban the

MAJOR GENERAL HENRY W. HALLECK

Halleck took over the occupation of Missouri in November 1861 and
cleaned up the mess made by his predecessor, Major General John C.
Frémont, by cracking down on abuses of power and replacing poor
officers with West Point professionals. (Library of Congress)

GENERAL ULYSSES S. GRANT

Grant won renown as a leader of conventional military forces, but he failed to combat insurgents effectively during the occupation of Tennessee because he lacked the extra leadership attributes required in counterinsurgency warfare. (Library of Congress)

BRIGADIER GENERAL ROBERT F. CATTERSON

Catterson, one of the most aggressive and successful counterinsurgency commanders during Reconstruction, led the state militia units that destroyed the Ku Klux Klan in Arkansas during 1868. (Library of Congress)

MAJOR LEWIS MERRILL
By diligently collecting intelligence and vigorously pursuing suspects,
Merrill rounded up large numbers of Ku Klux Klan members in York
County, South Carolina, in 1871. His success intimidated Klansmen
across the South. (Library of Congress)

GENERAL PHILIP SHERIDAN

After exceptional service as a commander of conventional forces in the Civil War, Sheridan foundered as a counterinsurgency commander during Reconstruction. His contempt for Southern whites led him to tolerate abuses of Southern civilians by federal soldiers, and his inflexibility kept him from gaining political influence with local Southern elites. (Library of Congress)

GENERAL ARTHUR MACARTHUR

The senior U.S. commander during much of the Philippine Insurrection, MacArthur generally left local commanders to their own devices, which yielded success because those commanders seized the initiative and led their men well. (U.S. National Archives)

BRIGADIER GENERAL J. FRANKLIN BELL

Rapidly promoted during the Philippine Insurrection for his exceptional leadership talents, Bell defeated insurgents by using harsh counterinsurgency measures while minimizing excesses against the civilian population. (Library of Congress)

RAMON MAGSAYSAY

Magsaysay (center), who became secretary of national defense and then president of the Philippines with American help, turned around the war against the Huk insurgents by firing weak commanders and inspiring his subordinates. (U.S. National Archives)

SIR HENRY GURNEY

As British high commissioner in Malaya from 1948 until his assassination in 1951, Gurney did not venture into the countryside to observe or to supervise, which resulted in poor decisions at the top and incompetence at the lower levels of leadership. (AP / World Wide Photos)

SIR GERALD TEMPLER

Templer suppressed the Malayan insurgents by ruthlessly replacing
ineffective commanders with talented officers gathered from elsewhere
in the British empire and by inspiring local commanders during
countless tours of the combat zones. (AP / World Wide Photos)

NGO DINH DIEM

During his first years in power, South Vietnamese president Ngo Dinh Diem built a new corps of South Vietnamese leaders, and when they came of age in 1962, they turned the tide of the war against the Viet Cong. But the successes were undone the next year when American-sponsored conspirators assassinated Diem and conducted massive purges. (U.S. National Archives)

GENERAL CREIGHTON ABRAMS

The commander of U.S. forces in Vietnam from 1968 to 1972, Abrams helped the South Vietnamese government compensate for the American drawdown by persuading South Vietnamese president Nguyen Van Thieu to oust weak South Vietnamese military commanders. (U.S. National Archives)

GENERAL CARLOS EUGENIO VIDES CASANOVA AND JOSÉ NAPOLEÓN DUARTE

As El Salvador's minister of defense, General Vides (left) revamped the Salvadoran military leadership in the mid-1980s, with little help from Duarte (right), El Salvador's president from 1984 to 1989. (Getty Images)

HAMID KARZAI

President Karzai (right) let family ties, friendships, and political connections influence leadership appointments in Afghanistan's police and civil service, empowering individuals whose misconduct in office alienated many of the traditional elites. (U.S. Department of Defense)

LIEUTENANT GENERAL DAVID BARNO WITH DONALD RUMSFELD AND DICK CHENEY

Barno (center), flanked here by Secretary of Defense Rumsfeld (left) and Vice President Cheney (right), found that some American commanders in Afghanistan adapted to counterinsurgency warfare without receiving any doctrine while others had to be steered in the right direction. (U.S. Department of Defense)

GENERAL ABDUL RAHIM WARDAK

The leadership of General Wardak (with sunglasses), Afghanistan's defense minister, enabled the officer corps of the Afghan National Army to improve over time while the rest of the government languished. (U.S. Department of Defense)

COLONEL H. R. MCMASTER

As commander of the U.S. 3rd Armored Cavalry Regiment, McMaster (right) permanently removed a large concentration of insurgents from the Iraqi city of Tal Afar through a combination of combat operations and appeals to local tribal leaders to bring their relatives into the police. (3rd Cavalry Museum)

LIEUTENANT COLONEL DALE ALFORD AND GENERAL GEORGE CASEY
Casey (right), commander of Multi-National Force—Iraq from 2004 to 2007, paid numerous visits to local commanders like Alford (left). As the commander of a Marine infantry battalion, Alford was the driving force behind the first major counterinsurgency victory in Anbar province. (Courtesy of Lieutenant Colonel Dale Alford)

MAJOR GENERAL JAMES N. MATTIS

Mattis, who commanded with distinction in both Afghanistan and Iraq, embodied the reliance of the U.S. Marine Corps on adaptive leadership, having once declared that "doctrine is the refuge of the unimaginative." (U.S. Department of Defense)

GENERAL DAVID PETRAEUS

While holding a series of key commands in Iraq and the United States, Petraeus (right) sought to improve the flexibility and creativity of Army leaders by challenging the U.S. Army's traditional personnel practices. (U.S. Department of Defense)

next morning feeling like an electric torch which has just been filled with new batteries."[38] Templer's magnetism and his attentiveness to the soldiers, police, and civil servants made him a popular man in all of the government's branches and at all levels. A young British officer described Templer as "dynamic, enthusiastic, energetic, and for someone in my position a hero, who was always open to ideas from junior officers like myself."[39] Templer's élan was contagious, permeating the top levels of the British leadership and working its way through them and down to the state and district officials.[40]

No less energizing were Templer's appearances before the public. During trips to the villages, he went into shops and alleys to talk with ordinary citizens, and at their conclusion he gathered the people together for a motivational speech in which he told them of the critical tasks that lay ahead.[41] At plantations and mines he lectured managers on the necessity of improving working conditions and told the laborers to work hard and resist Communist demands for strikes, but without coming across as domineering. On hearing Templer, one planter said, "Here was a man at least who knew what he wanted to do and how to do it." Templer's "visit was greatly appreciated and everyone on the estate had an opportunity of airing his views, asking questions and meeting him face to face. No previous High Commissioner had taken the trouble to do this."[42]

In Kuala Lumpur, Templer chided the Europeans for attending parties, playing golf, and going to the races instead of volunteering for activities in support of the counterinsurgency. The Communists, he told them, were working hard to destroy the Europeans and the existing order, not wasting time on the golf course. Templer published a list of volunteer opportunities, ranging from health-care providers to the Home Guard, and large numbers of Europeans signed on.[43]

Templer concluded that the security forces would benefit from common tactical doctrine, so he ordered the production of a doctrinal manual containing drills and techniques that had proven successful in combating the insurgents across Malaya. Entitled *The Conduct of Anti-Terrorist Operations in Malaya*, the manual was sent to army and police units in mid-1952.[44] The importance of this manual has been exaggerated, and the exaggeration has, among other things, contributed directly to the U.S. Army's emphasis on counterinsurgency doctrine in the early twenty-first century and to the attention afforded the publication of the *U.S. Army/Marine Corps Counterinsurgency Field Manual* in 2006. Templer's praise of the 1952 manual and the major improvements in the

British counterinsurgency effort after the manual's issuance misled analysts into believing that the manual was a leading cause of the improvements. The methods enumerated in *The Conduct of Anti-Terrorist Operations in Malaya* had, in reality, been disseminated and employed in Malaya long before the manual was printed. During the first years of the conflict, British veterans of Burma and Palestine had used many of these methods because they had used the same ones in those wars. In 1948 the British established a jungle warfare school in Malaya at which the instructors taught tactics derived largely from those employed in the war in Burma, and by 1949 the British were circulating pamphlets and a short manual derived from the experiences in Burma, Palestine, and the Boer War, as well as from discoveries made by innovative officers in Malaya.[45]

Operations in Malaya from 1948 to 1952 had engendered only modest refinements of the theories drawn from past conflicts. The principles and basic military methods employed by the British in this period were very similar to those enumerated in prior treatises, such as the *Small Wars Manual* published by the U.S. Marine Corps in 1940. The prescriptions in *The Conduct of Anti-Terrorist Operations in Malaya* were useful to newly arrived officers and soldiers with no knowledge of counterinsurgency but did not provide easy solutions to most counterinsurgency problems. They did not give officers surefire methods for accomplishing essential tasks like gaining the cooperation of allied leaders, organizing self-defense forces, winning the support of the population, motivating the troops, persisting in the face of difficulty, or adjusting methods in response to changing enemy tactics.[46]

The jungle warfare school emphasized to its students that the school could teach them basic tactics and techniques but that it was up to them to figure out whether, when, and how to use each one.[47] *The Conduct of Anti-Terrorist Operations in Malaya* itself acknowledged that successful military operations demanded excellent leadership, not just comprehension of methods. "Operations in Malaya largely consist of small patrols," it stated. "The success or failure of these operations therefore depends on the standard of junior leaders. . . . The type of junior leader required is a mentally tough, self-reliant hunter, determined to close with, and kill, the CT [Communist Terrorists]." The manual also noted that commanders above the platoon level had as a principal duty the monitoring, selection, and coaching of the platoon leaders. "The company commander plays the major part in the selection and training of the junior leader," it explained. "By operating with each platoon in turn, he can give help and advice to junior leaders, earmark future leaders and can generally do more in a few days to improve junior leadership than a cadre [training group] could do in three weeks."[48]

Templer considered his mission to be the implementation of the Briggs plan through better employment of methods already in place, rather than through major changes to those methods. Although he promoted doctrine, Templer was not doctrinaire but pragmatic and suspicious of abstractions, particularly theories that purported to apply everywhere. Rather than forcing his commanders to adhere closely to the new counterinsurgency manual, Templer granted them freedom to adapt general counterinsurgency principles to the specific environments they faced and the specific forces they possessed, both of which varied from one part of Malaya to another. So conscious was Templer of the dangers of imposing doctrine and micromanaging that he made special efforts to give key commanders maximum freedom of action. In the case of the district officers, the most critical of all the commanders, Templer removed both vertical and horizontal fetters, freeing them from the dictates of higher headquarters and other district officials. He gave them his phone number and told them to call if anyone interfered with their work so that he could put an end to the interference. To unblock district interagency committees that had been clogged by lack of consensus among members, Templer informed the committee members that they would be fired if they failed to reach agreement. This threat eliminated most of the gridlock; firings eliminated the remainder.[49]

Replacing poor leaders with good ones, unshackling leaders, and providing inspiration—that was the potent combination that enabled Templer to succeed where others had failed. Within a few months of his arrival, the results could be seen across the spectrum of counterinsurgency activities. In the field of intelligence collection, the heightened drive and ingenuity of Special Branch officers yielded more agents among the Min Yuen. Improved training inculcated intelligence tradecraft into the Special Branch officer corps more effectively, but without the right types of officers conducting and receiving the instruction, the training regimens would have achieved little more than previous ones.[50]

More and better intelligence meant more fruitful operations against the insurgents, but it did not guarantee success, for exploitation of the intelligence often required considerable skill on the part of the armed forces. Nor did it eliminate the need for patrols of the jungle based on educated guesses rather than firm intelligence, a type of operation that, as has been seen, demands leaders with particular attributes. In 1954, by which time the Special Branch had become highly productive, the average soldier still spent 1,000 hours on patrol before making contact with the enemy.[51] Fortunately for the British, improvements on the military side were as substantial as those on the intelligence side. Under Templer, military commanders evidenced increases in flexibility and creativity as well as initiative and dedication. As one of Templer's senior field commanders said, "Most officers I met were singularly free from hidebound prejudice. They rejoiced to use any conventional weapon in an unconventional way; and they were always ready to have a try with any unconventional weapon too."[52]

Because of the leadership upgrades in the civil service, police, and Home Guard, the counterinsurgents turned the New Villages and other resettlement areas from fertile insurgent breeding grounds into well-organized armed camps where insurgents could tread only at considerable peril. The police, assisted by civil officials and Home Guardsmen, investigated and rounded up thousands of members of the Min Yuen. With civil liberties still in suspense, the police employed searches without warrants, detentions without trial, and other police-state techniques, but they committed fewer abuses than before because of Young's overhaul of the police leadership. Policemen and civil servants were energetic and creative in restricting the movement and consumption of food. They established central kitchens and forbade citizens from purchasing any rice other than rice that had been cooked at the kitchens, which sharply reduced the amount of rice available to an individual and provided it in a form that spoiled in a few hours, before it could reach famished guerrillas in the jungle. Village shops were required to puncture cans at the time of sale to necessitate prompt consumption. As an additional means of increasing governmental control over the population, civil servants organized the election of village councils and authorized them to impose taxes and carry out public works projects. Templer's efforts to initiate larger social welfare programs were frustrated by a scarcity of funds, but the lack of such programs did little to inhibit the government's securing of control over the villagers.[53]

In Templer's first year, the government's armed forces not only halted the ascent of their Communist adversaries but shoved them down a precipitous decline. Whereas the government in 1951 had captured 927 weapons and lost 770, in 1952 it captured 1,170 and lost 487. The New Villages slowed the transfer of food from the Min Yuen to the guerrillas, severely impeding insurgent military operations. Since the jungle's few edible plants could at best sustain thirty guerrillas in one place for about two weeks, the guerrillas began to operate in groups of only three to fifteen people and spent most of their time looking for food instead of conducting military and political activities. In October 1952 the Communist Party ordered the guerrillas to undertake more ambitious attacks, believing that a shortage of attacks had undermined the guerrillas' morale and aided the government, but the guerrillas could not operate in groups of sufficient size to carry out the order. Government security forces easily repulsed their few feeble attempts to overrun the resettlement areas. In 1952 the insurgents for the first time failed to recruit as many people as they lost, beginning a trend that continued for the rest of the war. When Templer first arrived, insurgent incidents had averaged over 500 per month, and civilian casualties had averaged 100 per month. When he left, insurgent incidents were down to fewer than 100 per month, and civilian casualties to fewer than 20 per month. At the end of Templer's tour, insurgent strength stood at less than half of what it had been at the start.[54] Templer had turned the war around decisively, and for good.

Upon Templer's decision to step down in the middle of 1954, London decided to discontinue the concentration of military and civil powers in one man, convinced that improvements in the situation had rendered it unnecessary. Templer's civilian deputy, Sir Donald MacGillivray, assumed control of the civil side, while Lieutenant General Sir Geoffrey Bourne took command of military operations. This division of powers substantially reduced the efficacy of the counterinsurgency effort because the absence of a strong military leader at the top of the civil side led to regression. The civil service drifted back toward a business-as-usual attitude, and the district officers and other civil servants appointed under Templer were eventually rotated out and replaced by men of lesser aptitude.[55]

In the years following Templer's departure, the government was unable to deal a mortal blow to the Communists, but it did continue to make progress. By the end of 1956, the guerrillas had barely more than 2,000 men.[56] Malaya gained its independence on August 31, 1957, removing much of the Malayan Communist Party's appeal and drawing many Communist sympathizers to the parties of the non-Communist left. Malaya's first prime minister, Tunku Abdul Rahman, shared Templer's view that good government deserved precedence over self-government in a time of civil war, so he hired into his government the British, Australian, and New Zealand officers who until now had been conducting the war for the British government, a group that included most of the top officers in the army and police. In addition, large numbers of British, Australian, and New Zealand troops continued the hunt for the guerrillas.

In late 1957 and 1958 counterinsurgency operations destroyed some of the remaining guerrilla pockets, which allowed the government to concentrate its counterguerrilla forces in the few areas where the guerrillas refused to lay down their arms. Casualties and lack of food led to the surrender of several key guerrilla leaders, who convinced other guerrillas to surrender and provided information that led to further military reverses for the insurgency. Five hundred guerrillas surrendered in 1958, more than in any previous year. By the end of 1958, the number of guerrilla fighters had fallen to 350, which prompted the Communist Party to move most of its armed forces into southern Thailand, where they could recuperate and launch small attacks into Malaya. Scattered guerrilla and counterguerrilla operations persisted in the Thai-Malay border region into 1959 and beyond, but the insurgents ceased posing a significant threat to the well-being of the country.[57]

The perceived lessons of the Malayan Emergency have informed much of the advice provided to American counterinsurgents in the twenty-first century. As the foregoing assessment indicates, these lessons are in need of some revision. Contrary to popular belief, the ineffectiveness of the British counterinsurgents from 1948 to 1951 did not result from a failure to understand the problem or to identify appropriate countermeasures. Rather, it resulted from weak leadership. Following the outburst of Communist violence in June 1948, the British multiplied the number of policemen, but without sufficient attention to the quality of their leaders, committing the common error of presuming that effective forces can be created simply by providing funds and assigning a certain number of new personnel. Because of poor leadership, the expanded police forces were generally inept and, aside from occasional acts of indiscriminate brutality, inert. Through the Emergency regulations, the British government denied the people the protections of civil liberties, an appropriate enough response to the Communist threat, but one that allowed abuses to flourish in the absence of good leadership. The government's armed forces had considerably better officers than the police did at the start of the war, which translated into vigorous military operations and, in some cases, rapid adaptation of tactics to local conditions. Although the police failed to provide the armed forces with much intelligence on the insurgents, military operations succeeded in disrupting major guerrilla activities and denying the guerrillas the military initiative.

The Malayan Emergency demonstrates the critical importance of leadership at the top and the differences between good and poor leadership at that level. By refusing to visit the insurgency's equivalent of front lines—the villages and outposts and local headquarters—Gurney failed to inspire subordinates in the field or appraise their performance. Because of Gurney's preferred management style and the inferior quality of many junior leaders, the central headquarters micromanaged and produced an excess of paperwork at the expense of action. The addition of Briggs, a fine leader, to Gurney's leadership team failed to remedy this condition because Briggs was not given the authority required to impose change on sluggish bureaucrats. Nor, at the district level, did the district officers have the latitude to exert strong leadership, having been placed on interagency committees without the power to override uncooperative committee members.

When Gerald Templer took the helm in February 1952, he had the good fortune of receiving supreme authority over all civil and military organizations, which gave him the freedom of action that Briggs had never possessed. Templer, in turn, provided freedom to those below him. Although Templer issued doctrinal publications, he did not attempt to force specific methods upon local commanders, for he knew that success required autonomous and adaptive local leaders, capable of using their own judgment to determine whether, when, and how to apply doctrinal concepts.

By leaving the administrative duties of Kuala Lumpur to others, Templer was able to devote his time to the more important task of touring the country, primarily for the purpose of identifying leaders who deserved removal or promotion. He fired civil and military leaders at all levels, without concern for whether they were pleasant people or what it would do for their careers. Such callousness can be hard for compassionate people to stomach, but it did promote the greater good of effective counterinsurgency, and it saved the lives of counterinsurgents. The police and the civil service benefited the most from Templer's pitiless axe, for their leaders had never before been subjected to rigorous screening of the sort employed by vigilant military officers. To fill many of the holes created by the sackings, Templer brought in proven men from across the empire, a feat that depended upon a cooperative national government and a generally high level of talent among the officers and officials produced by British society and government in years past. Templer's accomplishments also illustrate superbly the value of energy and charisma in winning support from both government personnel and the population at large.

Templer did not introduce new counterinsurgency tactics or strategy. He executed existing tactics and strategy more effectively than before, by changing and inspiring the field commanders. Through this approach, Templer increased the initiative and inventiveness of the armed forces. The Special Branch of the police acquired much more intelligence thanks to Templer's addition of talented intelligence officers, and that intelligence presented new opportunities for the armed forces to eliminate Communists. Population relocation, which initially failed to stem the insurgency because of inadequate administrators and security forces, thrived under Templer because the new leaders of the civil service, the police, and the Home Guard possessed the attributes required to gain control of the resettlement areas and prevent misdeeds by local personnel. The government's leaders gained the support of much of the rural Chinese population through the establishment of security and the demonstration of integrity and empathy in governance—and not through the institution of social and economic reforms.

One more critical and underappreciated aspect of the Malayan Emergency was the strong performance of indigenous forces under foreign commanders. Both Templer, as British high commissioner, and Tunku Abdul Rahman, as the prime minister of independent Malaya, attained favorable outcomes by putting British and other foreign officers into leadership positions in the Malayan military, police, civil service, and Home Guard. Choosing good government over self-government in the short term, they defused the immediate Communist menace and ultimately attained a peace that would provide a long term in which Malayans could work on self-government free of the scourge of subversion.

CHAPTER 7

The Vietnam War

I n the early twentieth century, as in previous centuries, most of Vietnam's
leaders belonged to a very small elite that exceeded the rest of the population in social status, education, and wealth. Although the French had par-
titioned Vietnam into three colonies in the late nineteenth century, they had
not displaced the Vietnamese elite or fundamentally altered its relationship
to the Vietnamese masses. Concentrated in the urban population centers of
Vietnam, the members of the elite became more Westernized and modernized
with each year of French colonization, widening the gulf that separated them
from the peasants, who composed the vast majority of the populace.

As fate would have it, however, South Vietnam's first president, Ngo Dinh
Diem, grew up astride this gulf. Diem's father had served in the imperial court
as a traditional mandarin official, but he quit out of opposition to French policies, moved his family to the countryside, and took up farming. Diem learned
to grow rice in the premodern way, driving the plow with a water buffalo.
At the same time, he gained an understanding of the Vietnamese peasant's
mind, giving him a decided advantage over the Westernized Vietnamese elites
of Hanoi, Saigon, and other cities who aspired to guide the country's political
course.

Diem attended the School for Law and Administration in Hanoi and finished at the head of his class, which brought him an appointment as a district
chief, a position of considerable authority. Riding a horse in mandarin garb,
Diem crisscrossed his district to administer public projects and resolve disputes. A devout Catholic who shunned worldly possessions, he projected an

air of austerity and impartiality, two critical components of charisma in Vietnam because they elevated an individual above the corruption and favoritism commonplace among officials. At the extraordinarily young age of twenty-eight, Diem was promoted to the powerful and prestigious post of provincial chief.

In 1930, during a rebellion by the Vietnamese Communist Party, Diem arrested every Communist he could find in his province, but unlike some of his peers, he did not inflict gratuitous damage on the general population. So thoroughly did he impress the Vietnamese court in the succeeding years that Emperor Bao Dai appointed him minister of the interior in 1933. Within a matter of months, however, the French showed that they did not intend to increase Vietnamese autonomy as recently promised, so Diem quit. Returning to his home town of Hue, he read countless books and forged ties with other nationalists.

In World War II, Diem and his nationalist allies organized anti-French political subversion in league with exiled Vietnamese nationalists and, at one point, the Japanese. When the war ended, the Japanese occupation force folded, leaving a power vacuum into which Ho Chi Minh's Vietnamese Communists flowed. Ho asked Diem to serve as his minister of the interior, but Diem, wary of the Communists, insisted that he would take the job only if granted broad powers, which was more than Ho was willing to do. Soon the French returned to reclaim their colony. After a spell of peace and negotiation, they ran into armed conflict with Ho Chi Minh, which prompted them to ask Diem to serve in the colonial administration. He refused.

Diem sat out this war until its waning moments, in June 1954. At that juncture, the despairing French gave Vietnam an independent government in advance of the division of the country. Emperor Bao Dai named Diem the premier of what would soon become South Vietnam, an anti-Communist state opposite Ho Chi Minh's Communist North Vietnam. Rushed to Saigon, Diem inherited the colonial armed forces and civil administration, both of which had suffered enormous numbers of desertions as the war came to a close. Although Diem enjoyed much support among the South Vietnamese elite classes, the top leadership of the army remained in the hands of Frenchmen and Vietnamese Francophiles, who disdained Diem for his long-standing aversion to French rule, and the police were controlled by a group of gangsters called the Binh Xuyen.[1]

Viewing the prospects for South Vietnam as dire and the strategic stakes

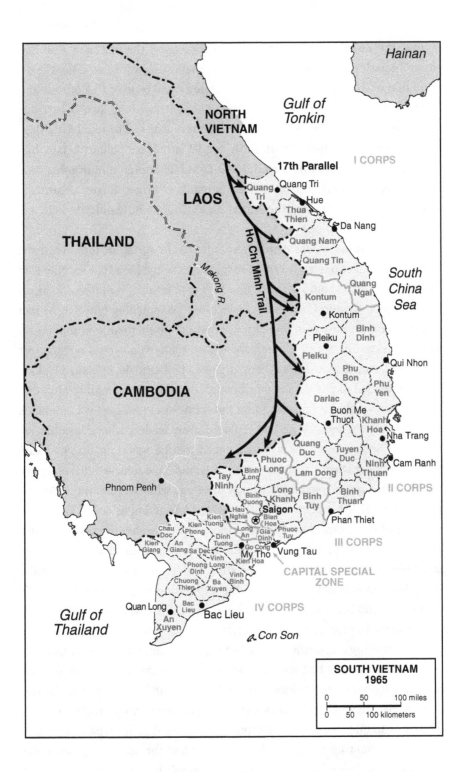

Hainan

Gulf of
Tonkin

NORTH
VIETNAM

17th Parallel   I CORPS

LAOS   Quang Tri
            Quang
            Tri   Hue
            Thua
            Thien   Da Nang

THAILAND   Quang Nam

                Quang Tin

                        South
                Quang   China
                Ngai   Sea

Mekong R.   Kontum

        Ho Chi Minh Trail   Kontum   Binh
                        Dinh
                Pleiku
                Pleiku   Qui Nhon

                        Phu
                        Bon   Phu
CAMBODIA   Yen

                Darlac
                        Buon Me
                        Thuot   Khanh
                                Hoa   Nha Trang

                        Quang   Tuyen   Cam Ranh
                        Duc   Duc   Ninh
                Phuoc Long   Thuan
            Binh
            Long   Lam Dong
Phnom Penh   Tay
            Ninh   Long   Binh   Binh   II CORPS
            Binh   Khanh   Tuy   Thuan
            Duong
            Hau   Saigon   Phan Thiet
            Nghia   Bien
    Kien   Hoa
    Tuong   Long   Gia
    Kien   An   Dinh   Phuoc   III CORPS
    Phong   Tuy
Chau   Dinh
Doc   Tuong   Go Cong Vung Tau
Kien   An   CAPITAL SPECIAL
Giang   Giang Sa Dec My Tho   ZONE
        Vinh   Kien Hoa
    Phong Long
    Dinh   Vinh
    Chuong Binh
    Thien   Ba
            Xuyen
Quan Long   Bac
    An   Lieu   Bac Lieu   IV CORPS
    Xuyen
Gulf of   Con Son
Thailand

SOUTH VIETNAM 1965
0   50   100 miles
0   50   100 kilometers

as high, the Eisenhower administration called upon the one man who had proved himself capable of rescuing such a situation, Edward Lansdale. The director of the CIA, Allen Dulles, gave Lansdale a small team of CIA officers and flew the bunch of them to Saigon to assist Diem. Before long, Lansdale struck up a close relationship with Diem similar to the one he had fostered with Magsaysay in the Philippines. Diem understood Vietnamese politics better than Lansdale or any other American did, but Lansdale tutored him in other vital subjects, such as piecing together the remnants of armed forces, organizing state finances, and handling the American embassy, whose officials were less than enthused with Diem.

Especially valuable was Lansdale's advice in the spring of 1955, when the Binh Xuyen and two heavily armed religious sects, the Hoa Hao and the Cao Dai, resisted Diem's authority and conspired to overthrow him. The American ambassador, J. Lawton Collins, coldly lectured Diem, telling him that he had to reach a compromise with those groups in order to win them over to the government's side. The South Vietnamese army, Collins said, would not support Diem in an armed showdown. Diem, urged on by Lansdale, informed Collins that he intended to put the insubordination down by force, maintaining that negotiations would be futile and that the army would follow his commands because in recent months he had replaced army leaders whose loyalties remained in doubt. Collins was so convinced that he was right that he made ready to support Diem's overthrow, and he would have achieved this objective if fighting had not erupted mysteriously in Saigon while he was away in Washington explaining his plans. Diem, with Lansdale acting as coach and salesman, seized the moment and ordered the army leadership to crush the Binh Xuyen and the two sects, which they did faithfully and effectively. The victory gave Diem a tremendous boost in prestige, and hence in support, among the South Vietnamese elites and gained the admiration of President Dwight D. Eisenhower and Secretary of State John Foster Dulles, who thereupon terminated American planning for Diem's removal.[2]

After meeting that challenge, the Diem government trained its weapons on the Communists who had stayed in South Vietnam after the division of Vietnam. Having buried their rifles and machine guns in burlap sacks at the end of hostilities, these Communists were now posing as innocent civilians and attempting to infiltrate government organizations and political parties. To stop them, Diem built up the civil administration and the security forces across the country, and together they tracked and demolished the Communist cells, rapidly in the cities and more gradually in the villages, eventually reaching the farthest corners of the countryside. Although Westerners often assumed that the crackdown alienated the peasants, it actually gained support for the government because it weakened the Communists and did not involve wanton excesses against innocent civilians. One Communist account described the situation thus: "By relying on force, [the South Vietnamese government] was temporarily able to stabilize the situation and increase the prestige of the counter-revolutionaries."[3]

Because the Communists were usually unarmed, the government was able to round them up without significant use of concentrated armed force. Diem, however, anticipated that the Communists would not remain peaceable forever, so he invested many of the government's human and material resources in the security forces. The head of the American advisory effort in the late 1950s, Lieutenant General Samuel "Hanging Sam" Williams, became Diem's closest American confidant after Lansdale's departure. Like Lansdale, and unlike some of the other Americans who served in Vietnam, Williams gained the ear of Diem and other Vietnamese because he knew how to coach them without appearing arrogant or imperious. Williams, and every other commander of the American military advisory effort, formed a high opinion of Diem, taking note of Diem's fortitude, judgment, ability to inspire, and knack for military strategy and tactics, characteristics underappreciated by many American civilians—first and foremost, Elbridge Durbrow, the U.S. ambassador to South Vietnam from 1957 to 1961. The quintessential Ugly American, devoid of empathy and tact, Durbrow openly displayed contempt for the Vietnamese and attempted to pressure them to take actions that would have worked far better in his native California than in Vietnam. His attitude and his proposals gravely undermined his influence as ambassador.[4]

With sound advice and encouragement, Williams assisted Diem and South Vietnam's top generals in removing inept leaders and squelching widespread insubordination. The officer corps, however, was so thoroughly stricken with incompetence in its upper layers that the lancing of boils here and there did not restore the patient to full health. Williams directed American military advisers to focus South Vietnamese army training on conventional warfare, for his greatest fear was an invasion of South Vietnam by large North Vietnamese conventional forces. The North Vietnamese army's conventional divisions, unlike bands of guerrillas, could seize Saigon and the rest of South Vietnam's centers of power by force of arms, and only conventionally equipped and trained

South Vietnamese regulars could stop them. Williams did not ignore the possibility of a guerrilla insurgency. Rather, he believed that counterguerrilla duty should belong primarily to local South Vietnamese militia forces—the Civil Guard and Self-Defense Corps—which had the advantages of superior intelligence sources and continuous presence in the same location. Both Williams and Diem sought to improve and enlarge these militias.

In the minds of Williams and Diem, the Civil Guard was to be a paramilitary force, armed with assault rifles and submachine guns and capable of mounting mobile operations against guerrillas, while the Self-Defense Corps conducted static defense of villages. They were overridden, however, by Ambassador Durbrow, who accepted the recommendation of a Michigan State University advisory team to equip the Civil Guard with pistols and nightsticks, like an American police force. Furthermore, Durbrow and the Michigan State team blocked a plan of Williams and Diem to put the Civil Guard under the military, which would have enabled them to replace poor leaders with military officers. The military leadership could not be entrusted with forces responsible for internal security, Durbrow declared dogmatically, because that would facilitate military domination of the government. The militia leadership thus remained replete with weak colonial-era leaders who condoned and perpetrated theft, corruption, and gratuitous violence.[5]

Leadership positions in the civil administrations, at every level, were similarly replete with colonial-era holdovers bereft of crucial attributes like initiative, dedication, and integrity. Diem had no choice but to rely on these men in the near term, because only they had the knowledge and experience to carry out such core administrative functions as taxation and public communications. "Generally speaking, the quality of my ministers is very poor," Diem admitted to one American. "Provincial chiefs sometimes do not get out and see all the people in their provinces; district chiefs often do not know what goes on in villages within their districts; and in the ministries in Saigon there are civil servants who never get out in the country to learn about the services which they head within their ministries in Saigon." As a result, Diem felt compelled to tell local commanders how they should do their jobs. "I have delegated, and delegated, and delegated," he explained, "but they have proven unworthy of the delegation of authority and responsibility time and again. This is why I feel constrained to step into the breach which exists and bring order out of the chaos."[6] Despite Diem's formidable leadership prowess and his deep understanding of counterinsurgency in the Vietnamese context, his micromanagement was unable to make up for the weaknesses of subordinates in the provinces.

In January 1959, at the Fifteenth Plenum of the Communist Party Central Committee, Ho Chi Minh decided that the crippling losses suffered by the Communists in the South demanded an armed insurrection. To avoid triggering a strong American reaction, Ho decreed that the Communists would at first attempt to win only small military victories and would concentrate on political organization in the villages. Larger offensives would take place at some distant date, to be determined by international conditions. For the remainder of the year, the North Vietnamese made ready for war, blazing infiltration trails through jungles and over mountains into the South, then sending men and matériel down the trails by foot.

The infiltrators burst into South Vietnamese villages at the beginning of 1960 and went on an extended killing spree that targeted government militiamen, officials, and supporters. Each month they racked up more than 150 assassinations, along with more than 50 kidnappings. The Civil Guard and Self-Defense Corps failed to repel the Communist guerrillas, or Viet Cong, as the South Vietnamese government called them, owing to inferior leadership and weaponry. Where the local government lacked resolute leadership, the assassination of a few civil officials or militiamen demoralized the rest of the government personnel and sent them fleeing their villages for the safety of the district or provincial capital, which opened the floodgates to Viet Cong intrusion. To supplant the village governments, the Viet Cong created shadow governments that recruited villagers, redistributed land, compelled the peasants to fork over rice as a form of taxation, and otherwise controlled the peasants' lives.

When the Civil Guard and the Self-Defense Corps crumpled, Diem sent the army into the villages to combat the insurgents. The army units did not fall to pieces as the militias had, because they had somewhat better leaders and much better weapons, but they could seldom locate the guerrillas for want of intelligence information or the willingness to venture into unsafe areas. When they did get near the guerrillas, they often attacked in large formations, whose approach was, like that of a herd of elephants, easily detected and evaded. South Vietnam's generals had disregarded recommendations from General Williams and other Americans to train the army in counterguerrilla warfare, sparking accusations that the army's difficulties were the result of inadequate training. But training deficiencies were far less important than leadership deficiencies. While training could impart valuable knowledge of counterguerrilla tactics, numerous officers already had such knowledge from the last war, and those who did not could learn quickly on the job if they were sufficiently adaptive. The army generally had trouble finding enemy guerrillas because its officers lacked the initiative, dedication, and organizational ability required for successful intelligence collection and patrolling, and it conducted excessively large military operations because its officers lacked imagination and flexibility. Diem remained unable to fix the army leadership in 1960 because the pool of capable and reliable replacements was still too shallow.[7]

In 1960 the Viet Cong won the allegiance of numerous villagers for two principal reasons. First, the Viet Cong's success in killing and driving off the government's representatives made a favorable impression on the peasants, who adhered to the ancient peasant tradition of gravitating toward the militarily stronger side in any contest. Second, the peasants were attracted by the excellent leadership of the Viet Cong, an attraction likewise rooted in tradition. The peasants looked for the leadership attributes that had been displayed by the best mandarins over the centuries, most notably competence and charisma, the latter comprising several components—impartiality, selflessness, and eloquence. In preparing for war in the late 1950s, the Communists had carefully selected and developed leaders to yield men with these characteristics. Diem was seeking to produce leaders with these same characteristics, but he had yet to produce them in quantity. People who had held power in colonial times still dominated the South Vietnamese leadership in the villages, and many of them clung to the habits of bad mandarins, abusing peasants, stealing public funds, and refusing to stand firm when attacked. In villages where the government and the Viet Cong were relatively evenly matched in strength and leadership, and only in those villages, was the Viet Cong's redistribution of land from the wealthy to the poor a major factor in causing peasants to join the insurgency.[8]

In some parts of the country, South Vietnamese militiamen and civil authorities did resist the initial Communist onslaught effectively, invariably because of strong governmental leadership. Over the course of 1960, moreover, Diem yanked some of the worst officials from their jobs and put in their place men who had less experience or less certain loyalties but possessed the will and skill to defeat the Viet Cong and the integrity and charisma to gain supporters by means other than force. Diem and his brother Ngo Dinh Nhu also created a political and paramilitary organization called the Republican Youth into which they funneled promising young leaders for development and accelerated promotion.[9]

The insurgency continued to grow, and the counterinsurgency generally remained frail, until the spring of 1962. At that point, in defiance of numerous prognostications that the gloom could never be lifted, the counterinsurgents began a period of rapid advancement and, in a matter of months, turned the tide of the war. A large increase in American military aid played a significant role in the turnaround, as did the arrival of thousands of new U.S. advisers, who taught military skills to the South Vietnamese and inspired them with energy and courage. These factors were not, however, sufficient for success. Across the border in Laos, where the government received an abundance of American military aid and advisers, the national armed forces were throwing down their American weapons and running at the first glimpse of the Vietnamese Communists, who were using Laos as their main channel of infiltration into South Vietnam.

The principal cause of South Vietnam's reversal of fortune, and of Laos's failure, was leadership. The quality of the leaders in the South Vietnamese armed forces and provincial administrations experienced a dramatic upturn during 1962 as the young men cultivated by Diem in the 1950s came of age and moved into critical commands. Rufus Phillips, a protégé of Edward Lansdale, described the change in local officials after he conducted a tour of the country in the middle of 1962. "Practically all of the officials I met in six provinces had assumed office within the last year," Phillips remarked. "Their conversation and their actions reflected a genuine desire to help the hamlet people and an understanding of their problems. Most of them were working long hours with energy and enthusiasm, inspecting their provinces during the day and going over papers at night."[10] Because of the command changes, government security forces more often conducted patrols, entered areas dominated by the Viet Cong, and operated at night. Military successes and better leadership of intelligence operations generated more intelligence on the insurgents, which in turn spawned more military successes.

The new generation of leaders provided, in addition, the leadership for the government's most important counterinsurgency initiative of 1962, the strategic hamlet program. To the novice observer, a strategic hamlet's most striking features were the physical barriers that surrounded it—bamboo fences, moats, barbed wire, and punji stakes. Far more important, however, were the people assigned to protect and administer the hamlet. Drawn from the Republican Youth and other dynamic governmental organizations, the strategic hamlet militias contained more men than the previous militia units did, and possessed much better leadership. Their commanders kept them in the hamlets twenty-four hours a day and organized fierce resistance to Viet Cong assaults, refusing to abandon the hamlets no matter how frequent the attacks. Strategic hamlet personnel recruited villagers, organized informant networks, and spoke at markets and homes about the superiority of the Saigon government. As a counter to the Viet Cong's land redistribution, they provided agricultural supplies like fertilizer and rat poison and helped the peasants with their labors. Rather than give the village governments control over the strategic hamlets, as in the past, Diem and Nhu delegated authority down to the hamlet level, the lowest administrative level, thus bypassing the aging incompetents in the village governments and the Saigon ministries.[11]

Although Diem masterminded the bulk of the leadership changes, he received valuable help from the Americans. In the second half of 1962, the chief U.S. military adviser, General Paul Harkins, urged Diem to punish, and if necessary replace, commanders who were not showing initiative in attacking the enemy, the leadership characteristic that seemed to remain in shortest supply. Traveling around the country almost every day in a small aircraft, Harkins dropped in on South Vietnamese military units with the regularity of a commanding officer to assess their strengths and weaknesses. He kept his advice private and had the knowledge, interpersonal acumen, and force of personality to enjoy Diem's respect.

"During the preceding week, I visited all the divisions," Harkins told Diem on July 18, 1962. "Leadership is lacking in platoons and companies, the very place where it is needed most — since these are the units which do the fighting." To bring more capable leaders into those slots, Harkins advised Diem to transfer officers from headquarters and logistical commands to combat units, reduce the length of officer training, and get professional men into the military in larger numbers.

Diem told Harkins, "I am concerned over the number of senior officers who have reached the height of their potential and who lack the education and initiative required in higher grades."

"Such men should be eliminated," said Harkins.

"The situation was inherited from the French, who were too easy and made colonels and lieutenant colonels who had no real capability or training," Diem remarked. "One of the difficulties in identifying incompetent officers lies in the fact that my generals do not want to recommend the separation of officers who are old friends." Despite the problems involved, "I am considering the thought of elimination."

During another meeting, Harkins narrated for Diem a story recently heard around the country, about a South Vietnamese battalion commander who had refused to attack a nearby Viet Cong force. When the commander was asked why he was not engaging the enemy, he responded, "As long as we don't bother them, they won't bother us."

"This commander is a lazy man," Diem told Harkins. Of late, Diem explained, he had been telling some of his commanders to be more aggressive and take more risks, but a number of commanders remained reluctant to attack.

"This is not right and is certainly no way to win," was Harkins's blistering response. "If commanders do not want to fight, they should come to you and tell you so, and you can find others who will."[12]

During the second half of 1962, Diem did sack those commanders who stubbornly resisted his orders to hunt down the enemy with vigor, replacing them with up-and-coming officers. South Vietnamese forces, resonating with the aggressiveness of their commanders, delivered one hard blow after another to the Viet Cong and broke their grip on large sections of the country. Repeated victories over large Viet Cong forces compelled the Viet Cong to stop concentrating in large numbers, which prevented them from overwhelming small government units and strategic hamlets. According to the Australian journalist Wilfred Burchett, a Communist sympathizer who lived with the Viet Cong during this period, Communist leaders believed that "in terms of territory and population, Diem made a considerable comeback in 1962," as government armed forces "registered a number of successes and held the strategic and tactical initiative."[13]

South Vietnam's armed forces and the strategic hamlet program continued to prosper during the first half of 1963. The regular armed forces and the militia forces increased in size as well as quality, with the total strength of each reaching approximately 215,000 men, and they conducted small operations with great frequency. The Viet Cong were losing 1,500 men per month, which would have depleted the 23,000-strong Viet Cong very rapidly had it not been for the arrival of a similar number of replacements from North Vietnam each month via the infiltration routes in Laos. Simultaneously, the number of villagers subjected to Viet Cong influence continued to fall.[14]

Diem's success in improving leadership quality and force size simultaneously was a remarkable feat, for rapid expansion of counterinsurgency forces normally results in degradation of overall leadership quality because leadership development lags behind unit creation. It was all the more impressive because Diem achieved it without eliminating loyalty as a criterion in command selection. Ever since 1954, military leaders had been plotting on and off against Diem, so he always retained some mediocre officers of definite loyalty in key commands that were close to Saigon, as protection against a coup. Journalists like David Halberstam and Neil Sheehan, who spent most of their time in and around the capital, loudly denounced the loyalty-based appointments and argued that merit should be the sole criterion. If some officers turned against Diem, they believed, it simply showed that he did not deserve to be president. This line of reasoning betrayed fundamental ignorance of the South Vietnamese elites—their fractious character ensured that certain individuals were always conspiring to overthrow the government regardless of its virtues. It also failed to consider the possibility that the men who overthrew the government would be inferior leaders or that they would purge massive numbers of capable government commanders for their loyalty to the replaced regime.

In the spring and summer of 1963 a group of politically motivated Buddhist monks, some of whom were Communist agents, launched a campaign of protest against the Saigon government in which they hurled baseless allegations of religious persecution. They demanded concessions and kept demanding them even after the government, under intense American pressure, granted many concessions and made innumerable other attempts at conciliation. To most South Vietnamese, in fact, the Diem government's concessions and its toleration of large public demonstrations signified a loss of prestige, for Vietnamese culture deemed weak the leader who did not quash his adversaries and maintain public order. The American press corps in Saigon, duped by misinformation from a Reuters stringer named Pham Xuan An who was actually a Communist spy, reported that Diem's heavy-handedness was creating dissension among the army's officer corps, when in reality the officer corps supported the suppression of the militant protesters.[15]

Accustomed to a state-controlled press, South Vietnam's elites presumed that the anti-Diem articles of Halberstam, Sheehan, Stanley Karnow, and other

American reporters represented the official U.S. position, which led some of them to entertain the idea of overthrowing Diem. The American journalists in Saigon also helped convince Ambassador Henry Cabot Lodge to incite a military coup. Lodge and like-minded officials were not certain who would become the new president and simply assumed that "the generals" would figure it out. It would be one of the most costly examples in history of inattention to individual differences in leadership ability. The military leaders, it turned out, did not want to overthrow Diem, but when Lodge informed them that the United States could not tolerate the current government, they agreed to a coup because they knew that South Vietnam could not survive without American assistance.[16]

The coup commenced on November 1 and continued into the early hours of November 2 as Diem's crack Presidential Guard held off the coup forces at Saigon's Presidential Palace. During the morning of November 2, convinced that further fighting would only abet the Communists, Diem ordered loyalist forces to lay down their arms. Lodge, who was worried that Diem and Nhu would be a menace to the successor regime, refused to facilitate their departure from the country, so the two brothers agreed to turn themselves in to the plotters, who sent a detachment of troops to collect them at a church, where they had gone to pray. On instructions from General Duong Van Minh, one of the top leaders of the coup forces, the soldiers killed Diem and Nhu in the back of an armored personnel carrier.

A committee of generals, headed by General Minh, took control of the country. Despite previous promises to liberalize the government and remove loyalty as a criterion in command selection, the generals purged huge numbers of Diem supporters from the government, throwing a number of them in jail. They ousted nearly all of the district and provincial chiefs, the leaders responsible for most of the counterinsurgency programs and organizations, including the strategic hamlet program, the militias, the police, and an assortment of economic development programs. They dissolved the Republican Youth, fired militia commanders, disarmed strategic hamlet militiamen, and replaced nine of the top twenty-two military commanders. The new generation of leaders, the bumper crop of talent that had rescued South Vietnam during the past two years, was systematically uprooted. In place of the expelled commanders, the junta put untested young men or older men who had failed past tests.[17]

The committee of generals spoke with eloquence of the classic counterinsurgency methods they intended to employ. They did not, however, build viable programs and organizations to replace those that they had destroyed, and they provided none of the direction and motivation that the new field commanders needed. Inertia took hold up and down and across the government. In December, Lodge himself conceded, "I am disconcerted by an apparent lack of drive in conducting the war. The members of the junta give me splendid clear-cut answers and say all of the right things, yet nothing much seems to happen." As a consequence of this collapse of leadership, South Vietnamese regulars stopped patrolling the countryside, militiamen quit, and village officials moved to district and provincial capitals. The Viet Cong regained the initiative by default and, with little effort, began moving back into the areas that they had lost in the preceding two years.[18]

Within three months of the coup, the Minh junta had put on such a stunning show of incompetence and self-destructiveness that influential Americans and South Vietnamese became convinced by the droves that the situation demanded another coup. At the end of January 1964, General Nguyen Khanh put out feelers to the Americans about staging such a coup and received the green light. On January 30, at four in the morning, Khanh and other dissatisfied generals sent tanks and armored cars to surround the homes of the government's top leaders. The coup forces took all of these individuals into custody without firing a shot and put them in prison. The head conspirators set up a new government with Khanh as chief of state.

Thirty-seven years of age when he took power, Khanh was an extraordinarily skillful and aggressive military leader. He had become the first commander of the Vietnamese National Army's elite airborne battalion in 1950 at the age of just twenty-three, and by the age of thirty he had been made a general. As the new chief of state, he moved more quickly and decisively than the committee of generals had. Yet Khanh lacked abilities that were critical to his new position. Despite years of distinguished service in the military, he did not have all the organizational skills necessary to run a national government effectively, which resulted in inattention to important matters and administrative drift. In the political realm, he lacked knowledge and judgment, which led him to rely for political advice on Ambassador Lodge, a man who knew American politics intimately and mistakenly assumed that this knowledge made him an expert on Vietnamese politics.

When Khanh asked Lodge whom he should appoint to a new cabinet, the ambassador responded, "One good rule of politics in any country is to include rather than to exclude, and to give all elements in the community a sense of participation." So Khanh appointed officials from every religious, political, and regional group. But diversity proved an inadequate substitute for quality. Identity-based appointments empowered individuals who lacked experience or talent and who spent much of their time bickering, backstabbing, and promoting their own group's narrow interests at the expense of others.[19]

Khanh initiated a new round of purging, a more useful one than the previous round, since he replaced many of the incompetent beneficiaries of the first purge with the capable Diem loyalists whose places they had taken. But then the Buddhists who had helped topple Diem began accusing Khanh of reviving "Diemism." Khanh, short on political smarts and determined to avoid Diem's fate for resisting the Buddhists, took to firing and imprisoning Diem loyalists.[20]

Khanh stabilized the South Vietnamese armed forces to a degree through personnel changes, but he kept in place more than a few officers whose dearth of flexibility and initiative led to a return to large, and largely barren, sweep operations. Khanh was not able to revive counterinsurgency programs in the hamlets, leaving the Viet Cong with unfettered access to the hamlets' resources. Important civilian officials in Washington, and later some historians, attributed the Viet Cong's strength at this time to the government's inattention to the use of political, economic, and social methods to gain popular support, which they ascribed to overemphasis on military affairs. That interpretation constituted a triumph of abstract theorizing over objective reality. Overemphasizing the military dimension was impossible when there was little or no security in the hamlets; the administrators of political, economic, and social programs could not function there if they could not be protected from Viet Cong bullets. Even with adequate security, the South Vietnamese government still would have been unable to do much with nonmilitary instruments of power, not because it was ignorant of good methods—its planning documents express full awareness of good methods—but because it lacked leaders who could implement those methods successfully.[21]

The only national counterinsurgency program that showed much promise in 1964 owed its success to the CIA, not to the Saigon government. Called the Counter-Terror Team program and later rechristened the Provincial Reconnaissance Unit program, it fielded small paramilitary teams in areas where other government forces refused to go. Although the CIA was able to lure unusually capable men into the rank and file with high pay, the principal reason for the program's success was the caliber of the South Vietnamese commanders whom the CIA handpicked for the program, the only South Vietnamese commanders anywhere who were appointed by Americans. By choosing the leaders, the CIA nullified the political and personal considerations that affected the selection of commanders for other units. Using advisers and informants within the units, CIA officers monitored the performance of commanders, admonishing or relieving commanders for ineffectiveness. Because of superior leadership, these teams operated more effectively than any other South Vietnamese forces, and because they operated in their home areas, they had better intelligence than any American forces. In time, it would become common for a 100-man Provincial Reconnaissance Unit to capture or kill several hundred Communists in a year while suffering few, if any, casualties. This program was too small, however, to have a major impact on the war as a whole.[22]

During the summer of 1964 the Communists were growing in strength not only in rural South Vietnam but also in the cities, where they had heretofore been very feeble. The urban police, like every other arm of the South Vietnamese government, had been debilitated by the post-Diem purges, and the Communists and other oppositionists exploited this weakness to the hilt. In August, Khanh attempted to reverse this state of affairs by ordering his security forces to prohibit public demonstrations, imprison individuals suspected of supporting the enemy, and execute terrorists and speculators. Buddhist and student groups—both of which were now heavily infiltrated by Communists—responded with riots that targeted government offices and Catholics, the latter because of their steadfast opposition to Communists and other subversives. Khanh lost whatever backbone he had possessed. Intimidated by the large crowds and the possibility of American disapproval, Khanh did not arrest the protesters but instead agreed to grant their demands, which included annulling all of the new anti-subversive measures. In a country that revered strongmen, Khanh's toleration of protests and his concessions caused him to lose face, demoralizing his supporters and encouraging his opponents to cause new trouble. "The emergency, and indeed any other laws, are being mocked," observed the British ambassador. "The grave element in all this is the failure of the Khanh regime to assert themselves even in the face of small demonstrations. In their desire to avoid appearing dictatorial they are showing themselves to be ineffective."[23]

As the Buddhists kept up the drumbeat of demands, Khanh fired more officers whom the Buddhists found objectionable, which prompted Harkins's successor, General William Westmoreland, to issue a warning that "actions best calculated to destroy the morale, the unity, the pride and confidence of the Armed Forces have transpired in a manner which leads me to believe that a relative free hand has been given to those who aim to destroy the Armed Forces." Khanh's capitulation to the Buddhists and his generally poor leadership sparked a coup attempt on September 13, which fizzled only because the U.S. embassy chose to back Khanh after the plotters, in conversations with American officials, revealed that they had no idea how to run the government. Because most military commanders remained neutral during the putsch or sided with the rebels, Khanh conducted a sweeping purge immediately afterward, sacking three of the four corps commanders and six of the nine division commanders.[24]

Khanh survived until February 1965, when the military leadership forced him out and sent him abroad with the face-saving title of ambassador-at-large. Though staunchly anti-Communist and generally unsympathetic to the Buddhist political activists, the generals settled, for the time being, on a civilian government led by Dr. Phan Huy Quat, a favorite of the militant Buddhists. Actively promoting the Buddhist political agenda, Quat relieved commanders who tried to rein in Buddhist protesters and imprisoned officers who criticized him for lenience toward suspected Communists. The officer corps, and hence the armed forces, reached new lows. The timing of this leadership disintegration could not have been worse for South Vietnam, for it coincided with the arrival in South Vietnam of the first wave of a North Vietnamese invasion. In the fall of 1964 the political calamities in Saigon, together with President Lyndon Johnson's tepid responses to North Vietnamese provocations and his campaign promises to keep American boys out of Vietnam, had convinced Hanoi to dispatch entire North Vietnamese army regiments for the purpose of conquering South Vietnam swiftly. Departing from the North in November 1964, the North Vietnamese army units commenced offensive operations in the South in the first months of 1965, concentrating thousands of troops at the point of attack and employing heavy weapons like pack howitzers and flamethrowers. These operations signified a shift in emphasis from guerrilla warfare to conventional warfare, and they had the intended effect, inflicting unprecedented casualties on the South Vietnamese army and forcing South Vietnamese commanders to operate in at least battalion strength.[25]

In May, Communist forces stepped up their attacks to still higher levels, with the objective of inflicting between 30,000 and 40,000 casualties on the South Vietnamese army by the end of the year. Losses of that magnitude, North

Vietnam's strategists believed, would permit Communist forces to take Saigon. In the first week of June, the North Vietnamese army and the Viet Cong dealt the government 1,876 casualties, the highest total for any week in the war. General Westmoreland, in a report dated June 7, observed that South Vietnamese soldiers "are beginning to show signs of reluctance to assume the offensive, and in some cases their steadfastness under fire is coming into doubt." South Vietnam would soon lose the war, Westmoreland asserted, unless large numbers of American troops stepped onto the battlefield, a course of action he strongly advocated.[26]

The military setbacks of early June also forced a showdown in the South Vietnamese government, between Premier Quat and the military. Meeting with Quat on June 11, fifty generals aired their dissatisfaction with the regime's failings, both political and military. After rounds of quarreling, as notable for their acidity as for their duration, Quat arose in exasperation and announced that he was resigning.

The generals promptly set about creating a new government, and the Buddhist agitators wasted no time in angling to bring to power their favorite general, Nguyen Chanh Thi. This time, however, the generals refused to play along, choosing instead Air Marshal Nguyen Cao Ky as prime minister and General Nguyen Van Thieu as the head of the ruling committee of generals. Appalled by the damage to the war effort caused by Buddhist conniving, these two officers immediately terminated the Buddhists' influence on personnel decisions and internal security policies. The Buddhist activists, and the political instability they engendered, had been throttled for good. Thieu was to remain at the top of the government for the remainder of the war, dumping Ky a few years later after a period of joint rule.

Ky was far from an ideal choice for prime minister. Though an accomplished military officer, the thirty-four-year-old Ky possessed little experience in civil governance, and his concentration on pressing affairs was as inconstant as his attention to his numerous love interests. His ivory-handled pistols and his favorite attire—a purple jumpsuit with purple socks and a purple scarf—symbolized his predisposition for style over substance. General Nguyen Van Thieu, on the other hand, had the marks of a formidable leader. At forty-two, he was much more mature and tactful than Ky and had recently demonstrated the savvy and interpersonal dexterity required to navigate the mazes and cesspools of Saigon politics. His talents as a military commander also exceeded Ky's and, along with his personality, had won him the respect of most of his military colleagues. During the political tumult of the past twenty months, Thieu had become one of the three generals whom American diplomats and military advisers regularly cited as an excellent candidate for chief of state.[27]

The new government energized the civil administration and fixed major problems that the preceding regimes had neglected. Within a few months, Ky and Thieu had stanched the political hemorrhaging of officers and undone some of the damage to the military and civil leadership. Headway in restoring the security forces and the administrative apparatus came slowly, however, because the machinery had been thoroughly corroded since November 1963 and now had to be repaired while in operation and under attack from powerful enemies. Through conventional battle, the Communists continued to deal the South Vietnamese army dreadful losses through June and into July, such that President Lyndon Johnson, at the end of July, assented to Westmoreland's recommendation to insert U.S. ground forces into the war.[28]

General Westmoreland, who until this point had devoted his time to helping the South Vietnamese forces wage war, took command of the U.S. combat forces that Johnson poured into the country. Ever since joining the Boy Scouts at age twelve, Westmoreland had stood out as a natural leader. His military bearing, granite jaw, and effortless self-confidence gave him considerable charisma, of the sort that made men do whatever he commanded, no matter the risk. Diligent and organized, he fit perfectly into the army culture when he entered West Point in 1933. During his West Point years, Westmoreland earned the Pershing Sword, bestowed on the cadet who had demonstrated the highest degree of military proficiency. While commanding artillery units in North Africa, Italy, and France during World War II, he demonstrated exceptional perseverance and unflappability in perilous straits. The late 1950s saw Westmoreland in command of the 101st Airborne Division, which established him as a member of the "Airborne mafia," a group of officers that dominated the army's top ranks by selecting each other for plum jobs.[29]

As troop ships bore American combat troops across the world's oceans to South Vietnam, Westmoreland told the Pentagon which generals he desired as division and corps commanders. Secretary of Defense Robert McNamara, Chairman of the Joint Chiefs of Staff General Earle Wheeler, and Army Chief of Staff General Harold K. Johnson all objected to some of his selections, but Westmoreland's persuasion and persistence broke their opposition. Most of Westmoreland's choices were Airborne officers or West Point graduates, or both, which were legitimate stamps of merit, but his strong preference for them provoked a certain number of accusations of cronyism and disregard for fine officers lacking those credentials.[30]

As part of his daily routine, Westmoreland invited junior officers for dinner at his villa to question them over steaks and gin-and-tonics about what they were seeing at their level. He made trips to the field at least three times a week, flying by helicopter to nearby locations and by fixed-wing aircraft to those farther away. Often he traveled to battlefields as soon as the fighting ended. During visits he asked tough, probing questions and issued stern warnings to officers who failed to produce the correct answers, creating no small amount of consternation. He did not, however, fire officers on the spot as other top commanders would have done. Fellow army officers, indeed, faulted Westmoreland for his willingness to forgive poor performance. When the commander of the 196th Infantry Brigade, Brigadier General Edward H. DeSaussure, incurred devastating losses through errors in judgment during Operation Attleboro, Westmoreland rejected the recommendation of one of his most trusted confidants, Major General William DePuy, to send DeSaussure on the next plane to the United States. Instead, Westmoreland transferred DeSaussure to the command of the 1st Field Force Artillery and allowed him to earn a subsequent promotion to major general. As one journalist noted, such actions ensured that Westmoreland was a figure "more popular than feared."[31]

Some Westmoreland critics found his refusal to fire substandard officers reprehensible in light of his toleration of commanders at lower echelons who relieved their own subordinate officers without hesitation.[32] Some of these commanders routinely tossed out subordinates, especially those commanding companies or platoons. Whether these removals were made wisely depended almost entirely on the judgment and integrity of the officer making the decision. A study of the relief of commanders by Brigadier General Thomas V. Draude concluded, "The decision of a higher commander to retain or reject his leaders at the fighting level is left to the higher commander's personal judgment. In this case, his judgment is not a matter of interpreting standard orders, guidelines, or principles as there are virtually none."[33] Draude found that commanders were usually relieved for weaknesses that became apparent before they resulted in a catastrophic failure, suggesting that commanders were, in general, vigilant in monitoring their subordinate commanders. He also discovered that a large proportion of the officers were relieved for failures that resulted from inexperience. Because of manpower shortages, captains with only twenty-four months in service regularly received company commands.

Draude observed that relief of commanders who were clearly poor leaders generally had a positive impact on a unit, but he also noted that some senior officers dissuaded subordinate commanders from bold and imaginative action by relieving commanders with great frequency and for relatively minor mistakes.[34]

In the second half of 1965, Westmoreland used heavily armed U.S. combat battalions to counterattack large Communist forces when they struck and to conduct search-and-destroy operations, in which the Americans hunted for large enemy units in remote areas. Search-and-destroy operations were to come under intense criticism because American forces often had trouble locating the enemy and because the presence of U.S. forces in the hinterlands kept them from participating in operations to secure the population. Westmoreland, the critics said, could not grasp the simple point that counterinsurgency forces should always stay close to the population. Such contentions might have had some merit had the war been merely a guerrilla war, but they were dangerously wrongheaded when advanced in the context of a war with a strong conventional component. During the last months of 1964, in adherence to standard counterinsurgency principles, Westmoreland had convinced South Vietnamese army commanders in Binh Dinh province to divide their forces into small detachments and disperse them across the villages to establish security and control the population. This approach at first gave the government a boost in the contest for the population's resources, but the enemy did not passively accept the deterioration of its position. Dispatching several large main-force units to Binh Dinh, the Communists attacked the small government detachments one at a time, so that in each case the Communists had overwhelming numerical superiority. Communist battalions mauled one village post after another. In early 1965, deprived of its intelligence sources in the villages, the government fell victim to concentrated surprise attacks on its district capitals. The provincial capitals and Saigon itself would have been next had the U.S. armed forces not saved the day.

The only way to foil such a rampage was to take the initiative from the Communists, which meant striking them with large mobile forces before they hit the small detachments. Thus, as Westmoreland concluded from the Binh Dinh experience, countering the Communists required both static forces to secure the villages and mobile forces to attack the enemy's conventional forces. Westmoreland decided to devote American troops to the mobile conventional operations away from the populace, because they had superior mobility and firepower, and let the South Vietnamese fight the guerrilla units in the village areas, because they had personal and ethnic ties to local communities that the Americans lacked.[35]

The American ground forces succeeded in accomplishing their first and most important mission, thwarting North Vietnam's conventional offensive. American units repeatedly decimated large Communist formations during the last months of 1965 through the skillful employment of highly mobile infantry backed by massive air and artillery strikes. These operations compelled the North Vietnamese to operate in smaller units, scale back their offensive activities, and abandon plans for the swift seizure of Saigon. Although those changes made Communist forces somewhat less vulnerable to American power, the Americans continued to inflict crushing defeats on the North Vietnamese army and the Viet Cong in 1966 and 1967. The North Vietnamese, however, kept feeding new soldiers and matériel into South Vietnam through Laos and Cambodia, which enabled them to keep fighting and killing Americans, thereby eroding support for the war among the American people, who were far less inclined to tolerate casualties than was the ruling circle in Hanoi.

From the middle of 1965 to the end of 1967, in accordance with Westmoreland's division of labor, the South Vietnamese government diverted much of its regular army to counterinsurgency in the villages. Familiar signs of poor leadership could be found in the army across the country—mistreatment of the civilian populace, desertion, application of inappropriate tactics, and reluctance to pursue the enemy. In I Corps, which consisted of the northernmost provinces of South Vietnam, U.S. Marines attempted to compensate for the lack of leadership in the South Vietnamese security forces by attaching Marine squads to local militia platoons and putting the combined units under Marine command. The Combined Action Program, as it was called, substantially improved the performance of the militiamen and cut desertion rates from 25 percent per year to almost nothing.[36] A contemporaneous study, based on interviews with numerous Combined Action Program officers, noted, "The major variable affecting the performance of military operations is the leadership ability of the Marine squad leader. This man is the key to the entire operation, and on his capabilities all else hinges." If this leader gave in too much to the opinions of his men or committed errors that caused his men to lose their respect for him, then the unit "goes slack and becomes not only ineffectual or a liability, but also quite vulnerable to the enemy."[37] The Combined Action Platoons meted out heavy losses to the Viet Cong and gained the cooperation

of numerous villagers, even though they spent little time on civic action programs of the sort often viewed as essential to successful counterinsurgency.[38]

The Combined Action Program's most enthusiastic advocates argued that
the United States could win the war by assigning far more troops to Combined Action Platoons. Westmoreland and some leading civilians rejected
that recommendation, and with good reason. Expanding the program would
have pulled American forces away from search-and-destroy missions, which
would have allowed Communist forces to mass against the dispersed Combined Action Platoons as they had done to South Vietnamese forces in Binh
Dinh in 1964. As it was, with numerous large U.S. units shielding the populous areas and disrupting major enemy operations, Communist forces overran
many Combined Action Platoons. The program was a short-term fix, useful
for helping turn South Vietnamese forces around, but unhelpful in the long-
term development of South Vietnamese leadership, for it allowed the Vietnamese to hold the enemy at bay without having to correct their leadership
problems.[39] As the future was to show, the South Vietnamese had the potential
to provide the necessary leadership in the villages without extended American
tutelage of the sort provided by the Combined Action Platoons.

Another American-driven effort to restore governmental presence in the
villages, begun in 1966, was the Revolutionary Development Cadre program.
Similar in concept to the strategic hamlet program, it put fifty-nine-man
teams into hamlets on a permanent basis and directed them to carry out the
full spectrum of military and political operations. It failed because it lacked
the element that had vaulted the strategic hamlet program to success: strong
leadership. Seeking to expand the number of teams rapidly, the program's
South Vietnamese leadership chose team commanders with haste and insufficient regard for merit. Because of inferior commanders, the Revolutionary
Development Cadres usually fought poorly or fled when the enemy attacked.
Once attacked, they often stopped living in a village altogether, operating instead from a secure base outside the hamlet, leaving the Viet Cong free to
prowl after dark. This dysfunction led eventually to the abandonment of the
original concept; the teams were downsized and attached to units that had
better security capabilities.[40]

The U.S. Agency for International Development and other civilian agencies of the American government implemented a plethora of nonmilitary
programs that benefited the rural populace, initially through a chain of command separate from that of the military officers responsible for pacification.

Oftentimes the civil and military organizations did not collaborate or even tell each other what they were doing. As a consequence, they sent mixed messages to the South Vietnamese and interfered with each other's efforts. Most problematically, the civil organizations implemented programs without adequate military protection. Civilian agencies vehemently opposed plans to put their people into the military chain of command, arguing that the military would misuse their skills and resources, so intervention at the presidential level was required to bring about change. In the spring of 1967, President Johnson authorized a new organization, called Civil Operations and Rural Development Support (CORDS), that put all the pacification personnel and programs—save those of the CIA—under a single adviser at the provincial or district level. CORDS fell within the military command structure, but some of the top provincial and district advisers were civilians. At the national level, Westmoreland left CORDS in the hands of a new civilian deputy, Robert Komer, for Westmoreland preferred to focus his energies on the big-unit war and the American forces that dominated it, which he found more exciting than pacification. Belying the fears of the civilian agencies, CORDS bolstered civil-military collaboration and improved the effectiveness of numerous counterinsurgency initiatives.[41]

To address another perceived weakness in the counterinsurgency effort, Komer and senior CIA officers created the Phoenix program, an interagency intelligence program focused on the leadership of the Viet Cong shadow governments. If the Viet Cong's leaders could be eliminated, the argument went, then the followers would become disorganized or collapse outright. The Phoenix program created coordination centers where representatives from American and South Vietnamese agencies could share information on the shadow governments, thereby corroborating single-source information, diminishing duplication of effort, and connecting intelligence organizations to operational forces.

Surgical targeting of the shadow governments proved impossible, however, for life had by now become so dangerous for Viet Cong leaders that they rarely went anywhere without a sizable contingent of soldiers or guerrillas. Most agencies did not want to share their secrets with the Phoenix centers, for fear that Viet Cong spies in the centers would discover their sources, that the information would be misused, or that due credit would not accrue to them for their intelligence work. Overcoming the resistance of intelligence officers almost always required orders from their immediate superiors; thus, intelligence was certain to flow into the centers only when a single person commanded multiple agencies, and only if that person was enterprising and conscientious. Otherwise, intelligence agencies shared information through Phoenix centers only in the few places where the leaders of different agencies had sufficiently close personal relationships with one another.[42]

Leadership was critical for intelligence collection itself—for all police, paramilitary, militia, and military organizations that tried to locate insurgent forces in and around the villages. Most South Vietnamese intelligence organizations suffered from a chronic shortage of experienced and talented leaders because the South Vietnamese army received top priority in the allocation of new personnel, and it assigned the best leaders to combat units, although this problem was often mitigated by strong combat commanders who invested much time in intelligence collection. Good leaders trained and motivated their men to obtain information from informants and agents, and consequently their subordinates usually succeeded in collecting large amounts of reliable information. Poor leaders invariably failed to produce results. Good leaders caught governmental personnel and private citizens who claimed that personal enemies were Viet Cong by seeking corroboration from other sources before authorizing detentions and by reviewing all evidence when trying detainees. The leaders themselves were not normally tempted to affix the Viet Cong label to personal enemies, because Saigon assigned commanders to areas other than their home areas for the express purpose of keeping them out of local squabbles.[43]

During the Tet holiday in January 1968, the Communists tried, like the Greeks at Troy, to win by trickery what they had not won in battle. In violation of a holiday ceasefire, swarms of Viet Cong attacked most of South Vietnam's cities and towns, exhorting the citizenry to rise up in support of the revolution as they passed through. But the urban populations were as hostile to the Communists as they had always been. Instead of joining the revolutionaries, people reported their location to the government. When Viet Cong forces had fought in the jungles and forests, they had attacked quickly and withdrawn just as fast, making no attempt to hold on to territory or installations. Now, in the cities, they tried to hold intersections and buildings, which turned into the anvils on which the hammer of South Vietnamese and American firepower smashed them. Sustaining horrendous losses while clinging to fixed positions, the Viet Cong suffered further losses when they fled, as the relatives of government personnel reported their movements to the security forces. Within a few days, the Communists had been vanquished in all of the towns and cities except Saigon, where they held out for two weeks, and Hue, where they hung on for a month, during which time they massacred several thousand civilians.[44]

General Westmoreland incurred much undeserved blame for not anticipating the Tet Offensive and received little credit for crushing it, which may be the principal reason behind President Johnson's decision to bring him home in June 1968 and turn command over to Westmoreland's deputy, General Creighton Abrams. The son of a mechanic for the Boston and Albany Railroad, Abrams was a native of western Massachusetts. In high school he was the captain of the undefeated football team, class president, class orator, editor of the school newspaper, and president of the scholastic honor society. Everyone in the school liked Creighton Abrams. He had to turn down a scholarship to Brown University because his family could not afford the books and other expenses, so fate brought him to West Point, into the class of 1936. He only made it to the third string of the West Point football team because his intelligence and athleticism could not make up for the fact that he was five feet nine inches tall and weighed 165 pounds. Still, he allocated more effort to sports than to academics, graduating 185th in a class of 276.[45]

His first moments of military glory came during the breakout from Normandy in the summer of 1944, when, as the 37th Tank Battalion commander, he displayed the aggressiveness of a piranha and the audacity to match. His tank was always at the front, engaging the enemy with the hatch open and Abrams sticking out from the waist up. With all the German tank shells and machine gun rounds sent in his direction, few expected him to live very long. Abrams insisted that all of his tanks fight with their hatches open so that the crews could see what was going on around them. Once, when he found one of his tanks with the hatch closed, he threatened to weld it shut. His men were always prepared and organized and hungry for a fight. One journalist remarked that Abrams could "inspire aggressiveness in a begonia."[46] Time and again, the tanks under his command bested German Panther and Tiger tanks despite the superiority of the German main guns and armor.

As the U.S. Army advanced toward the German heartland, the 37th Tank Battalion regularly breached the enemy line ahead of every other American unit, and Abrams kept the battalion in the enemy's rear for hours or even a few days at a time, wreaking havoc on German logistics. Abrams became a national hero during the Battle of the Bulge by leading his tanks into Bastogne, the crux of the battle, to relieve the beleaguered American garrison. His stunning exploits made him a favorite of General George S. Patton, who was reported to have said, "I'm supposed to be the best tank commander in the Army, but I have one peer—Abe Abrams. He's the world's champion."[47]

As a general officer, it was intellect and charisma that elevated Abrams above the rest. General Phillip B. Davidson, the top intelligence officer in Vietnam for both Westmoreland and Abrams, attested that Abrams "had that rare quality, common sense, the knack of going straight to the heart of the problem, and insisting on a simple and workable solution. Woe to the briefer who gave Abrams some involuted theory or complex statistical mish-mash." Throughout the army's officer corps, it was regularly said that "Abe is the smartest officer in the army."[48] Abrams's charisma defied precise description, but it was extremely powerful in gaining him the affection and labors of his men. To enhance this appeal, he publicly cultivated the air of a beer-swilling, cigar-chewing tough guy, although in private he listened to Mozart and Wagner, enjoyed fine food and wine, and devoted many hours to serious books of history and philosophy.[49]

Throughout his time as the commander of American forces in Vietnam, Abrams filled much of his schedule with inspections throughout the country, often providing no advance notification. When officers attempted to give Abrams the customary briefing, he ordered them to desist. "To hell with the briefing—let's just talk!" he would say to young officers who greeted him upon landing. "Just take me out and show me what the problem is."[50] At his headquarters in Saigon, Abrams continued Westmoreland's practice of inviting young officers to dinner to glean information and insights from them. Unlike Westmoreland, Abrams did not demonstrate a strong preference for West Point graduates or Airborne officers when dispensing jobs and tasks, and he looked askance at those who thought such affiliations made them more deserving. As Westmoreland's division and corps commanders completed their tours, Abrams chose their replacements from groups of officers who had been nominated for command.[51] The subsequent effectiveness of these commanders indicates that Abrams chose well.

Soon after taking over for Westmoreland, Abrams directed U.S. forces to operate more often in small units in the populous areas and in tandem with South Vietnamese forces. As a matter of principle, Abrams believed that American combat troops should become more involved in population security, but his decision was also the product of the changing security situation after the Tet Offensive—the crippling of the big Communist forces reduced the need for search-and-destroy operations and lowered the risks of small-unit operations. Ultimately, Abrams's attempts to change tactics from the top were constrained by his insistence on decentralization of command authority. Recognizing that the war varied enormously from one place to the next, Abrams let his division commanders decide how often to deploy troops in small and large groups and how much firepower to use. "The kind of war that we have here can be compared to an orchestra," Abrams said on one occasion. "It is sometimes appropriate to emphasize the drums or the trumpets or the bassoon, or even the flute." Some officers still spent most of their time beating the drums of search-and-destroy, which could be justified by the need to stymie the North Vietnamese army units that continued to flow in through Laos and Cambodia. In the complex environment of Vietnam, it was often very difficult to determine from on high that a commander needed to substitute the bassoon or flute for the drums, and therefore Abrams usually suggested methods to his commanders rather than dictating them. Those commanders were, after all, men whom he had picked because he trusted their abilities. Their judgment and flexibility and creativity, not his, would decide whether the proper instrument was played. For the most part, it was.[52]

Many analysts of the U.S. military in Vietnam have maintained that the conventional organization and culture of the armed forces, especially the army, severely hindered the use of those forces in counterguerrilla operations. Yet in the post-Tet period, plenty of U.S. Army officers, as well as Marine Corps officers, shifted swiftly and effectively from large search-and-destroy operations to small counterguerrilla operations on account of their flexibility and aptitude for improvisation. Most had the good sense and interpersonal skills to find South Vietnamese government personnel and informants who could help them locate the Communists. In populous areas where American forces began operating in small groups, security usually improved significantly, provided that large Communist forces did not intrude.[53]

The largest leadership challenge confronting American commanders in the village war was preventing their troops from mistreating the civilian population. A minority of combat commanders were not equal to the challenge, and a tiny minority, of whom the most egregious by far was Lieutenant William Calley of My Lai infamy, encouraged violence against civilians. Abuse of the civilian populace was more common among support units, which sometimes served as the dumping ground for officers and enlisted men who plainly lacked the character to be entrusted with combat duty. Some support units acquired a reputation for running peasants off the road with their trucks, disrespecting passersby, and shooting water buffaloes for sport.[54]

During Abrams's tenure, South Vietnamese counterinsurgency commanders improved dramatically in every way, and so did the personnel under their command. Generally speaking, the South Vietnamese had sought to employ the right types of counterinsurgency methods in the few years preceding Abrams's arrival, but only now did they have the leadership to implement them successfully. As one Communist document from 1970 explained, "The general enemy scheme remains basically the same," but "it is now implemented more energetically, more skillfully, and more bluntly." Better leadership, and the military successes it produced, swept the Viet Cong out of the villages and inspired the villagers to assist the government.[55]

Three factors account for the remarkable transformation of South Vietnam's leadership in the late 1960s and early 1970s. The first was the Hue massacre, which brought home to South Vietnam's elites the gruesome fate they would suffer if the war were lost. Second was the reduction of American force levels, which convinced the South Vietnamese leaders that they had to act with vigor and perseverance to prevent slippage in the fighting and avoid ultimate defeat. For President Thieu himself, it also meant that he had to appoint winning commanders. The third factor was American persuasion and pressure, judiciously applied, which induced Thieu to make numerous command changes.

After some months in Vietnam, Komer decided that fixing the leadership was the key to fixing South Vietnam's armed forces and thus made it his number one priority. "I started out looking at Vietnam as a problem in resource allocation, and ended up looking at Vietnam more as a problem in getting the right Vietnamese in the right jobs," Komer said. "It was much less a question of the size of the ARVN [South Vietnamese army] or the size of the Vietnamese Civil Service than of the qualities of leadership." Komer's influence with the South Vietnamese was sharply limited, though, by his arrogant and abrasive personality, which earned him the nickname Blowtorch. Komer's successor at CORDS, William Colby, also recognized the importance of leadership and, being more likable and empathetic than Komer, was able to persuade President Thieu to replace numerous officers whom CORDS advisers had identified as poor leaders. Colby was especially effective in engineering replacements of district and provincial chiefs, who, as in times past, were the linchpins of pacification. Of 20 provincial chiefs relieved from 1968 to 1971, CORDS had requested the removal of 14. Of 124 district chiefs relieved in the same period, CORDS had advocated replacing 84. The steep rise in the quality of the district and provincial chiefs had an electrifying effect on the militia forces, which grew from 418,000 to 680,000 men between 1967 and 1972. As in the early 1960s, the South Vietnamese were able to increase their forces in quantity and quality at the same time.[56]

Whereas General Westmoreland had focused almost exclusively on U.S. forces once they entered the ground war, General Abrams gave great attention to South Vietnamese forces and their American advisers and regularly implored President Thieu to replace subpar commanders. Like William Colby, Abrams used superior social skills to obtain cooperation from Thieu and other high South Vietnamese leaders. Changes of key commanders in the South Vietnamese army worked the same magic as the substitution of district and provincial chiefs did. A prime example was the ARVN 7th Division in 1969, which had fallen flat after American forces vacated its operational area because of officers who displayed no initiative and made costly mistakes that went unpunished by the division's commander. U.S. Defense Department analyst Thomas Thayer described what followed: "President Thieu relieved the division's commander and appointed an aggressive brigade commander from the ARVN airborne division to the job. No other measures were taken nor was additional support furnished." The new division commander replaced two regimental commanders and demanded that the regimental and battalion commanders operate more often on their own initiative. "The new commander quickly turned the division into an effective fighting unit," reported Thayer, "furnishing strong evidence that replacing a poor commander with a good one was the best way to improve a poor ARVN division."[57]

Commenting on the South Vietnamese army as a whole in November 1969, Abrams reached the same conclusion. "Leadership—where that's good, they're good," said Abrams. "Where it's mediocre, they're mediocre. Where it's piss poor, they're piss poor. It's just that simple. We've had some very dramatic examples here of where one man has changed—one man, just the commander, and in a month and a half's time you've got an entirely new outfit. Used to be flat on its ass, wouldn't go anywhere, couldn't fight. Only changed one man—transformed the whole thing."[58]

American efforts to pressure South Vietnamese commanders directly were much less successful. Wary of appearing subservient to foreigners, the South Vietnamese usually became less likely to adopt a course of action when an American adviser recommended it unless the recommendation came in the most inconspicuous and subtle of fashions. At one point, the Americans tried to spur the South Vietnamese on by assigning them quotas of Viet Cong cadres to be captured or killed, but the South Vietnamese either fabricated statistics to meet the quotas or ignored them.[59]

From 1969 to 1971 the invigorated South Vietnamese forces and their American allies eliminated the remaining South Vietnamese insurgents by killing them, capturing them, or driving them to defect through the national amnesty program. The war ceased to have a significant component of insurgency by the end of 1971, becoming a purely conventional war between the armed forces of North Vietnam and South Vietnam.[60] At the end of March 1972, by which time President Richard Nixon had completed a phased withdrawal of all U.S. ground forces, a whopping fourteen North Vietnamese army divisions slashed into South Vietnam in a three-pronged offensive known to Americans as the Easter Offensive, to North Vietnamese as the Strategic Offensive, and to South Vietnamese as the Summer of Fire. Making liberal use of armor and artillery, the North Vietnamese overran Quang Tri, the northernmost province of South Vietnam, and advanced on two pivotal provincial capitals, Kontum and An Loc. Seeing the deficiencies of some of the South Vietnamese military commanders, President Thieu replaced a few key ones with outstanding officers from other commands, and they quickly restored the fighting spirit in the South Vietnamese army units. In the next few months, with the support of U.S. air and naval power, the South Vietnamese blunted the remaining North Vietnamese assaults and drove the invaders from the populous areas they had seized. On account of the Saigon government's control of South Vietnam's villages, it alone could rely heavily on villagers for recruits, food, and intelligence, which proved to be critical assets during the offensive.

In the end, however, the obliteration of the insurgents did not save South Vietnam from defeat. President Nixon withdrew America's remaining advisory and support personnel from South Vietnam in January 1973 in return for North Vietnamese promises to end the fighting and repatriate American prisoners of war, while promising President Thieu that the United States would come to South Vietnam's assistance if the North Vietnamese launched another major offensive. But when 550,000 North Vietnamese army troops attacked two years later, Nixon was out of office because of Watergate, and the U.S. Congress prevented his successor, Gerald Ford, from fulfilling Nixon's promise. The Congress also refused to provide South Vietnam with the fuel, equipment, and supplies required to repel a massive enemy force, which, thanks to its more reliable allies, possessed state-of-the-art artillery, 600 tanks, and all the oil and ammunition they needed. The final defeat of South Vietnam came on April 30, 1975, when a North Vietnamese tank crashed through the gate of the Presidential Palace in Saigon. South Vietnamese leaders who had not escaped or perished were either executed immediately or incarcerated for many years in "reeducation camps," where huge numbers died.

For those pondering counterinsurgency present and future, the Vietnam War illuminates the challenges of constructing new security forces from the ruins of the old. As South Vietnam attempted to build police, militia, and military forces after the armistice in 1954, leadership development constituted the most formidable task by far. Until President Diem could raise a new crop of leaders, he had to rely on the leaders inherited from the French colonial regime, who were generally so bad that Diem could not wring good performances from them through any amount of exhortation, dictation of counterinsurgency principles, or micromanagement. Recruiting a new generation of leaders and providing them with sufficient experience for important counterinsurgency commands took seven years.

Once this new group of leaders was ready, Diem came up with creative organizational devices to advance them past older leaders who, being human, were averse to relinquishing their powers. He channeled many of the younger leaders into a new organization, the Republican Youth, which had a chain of command that bypassed stagnant national ministries and village administrations. He flooded the Ministry of Defense with new talent and transferred control of a vital militia force, the Civil Guard, to that ministry after overcoming long-standing American opposition to the transfer, thereby circumventing the Ministry of the Interior.

Americans regularly denounced South Vietnam's presidents for appointing certain commanders for reasons of political loyalty rather than merit, but the criticism was often misplaced. The president needed loyal armed forces in a country with powerful centrifugal forces. Diem would have been forced from power well before 1963 had he not enjoyed the support of key military commanders, and he would have been replaced by someone of lesser quality who would have purged good officers, as indeed happened when the military overthrew him in 1963. In further illustration of the perils of a change in government, the post-Diem purge intensified rivalries and animosities within the South Vietnamese elites, fostering additional coups and purges that laid the

South Vietnamese leadership so low as to invite a North Vietnamese invasion and require an emergency American intervention. Any South Vietnamese president had to consider both loyalty and merit in appointments and strive for a balance that enabled the government to withstand attacks from without and from within.

Purely merit-based selection worked very well on a small scale in the one South Vietnamese organization with leaders selected directly by Americans, the Provincial Reconnaissance Units. By scrutinizing the leadership qualities of South Vietnamese officers and disregarding political considerations, the Americans consistently installed superb leaders in these units. In the case of the Combined Action Platoons, South Vietnamese militiamen took their orders from American commanders, which was not quite as effective because of barriers of language and culture but still elicited strong performances from militiamen, provided that the commanders had the requisite leadership traits.

At various times in the war, outside observers advocated direct American control of the entire South Vietnamese armed forces, a very alluring course of action in light of the successes of the Provincial Reconnaissance Units and the Combined Action Platoons. Top South Vietnamese and American leaders consistently scotched this proposal, however, viewing it as an affront to South Vietnamese sovereignty and nationalism and as an impediment to South Vietnamese self-sufficiency. Both South Vietnamese and Americans viewed the U.S. presence in Vietnam as limited in duration, which meant that the South Vietnamese government had to learn how to choose its own commanders. In addition, the South Vietnamese understood their country's internal politics and political personalities far better than the Americans did, giving them a decided advantage in judging the political impact of command appointments, although the Americans sometimes did play an invaluable role in recommending changes of commanders.

At the highest level of the South Vietnamese government, the United States wielded a strong positive influence when the top American officials in Saigon enjoyed good personal relationships with the South Vietnamese president and did not try to pressure him into adopting American solutions to his problems. Included in this category of Americans were Edward Lansdale and Samuel Williams, who helped Diem tackle unfamiliar political and military problems, and Paul Harkins and Creighton Abrams, who motivated Diem and Thieu, respectively, to attack the enemy aggressively and remove weak officers.

Americans who did not build strong personal relationships with the South Vietnamese, like Elbridge Durbrow and Henry Cabot Lodge, obtained scant cooperation from the South Vietnamese and, through pressure tactics, often caused the South Vietnamese to do the opposite of what was desired. Unable to see South Vietnam through Vietnamese eyes, these Americans further undermined their standing with the Vietnamese by promoting a host of counterproductive measures. Among the most shopworn was a "broadening" of the South Vietnamese government by installing representatives of every population segment. On the few occasions when the South Vietnamese felt sufficiently indebted to the Americans to follow this advice, they came to regret it, for the representatives were incompetent or concerned only with advancing their own faction's parochial agendas.

General William Westmoreland's critical flaw was his inattention to the quality of South Vietnamese military commanders. Permitting the South Vietnamese to solve their leadership problems entirely on their own promoted South Vietnam's sense of independence, but it forfeited the very large gains that could be had by promoting the replacement of inferior commanders, gains that Westmoreland's successor realized. Westmoreland exemplified the leader whose compassion for subordinates prevented him from relieving those who, for the greater good of the cause and the lives of their men, deserved to be relieved. Westmoreland, moreover, did not give due consideration to the problems created by disunity of command among counterinsurgency agencies. Fortunately for him, others did, and they persuaded President Johnson to form CORDS, which, by placing civil and military agencies into a single chain of command, made it possible to achieve close civil-military collaboration and hence hastened the annihilation of the insurgents.

The activity that most set General Abrams apart from Westmoreland, and that bore the most fruit, was Abrams's judicious coaxing of President Thieu to replace commanders. Abrams also sought to alter American tactics by boosting the number of small operations in populous areas, and American forces did indeed operate much more often in small units than before, with their officers usually demonstrating the necessary attributes of counterinsurgency leadership. But many of the American forces made few or no tactical changes. Abrams's ability to change tactics from the top was seriously constrained by the ongoing need for large, mobile operations against big North Vietnamese army units and by his own recognition of the need for decentralized command. The counterinsurgency as a whole did not undergo a major shift in methods under

Abrams; the major shift was in the number of American troops allocated to securing the populous rural areas. The American troops who were transferred to population security employed essentially the same methods that hundreds of thousands of South Vietnamese troops were already using.

Much misunderstanding of counterinsurgency in Vietnam has arisen because of a lack of awareness that Communist armed forces regularly massed for large conventional attacks, a feature that sharply differentiated this war from insurgencies that never advance beyond the guerrilla phase. The intermingling of the Communist regular and irregular forces and the ability of the regular forces to switch back and forth between regular and irregular warfare demanded that the counterinsurgents employ mobile conventional forces to engage enemy regulars, as well as less heavily equipped static forces to keep the guerrillas out of the villages. At least some of the commanders of the counterinsurgent conventional forces needed proficiency in both regular and irregular warfare, along with the judgment to know when to use each and the flexibility to transition readily from one to the other.

South Vietnam's inability to resist the insurgents effectively during certain periods of the war resulted from neither bad doctrine nor a misunderstanding of the enemy nor lack of emphasis on nonmilitary programs. It resulted from bad field leadership. Variations in the South Vietnamese government's overall success against the insurgents coincided exactly with changes in the overall quality of South Vietnamese leaders—from the sharp upturn in 1962 as new leaders came of age, to the precipitous drop following the overthrow of Diem in November 1963, to the slow climb brought on by the installation of the Thieu-Ky government in 1965, to the more dramatic and sustained ascent after the Tet Offensive of 1968. How these shifts in leadership quality occurred demonstrated one more trend with broad implications: major changes in leadership quality were driven by the actions of the counterinsurgents themselves.

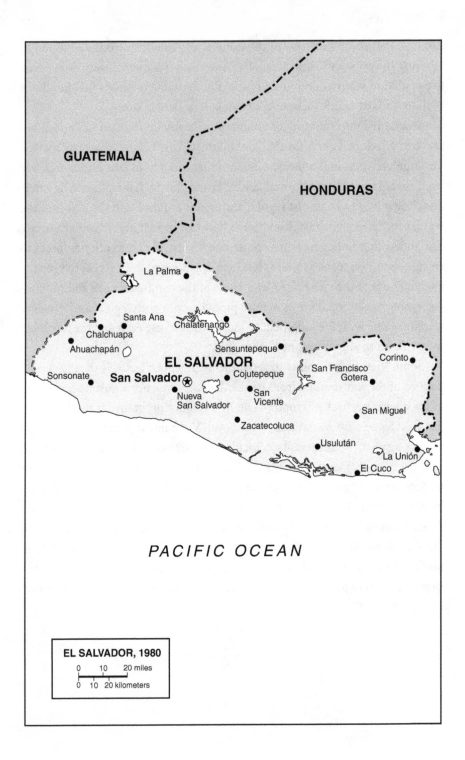

GUATEMALA

HONDURAS

La Palma

Santa Ana
Chalatenango
Chalchuapa
Ahuachapán
Sensuntepeque
EL SALVADOR
Corinto
San Francisco
Gotera
Sonsonate
San Salvador
Cojutepeque
Nueva
San Salvador
San
Vicente
San Miguel
Zacatecoluca
Usulután
La Unión
El Cuco

PACIFIC OCEAN

EL SALVADOR, 1980

0   10   20 miles

0   10   20 kilometers

CHAPTER 8

The Salvadoran Insurgency

A country the size of Massachusetts, with the highest population density in Latin America, El Salvador had 3.9 million people when war broke out in 1980. Dominating the country was a small, wealthy elite that owned 70 percent of the land and relied on the army for protection against its enemies, foreign and domestic. The army was headed by a different small group of men, who also enjoyed considerable wealth, but they were nouveaux riches of lower-middle-class birth, which kept them off the invitation lists for the balls and weddings of El Salvador's high society.[1]

Domestic enemies had been on the rise in the 1970s. The peasants were restive, stirred up by Communists and by preachers of "liberation theology," a doctrine that advocated political radicalism by invoking the unusual claim that Jesus had been a left-wing political activist. Revolutionary fervor gripped some of the country's most gifted and well-educated youth as radical university professors and high-school teachers recruited their students into subversive organizations. But where the revolutionary elites were largely motivated by abstract political and religious ideas, the peasants saw revolution as the solution to a concrete problem, the misconduct of El Salvador's security forces. Devoid of concern for civil liberties and inclined toward cruel and unusual punishments, the security forces committed innumerable acts of brutality against suspected rebels and innocent civilians alike.[2]

When Jimmy Carter became president of the United States in 1977, he declared that America's allies should afford their peoples all of the rights and privileges that the United States granted its people. He put the Salvadoran government on notice that it would have to comply with American human rights standards in order to keep U.S. aid flowing into its treasury. The proud Salvadorans could not abide such Yankee self-righteousness and intrusiveness, even if it came from a Georgia peanut farmer rather than a Boston Brahmin or a Manhattan blueblood, so they refused that condition. The Carter administration, very uncompromising in its early days, cut off aid.[3]

In October 1979 the Salvadoran president, General Carlos Humberto Romero, was ousted by young officers who shared the Carter administration's vision for El Salvador—they favored democracy, respect for human rights, an end to corruption, and redistribution of land from rich to poor. The new government reached out to moderates and even to the militant left. But the junta did little to fulfill its bold promises during its first months in power, owing to its own shortcomings and the obstruction of conservatives and right-wing extremists in the armed forces. The junta was unwilling to coerce or oust these rightists because the traditions of the Salvadoran officer corps forbade it. These traditions, of inordinate importance to the government and the army, originated in one military school in San Salvador.[4]

Located in a few cement buildings on a noisy city street, the Salvadoran military academy looked like a set of warehouses or administrative buildings. Called the Captain General Gerardo Barrios Military School, it took its name from a Salvadoran officer who had led the expulsion of the American adventurer William Walker from Nicaragua's presidency in 1857. All officer candidates for the army and the three internal security forces—the National Police, the Treasury Police, and the National Guard—attended the academy and at graduation became members of a single officer corps. Admission into the military academy was highly competitive. For lower-middle-class boys, it offered more than any other job or school available to them—cadets received four years of free education, followed by a well-paid job, higher social status, and plentiful opportunities for graft.

Instructors at the military academy focused on physical training and administered very little training of the mind. The numerous cadets who failed to reach graduation were thrown out for physical, not mental, inadequacies. In the classroom, cadets learned primarily by rote memorization, and they were taught to obey orders without analyzing or questioning them, a type of instruction that discouraged initiative and left junior officers with little preparation for situations that demanded personal judgment or creativity. In developing innovative methods of warfare, crafting propaganda for domestic consumption, and gaining the sympathies of foreigners through public relations, the academy's products would be much inferior to their opponents in the insurgency that boiled up in 1980.[5]

During their four years in the academy, Salvadoran army officers were imprinted with a loyalty to the officer corps above all else, and to their own graduating class, or *tanda*, above the rest of the officer corps. This fealty, combined with a cultural aversion to confrontation, kept Salvadoran officers from punishing fellow officers for mistakes and crimes. Even the worst offenses, such as abetting the enemy or murdering civilians, did not get officers kicked out of the officer corps, although they typically led to assignments as attachés in obscure and undesirable foreign countries. The culture of the officer corps also dictated that officers avoid making major changes of any kind, so as not to offend officers predisposed to the status quo. It was for this reason that the junta of 1979 declined to implement its ideas on land reform, democracy, and other political issues in the face of opposition from the rightists.[6]

Three main revolutionary groups had already engaged in violent opposition prior to the October 1979 coup. They held their weapons in abeyance during the first months of the new regime, waiting to see whether it would make good on its vows of change. If, as some insurgents speculated, the factions in the officer corps and government set upon each other, the insurgents could exploit the situation as Lenin had done in Russia in 1917. By the end of 1979, however, the government's failure to deliver change and its opposition to radical leftists convinced the revolutionaries to pursue their aims by force of arms.

In early 1980 the junta did get moving on some of the promised reforms, muting opposition from rightist officers by securing from the Carter administration $5.7 million in "non-lethal" military aid, which consisted of trucks, communications equipment, and uniforms. The junta agreed to the nationalization of banks and the redistribution of land from well-to-do landowners to peasants who owned no land. But the government implemented the reforms sporadically and often improperly, generating animosity among landowners and others on the right. Some farmers with small holdings had to relinquish land, and only 10 percent of the landowners who were stripped of their land received compensation.[7]

The drastic character and poor implementation of these reforms came together with the rise of the insurgency to produce a maelstrom on the political right. Far-right military officers maneuvered to relieve reformist officers of their commands and send them abroad as embassy or consulate attachés. They sanctioned, and in some instances participated in, what became known as death squads. Composed of soldiers and other militant citizens dressed in civilian garb, the death squads gunned down suspected insurgents and insurgent supporters on a large scale. At times, soldiers were brazen enough to perpetrate such murders in uniform. According to most American sources, the large majority of the estimated 8,000 to 9,000 civilians killed in 1980 were the victims of either rightist death squads or government forces.[8]

Over in Cuba, Fidel Castro was working to unite the Salvadoran leftists under Communist leadership, in the belief that El Salvador was an important battlefield in the struggle to spread Communism across Latin America. In December 1979, Castro had brought a handful of Salvadoran revolutionary groups to Havana and encouraged them to unify, which led to the formation in October 1980 of a unified front organization, the Farabundo Martí National Liberation Front (FMLN). Named after a famed Salvadoran Communist, the FMLN was avowedly Marxist-Leninist in its ideology.[9]

The depletion of the ranks of the insurgents by the Salvadoran military and the death squads in 1980 convinced Castro and the FMLN leadership that a mighty offensive had to be launched in the near future, while the revolutionary organizations still had some life in them.[10] Castro and Nicaraguan Communists from the Sandinista regime assisted the FMLN in planning the offensive, which they dubbed the "final offensive" in the expectation that it would overthrow the Salvadoran government in short order. During the last months of 1980, insurgent forces trained for the offensive in Cuba, and both Cuba and Nicaragua provided the insurgents with weapons to carry out the attacks. The offensive was scheduled to begin on January 10, 1981, and end before Ronald Reagan's January 20 inauguration as Carter's successor, in order to seize the prize before the United States could increase its military assistance—the rhetoric of the staunchly anti-Communist Reagan had made clear that he would be more supportive of the Salvadoran government than Carter had been. "It is necessary," the insurgents resolved in early January, "to launch now the battles for the great general offensive of the Salvadoran people before that fanatic Ronald Reagan takes over the presidency of the United States."[11]

The "final offensive" began on January 10 with simultaneous attacks on government offices and military installations across El Salvador. Surrounding the government's armed forces at fixed positions, the insurgents attacked head-on, orange fire flowing from their Communist-bloc automatic rifles and submachine guns. Insurgent leaders had hoped that reformist military officers and urban civilians would flock to their side, and they might have succeeded if that hope had been realized. As it turned out, however, neither group assisted the revolutionaries in appreciable numbers. The army's officer corps, to the surprise of its detractors, displayed resolution and competence in defending the offensive's targets, preventing the insurgents from overrunning more than a few.[12]

The situation, nevertheless, seemed dire enough at first that Carter, on January 13, chose to restore all nonlethal military aid to the Salvadoran government in spite of his ongoing dissatisfaction with Salvadoran human rights practices. The next day, the U.S. National Security Council approved $5.9 million in lethal aid, the first such aid since 1977, and Carter used the emergency provisions of the Foreign Assistance Act to send the aid without congressional authorization. On January 16, in another agonizing decision, Carter suspended aid to Nicaragua because of accumulating evidence that the Sandinista government was transporting arms to the Salvadoran insurgents, ending an ill-starred policy of courting the Communist Sandinistas with aid and goodwill.[13] Having begun his term deploring the "inordinate fear of Communism which once led us to embrace any dictator who joined us in that fear," Carter ended his presidency supporting undemocratic anti-Communists in El Salvador and Nicaragua, based on a well-justified fear of Communist expansionism.[14]

The aid authorized by Carter had no impact on the outcome of the offensive, for the insurgents abandoned their attacks after just one week and retreated, with thoroughly deflated spirits, into the countryside. Aside from a few guerrilla and terrorist attacks here and there, they spent the next months developing revolutionary base areas in the mountains and the jungles where government forces did not venture. They made logistical preparations for future offensive actions and sent their best cadres for military training in Cuba and Vietnam, which, along with Nicaragua, were to be their principal suppliers of weapons and ammunition in the coming years.[15]

The Salvadoran government, meanwhile, doubled the size of its army, from 10,000 to 20,000, and sent soldiers out to cut the insurgency's supply lines and kill insurgents and their supporters. This approach would have accomplished a good deal if the soldiers had executed it with resolve and skill, but they manifestly did not. Salvadoran officers, who were assigned to commands based on seniority and political reliability, were generally lacking in aggressiveness, dedication, and basic military proficiency. They avoided night operations, and on the weekends they left their troops in order to spend time with their families in San Salvador. American military advisers, accustomed to working through the night and living away from home for months or years at a time, derided the Salvadoran army for fighting "a nine-to-five war." The insurgents, with assistance from informants among the peasants, regularly outfought the government forces. As the war intensified in the spring, insurgent weapons shredded government units and reduced the government's control over the rural population. The counterinsurgent armed forces incurred a staggering 1,300 casualties during the first six months of 1981. After the insurgents captured the town of Perquín in July 1981, government forces ceased offensive operations and concentrated on static defense, which deprived them of the initiative and hence made them even more vulnerable to concerted enemy attacks.[16]

In Washington, Ronald Reagan ratcheted up aid to the Salvadoran government while his belongings were still moving into the White House. During February 1981, the Reagan administration granted El Salvador $25 million in new military aid, more than it allocated to the rest of Latin America combined, in addition to setting aside $19.5 million for CIA covert operations in El Salvador. The military aid paid for new Salvadoran military facilities, new M16 automatic rifles to replace the stocks of old G3s, and scores of helicopters and fixed-wing aircraft. In addition, Reagan dispatched twenty-six U.S. advisers to El Salvador, augmenting the twenty-eight sent by Carter late in his term, and authorized the advisers to train Salvadoran units. The Reagan administration forbade the advisers from taking action against the enemy or accompanying Salvadoran units into the field, both of which would have brought the War Powers Resolution to bear. The administration also kept them from working with the National Guard, the National Police, the Treasury Police, and the self-defense units, organizations that needed help even more than the army because they were repositories for the roughest and cruelest men of the rural townships and were reportedly the primary suppliers of death squad members.[17]

In recognition of the need to improve the Salvadoran officer corps, the United States brought all graduates of the Captain General Gerardo Barrios Military School to Fort Benning, Georgia, to attend either the School of the Americas or the U.S. Army Infantry School. Hundreds of Salvadoran officer candidates spent three months in training at Fort Benning in lieu of attending the Salvadoran military academy in order to produce new officers for the mushrooming Salvadoran armed forces. The training and education programs in the United States de-emphasized the activities stressed at the Salvadoran military academy, such as squat jumps and parade dress formations, and instead focused on independent and innovative thinking, counterinsurgency theories, and benevolent treatment of civilians and enlisted soldiers.[18] According to most observers, Salvadoran officers were persuaded to adopt American views on these subjects during their time in the United States, but upon their return to El Salvador they came under pressure from senior Salvadoran officers to revert to the old ways of doing business. Some accounts contend that the returnees abandoned most of what they had learned in the United States, while other accounts sharply dispute that claim.[19]

One of the widest divergences between American and Salvadoran counterinsurgency practices was the size of operations. American trainers and advisers urged the Salvadoran army to conduct small patrols, arguing that big operations were much easier for the insurgents to evade. Salvadoran army officers, on the other hand, thought that small patrols were for other security forces. The army's main concern, as they saw it, was fighting big battles, as it had done in 1969 after a clash between Salvadoran and Honduran soccer fans produced the seven-day "Soccer War." During the first years of the insurgency, the Salvadoran army commonly sent soldiers out in groups of several hundred or more. Over time, however, as the army failed over and over again to locate insurgents, Salvadoran officers experimented with small-unit actions and, finding them successful, adopted them as standard practice.[20]

With respect to other counterinsurgency methods, the Salvadorans remained convinced that the Americans did not have all the answers. Indeed, American advice turned out to be unsound on more than a few occasions, and the extent of American advice was limited by the prohibition against American participation in combat operations, which prevented the advisers from understanding all the challenges that had to be met. General John R. Galvin, the commander in chief of the U.S. Southern Command from 1985 to 1987, said later, "I don't think that the Salvadorans felt that we had a corner on the market of counterguerrilla operations by any means. I think that we were assisting them by basically providing resources for the fighting and, to some degree, the doctrine of counterguerrilla operation. But a great deal of that doctrine was also being produced in the form of the 'School of Hard Knocks' as the Salvadoran armed forces went out to fight the war."[21]

American trainers at Fort Benning and American advisers in El Salvador spent much of their time imploring Salvadoran officers to end human rights abuses and sever all ties with the death squads. When the Salvadorans first asked why they should heed this counsel, the Americans explained that the security forces needed to hold the "moral high ground." The Salvadorans found that argument unconvincing and stuck to their old habits. The Americans then started emphasizing the practical benefits of respecting human rights—obtaining intelligence from appreciative civilians and from prisoners who had not been executed, as well as retaining the support of the United States. Those points proved much more persuasive and led to a gradual reduction in abuses.[22] At various times, moreover, senior American diplomats and military officers coerced the top Salvadoran leadership into stopping human rights abuses by local commanders, with the advisers in the field serving as verifiers of compliance. Near the end of the war, one of the top insurgent leaders remarked that for the insurgents, "the most damaging thing that occurred during the war was putting American trainers in the [El Salvador armed forces] brigades." The presence of these Americans, he said, reduced human rights violations, which lowered the number of men desiring to join the insurgency.[23]

Among the leading cause of ulcers for American advisers was the reluctance of Salvadoran officers to take the initiative. Another was the Salvadorans' refusal to adopt leadership techniques that were standard in the U.S. military, such as maintaining a sense of urgency and visiting troops regularly to supervise execution of orders. What modest advances the advisers did make in strengthening Salvadoran leadership capabilities often stemmed from advisory emphasis on very basic matters and careful circumvention of the impediments to change. Some advisers induced their counterparts to take on traits by displaying those traits themselves. Particularly successful in this regard were advisers from the U.S. Army Special Forces, who, by virtue of the organization's personnel policies and philosophy of decentralized command, possessed an unusually high degree of initiative and creativity.[24]

Perceptive Americans recognized early on that the Salvadoran army was not selecting its best officers as commanders. Although U.S. advisers could not observe military operations in the field, Americans from the attaché's office were permitted to do so, and they collected invaluable information on particular units and commanders. Senior American officers made a regular habit of telling the Salvadoran Defense Ministry to reward talent and hard work and remove incompetence and sloth, although the ministry's leadership at first paid them little heed.[25]

To alleviate the problems caused by inadequate junior leadership, the Americans pressured the Salvadorans to build a noncommissioned officer corps. Salvadoran military leaders, who had never had noncommissioned officers, deemed it too radical a change to military culture. They created a noncommissioned officer corps only because the Americans insisted, and did everything possible to render it impotent. Rather than making NCOs out of enlisted men who were better leaders than others, the Salvadorans gave the NCO title to those who had served longer than others, and assigned them no real leadership duties.[26]

In early 1982, Colonel John Waghelstein arrived in San Salvador to assume command of the U.S. advisory group. He found that most of the government forces were in the same static defensive positions they had occupied for months, leaving the insurgents free to roam the countryside and consolidate their control over the population. The few army units that journeyed into the rural areas were ambushed almost without exception. This sorry state of affairs, Waghelstein concluded, was purely the result of bad leadership. "Out of 14 departments," Waghelstein recalled, "only two departmental commanders were worth a damn, and the others were sitting on their buns waiting for something to happen." In addition to demonstrating initiative, the two good departmental commanders differed from the others in that they were making progress in organizing self-defense forces. The officer corps contained lieutenant colonels who were better leaders than most of the departmental commanders, but Minister of Defense José Guillermo García refused to put them in command because they did not belong to his tanda, whereas most of the departmental commanders did.[27]

The best departmental commander, in Waghelstein's opinion, was Lieutenant Colonel Sigifredo Ochoa Perez. "He was the guy we wanted everybody else to be like," Waghelstein said. "Ochoa's units would go out and stay out and they would rotate them out in the field, not in the barracks, but in the field, which is a distinct difference. . . . So you always had a presence out there and they never set up in one place for very long." Ochoa gained the assistance of churches and schools in combating the insurgents, and he organized effective psychological operations and public works projects.[28]

The only elements of the Salvadoran security forces that were rich in good commanders were the army's quick-reaction battalions, elite units that were shuttled around the country to deal with crises or take offensive action. Foremost among their commanders was Lieutenant Colonel Domingo Monterrosa.

An extraordinarily imaginative officer, Monterrosa made superb use of air assets, outmaneuvering insurgents with heliborne troops and pelting them with rockets and bombs from attack aircraft. He consistently hit the enemy before being hit and pursued the enemy long after other officers would have given up. Monterrosa also convinced numerous insurgents to defect by creating an amnesty program that treated defectors with benevolence, a break from the past practice of killing any and all insurgents. Waghelstein commented, "Monterrosa was everybody's ideal of a blade. He was the spearpoint. He was the one who was always at the front with the kerchief and the plumes." Monterrosa's quick-reaction battalion "was a different unit, different philosophy, different way they were trained, and particularly a different leadership. That style of leadership was stamped on all the subordinates. Monterrosa's subordinates emulated him."[29]

Waghelstein made the replacement of weak departmental commanders a top priority and stressed it constantly in discussions with Defense Minister García. In the fall of 1982, García promised to remove three of them, but at the last minute reneged, declaring that he could not get by without their support. The only departmental commander he could afford to upset, in his opinion, was the exceptionally capable Ochoa. García maneuvered to sideline Ochoa as part of an effort to undercut allies of Roberto D'Aubuisson, the founder and leader of the right-wing ARENA party. But when García canceled plans to send Ochoa to an important position in Washington and instead ordered him to a worthless posting in Uruguay, a virtual exile, Ochoa refused to accept the reassignment, setting up a showdown that would determine the future direction of El Salvador's armed forces.

The Americans had backed García's previous firings of D'Aubuisson's allies, because D'Aubuisson had been heavily involved in death squad murders, but they did not back García in this instance, because Ochoa was such an effective leader and García was showing himself to be more and more ineffective. A group of young officers known as the Praetorians, who scoffed at the officers of García's generation for their reluctance to fight but who were not aligned with the D'Aubuisson faction, backed Ochoa for reasons of personal friendship and professional respect. The combination of Americans and Praetorians spelled doom for García. He was forced into retirement, and Ochoa went to Washington as originally scheduled.[30]

For the rest of 1982 and the first months of 1983, the departmental commanders remained weak. Their persistent inertia permitted the insurgents to move across the country at will and concentrate overwhelming forces at fixed positions. In January 1983 insurgent forces overran a 300-man garrison and a 500-man garrison while advancing on the provincial capital of San Francisco Gotera. The Salvadoran army countered by sending 6,000 troops, including all three quick-reaction battalions, to San Francisco Gotera. Although that move ensured the safety of the provincial capital, it left the rest of the country highly vulnerable, a reality that the insurgents exploited by capturing Berlín, a city of 40,000 in the eastern part of the country, and holding it for three days. Guerrillas swallowed up new swaths of the countryside, expanding their "liberated zones."[31]

In the middle of the year, the Salvadoran government massed its best forces in San Vicente province for an American-designed national counterinsurgency campaign. According to the campaign plan, the government's armed forces would drive the insurgents out of one province and allow civil authorities and militias to take charge of reconstruction, then move on to an adjacent province to do the same thing, expanding the pacified area like an oil spot until the entire country had been saturated. But the insurgents outwitted them again. By launching attacks in areas denuded of forces for the San Vicente operation, the insurgents compelled the government to remove troops from San Vicente to defend those areas, which in turn enabled the insurgents to demolish the new schools and roads and self-defense forces that had just been built in San Vicente.[32]

Americans in El Salvador and Washington spent much of 1983 warning that El Salvador would soon fall to the revolutionaries unless the United States provided more aid.[33] The outlook was bleak indeed. Yet it proved not to be American aid that saved the day but a transformation of the Salvadoran officer corps. The two seminal events in this transformation occurred in May 1983, although their impact was not felt until some months later. The first was at Quebrada Seca, where the insurgents were holding prisoners from the Salvadoran army. Standing over their captives, insurgent gunmen shot forty-two of them in the head at point-blank range. The U.S. media, which overwhelmingly opposed the Salvadoran government and the Reagan administration's support for it, gave scant coverage to the incident, but its influence on the Salvadoran armed forces was profound. News of the slaughter enraged Salvadoran officers and soldiers, and that rage drove them to more aggressive action. The killings also put a halt to surrenders by the Salvadoran forces, who until now had raised the white flag in large numbers, having heard that the insurgents would take their weapons and uniforms but let them keep their lives. Now it was a fight to the death.[34]

The second, more momentous event was the installation of General Carlos Eugenio Vides Casanova as minister of defense. The appointment was the product of internal politics rather than merit—Vides was chosen because he was one of the few officers who was palatable to both the D'Aubuisson faction and a group of influential officers whom former Defense Minister García had implanted in the senior leadership. Vides's prior record did not give much reason for optimism. During his stint as commander of the National Guard, guardsmen had committed murders by the bushel, often as members of death squads. Vides lacked experience commanding troops in the field, which earned him the nickname "Señorita Casanova" among other officers. He was, however, reputed to be a man of honesty and moderation who favored political and military reform.[35]

Vides soon showed himself to be the falcon to García's turkey. In stark contrast to his predecessor, Vides regularly went into the field to find out what was actually happening. He pressured officers to prevent their troops from mistreating civilians. In selecting commanders, he put merit ahead of tanda, a bold and controversial move that risked his continued presence in his job— and ultimately reaped huge rewards.[36]

Senior officers who were heavily invested in the status quo might have taken action to stop Vides had it not been for several glaring military debacles in late 1983 that illuminated the dire need for change. In each case, at El Tablon, El Paraíso, and the Cuscatlan bridge, the Salvadoran forces suffered defeat because their leaders failed to conduct standard patrols and reconnaissance. In the most crushing of these defeats, at El Paraíso, 800 insurgents overran the headquarters of the 4th Infantry Brigade, killing more than 100 government troops and taking 162 prisoners. At the Cuscatlan bridge, the only remaining bridge linking the eastern half of the country to the western half, the 400 government defenders fled as soon as they came under attack.[37]

During the last two months of 1983 and the first months of 1984, Vides overhauled the command structure and conducted a wholesale relief of commanders. He appointed six brigade commanders to replace the twenty-six separate commanders who had reported to the Defense Ministry. The old system had served the defense minister's interests by keeping any one commander from having enough power to oust him or launch a coup, but it had left the Defense Ministry with too many people to supervise effectively. Vides appointed

Colonel Adolfo Onecifero Blandon, a Praetorian known for aggressive combat leadership, as chief of staff of the armed forces and moved other Praetorians into important command slots. Decentralizing power, Vides and Blandon left brigade commanders to decide which counterinsurgency methods to use in their operational areas while still urging them to action and watching their performance. Blandon chastised commanders who did not spend time in the field or take the initiative, and kept an eye out to make sure that those weaknesses were corrected. Within a few months, these leadership changes had enlivened the armed forces and boosted their military skills, resulting in much more military success.[38]

Vides received another club with which to beat hidebound officers when Vice President George H. W. Bush visited El Salvador at the end of 1983. Saying that he spoke for President Reagan, Bush informed Salvadoran leaders that the United States would discontinue aid if they did not put a stop to the death squads and fire a list of military commanders who, according to U.S. intelligence, were complicit in death squad killings. In addition, Bush said, the Salvadoran government would lose American assistance if it did not complete the implementation of land reform, provide security for the coming national election, and abide by the electoral results. In a more positive vein, Bush said that if the Salvadoran government met all of these conditions, the United States would send additional aid in order to make possible "a winning effort."[39]

Although far-right officers objected to the American demands, the army complied with all of them except for expelling the military officers on the vice president's list. Some officers, especially those newly appointed by Vides, were already demonstrating increased respect for human rights and democracy; others went along glumly. Government human rights violations plummeted in early 1984, and death squad murders fell from 140 per month to 35 per month. In light of this progress, the Americans let slide the government's refusal to fire the offending officers, and they increased the level of aid.[40]

In 1984, despite all of the positive changes wrought by Vides and Blandon, many Salvadoran units were still held back by a shortage of good leaders. The continued expansion of the armed forces, to a strength of 42,000, stretched further an already thin officer corps.[41] When Colonel James J. Steele became head of the advisory group early in the year, he discovered that first lieutenants were commanding battalions and second lieutenants were commanding companies, while platoons did not seem to have leaders at all. "As you expand a force in a crisis you have to keep in mind what it takes to continue to lead that force effectively," Steele observed. "We've probably expanded here too quickly for the leadership." As in past counterinsurgencies, the ease of recruiting and equipping enlisted men encouraged unsuspecting planners to expand the forces with a rapidity that officer development could not match. Steele commented, "When you expand a force like that, if you have someone like the U.S. helping you, you can provide uniforms and weapons for the soldiers. There are a lot of people in El Salvador, and recruiting is not such a major problem. But you don't build battalion commanders, company commanders, platoon leaders, and first sergeants in six months. You don't do that in a year!"[42]

Steele also criticized the policy of determining the size of the Salvadoran security forces by multiplying the enemy's strength by ten or fifteen or twenty, a method popularized by counterinsurgency theorists. It failed to take into account the possibility that fewer forces with a higher density of good leaders might be better than more forces with a lower density of good leaders. Steele remarked, "Anybody who gets caught up in this business of a 10 to 1 force ratio to beat an insurgency is naïve. I'd like to get my hands around that guy's throat! It's so simplistic! Every country has its own force ratio. It's a product of how good the troops are, how bad the guerrillas are, how many leaders you have to begin with, and a whole host of considerations."[43]

Colonel Lyman C. Duryea, the American defense attaché in El Salvador at this time, articulated another reason for the ongoing leadership inadequacies: a deficiency in basic military skills among Salvadoran commanders at the battalion level and above. Some of these commanders had attended the U.S. Army's Command and General Staff College in Fort Leavenworth, Kansas, but the instruction they received there was too advanced and too theoretical for them. What they needed were the nuts and bolts of small-unit operations and counterguerrilla warfare. The junior leaders, on the other hand, knew the nuts and bolts because they had been trained at the less advanced American schools in training regimens created by the Reagan administration. Duryea concluded, "The way we're going now it will take a full military generation — which I define as about 20 years — and maybe more, before we get a trickle-up effect and we start seeing professionalism at the battalion command level. . . . We can train the cadets and the troops all we want, but until we reach the guys in the positions of command, the training that we give the young soldiers and the young cadets won't get employed because they immediately forget all of the good things they've learned and adapt to the bad habits of their own chain of command."[44]

Large insurgent attacks continued into 1984. Despite the ongoing leadership problems, the Salvadoran military had improved its prowess to the extent necessary to foil the enemy's initiatives. When insurgent forces surfaced, whether in the mountains or on the plains, the army massed forces using American helicopters and backed them with the firepower of American A-37 close-air-support aircraft and UH-1M and MD-500 attack helicopters, but the Salvadorans had to do the essential ground fighting themselves. In a string of major battles, the Salvadoran armed forces sent large insurgent troop concentrations into retreat with long casualty lists. Insurgent desertions increased sharply in number. By the end of the year, the sting of these defeats had caused the insurgents to revert to small hit-and-run attacks and terrorist strikes, which put a decisive military victory beyond reach, at least for the time being.[45]

The government's security forces prevented the insurgents from interfering with the national election of 1984, an event with critical implications for the war and the future of the country. In the race for the presidency, Roberto D'Aubuisson of ARENA held the early lead over José Napoleón Duarte of the Christian Democratic Party. The Reagan administration feared that D'Aubuisson, with his history of involvement with death squads, would blight the Salvadoran government's image in the United States and obstruct the sorts of reforms the Americans deemed necessary. He might well send pro-reform officers into virtual exile in embassies on the other side of the world. Reagan therefore authorized the CIA to pour several million dollars into the election campaign to promote Duarte. The impact of the CIA's money is impossible to determine with precision, but there is reason to suspect that it decided the outcome, for Duarte overtook D'Aubuisson after the CIA money began to flow, and he received more votes on election day.[46]

The illegitimate son of a tailor, Duarte had attended Notre Dame University in Indiana using money his father had won with a lottery ticket. He had served three terms as the mayor of San Salvador, starting in 1964, and had headed the government briefly near the start of the insurgency, overseeing the implementation of agrarian reform and nationalization. His election in 1984 gave El Salvador's cause a badly needed lift in the United States. American liberals, who until now had been skeptical of the cause, found the relative cleanliness of the election impressive, as they did Duarte's reformist outlook. As a consequence, the U.S. media produced stories that reflected favorably on the Salvadoran government, and the U.S. Congress became more amenable to providing aid to El Salvador.[47]

After assuming the presidency, Duarte undertook new measures to stop the death squads, including the elimination of several government security groups that had been linked to them. Death squad murders fell to less than a dozen per month.[48] Duarte and his party, however, failed to bring to life most of the other reforms they had advocated, mainly on account of inefficiency and corruption. They did not punish any perpetrators of death squad violence. They did not organize viable counterinsurgency initiatives to regain control over the populace. Even after the 1985 elections, which for the first time gave the Christian Democrats simultaneous control of the presidency, the legislature, and the judiciary, they accomplished little. The public recognized this poor national leadership for what it was, and disillusionment set in, leading to a decline in support for the Christian Democrats that led to their fall from power a few years down the road.[49]

In 1986 the precipitous growth of El Salvador's security forces came to a halt, with their total strength peaking at 56,000, and the stretching of the officer corps ended. Units began receiving more officers as new officers graduated from training courses. As the leadership solidified, Salvadoran forces operated increasingly in small numbers and at night, inflicting serious losses on the insurgents and disrupting their operations by keeping them on the run. But numerous units still had subpar commanders, in part because the tanda obsession made something of a resurgence, with various academy classes from the 1960s occupying their time jockeying to get the largest number of the most coveted jobs in the armed forces. The government, moreover, made little progress in creating self-defense forces or undertaking civic action. The insurgents, despite heavy casualties, continued to make numerous small attacks and assassination attempts in 1986 and the two succeeding years.[50]

In 1987, in a stunning break with the past, the Salvadoran government allowed leftist political leaders to return from exile and participate in politics — including the leaders of several socialist parties that supported the insurgents. Although American critics continued to argue that the insurgents enjoyed widespread popular support, the political parties allied with the insurgents actually had very little support among most segments of the population. Their terrorist acts against the civilian population and their dictatorial methods in areas under their control had alienated huge numbers of Salvadorans, and the improved conduct of government personnel had increased pro-government sentiment.[51] The contestants in the next election who worried the U.S. government were not on the left but on the right. The popular Alfredo Cristiani had replaced D'Aubuisson as the head of ARENA, and he became the frontrunner in the 1989 presidential race. Although Cristiani himself had not been directly linked to the death squads, the ARENA party remained tainted by that association in the eyes of many Americans. But Cristiani's lack of death squad ties, along with his perfect English, sophistication, and Georgetown University diploma, eased the U.S. government's concerns to a sufficient degree that it did not try to block his election as it had with D'Aubuisson.

Cristiani won the March 1989 presidential election in a landslide, receiving 54 percent of the vote versus 37 percent for the Christian Democrat candidate, Fidel Chávez Mena. The leftist Democratic Convergence, comprising political groups sympathetic to the insurgents, won just 4 percent. Once in power, Cristiani and ARENA proved much more competent than Duarte and the Christian Democrats. They cut down on corruption and instituted free-market reforms that revitalized the economy.[52]

Cristiani's first critical challenge came in November 1989 in the form of a major insurgent offensive. The insurgents were seeking to overthrow the new government and believed that if the offensive fell short of that objective, it would at least compel the government to accept terms favorable to the FMLN in negotiating an end to the war, such as giving pro-FMLN politicians positions of power in the government. As in 1981, the insurgents were counting on civilians to rise up in support of the revolution.[53]

On November 11, 1989, the same day that East and West Germans tore down the Berlin Wall, 2,000 insurgents attacked the center of governmental power, San Salvador, with assistance from the leftists whom the government had allowed to return in 1987. They occupied several neighborhoods and held them for days. But the masses did not rise up in support of the revolution, and the government reacted strongly. Salvadoran troops hunted the insurgents up and down the streets of San Salvador. The Salvadoran air force bombed entire neighborhoods that the insurgents had commandeered, causing extensive loss of life among civilians who were not aligned with the insurgents, but Cristiani, demonstrating the fortitude and sense of urgency that had been lacking in the previous president, launched an investigation and relieved the commanders who had ordered the profligate bombing.[54]

During the insurgent onslaught, government security forces rounded up opposition political leaders, labor union activists, and leftist clergy. Death squads, in whose company could be found a certain number of government security force personnel, murdered some civilians who were suspected of abetting the insurgents.[55] Their victims included six Jesuit priests at San Salvador's Universidad Centro Americana, practitioners of liberation theology who, according to army and police reports, had passed information to the insurgents. In a conversation with an American adviser, a Salvadoran officer divulged the name of the Salvadoran army commander who had instigated the killing of the Jesuits. It was a sign of major progress—in earlier days, Salvadoran officers would not have taken any action that could have caused such serious harm to a fellow officer, especially on a human rights issue. But when word of the Salvadoran government's complicity in these murders reached the American Congress, a deafening outcry shattered the bipartisan consensus in support of the war. The House and the Senate cut annual military aid to El Salvador in half, from $85 million to $42.5 million. The Bush administration demanded that the Salvadoran government punish the guilty officers, a very tall order considering that no Salvadoran government had ever punished military officers for political violence against civilians. The Salvadoran military attempted to derail investigations into the killings by lying and by destroying evidence, but Cristiani, whether because of U.S. pressure or his own convictions or a combination thereof, arrested several officers and enlisted men and sent them to trial for the killings. Salvadoran courts eventually convicted two of the officers for murder and sentenced them to thirty years in prison.[56]

The government's armed forces completed the defeat of the insurgent offensive at the beginning of December. The attack on San Salvador was to be the last serious offensive by the insurgents, although the war had not yet neared its end. The defeat of the Sandinistas in the Nicaraguan elections of February 1990 and the crumbling of Communism in eastern Europe soon deprived the insurgents of logistical support, dashing their hopes of taking San Salvador by force or obtaining a power-sharing agreement. At the same time, the insurgent offensive had made the Salvadoran elite and the U.S. government less confident of completely wiping the insurgency out militarily, and they were hence more amenable to negotiations. In April 1990 the government and the FMLN entered into talks to end the war, beginning nearly two years of what the Communists termed "fighting while negotiating." Peace finally came in February 1992, with the insurgents agreeing to disband their armed forces and discontinue all violence, and Cristiani agreeing to halve the armed forces, create a civilian police force separate from the military forces, allow a U.N. commission to investigate human rights abuses, and authorize an independent board to remove Salvadoran military officers guilty of human rights

violations. The last provision nearly provoked a military coup; Cristiani narrowly averted it by extending the retirement dates of the officers in question
and sparing them from public humiliation.[57] American advisers continued to
work with the Salvadoran armed forces following the armistice, an arrangement that the FMLN actually welcomed. As James LeMoyne of the *New York
Times* reported, the erstwhile rebels believed that "American military advisers
are needed to keep the Salvadoran military in line."[58]

Death squads did not resurface after the hostilities ceased. Cristiani abol-
ished the National Guard and the Treasury Police, the governmental organizations that had been most heavily involved in the death squads in earlier years.[59]
Members of the new civilian police force suffered from the traditional mala-
dies of corruption, disrespect for the population, and apathy. Nevertheless, the
new police constituted, in the words of one expert, "one of the most ambitious
reform efforts, and progressive public security forces, in Latin America."[60] The
government respected freedom of the press and the academe and conducted
elections fairly. The FMLN, which shed its Marxist-Leninist ideology and embraced liberal democracy, claimed the largest representation in the National
Assembly in 2000 and since then has been neck-and-neck with ARENA.[61]

In the twenty-first century, the Salvadoran experience has often been cited
as an excellent model for contemporary practitioners of counterinsurgency,
particularly those advising foreign governments. Although the dissolution of
the Salvadoran insurgency was in part the result of Communism's global collapse, the Salvadoran government and its American advisers are rightly acclaimed for strengthening El Salvador's security forces, dealing major military
losses to the insurgents, and curbing human rights violations by governmental
personnel. American advisers and American training clearly helped improve
the basic military proficiency of Salvadoran officers, especially in the early and
mid 1980s, which was no small achievement, and they had a more limited
impact on the initiative and organizational skills of those officers. Without a
doubt, persuasion and pressure from American advisers, trainers, and diplomats served as the main brakes on Salvadoran human rights violations over
the course of the war. Had the Americans not convinced Salvadoran leaders
that human rights violations impaired the war effort, and had they not con-
vincingly threatened to terminate aid in the absence of improvement on that
score, the murders, torture, kidnappings, and disappearances would probably
have continued at the same rates.

American pleas for the replacement of weak Salvadoran commanders, on

the other hand, elicited much less cooperation. The Salvadorans were more resistant to changes in their personnel system, and American policymakers did
not push them hard on this issue because they did not appreciate the importance of leadership or because they wanted to expend most of their limited influence on human rights, a paramount issue given that congressional support
hinged on it.

Credit for improving the quality of Salvadoran commanders in the mid-
1980s belongs chiefly to changes at the top level of the Salvadoran government. Most important was the appointment of a new defense minister, Carlos
Eugenio Vides Casanova, whose selfless commitment to improving the armed
forces made it possible to substitute merit for tanda and personal loyalty—
the traditional banes of the officer corps—in personnel decisions. Vides also
broke down the long-standing centralization of command, which had stifled
initiative. The CIA-supported election of José Napoleón Duarte in 1984 promoted stability and gained El Salvador the full approval of the American government, preventing the sort of leadership tumult that had plagued South
Vietnam twenty years earlier.

Although the Americans persuaded numerous Salvadoran officers to accept classic counterinsurgency principles, the Salvadorans demonstrated considerable independence in selecting counterinsurgency methods, especially in
the military realm, in no small part because of the American policy of forbidding American advisers from accompanying Salvadoran forces into combat.
The national counterinsurgency strategy that the Americans convinced the
Salvadorans to implement in 1983 ended in disaster, disproving the theory,
fashionable again today, that pooling national resources in support of a national, geographically prioritized strategy will cure many of counterinsurgency's ills. In removing forces from one area to concentrate them in another,
the strategists failed to anticipate that the insurgents would counter by moving
forces in the opposite direction, away from the concentrated counterinsurgent
forces and toward areas depleted of counterinsurgents. This reality reinforces
the view that counterinsurgents must have good local commanders spread
out across the country, with significant forces continuously at the disposal of
each.

The growth of the Salvadoran security forces showed the perils of rapid
force creation. At some point, adding more counterinsurgency troops became
counterproductive because the leaders with sufficient talent and experience
were spread too thinly and the ratio of strong leaders to weak leaders was

too low. El Salvador's expansion of its security forces from 10,000 in 1980 to 56,000 in 1986 went well beyond that point.

The shortage of good officers was especially pronounced at the battalion level, a critical problem given that a battalion commander was usually the senior local commander. The Salvadoran military had not developed enough officers in preceding years to staff so many battalions, and the officers whom it had produced had been screened according to the wrong criteria and given inappropriate training and education. Only occasionally had the old system yielded excellent officers, like Ochoa and Monterrosa. The deficiencies in initiative, dedication, and integrity among field-grade officers also had deep roots in culture and personality, making them especially difficult to remedy. The officers who could be improved dramatically by excellent Salvadoran leaders and American advisers were the younger ones, and they required years of cultivation and experience before they could occupy key commands. Colonel Duryea overstated the case in saying that it would take twenty years to produce adequate battalion commanders—the American advisory effort had begun five years earlier, and it does not necessarily take twenty-five or even twenty years to produce a good battalion commander. But it usually takes at least ten or fifteen. Those desirous of building brand-new security forces in the third world, and those who would criticize them, should take note.

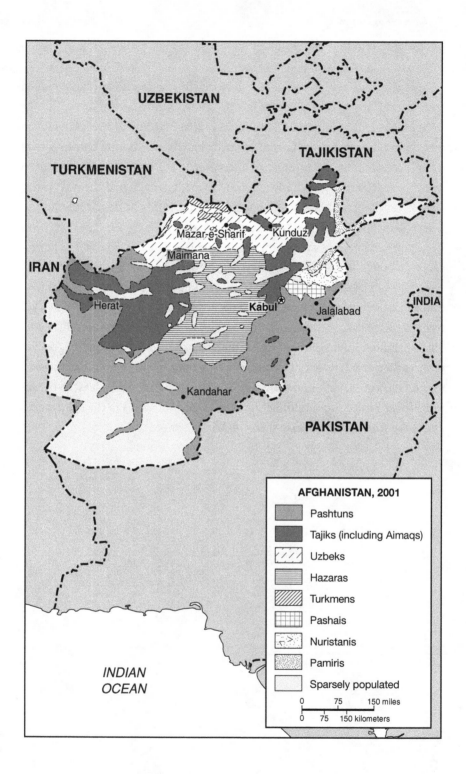

UZBEKISTAN

TURKMENISTAN

TAJIKISTAN

IRAN

Mazar-e-Sharif

Kunduz

Maimana

Herat

Kabul

Jalalabad

INDIA

Kandahar

PAKISTAN

INDIAN
OCEAN

AFGHANISTAN, 2001

Pashtuns

Tajiks (including Aimaqs)

Uzbeks

Hazaras

Turkmens

Pashais

Nuristanis

Pamiris

Sparsely populated

| 0 | 75 | 150 miles |

| 0 | 75 | 150 kilometers |

CHAPTER 9

The War in Afghanistan

The path to the catastrophic attacks of September 11, 2001, winds through the Soviet invasion of Afghanistan in 1979 and the ensuing Soviet-Afghan War. Intent on bleeding the Soviets, the United States supplied arms to the Islamic rebels of diverse motives and morals who waged bitter war on the Soviets and their Afghan allies across the 1980s. The Soviets and the Communist Afghan government, neither of them hindered by a free press or a voting public, imposed draconian punishments on the insurgency's civilian supporters but failed to break the insurgents' will, so the bloodshed dragged on. The first people to have their collective will broken were the Soviets, who withdrew their forces from Afghanistan in 1989. But the war did not end there. Afghan Communists retained control of the government, and they continued to fight the insurgents for another three years before succumbing to enemy blows. By the time the Afghan Communist government was vanquished, the Soviet Union itself had perished, and because of its demise, American assistance to the rebels had ended. Whether continued American aid could have saved the rebels from themselves is, however, doubtful.

Once the Afghan Communists had been dethroned, the rebels turned their weapons on each other. Young warlords, emerging at the helms of rival factions, seized control of resources and public services, trafficked in narcotics, made lucrative businesses of extortion, and committed atrocities against their opponents. Pakistan, Saudi Arabia, Russia, and Iran backed the factions that they considered most conducive to their own security concerns. Eventually the Pakistanis and Saudis settled on a group of Pashtuns called the Taliban, grim enforcers of a legal code that combined the most extreme elements of the Quran and traditional tribal law. The Taliban tortured men whose beards were insufficiently long, beheaded women who did not wear burqas, and sawed off the arms of thieves. By combating criminals and warlords, they held out the promise of order restored, which was alluring to people tired of omnipresent extortion, theft, and violence. Between 1994 and 1996, Taliban fighters subdued most of the warlords and gained control of the national government, in the process committing numerous atrocities against non-Pashtuns. They were unable, however, to vanquish the Northern Alliance, a collection of Tajik warlords supported by Russia and Iran. The Pashtun population's initial admiration of the Taliban, moreover, eventually turned to sullen resignation, and in some cases armed opposition, as the full weight of Taliban justice crashed down on them.[1]

In 1996 the Taliban welcomed into Afghanistan the Saudi terrorist Osama bin Laden and his Al Qaeda followers, whose variant of radical Islam was similar to the Taliban's. It seemed a perfect partnership—Al Qaeda needed sanctuary from foreign counterterrorists, and the Taliban needed Al Qaeda's help in combating the Northern Alliance. But the marriage did not end in happiness. For a few years, bin Laden was able to perpetrate terrorist attacks against American targets without sparking U.S. intervention in Afghanistan, but the attacks of September 11 were too horrific to be ignored. The shocking collapse of the World Trade Center and the deaths at the Pentagon and Shanksville, Pennsylvania, prompted the administration of George W. Bush to send the Taliban an ultimatum: hand over bin Laden and the other Al Qaeda leaders harbored in Afghanistan or face the wrath of the U.S. military. The Taliban's rejection of American demands sealed their fate.

With American interest in Afghanistan's internal affairs rejuvenated, the United States forged a military partnership with the Northern Alliance. In the months leading up to September 2001, the Northern Alliance's armed forces had been pushed into two mountainous areas of northern Afghanistan. They had just 12,000 fighters and 10,000 militiamen left, compared to the Taliban's 50,000 regulars and 40,000 militiamen. American air power, however, more than overcame that disparity in the offensive that the Americans and the Northern Alliance launched together in early October. American B-52 and B-1B bombers and F/A-18 fighters began the onslaught by depositing precision-guided munitions onto Taliban air defenses, command-and-control centers, and airfields. A week of unrelenting bombing reduced the power centers of the military and the government to smoking holes in the ground and caused the death or desertion of huge numbers of Taliban troops. Northern Alliance forces, accompanied by 350 U.S. Special Forces soldiers and 100 CIA officers, then advanced on the ground, supported by AC-130U Spectre gunships and other aircraft lurking in the skies. On November 9, the Taliban's defenses in the north began collapsing, and the capital city of Kabul, perched among the mountains more than one mile above sea level, fell on November 13. The Taliban leaders fell back on Kandahar, their spiritual home, but had to surrender it on December 6. In company with their Al Qaeda compadres, they fled into the mountains of eastern Afghanistan, with some continuing on to Pakistan.[2]

At a U.N.-brokered conference of Afghan political groups in Bonn, Hamid Karzai was selected to head a provisional Afghan government. A Pashtun, Karzai commanded widespread respect as the son of Abdul Ahad Karzai, a prominent political figure and chief of the Popolzai tribe until his assassination by the Taliban in 1999. During the war against the Soviets, Hamid Karzai had gone to Pakistan, where he served as a leader of a moderate nationalist group. He had worked to obtain foreign funding for the anti-Soviet rebels, although he was uncomfortable with the Islamic fanaticism he saw in some of the other Afghan factions that were backing rebels. The Americans involved in financing and supplying Afghan rebels took a liking to Karzai because he had a pleasing personality, spoke English, and espoused a moderate nationalism that differed sharply from the extremism of other Afghan elites. Karzai made a number of trips to Afghanistan to conduct military operations, but he was mainly a political leader, not a military leader. Following the fall of the Afghan Communist government in 1992, Karzai became deputy foreign minister, remaining in Kabul until 1994, when the crumbling of the government convinced him to return to Pakistan. The rise of the Taliban at first struck him as a positive development because of their commitment to law and order, but within a few months he soured on them as news of their fanatical cruelty spread.

A few days after the September 11 attacks, Karzai reentered Afghanistan and organized armed resistance against the Taliban. He remained in the country while other Afghans debated in Bonn, although he did speak to the conference by satellite phone from the mud house serving as his temporary quarters. Flown by U.S. military aircraft to Bagram a few days after the Taliban's surrender, Karzai drove to the Arg Palace in the dark of night, without any of the fanfare that his supporters had recommended. He quietly took up the duties of chief of state the next day. Karzai called for national unity and reconciliation, believing that most of the Taliban's followers had been duped into joining and ought to be forgiven. While vowing to apprehend those "who still use the Taliban cover to disturb peace and security in the country," Karzai promised amnesty to "the ordinary Taliban who are real and honest sons of this country."[3]

The United States and its allies did not deploy large occupation forces to Afghanistan, out of concern that it would arouse xenophobia or put the U.S. military into the nation-building business that President Bush had foresworn in the presidential campaign of 2000. To run the country and combat the remnants of the Taliban and Al Qaeda, therefore, the United States and Karzai had to rely on the warlords who had fought the Soviets and then each other and then the Taliban. These individuals received control of the provincial governments and filled numerous jobs in the ministries in Kabul, with ominous consequences for the nation's future. Time had done little to alter the character of these warlords; many were vicious men who put personal gain before the good of the country, committed atrocities, engaged in mobster activities, and showed an inability to cooperate with others. The warlords backed Karzai as interim president because he did not have a militia of his own and hence could not push them around.[4]

The United States and its Western allies funded the enlargement of the warlord militia forces, which were renamed the Afghan Militia Forces (AMF). Within six months, the warlords had over forty divisions and several dozen separate brigades, with a total of 200,000 men, far more than the national armed forces. Although the militias advanced the government's cause in some areas by providing security and jobs for the local people, too often they produced alienation through their criminal activities and abuses of power. Worries about the dubious character of the AMF's leaders soon prompted Afghanistan's foreign patrons to seek the subordination of the militias to Karzai's government, which the warlords opposed successfully for some time.[5]

The United States eventually skirted this opposition by convincing the warlords to take leadership positions in the police and move their troops from the AMF into the police forces. By this route, Northern Alliance warlords came to dominate the leadership of the police, and they coalesced in resisting efforts by the Interior Ministry in Kabul to exercise authority over them. The ministry's efforts became more assertive in January 2003, when Karzai replaced the ineffectual interior minister, Taj Mohammed, with Ali Jalali. Vowing to make major improvements in the police and the rest of the ministry, Jalali made police chiefs and provincial governors out of people who were neither members of the Northern Alliance nor warlords. He was unable, however, to pry the Northern Alliance from the trenches they had dug for themselves within the ministry. Although he replaced twenty-two of thirty-two provincial governors, most of those whom he fired became leaders in other provinces on account of political pressure from the warlords and their foreign patrons. Many of Ali Jalali's attempts to bring new blood into the police leadership and the ministry's headquarters were likewise stymied.[6]

When the major foreign powers had divided key reconstruction tasks among themselves, responsibility for the police went to the Germans, who, it was hoped, could impart some of their Teutonic precision and efficiency to the Afghans. The Germans set up a program to train a small number of police chiefs for three years, providing a course similar to that given to German police officers. The Germans later explained that their plan was "to start with the backbone, that's why we started with the leaders."[7] In principle, the German approach made good sense, but it did not align with Afghan realities. The training program was too long and the number of trainees too small to meet the urgent demand for capable police leaders. As Robert Finn, the American ambassador to Afghanistan until November 2003, observed, "The Germans produced a program to produce German police, which will be perfect in four years, but everybody will be dead by then."[8] The Germans put a ceiling of 62,000 on the police force by using the same ratio of police to citizens that existed in Germany, failing to take into account that Germany had a far higher population density and that no armed militias were assassinating government officials or torturing unfriendly civilians in Bavaria or Saxony. Afghanistan was left with fewer police forces per capita than any other country in the region, and far fewer than Iraq.[9]

In November 2003 the United States hired private security contractors to produce rank-and-file policemen quickly and in large quantities, directing them to establish police training centers with condensed nine-week training programs. Thirty-two thousand new policemen were pushed through training by the end of 2004 and 71,000 by July 2007. Outside observers often found fault with the private contractors responsible for training, characterizing many as "cowboys" who were much more interested in thrills and money than in rescuing the indigenous government. Their police training programs were short not only in duration but also in substance, and they failed to identify strong candidates for leadership. As one observer said, "The Germans are creating high quality—but too few. . . . The other side, the U.S., churns out a conveyor belt where quality is not an issue."[10]

General Muhammad Fahim, who had led the Northern Alliance army to victory over the Taliban, assumed the critical position of defense minister in the Karzai government. He turned the ministry into a house of corruption, with himself as the top beneficiary. An ethnic Tajik like most of the Northern Alliance commanders, Fahim packed the officer corps with Tajiks. Of the thirty-eight generals whom he appointed to the new General Staff, thirty-seven were of Tajik ethnicity. In 2003, American pressure caused the ministry to institute ethnic quotas in the officer corps and to bring back into service non-Tajik professional officers with British or Soviet military training. It was one of the few American initiatives the Afghans neither thwarted nor diluted; within three years, the army's ethnic makeup mirrored that of the country as a whole. The quota system put some fine Pashtun officers on the government side and enabled the government to recruit more Pashtuns into the army. But it also entailed placing ethnicity above merit in some cases and consequently led to the advancement of some weak non-Tajik officers.[11]

The Afghan civil service received less attention than the police or army, and soon after the war it reached an advanced condition of chaos. In 2002, spurred on by the World Bank, the Afghan government promulgated a public administration reform program that featured merit-based recruitment and appointment as well as bureaucratic streamlining. But the official rhetoric and instruction failed to curb the Afghan preference for dispensing civil service appointments to family members, friends, and political allies. Government officials cheated the merit-based processes by divulging recruitment test answers to their preferred candidates and by various other scams. Top-level officials who should have prevented such behavior condoned it and sometimes engaged in it themselves. Lamented one ministry employee, "I think in this ministry nobody wants real changes, because even the minister wants to put his own relatives into positions."[12]

The limbs of the new government had precious little time to grow strong before they had to grapple with subversion. In September 2002, insurgents commenced improvised explosive device (IED) attacks and rocket and mortar bombardments, at first concentrating on U.S. bases and subsequently striking at the Afghan government and its supporters. Recruited in Afghanistan and Pakistan and provided covert aid and sanctuary by the Pakistani government, the insurgents lacked unified leadership and common long-term objectives and thus could be said to constitute multiple insurgencies. Among the ranks of the insurgents stood not only members of the former Taliban government and remnants of Al Qaeda but also rebellious Pashtun groups like the Haqqani Network and Hezb-e Islami Gulbuddin. Some of these groups were concerned only with local or national politics or the removal of American forces from Afghanistan while others desired a global Islamic holy war. Because of the difficulty of distinguishing the various factions from one another, their opponents gave them the umbrella name of "neo-Taliban."[13]

Concentrated in Pashtun areas, the neo-Taliban fed off Pashtun resentment of the Tajiks of the Northern Alliance, some of whom had pillaged, raped, and murdered in Pashtun communities in late 2001 and 2002 in retaliation for past Taliban atrocities. Many Pashtuns thought that Karzai, though himself a Pashtun, had given too much governmental power to the Tajiks. As in the early 1990s, the insurgents appealed to people's desire for order, offering deliverance from lawlessness fostered by the inadequacies of the government. All of these factors drove tribal elders and other local elites into insurgency, and they brought with them the other elements of society, who tended to choose the side taken by the elites whom they most respected.[14]

Karzai did not at first take the insurgent threat with sufficient seriousness. In 2004 he pressed for inclusion of former Taliban members in the new Afghanistan, asserting that the only dangerous people were 150 or so hard-core Taliban who had ties with Al Qaeda. His lenience allowed subversives time and space to prepare for intensified armed activities. At the local level, the warlord-dominated militia and police forces demonstrated neither the will nor the capability to prevent the growth of insurgency, and foreign forces and Afghan National Army soldiers were far too few in number and too short on information to fill the void left by police and militia units that were worthless or worse. The rapid defeat of the Taliban army in 2001 had convinced American prophets of technological advancement that new technologies had enabled the United States to find and destroy its enemies from the air, making large ground forces unnecessary, but the neo-Taliban easily avoided detection by America's high-tech intelligence and surveillance devices. They possessed no heavy equipment or tanks that were obvious from the air, nor did they wear uniforms that distinguished them from the rest of the population.[15]

Slowly the insurgents spread into the villages, killing or driving away government personnel and supporters while forming shadow governments. Free to attack at times and locations of their choosing, guerrillas struck superior forces at sites from which a quick and untraceable getaway could be made. For the counterinsurgents, this state of affairs carried a strong risk of crippling morale and stimulating indiscriminate violence against the civilian population, a risk that could be averted only through sound leadership. As Colonel Bernd Horn, commander of the 1st Battalion of the Royal Canadian Regiment during the first years of the conflict, explained: "The inability to hit back can cause the soldiers to feel impotent. It can build frustration, fear and a sense of futility, if not hopelessness. When casualties occur, particularly deaths, morale is dealt another severe blow. As such, the leadership challenge to maintain the aim and mission focus, as well as the overall initiative in the campaign, is immense and critically important. Coupled with the need to sustain morale, particularly in light of the factors aforementioned, is the leader's role in ensuring that soldiers continue to practice a healthy outlook in regards to the local population."[16]

Most of the U.S. forces in Afghanistan during the first stages of the insurgency arrived with little, if any, knowledge of counterinsurgency. They therefore did a lot of learning by doing. Commanders with creativity, flexibility, judgment, and initiative figured out quickly how to swim in the unfamiliar waters into which they had been thrown. Lieutenant General David W. Barno, who took command of all coalition forces in Afghanistan in October 2003, said, "Our forces in the field once again demonstrated their remarkable ability to adjust to changing situations with only general guidance—and deliver results. When I asked a superb battalion commander how, in the absence of doctrine, he was able to shift his leaders toward a largely new COIN [counterinsurgency] approach in the middle of their combat tour, he laughed and said: 'Easy, sir—Books-A-Million.Com!' Reading classic counterinsurgency texts in the field became a substitute for official doctrine."[17]

Afghanistan's kaleidoscopic physical and human landscapes heightened the importance of adaptivity and further reduced the value of doctrine. Captain Jeremy Turner, a company commander in the 82nd Airborne Division in Kandahar, commented that insurgent and counterinsurgent methods varied widely from place to place because "the mountainous terrain acts to isolate populations from one another, creating different paradigms within each valley. In one valley, there may be a heated rivalry between two warlords of different tribes or subtribes. . . . In the next valley, those two warlords may be virtual unknowns, and, instead, drug trafficking and smuggling could be a major problem. . . . In the next, it could be corruption in the police force, and in another area, the problem may be hard-core jihadists and Taliban forces."[18]

Not all American commanders adjusted well to the new environment. It was not because they were in general poor leaders; they were, in fact, among the most carefully selected officers in the country's history. The American armed services, having become relatively small, all-volunteer forces after the Vietnam War, had in recent years maintained high entrance standards for officer candidates. In the wake of the Vietnam War, promotion and command selection had been centralized, taking decisions away from individual senior officers and giving them to boards of officers that reached decisions based on written evaluations, which stopped senior officers from advancing their protégés and members of their organizational cliques ahead of more deserving officers. In addition, staff officers and noncommissioned officers were better prepared than in the past to carry out leadership tasks that might be neglected or botched by a weak commander, although this improvement did not by any means obviate the need for a strong commander.[19]

The problem was that many commanders, especially in the regular army, were deficient in flexibility, creativity, and other attributes of greater value in counterinsurgency than in conventional warfare. The importance of those attributes could be seen in the contrast between Special Forces officers, who often possessed them, and regular army officers, who often did not. Near the American base at Bagram, the author Robert D. Kaplan found Special Forces officers working closely with the local Afghans, wearing beards to gain status with them, and thriving on rapid decentralized operations. The leaders of the army regulars, by contrast, kept their troops inside large bases, forbade the wearing of beards, placed restrictions on operations in order to reduce the risk of casualties, and instituted lengthy bureaucratic processes that forced the delay or cancellation of numerous operations.[20]

Early in the war, commanders lacking flexibility and creativity tended to operate from a few large bases, from which their troops flew out for large operations lasting a week or two and then flew back. These raids inflicted significant losses on the insurgents but failed to stop them from recruiting new members and increasing the strength of the insurgency. When Lieutenant General Barno took command of the coalition forces, he concluded that many of the commanders in the provinces needed to shift to the mission of population security. He assigned American units control of specific geographic areas and instructed them to send small detachments into Afghan villages to live among the people and patrol relentlessly. This change put commanders in a much better position to combat the insurgents, but it did not guarantee that they would destroy them—ultimate success still required commanders with the right attributes.[21]

Among the more imaginative of the American initiatives in Afghanistan was the creation of the eighty-person Provincial Reconstruction Teams, which the U.S. Army established in 2002 to alleviate the poor governance and unemployment that were helping the insurgents gain traction with the population. Intended to marshal the full range of counterinsurgency expertise in the U.S. government, they were composed of armed soldiers and members of U.S. civilian agencies who were responsible for all types of nonmilitary counterinsurgency activities. The teams were placed in the right provinces—those with the highest potential to become insurgent breeding grounds—but they were based near provincial capitals, which sharply restricted their clout in the countryside.[22]

The Provincial Reconstruction Teams attempted to build relationships with local Afghan leaders, both official and unofficial, which required not only good social skills but also considerable patience. "Winning over a population is, in part, winning over the leadership," said Captain Dennis Sugrue. "You do this through developing relationships. One thing that won me a lot of ground initially was sitting and spending two hours to conduct a 10-minute meeting. That's difficult for Americans to do."[23] The teams gave local Afghan leaders much of the responsibility for distributing aid. At times this delegation did more harm than good—the aid did not always make the trip from the leader's warehouse to the homes of the intended recipients, and the power to dispense it strengthened warlords known for corruption, drug trafficking, and human rights violations. To their credit, some Provincial Reconstruction Team commanders were able to effect the removal of governors and police chiefs who misused the aid. Unfortunately, the replacements were frequently no better.[24]

In 2003 and 2004, U.S. military advisers and aid helped eliminate many of the problems in the Afghan National Army. The Americans struggled, however, to find good leaders and pull the Afghan leadership away from the highly centralized command model that had been learned from the Soviets.[25] The United States and its foreign allies had very little success in fixing the pieces of the Afghan government that lay outside the Ministry of Defense. As part of its global war against illicit narcotics, the U.S. government tried to help the

Afghans reduce opium output. Afghan farmers and the warlords who served as middlemen were drawn to opium farming because profits went as high as US$1,000 per kilogram, as opposed to $1 per kilogram for rice or wheat. Much of that profit ended up in the pockets and bank accounts of the neo-Taliban, who pulled in hefty fees for protecting opium farming and trafficking, and corrupt government officials, who accepted bribes to look the other way. In May 2004 the United States assisted the Interior Ministry in establishing a Central Poppy Eradication Force, whose staff of 700 were trained by the private security company DynCorp, and directed funds to provincial governors for poppy eradication. Yet Afghanistan's opium production continued to rise.[26]

The police continued to flicker dimly, but did shine in a few areas because of the talent of outstanding leaders. The best was the police chief in the northern steppe city of Mazar-i-Sherif, home of the blue-tiled tomb of the fourth caliph. Few places in Afghanistan presented so tangled and complicated a web of human interaction as Mazar-i-Sherif. Pashtuns, Uzbeks, Tajiks, Hazaras, and Turkmens all mingled and connived while Russia, Iran, and China probed and plotted in pursuit of their own interests. When Muhammad Akrem Khakrez-wal became the city's police chief, he stamped out widespread violence and crime with remarkable speed by putting police on the streets and gaining the cooperation of every ethnic group. Highly sociable, he cultivated relationships with the ethnic leaders and studiously avoided any semblance of corruption, knowing that it would demolish those relationships. He later became chief of police in Kabul and seemed headed to be the next minister of the interior when he was assassinated during a trip to Kandahar, apparently by Pakistanis operating in league with the Kandahar governor, a notorious warlord named Gul Agha Shirzai.[27]

On October 9, 2004, the Afghan people voted Karzai into power as the first permanent president of the new Afghanistan. No longer was Karzai at the mercy of warlords, or at least not entirely. Karzai fired his most powerful and troublesome minister, Defense Minister Fahim, and wrested control of the militia forces in the Kabul area from the Northern Alliance. For his new defense minister, Karzai selected General Abdul Rahim Wardak, a capable professional soldier of Western orientation. He relieved other warlords from provincial governorships, militia commands, and leadership positions in the central ministries. Some of these individuals went to unimportant, face-saving desk jobs, but Karzai assigned a large number of others to important commands, albeit in areas remote from their original preserves. Many warlords, moreover, refused to subordinate themselves and their supporters—some of whom were still in militias—to the new central government. They foiled efforts to transform militia forces into National Army forces by sending the central government and the coalition their weakest troops and their most dilapidated weapons. Fearing heavy bloodshed, Karzai rejected the idea of bringing these warlords into line by force.[28]

In 2005 the neo-Taliban gained momentum as fighters and supplies streamed in from Pakistan. Not until 2006, however, did the frenzy truly begin. The average number of insurgent incidents per month hit 600 in 2006, up from 130 per month the previous year. The neo-Taliban perpetrated 139 suicide attacks in 2006, compared with 17 in 2005. Viewing education as a critical weapon of the counterinsurgents, the neo-Taliban killed teachers and students and torched schools. In an unprecedented show of audacity, the insurgents placed mines near U.S. and NATO outposts. Insurgent forces gathered in large numbers for assaults on government and foreign military forces and in a few cases stepped into pitched battles.[29]

The booming opium industry provided the neo-Taliban with the means to buy the services of thousands of Afghans in 2006. Exploiting widespread unemployment, they co-opted tribal leaders by offering to pay tribesmen who joined their forces between US$200 and US$600 per month, far more alluring than the US$50 or US$60 per month that policemen and soldiers earned. Another leading cause of increased support for the insurgents remained the misbehavior of government personnel. The most commonly cited grievances against government leaders were favoritism toward certain tribes, preferential dispensation of land and water, physical abuse, and theft of state property and money.[30]

Adding to the government's problems at this time was a wholesale change of ministerial leadership. In early 2006 nearly all of the cabinet ministers left, either because Karzai ousted them or because they had become disillusioned with the Karzai government. A large majority of the departing ministers were experienced technocrats intent on improving the government, whereas their replacements were novices inclined to defer to Karzai. Critics said that Karzai made the changes because he wanted a weak cabinet of yes-men whom he could keep in his palm. Karzai said that he was merely meeting the demands of the newly elected parliament. Fortunately for Afghanistan, one key minister survived the purge, Defense Minister Wardak. His continued presence ensured that the Afghan National Army remained the country's most competent and least abusive entity in the years to come.

In 2006, the Afghan National Army continued to improve in quality, but major leadership deficiencies remained. U.S. advisers often took command of Afghan army units because of the gross inadequacy of their Afghan officers.[31] Where the Afghan police had adequate leaders, they performed reasonably well, often providing NATO forces with intelligence in exchange for supplies, equipment, money, and other items that the Interior Ministry failed to provide.[32] As before, however, good police leaders were scarce. The civilian population consistently reported the police to be the principal perpetrators of robbery, kidnapping, and other crimes. Police routinely took bribes to release prisoners or to turn a blind eye to drug trafficking, and at checkpoints they shook down truck drivers and arrested innocent civilians to hold for ransom. Police chiefs either directed the nefarious activities or allowed subordinates to provide the direction, and they forced local policemen of integrity to participate by threatening to fire them if they did not.[33]

Foreign patrons, distraught at the police's appalling behavior, compelled the Ministry of the Interior to implement a police reform program in 2006. The program mandated that corrupt and inept policemen be removed and that the bloated officer corps be cut in size. Because senior police positions had been disbursed liberally as political favors, field-grade and general officers outnumbered sergeants, so huge numbers of colonels and generals had to be removed and the number of rank-and-file patrolmen had to be increased by nearly 10,000. The review board that evaluated officers took into consideration their experience, ethnic diversity, interviews, and a written examination designed to test analytical abilities, ethics, and management style. The police officers rated highest kept their jobs; the others were demoted or fired. This process weeded out large numbers of poor officers but did little to improve the overall quality of police leadership. Karzai repeatedly circumvented the system in order to protect officers with records of human rights abuses, corruption, or incompetence, because of political or personal considerations or, according to some accusers, bribery. International outcries forced Karzai to get rid of some of these people, but not enough. In another gesture of reform that was more flimflam than fix, Karzai agreed to set up a board to approve senior leadership appointments but brought few appointments to this board for approval.[34] As a senior Ministry of the Interior official remarked in late

2006, "It is very difficult to make progress when people are appointed based on personal connections. We try to hire professional police based on merit but we are not able to. There is political pressure from senior officials to hire their relatives and friends."[35]

In response to pressure from NATO countries, Karzai fired several provincial leaders in the south and replaced them with more reputable individuals. Some of the new leaders, however, turned out to be as inept as their predecessors had been corrupt. And as usual, some of the unsavory officials whom Karzai relieved ended up in positions of authority elsewhere. Karzai did make a major step forward when he fired the chief justice of the Afghan Supreme Court, Fazel Hady Shinwari, an atrociously corrupt man whom Karzai had appointed as part of a political deal with an Islamic leader. During the ensuing six months, the new chief justice, Abdul Salam Azimi, fired or imprisoned eight judges and four clerks on grounds of corruption and investigated 6,000 questionable cases. Karzai also appointed a new attorney general, who prosecuted corrupt government officials and fired corrupt prosecutors.[36] On the other hand, Karzai's Anti-Corruption and Bribery Office, which had a staff of 140 people, did not convict a single person in 2006. Karzai failed to prosecute or remove any of the numerous drug traffickers in his cabinet and parliament. Among those widely believed to be involved in corruption was Karzai's own brother, Ahmed Wali Karzai, a government official in Kandahar. Western officials repeatedly advised the president to send his brother out of the country, to no avail.[37]

In 2006, foreign governments, the United Nations, and international charities poured money into social and economic programs aimed at mitigating the problems of poverty and isolation in the hope that they would make the people less receptive to the neo-Taliban. But no amount of spending could make up for the poor quality of the Afghan administrators and policemen in the provinces. "Schools or clinics are useless if people hate the district level administration," an Afghan civil society representative said.[38] Nor could it make up for the inability of the government to protect them from insurgents, criminals, and wicked policemen. As an Afghan researcher in southern Afghanistan remarked, "People don't care if the roads built are paved with gold. They would rather have security."[39] Afghans wanted to support the side that could bring order and defeat its armed rivals—and often that side was the neo-Taliban.[40]

NATO military forces were more visible in 2006 than in past years, although many labored under severe restrictions from their governments, preventing them from participating in combat or operating in areas of insurgent activity. NATO commanders received ten pages listing all the restrictions, and they had to obtain clearance from home capitals before employing NATO forces in certain types of missions.[41] Still, NATO was able to put its least restricted forces—those of the United States, Canada, the United Kingdom, and the Netherlands—in the places where they could be most useful. Thousands of Canadian and British troops moved into southern Afghanistan to combat the neo-Taliban insurgents where they were strongest. Dispersing among the population, the Canadians and British weakened the neo-Taliban's grip through military operations and community development. In the middle of 2006 insurgent forces in the south responded with large attacks, compelling the Canadians and British to concentrate their forces for major combat. Although this concentration of troops undermined Canadian and British control of the population, it led to big battles that produced heavy insurgent casualties, frustrated an insurgent plan to seize the city of Kandahar, and ultimately permitted Canadian and British forces to return to population control operations under more favorable circumstances than those prevailing when they left.[42]

Lieutenant Colonel Ian Hope, commander of Canada's Task Force Orion in Kandahar from January to August 2006, recorded the leadership lessons he learned during the neo-Taliban offensive. "Operational tempo and effectiveness were almost entirely dependent upon the personalities of the commanders," Hope wrote. "I trusted the subordinate commanders to demonstrate an aggressive spirit and maintain operational initiative through offensive action. Not all people are equal in this regard and the Army must learn that robustness and determination are not nice-to-have qualities in manoeuvre commanders; they are core qualities, and we must work hard to select the few who have the tenacity to sustain a high level of resolve in the face of danger." Summing up the unit's experience, Hope stated, "Under the baking Afghan sun we are rediscovering, by way of pain, that the first determinants in war are human. In combat, the power of personality, intellect and intuition, determination, and trust outweigh the power of technology, and everything else. This stark reminder comes after 30 years of the Canadian Army following obediently the lead of our allies in combat development and falling victim to the seduction of the microchip."[43]

The counterinsurgents killed an estimated 3,500 neo-Taliban in 2006, yet the insurgents appear to have replaced all of their losses through recruitment in Afghanistan and infiltration of insurgents from Pakistan. They entered 2007 with an armed strength estimated at 7,000 to 12,000. Insurgent attacks in 2007 outpaced those of the previous year, with most coming in the form of guerrilla warfare or terrorism — the insurgents had learned the futility of provoking large battles. The neo-Taliban continued to enlarge the area under their control in the south while simultaneously expanding their presence in the north, northeast, and west.[44]

In 2007 the Afghan National Army improved further under the guidance of Defense Minister Wardak and the influence of U.S. military advisers. The police continued to flounder, even though the United States ponied up $2.5 billion for the police and shifted hundreds of U.S. advisers from the army to the police. Coalition forces and the Afghan army did not have enough troops to stay in large areas on a permanent basis, so once they cleared an area they usually had to turn it over to Afghan policemen, who were likely to lose it again. The pay of police officers was raised to seventy dollars per month, but it was still too meager to curb corruption or undermine the attractiveness of neo-Taliban salaries. According to one estimate, 80 percent of the police force was complicit in the drug trade during 2007. The government prosecuted several hundred small-time drug dealers and seized several heroin labs, but it convicted none of the drug-trafficking kingpins — the few dozen individuals who controlled the majority of the drug trade. Opium production increased by 34 percent over the previous year.[45]

Insurgent activity rose again in intensity in 2008, creeping further into northern and western Afghanistan even as the number of international troops increased to nearly 70,000, of whom 32,000 were Americans. The full extent of the neo-Taliban's growth was difficult to ascertain because the NATO forces in northern and western Afghanistan, still shackled by restrictions from their national governments, were not actively combating the insurgents. Their detachment notwithstanding, the Afghan counterinsurgents in the north fought doggedly against the neo-Taliban because the Afghan corps commander was an excellent leader, but the counterinsurgency languished in the west, where the corps commander was weak.[46]

Despite the ongoing improvements in the Afghan National Army, lack of initiative among army commanders remained a major problem in 2008. As in years past, U.S. advisers kept urging the Afghans to reduce the centralization of authority, but their words often bounced off their counterparts. Afghan field commanders remained reluctant to act without authorization from higher authorities, and senior commanders made critical decisions that should have

been made by the officers on the scene. In terms of personnel changes, political and ethnic considerations remained major obstacles. Colonel Jeffrey M.
Haynes, head of the U.S. Marine advisory group in Afghanistan in 2008, remarked, "The number one challenge for the Afghan National Army is the fact
that corps and brigade commanders cannot readily make officer personnel
moves without having to consider ethnic group and the Ministry of Defense
approval process. This makes it very difficult for the corps commander to put
the most qualified officers in command positions."[47] Only one of the Afghan
National Army's forty-nine battalions was deemed capable of conducting all
of its functions independently. Another eighteen were considered capable of
performing all functions with foreign assistance, usually in logistics, intelligence, or planning, while fifteen were considered competent at some functions
with foreign support.[48]

At the highest levels, the United States was giving the Ministry of the Interior the attention that the Ministry of Defense had received in prior years,
with American diplomats and military officers filling advisory roles where
Europeans had performed inadequately in times past. The Americans beseeched and pressured Karzai and the minister of the interior to relieve bad
police chiefs, and they did obtain some replacements. With the assistance of
the United States and other foreign allies, the Ministry of the Interior organized a program called Focused District Development, in which the ministry
temporarily inserted elite police forces into an area and withdrew the existing police for vetting and training. Most of the leaders were ousted from the
existing forces because they were incompetent or abusive or had shown par-
tiality toward their own tribes in enforcing the law. The central government,
not the provincial governors or other local power brokers, selected the new
police chiefs, and it purposefully chose men who did not have local connections in order to prevent tribal favoritism. In many instances, the entire police
force was replaced. Policemen were no longer paid through the governor but
received their paychecks directly, ending the governors' regular practice of
keeping cuts of policemen's pay for themselves. The preliminary results of the
Focused District Development program were mixed, with some reports indicating that it had improved police leadership and performance and others that
the new police leaders and units were little better than the old. Projected to
take five years to cover the country, the program was progressing gradually as
of mid-2008.[49]

Numerous civil servants in the provinces remained as guilty of corruption

and incompetence as the police despite new exhortations from Kabul to institute meritocracy and end abuses in the civil service.[50] Sarah Chayes, a former
National Public Radio reporter who took up residence in Afghanistan and became a confidante of top Afghan officials, noted that provincial officials from
a variety of ministries were creating enormous discontent through their misconduct. For example, health officials routinely gave the stamp of approval to
bad pharmaceuticals from Pakistan in exchange for bribes. When donors sent
good medicines to hospitals, the hospital officials sold them at the local bazaar
and used the bad Pakistani versions to treat the hospital patients. With officials
from the Education Ministry, it was commonplace to retain for personal use
the food that relief agencies had sent for local schoolchildren. According to
Chayes, "Every time any person has to interact with any government department, to get a driver's license, a death certificate, to register a cooperative, to
get goods out of customs, to run a business, you name it, a 'bribe' is extracted
at every step of the way. Then the person who got the lower-level agents their
jobs will come around at the end of the day to pick up his cut." Chayes believes
that Afghanistan has reservoirs of people outside government who could, with
foreign mentoring, provide the leadership required to set the country aright,
although she doubts that many will be willing to serve in the government as
long as the leadership in Kabul remains the same.[51]

Most of the government ministries in Kabul were still in the hands of
individuals without the necessary integrity or experience, who had received
their positions because of familial, tribal, or political connections. Doctor Sultana Parvanta, who resigned as planning director of Afghanistan's Ministry of
Urban Development and Housing because of disillusionment with the Karzai
government, blamed the leadership of the ministries for much of the rampant corruption. "The Afghans have a saying that no one can ask for bribes
and practice corruption in an office or institution if the boss is not approving
the deals and also taking a cut," she remarked. "These ministers are allowing
predatory practices." The West, Parvanta believes, ought to wield its influence
to bring better leaders into the central government. "We need competent, courageous, and honest leaders who have a vision and love for the country. This
dedication to the welfare of the people and the country must outweigh the love
for self, money, power, and benefits to a small group of people."[52]

Hamid Karzai's ascension to power after the fall of the Taliban illustrates
several leadership perils that may spring up elsewhere, in some other dis-

tant land where the West believes its interests to be at stake. Karzai was the sort of figure with whom Western diplomats and journalists felt comfortable—English-speaking, cultured, conciliatory, and gentle. But qualities that appealed to those cosmopolitan elites were not the qualities required to rule Afghanistan. As in South Vietnam in the 1950s and 1960s, the central government faced challenges to its authority from factions more concerned with self-aggrandizement than national solidarity, and taming these factions often required confrontation rather than conciliation, aggressiveness rather than gentleness.

Karzai, in league with Western countries that understood Afghanistan's elites only superficially, empowered warlords whose criminal tendencies and inability to govern opened the door to insurgency. The United States and its NATO allies belatedly identified the damage caused by warlord leadership and spent years coaxing Karzai and his ministers to dislodge the warlords from the government. Convincing the Afghans to fire leaders was exceeded in difficulty only by the task of identifying leaders who deserved to be hired. In a country ravaged by decades of cruelty and death, with only a faint heartbeat of nationalism, the supply of integrity and dedication was short, not merely in the warlord class but in all classes of society. Replacement leaders were often no better than their predecessors and, in many cases, were merely bad leaders who had been shuffled over from other jobs.

Western pressure caused the Afghans to adopt merit-based hiring and promotion systems, but these systems could work only with the cooperation of top Afghan leaders, and most of those leaders cooperated only partially or not at all. Karzai and his ministers steered friends, relatives, and political allies into leadership jobs, making cunning use of subterfuge to conceal their dishonesty from foreign onlookers, and they seldom rewarded officers who had distinguished themselves at lower levels of command by appointing them to higher positions of authority.[53] Although political considerations deserved to trump merit in some leadership appointments, merit could not be discounted too often without jeopardizing the viability of the state, which is what occurred under Karzai.

The Afghan National Police became a black hole for Western money and training programs. By paying minimal attention to leadership quality, the U.S. government and private security contractors ensured that the police would prey on the population and cower before the enemy. Bad police leadership also translated into high rates of desertion and absenteeism and the disappearance of equipment.[54] The princely sums of money thrown at social and economic development programs were largely squandered, too, because poor police leadership and poor administrative leadership resulted in corruption, mistreatment of civilians, lawlessness, and free rein for the insurgents to destroy development projects and kill government employees. The Focused District Development program has, in its early stages, achieved improvement in a portion of the targeted districts by replacing bad police chiefs with centrally selected officers lacking local tribal connections. Whether it will transform the police across the country has yet to be determined.

Over the course of the war, the United States and its allies have made much more headway with the Afghan National Army than with the police, principally because of Defense Minister Abdul Rahim Wardak, a shrewd man with a strong commitment to the betterment of the army's leadership. Foreign insistence on ethnic diversification of the officer corps has had a salutary effect as well, though of less importance. Breaking the Tajik stranglehold on the military leadership reduced Pashtun alienation with the government and attracted Pashtun military-age males to the armed forces, men who might otherwise have sided with the insurgents. In terms of leadership quality, the effects were mixed, for commands went not only to competent non-Tajiks who had been unfairly excluded but also to non-Tajiks who were less capable than the Tajiks they replaced.

Although the Afghan government managed to conceal some of its chicanery, the Americans were well aware that it regularly flouted the ideals of meritocracy in selecting its leaders. American personnel on the ground saw an urgent need to oust bad Afghan commanders—a startling 96 percent of the Afghanistan veterans surveyed in the 2008 Counterinsurgency Leadership Survey believed that the United States needed to do more to get the right Afghans into leadership positions.[55] In theory, the United States could have used its position as Afghanistan's principal benefactor to bully Karzai into enforcing merit-based personnel policies or to achieve Karzai's removal by means of a coup or forced resignation. But in reality the United States lacked the necessary leverage to compel Karzai to change, and it was unwilling to force him out. Countless pledges by the U.S. executive and legislative branches to protect Afghanistan had shown Karzai that the Americans would not make good on a threat of withdrawing aid, and countless professions of commitment to democracy and national sovereignty had shown that the United States would not remove him from office. The United States now must ask itself whether punctilious respect for democracy and national sovereignty is worth the death and destruction that flow from poor Afghan leadership. If it is not worth the cost, then the United States must seek new ways of bringing better national leadership to power in Kabul's lofty heights.

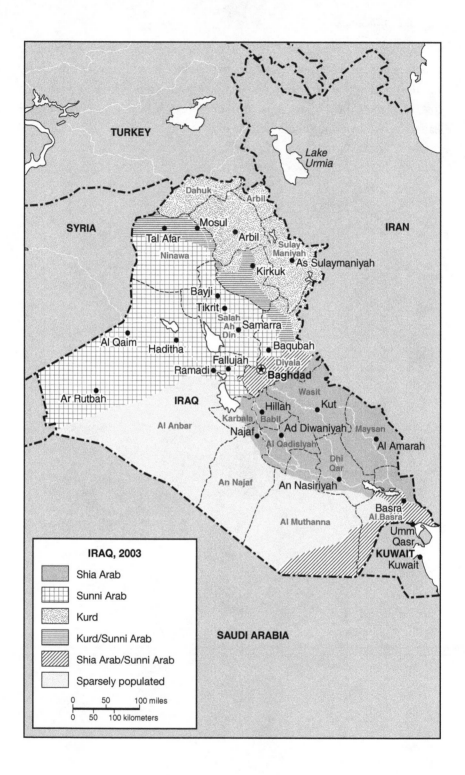

CHAPTER 10

The Iraq War

The United States had not yet perceived the gravity of the neo-Taliban menace when it embarked on another war that would make an unexpected turn into counterinsurgency. Extremely sensitive to terrorist threats after the 9/11 catastrophe, the Bush administration became convinced, from largely erroneous intelligence, that Iraq possessed weapons of mass destruction that could be transferred to Al Qaeda or other anti-American terrorists. Administration officials believed, moreover, that overthrowing President Saddam Hussein and holding elections for new Iraqi leaders would start a wave of democratization across the Middle East that would end governmental repression, an alleged catalyst of terrorism. This vision of a democratic Iraq had momentous and unintended consequences for the subsequent counterinsurgency.

The planning for the invasion of Iraq likewise held unseen ramifications for the counterinsurgents of the future. Because expeditionary military forces take many months to mobilize and transport across the world, the number of troops assigned to the invasion force would put a ceiling on how many forces could be assigned to occupation duty immediately after the war. Believing that technological advances had reduced the need for ground troops, Secretary of Defense Donald Rumsfeld sought to minimize the number of American troops sent to Iraq in order to hold down American costs and limit the American commitment. After haggling with the uniformed military, the Office of the Secretary of Defense settled on 145,000 ground troops, most of them American or British.

In September 2002, with the whirlwind of war drawing nearer, Rumsfeld assigned responsibility for postwar occupation planning to the Office of Special Plans, under the leadership of the undersecretary of defense for policy, Douglas Feith. The task demanded fine-tuned practical judgment and excellent organizational skills, neither of which could be found in Feith's possession. Feith devoted inordinate time to abstract theorizing and to the minutiae of memoranda while neglecting the basic tasks of managing his own organization, not to mention pulling together the resources of the U.S. government to run a country of 27 million people. Gary Schmitt, an associate of Feith's who shared his neoconservative political views, said that Feith "can't manage anything, and he doesn't trust anyone else's judgment."[1]

In January 2003, Rumsfeld and Feith created the Office of Reconstruction and Humanitarian Assistance (ORHA), which would go into Iraq immediately after the war to take control of governance and provide humanitarian relief. To head ORHA, they chose Jay Garner, a retired U.S. Army lieutenant general who had led Operation Provide Comfort, the relief effort that assisted Iraqi Kurds at the end of the 1991 Gulf War. Feith inserted a former law partner of his, Michael Mobbs, into the position of chief of civil administration for ORHA, even though Mobbs had no experience in this area. One member of Garner's staff said that Mobbs "couldn't have led a platoon."[2] Mobbs "didn't know what to do," commented a former ambassador. "He just cowered in his room most of the time."[3]

Garner planned to pay the salaries of Iraqi government and military employees after the war in order to keep the country running and ensure that Iraqis did the lion's share of the reconstruction work. Ten days before the invasion, Frank Miller of the National Security Council informed President George W. Bush that the Iraqi army and police would remain intact after the war and that only the top 1 or 2 percent of Saddam Hussein's Baath Party would be barred from service in the new Iraqi government. Bush and other top administration officials gave their approval to those plans.[4]

Rolling into Iraq on March 20, the coalition forces annihilated the Iraqi army in three weeks, suffering fewer than 200 fatalities while inflicting approximately 100 times that many on Iraq's armed forces. The world marveled at the power of the U.S. military, and Saddam Hussein went into hiding. Basking in the sunshine of victory, General Tommy Franks of Central Command predicted that a functioning Iraqi government would be in place within thirty to sixty days and that most American forces could be withdrawn within six months, for the Iraqis would be taking up most of the burden of reconstruction. Underlying these predictions was the assumption that Iraqis of all types would submit to the authority of the new Iraqi government and stay out of trouble.[5]

Iraq needed little time to depart from this script. Following the capitulation of Saddam Hussein's regime, law enforcement collapsed, and the people of Iraq, having no experience of freedom, reacted to their liberation by engaging in widespread looting, theft, and violence. Looters tore the innards out of government buildings, down to the water pipes. Others sawed down power lines and towers and sold the copper and aluminum in Iran or Kuwait. Anyone who drove a car ran a serious risk of being carjacked. American forces, so mighty in battle, did nothing to stop the petty mayhem because neither Franks nor ORHA nor Feith had provided directives or authorizations to restore order. As a consequence of the decision to keep the invasion force small, the U.S. military had few troops outside the largest metropolitan centers and was especially thin on the ground in Anbar province, heartland of the Sunni Arabs, the people who had long dominated the country's leadership and who therefore most resented the American conquest.[6]

Despondence took hold among Iraqis, who came to embrace the old Arab proverb "Better forty years of dictatorship than one day of anarchy."[7] Iraqi pleas to the Americans to impose martial law came to naught. At a meeting organized by Garner in late April, a tribal leader rose to his feet and said to the Americans, "We need a decision maker. We need you to appoint a government that can determine our future. We can't have this chaos. It is up to you to appoint somebody to do something."[8] But Garner and ORHA failed to take charge. Garner and his staff made little effort to identify or communicate with Iraqi leaders who could help calm the situation or Iraqi experts who could help restore essential services like electricity and water. The top British official in Iraq reported to London that ORHA "is an unbelievable mess. No leadership, no strategy, no coordination, no structure, and inaccessible to ordinary Iraqis."[9] Iraqis saw the chaos as evidence of American incompetence or malevolence, and many turned against the United States as it wore on.[10]

In late April, after receiving complaints that "Garner just isn't pulling things together," Bush relieved Garner and dissolved ORHA. He sent out L. Paul Bremer to head a new organization called the Coalition Provisional Authority (CPA), with a mandate to run the affairs of Iraq, employing American CPA staff and Iraqis of his choice, until the Iraqi people elected a permanent government. An experienced diplomat, Bremer looked a good deal younger than his sixty-one years of age, and he was by all accounts an energetic and tireless worker who displayed confidence and perseverance at times of crisis. Americans and Iraqis alike found him charismatic. Larry Diamond, a Stanford professor of political science who joined CPA, said of Bremer, "A skillful, take-charge leader, he would quickly come to be seen in Baghdad as a man in control. The contrast to the inarticulate, laissez-faire Garner could not have been more striking."[11]

Diamond also observed, however, that Bremer "was alternately (and at times simultaneously) engaging and domineering, charming and patronizing, informal and imperial, practical and inflexible, impressive in his grasp of detail and yet incessantly micromanaging."[12] Bremer's insistence on involving himself in low-level decisions produced lengthy delays in the disbursement of money for reconstruction projects, the equipping of Iraqi security forces, and the payment of Iraqi officials' salaries. He structured his organization poorly, creating isolated vertical lines of authority that prevented the different parts from working together. Bremer did not do well in choosing the people to run CPA, either, although this problem was in part the fault of officials in Washington who hired CPA staff members, for they did not aggressively recruit well-qualified personnel and in total sent only 600 hires to Iraq—far too few to oversee the multitudinous activities in CPA's charter. Much of the CPA staff consisted of young political appointees who possessed little to no relevant experience, and although some were highly dedicated and worked eighteen-hour days, others had little interest in the work and spent as much time as possible at bars and parties in the Green Zone, the heavily guarded neighborhood in central Baghdad where CPA was headquartered.[13] It is hard to imagine such a state of affairs prevailing under a stern and flinty leader like High Commissioner Gerald Templer in Malaya.

Bremer, in conjunction with Feith and other Pentagon civilians, made disastrous errors at the outset as a result of poor judgment and lack of empathy. Within ten days of arriving, Bremer announced two policies that he and Pentagon officials had masterminded: banning the four top layers of the Baath Party from governmental service and disbanding the Iraqi security forces. Inspired by the far-reaching de-Nazification program after World War II, the de-Baathification edict went well beyond what President Bush had approved, sweeping up not merely top executives but mid-level officials, schoolteachers, and physicians. As many as 100,000 government employees, most of them Sunnis, lost their jobs.[14]

In dissolving the Iraqi security forces, Bremer put out of work 385,000 members of the armed services and another 335,000 who had served in the police, presidential security units, or other internal security forces. Bremer and Walter Slocombe, a Clinton-administration undersecretary of defense, had decided to disband these forces and start from scratch in order to purge "Saddamism" and end Sunni dominance. Only after considerable damage had been done did Bremer agree to pay the discharged personnel, and he did not rehire most of them into the new armed forces, leaving them with no real commitment to the government and plenty of spare time to get into trouble.

U.S. military leaders in Iraq were furious at these two decisions, which Bremer had made without even consulting them. They argued that these policies needlessly swept away many of the Iraqis who, in the preceding weeks, had been industrious in getting the country back on its feet. American commanders on the ground were convinced that the leaders of Iraq's security forces had accepted their defeat and were willing to restore order in accordance with American designs as long as the Americans kept them in power and paid their salaries. Some of these Iraqis, in fact, had joined the Baath Party only because it had been a prerequisite for career advancement, and some of the best army officers had not even been Baathists, for the Baath Party frequently shunned officers with skill and drive as potential threats. American military officers also predicted that disfranchising all of the Saddam-era elites would drive men with leadership talent and military experience into armed rebellion, a prophesy that came true in a matter of months. Iraq's long-standing elites were in no mood to sit idly by while Americans and Shiites and Kurds took over leadership of the country. Unlike the Nazis in 1945, who had sustained enormous casualties and seen their homeland smashed in a world war spanning nearly six years, the Sunni elites had large reserves of manpower, and many were not convinced that they had been beaten militarily—the war had not even touched most of Iraq's territory. When insurgent violence erupted across Iraq in August 2003, it would be organized primarily by former Baath Party and security force leaders.[15]

De-Baathification and the disbandment of the Iraqi security forces destroyed a central element of the original American design for postwar Iraq, the reliance on Iraqi rather than American labor to carry out most reconstruction tasks. Without retaining hundreds of thousands who had served Saddam Hussein, it was impossible to field massive numbers of administrators, policemen, and soldiers within a few weeks or months. And creating leaders was a far more daunting proposition, given that nearly all of the experienced leaders had just been banned from service and that officers take years to produce.

Bremer could at least have sped up the construction process if he had been more discerning in selecting the Iraqis who would form the new governmental elite. Bremer's understanding of the various individuals and groups was handicapped by his refusal to consult American officials who had studied Iraq for many years, a refusal apparently rooted in those officials' skepticism about democratizing Iraq. Bremer gave key jobs to Iraqi exiles who seemed charming to uninitiated Westerners but who, in the opinion of most Iraqis and many Western experts, were hopelessly out of touch or were more concerned with sectarian or private interests than with national ones. Bremer and others in CPA also handed influential positions to Iraqi civil servants who had been ousted by Saddam, on the assumption that they had been removed because of principled opposition to the illiberal and inhumane practices of Saddam's regime. Ali Allawi, the interim Iraqi minister of defense during the CPA era, remarked, "One of the facts that later became established, often through bitter experience, was that not all those bureaucrats who had been sidelined were worthy of high office. Some had been dismissed for malpractice, corruption or incompetence." Concerned mainly with rapid increases in force size, CPA often allowed local politicians to select police and National Guard commanders and did not check the backgrounds or capabilities of those selected, many of whom were insurgent sympathizers or political hacks without leadership potential. A postmortem by the inspectors general of the State and Defense Departments found that in the initial development of the Iraqi Police Service (IPS), the focus on enrolling large numbers of recruits "overshadowed the need to ensure the IPS has effective, committed leadership." Nor did CPA remove many of the Iraqi leaders after they manifested their incompetence, corruption, or disloyalty.[16]

With CPA understaffed and concentrated in Baghdad, the widely stretched coalition military forces assumed by default most of the responsibility for resuscitating and running the country. U.S. military commanders served as mayors and city managers and economic planners and tried to involve Iraqis in local government, in some cases via elections. Bremer frequently countermanded decisions by local military commanders even though no CPA staff were on the scene to assess whether local realities justified those decisions. In addition, Bremer retained tight control over reconstruction money rather than delegating it to local commanders and was slow to dispense it, which military officers endlessly cited as a severe hindrance to reconstruction efforts.[17]

The U.S. armed forces in Iraq were not under Bremer's command but under that of Lieutenant General Ricardo Sanchez. Despite never having commanded above the division level before, Sanchez was given command of all U.S. forces in Iraq in June 2003, ahead of officers who ranked higher than him in seniority, relevant experience, and ability, apparently because top U.S. leaders thought that he would merely oversee a short and easy occupation. As fate would have it, Sanchez received the most important command in the U.S. military since the Vietnam War.

The *Washington Post*'s Tom Ricks aptly wrote of Sanchez, "The opinion of many of his peers was that he was a fine battalion commander who never should have commanded a division, let along a corps or a nationwide occupation mission." He spent too much time on little details. As a State Department official commented, with Sanchez it was "all trees, no forest." Rather than visiting units in the field to check on their activities, he insisted that they send him numerous statistical measures of progress. Lacking empathy and sociability, Sanchez alienated Bremer, other senior U.S. officials, his subordinates, the press, and numerous Iraqis. He made such a poor impression on General John Abizaid, his commanding officer, that Abizaid regularly flew to Iraq to take charge of crises and make decisions himself.[18]

Although Sanchez micromanaged, he usually micromanaged one small issue at a time, leaving most other matters to subordinate commanders. He allowed his division commanders to select counterinsurgency approaches in their areas, a sensible policy considering the variations in the population and the opposition across Iraq. But Sanchez neglected a critical element of decentralized command—oversight. Seldom checking on the division commanders, not to mention brigade or battalion commanders, Sanchez was unable to determine how well they were leading.[19]

Some of the military commanders crafted much better approaches than others. In general, Marine commanders outdid Army commanders in this regard. The Marine officers who served in Iraq in 2003 had received much more training and education in counterinsurgency than had most of their Army counterparts, a legacy of the Marines' historic involvement in counterinsurgencies and other forms of irregular conflict. In the decade prior to the Iraq

War, the top Marine Corps leadership had emphasized initiative, creativity, and flexibility in grooming Marine commanders for what the service termed the "three block war," in which Marines were carrying out humanitarian assistance on one city block, conducting low-intensity military operations on the next, and fighting a high-intensity war on the third. Less deferential to doctrine and standardization than was the Army, the Marines did not employ premanufactured solutions to counterinsurgency problems; rather, they possessed a familiarity with the subject that gave them a range of solutions to consider employing and, if necessary, adapting. Because of organizational culture and decentralization of command, Marine officers were accustomed to adapting to complex and unfamiliar problems on their own.[20] In addition, the Marine Corps generally outdid the Army in keeping weak leaders out of its officer corps, so the average officer was of higher quality—which is not to say that all Marine officers were suited to counterinsurgency, for some were seriously deficient in the traits required for success.[21]

The 1st Marine Division had taken Baghdad during the war and then occupied Saddam Hussein's hometown of Tikrit. In the middle of the spring, it trucked down to southern Iraq under the command of Major General James "Mad Dog" Mattis, the most celebrated Marine officer of the early twenty-first century. At once charismatic and cerebral, Mattis was an outstanding motivator whom the Marines in Iraq saw everywhere and at all hours, and a brilliant tactician and strategist who was constantly prowling the front lines and scanning his large military history library for new ideas on vanquishing the enemy. Marines idolized Mattis. Large segments of the American public admired his blunt talk and his passion.

In the tradition of the Marine Corps, Mattis prized familiarization before war and adaptation in war. His division's successes in occupation duty were made considerably easier by their familiarity with the sorts of challenges they were likely to encounter. In addition to studying counterinsurgency over the course of their careers, the division's officers had, prior to the war, participated in a planning exercise for the occupation of a defeated Iraq. Lieutenant General Michael Hagee, commander of I Marine Expeditionary Force, had ordered the exercise when it became clear that General Franks's Central Command was not going to give him planning or guidance for the postwar occupation.[22]

After arriving in southern Iraq, Mattis sent the division's M-1 tanks, armored personnel carriers, and artillery to Kuwait to prevent his Marines from using heavy firepower that might unnecessarily arouse the locals. He told his

Marines to avoid persecuting former Saddam supporters in revenge for friends killed or maimed during the war and to concentrate on gaining the population's assistance in identifying and isolating miscreants. Some Marines cleaned city streets and restored electrical power while others conducted armed patrols, all of them building relationships with local leaders and gathering information from the citizens. Marine commanders dissipated hostile crowds through carefully chosen words and force of personality. When unemployed former Iraqi soldiers demonstrated in public, Marine officers met with them, listened respectfully to what they had to say, and convinced them to desist.[23]

U.S. Army Special Forces officers, located predominantly in northern and western Iraq, also distinguished themselves in preventive counterinsurgency. Major Jim Gavrilis, who like most Special Forces officers had expertise in this type of work, entered the town of Ar Rutbah on April 9 after directing the air strikes that erased Saddam's military installations from the town map. He immediately sought to cultivate the local leaders and the government and army personnel, having tea and fire-cooked pita bread with Bedouins in the desert, meeting police officers in the town for utensil-free meals. Gavrilis kept the police and civil administration running by speaking with their leaders and paying the salaries of all the employees. He did not purge Baathists, but he did require them to denounce the Baath Party in writing and pledge allegiance to the new Iraq. To convince sheiks and imams to help maintain order, Gavrilis provided relief supplies. Gavrilis said, "I focused more on security and governance than on economics," and added that economic prosperity and provision of essential services depended upon security and governance.[24]

Of the commanders of U.S. Army regulars who were first assigned to occupation duty, a few had extensive familiarity with counterinsurgency, which helped permit a smooth transition into counterinsurgency operations. One of them was Major General David Petraeus, whose 101st Airborne Division was sent to the city of Mosul after taking part in the conquest of Baghdad. The son of a Dutch sea captain who had fled to New York at the outbreak of World War II, Petraeus entered West Point in 1970, near the end of American involvement in the Vietnam War. Hard work, natural talent, and ambition propelled Petraeus into the top 5 percent of his class. A note in the academy yearbook read, "A striver to the max, Dave was always 'going for it' in sports, academics, leadership, and even his social life." At Ranger School, he won all three of the prizes awarded for merit. In the real world of the Army, Petraeus attained accolades and promotions well ahead of his peers.

One of the defining moments in his life came in 1991, when, as a battalion commander in the 101st Airborne, he was observing a live-fire exercise. A rifleman participating in the exercise tripped and fell with his finger on his trigger, accidentally discharging a bullet that struck Petraeus just above the name tag on the right side of his chest, tearing out part of a lung and leaving a gaping exit hole in his back. Rushed to the hospital at Fort Campbell, Petraeus had a tube pushed into his chest to clean out debris and bacteria, an extremely painful procedure. Brigadier General Jack Keane, who was on hand, remarked, "Normally a guy screams and his body comes right off the table. All Petraeus did was grunt a little bit. His body didn't even move. The surgeon told me, 'That's the toughest guy I ever had my hands on.'" The Army flew Petraeus by emergency helicopter to Vanderbilt University Medical Center in Nashville, where he underwent five hours of surgery under the scalpel of Dr. Bill Frist, later the majority leader in the U.S. Senate. He recovered far sooner than expected. "Petraeus recuperated at the Fort Campbell hospital and he was driving the hospital commander crazy, trying to convince the doctors to discharge him," Keane recounted. "He said, 'I am not the norm. I'm ready to get out of here and I'm ready to prove it to you.' He had them pull the tubes out of his arm. Then he hopped out of bed and did fifty push-ups. They let him go home." Petraeus remained in superb physical condition after the accident. Twelve years later, at the age of fifty, he ran an Army ten-mile race in sixty-four minutes.[25]

Along the way, Petraeus earned a doctorate at Princeton. Because he wrote his dissertation on the lessons of the Vietnam War, his understanding of the counterinsurgency methods applied in Vietnam was credited for his triumph in Mosul. Yet Petraeus implemented some methods in Mosul that were very different from those employed in Vietnam. He had the astuteness to recognize the differences between Vietnam and Iraq and the creativity to come up with new solutions.

Petraeus began the occupation of Mosul by airlifting enough soldiers into the city to halt the looting and other forms of disorder. He and his staff met every day with Iraqi leaders and managers and gained their cooperation through personal magnetism and offers of reconstruction assistance. It was no mean task in a city containing 110,000 former Iraqi army soldiers who had plenty of reasons to hate the Americans. Petraeus facilitated reconstruction by hiring Baathists into middle-management jobs—in defiance of Baghdad's de-Baathification order. Once he had squeezed money out of Bremer, he challenged his brigade commanders to outspend one another on infrastructure and economic projects. An empathetic leader, he insisted that his troops respect local customs, ordering them, for instance, to wait at the door of a house for the man to come out rather than barge in unannounced and needlessly insult the family's honor. Petraeus improved the living conditions in prisons, cracked down on interrogators who beat detainees, and invited Iraqi religious and civic leaders to see the prisons with their own eyes.[26]

One of the most important leadership challenges, Petraeus found, was allocating unanticipated leadership tasks to subordinate commanders and staff officers. All of his officers had new duties on top of those for which they had been trained. The trick was to match tasks to personalities. "One of the jobs of a leader is to employ everybody in his organization in the best way possible to get the most out of them, to help them be all they can be," said Petraeus. "In other words, the S-3 (operations officer) must do the S-3 business, but it may be that [the commander] also can use the S-3 to engage with certain leaders because he's really good at it. Or maybe not, maybe the S-5 (civil affairs officer) has to do it, or the deputy commander."[27]

Most of the U.S. Army commanders knew little about counterinsurgency at the start of the occupation. Those who were not creative or flexible gravitated toward relatively simple counterinsurgency methods of questionable utility— brief forays into hostile territory, highly destructive attacks on suspected insurgent hideouts, and mass arrests. On the other hand, creative and flexible officers soon came up with effective methods. To find methods that might be worth trying, battalion and company commanders read books and articles on counterinsurgency, tapped Reservists and National Guardsmen with pertinent expertise, and sent e-mails to experts back in the United States. Using these ideas and their own ingenuity and judgment, they produced methods tailored to local conditions. They formed city councils, funded small businesses, organized community policing, repaired damaged infrastructure, and performed a myriad of other previously unencountered tasks. They devised innovative countermeasures whenever the insurgents adopted new IED technologies and tactics, and they invented schemes for collecting intelligence—disguising soldiers as water and sewer surveyors, for instance.[28] Major General Peter Chiarelli, who commanded the Army's 1st Cavalry Division during one of the first counterinsurgency campaigns in Baghdad, attributed the division's achievements primarily to the ability of small-unit leaders to adapt.[29] Petraeus later observed, "The key to many of our successes in Iraq, in fact, has been leaders—especially young leaders—who have risen to the occasion and taken on tasks for which they'd had little or no training, and who have demonstrated enormous initiative, innovativeness, determination, and courage."[30]

Some division and brigade commanders played a large role in promoting adaptation by encouraging battalion and company commanders to improvise and by persuading or compelling the less creative and flexible ones to rely less heavily on conventional military operations.[31] Eliot Cohen, an expert on military leadership and a frequent consultant to the nation's top military and political leaders during the Iraq War, remarked that "the character of individual military commanders, at the division level and often below, had large consequences for the conduct of military operations. The 101st Airborne Division, 1st Cavalry Division, and 1st Armored Division under Generals Petraeus, Chiarelli, and Dempsey adapted remarkably quickly to the counterinsurgency mission, pursuing a combination of reconstruction and focused violence which achieved notable successes in restoring some semblance of normality in their areas of operation."[32]

As in countless prior counterinsurgencies, understanding tried-and-true counterinsurgency principles and methods was no guarantee of success. Without critical leadership attributes, leaders could not turn ideas into productive actions on the streets of Iraq. A squadron commander from the 3rd Armored Cavalry Regiment (ACR), for example, professed the importance of gaining popular support but failed to gain popular support or stem the insurgent tide because he could not induce his soldiers to treat the population with respect. His troops ransacked homes without cause. They stopped civilians at gunpoint and dumped their breakfasts out of their baskets while asking them questions and yelling obscenities. Four soldiers from the 3rd ACR beat a former Iraqi general to death in November 2003, and other soldiers from the regiment were accused of stealing thousands of dollars from Iraqis. A captain from the 3rd ACR kicked prisoners in the ribs, hit prisoners with baseball bats, and rudely berated Iraqi government leaders. Only belatedly did the regiment's leadership begin punishing offenders. Some officers attributed the abuses to the regimental commander's excessive sympathy for the men in the regiment, which violated one of the cardinal rules of military leadership—that officers should maintain an emotional distance between themselves and their subordinates in order to prevent undue lenience.[33]

American commanders without sociability, charisma, empathy, or flexibility failed to cultivate local Iraqis through civic action and personal interaction. If they did not gain cooperation from Iraqis, they could not tell insurgents apart from ordinary civilians and ended up detaining large numbers of innocent Iraqis, which increased popular sympathy for the insurgents, and releasing most of the detainees for lack of evidence, which put real insurgents back on the streets. Inadvertently or not, they authorized actions that Iraqis considered taboo, such as body searches of women.[34]

American officers lacking in integrity allowed their troops to run Iraqi civilians off the road and beat suspicious civilians. Although Americans back in the United States often ascribed such misbehavior to the character of the troops who engaged in it, most military officers laid blame on the commanders for failing to maintain discipline.[35] The single most damaging occurrence of American misconduct, the prisoner abuse scandal at Abu Ghraib, resulted from a clear failure of leadership in one Army Reserve unit, the 800th Military Police Brigade. Reserve and National Guard units, it is worth noting, had the most serious leadership problems of the U.S. forces sent to Iraq because of less rigorous screening of officers; a significant number of their officers performed so poorly in command positions that they had to be reassigned to lesser duties.[36] The officers of the 800th Military Police Brigade did not have the dedication and organizational ability to perform the simple task of keeping watch over the enlisted soldiers and NCOs who committed the abuses. As Brigadier General Huba Wass de Czege, one of the military's foremost thinkers, put it, "Anyone who has served for even a short while in troop command realizes how 'not much good happens' after midnight when bored young troops go unsupervised and are open to temptation. It's simply inconceivable how any experienced commander could have left this flank unguarded. He should have had his trusted agents visit at all hours of the day and night."[37]

The vast majority of American units did not suffer from the leadership problems that led to Abu Ghraib, and their troops did not commit such crimes.[38] Thanks largely to insurgent superiority in the realm of public communications, however, Abu Ghraib and a few other incidents created a widespread belief among Iraqis that misbehavior was the norm for American forces. Spreading the truth and countering insurgent propaganda required creativity and cultural understanding that were not always at the disposal of American commanders, whether at the local level or in Baghdad. Central headquarters required lengthy and difficult approval processes that blocked the dissemination of information or delayed its release until it was out of date, whereas the insurgents put out CDs and DVDs with their false or exaggerated tales of American misdeeds within twenty-four hours of their alleged occurrence, and their contents made their way rapidly to the whole Iraqi population through its principal sources of information—satellite television channels and marketplace chatter.[39]

Insurgent violence spiked in the spring of 2004, thanks to the emergence of a new Shiite insurgent group called Jaish Al Mahdi, or Mahdi Army, under the guidance of the virulently anti-American cleric Muqtada Al Sadr. Relying primarily on urban guerrilla warfare and terrorism, the various insurgent groups aimed most of their blows at the nascent Iraqi security forces, which were less heavily protected than American forces and posed a greater long-term threat. Except in the few cases where they had good commanders, the Iraqi security forces performed disastrously. If insurgent attacks did not kill them first, they either sat still, deserted, or joined the insurgents.[40]

The spring attacks confirmed what others had been saying for many months, that CPA's development of Iraqi security forces was a complete failure. A large chorus of Americans recommended that the U.S. military take control of the Iraqi armed forces. Despite Bremer's strong objections, Secretary of Defense Rumsfeld decided in June 2004 to transfer responsibility for the Iraqi armed forces from CPA to a new military organization headed by Lieutenant General David Petraeus. The choice of Petraeus was a wise one, for Petraeus recognized the extraordinary importance of leadership selection, and he was adept at solving large and complicated problems. "In an Iraqi unit, the leader is really of paramount importance," Petraeus told Greg Jaffe of the *Wall Street Journal*.[41] Later, after he had held command of the security assistance program for many months, Petraeus told Julian Barnes of *U.S. News and World Report* that "the key ingredient, increasingly, has become Iraqi leadership rather than another heavy machine gun." In Petraeus's view, as reported by Barnes, "the decision of who should lead battalions or companies has proved to be the most important."[42]

In his new position, Petraeus devoted much of his time and energy to identifying the most suitable Iraqis to command the Iraqi army units. Among the biggest obstacles he faced were the ongoing politicization of leadership selection, the murder of prospective commanders by insurgents, and the lack of Iraqis with leadership experience. The last of these was the biggest obstacle. "You don't grow battalion commanders or command sergeants major in a year or two," Petraeus said ruefully, echoing his predecessors in Vietnam and El Salvador.[43] Petraeus and his staff sculpted a military academy that, a few years later, would be putting out 1,000 lieutenants per year, and they created equivalents of other U.S. Army leadership development institutions, including a war college, a staff college, a strategic studies institute, and a training and doctrine command. The American military advisers under Petraeus turned out to be better at developing Iraqi military forces and leaders than the civilians who had preceded them had been, although they varied widely in quality because the U.S. Army's personnel system did not consider advisory duty a high priority.[44]

The spring debacle also resulted in an authorization from Bremer to recruit Saddam-era military officers into the Iraqi army and police. Pressure from the bottom, from Iraqis and Americans appalled by the ineptitude of the security forces in their districts, convinced Bremer to make this policy reversal, in the face of strong opposition from the Iraqi ministries in Baghdad and several senior officials in Washington. In some instances, the results were immediate and spectacular. Mark Etherington, a CPA adviser, recounted that the Iraqi provincial council in his province chose to replace the police leadership with officers from Saddam's army because "the problems which we faced in our daily work could be boiled down to a single irreducible minimum — the inability of our local police force to carry out its tasks." As soon as the new chief took office, he fired fifty-five policemen guilty of incompetence, corruption, or perpetual absence. The rest of the policemen began patrolling the streets and performing their assigned duties, and within six weeks, policemen were participating in operations with an American armored cavalry squadron. Etherington said of these developments, "We saw them with incredulity and rejoiced."[45]

General Sanchez departed in mid-2004, to be replaced by General George W. Casey, Jr., a thoughtful and level-headed officer who was the son of Major General George W. Casey, the highest-ranking American officer killed in the Vietnam War. Casey's arrival heralded a major improvement at the top level of the American command. Allocating much of his time to firsthand observation of the war, Casey visited four U.S. battalions every week, eventually making it to every combat arms battalion. He spent even more of his time working with the Iraqi leadership on developing the Iraqi armed forces.

Casey formed an in-house think tank out of nine distinguished military officers with doctorates, of whom the leading counterinsurgency expert was Kalev Sepp. A retired Special Forces officer, Sepp had served as an adviser during the Salvadoran Insurgency and had later obtained a doctorate in history from Harvard. Sepp told Casey that U.S. forces needed to put more effort into engaging the Iraqi citizenry, controlling the population centers on a continuous basis, and guarding Iraq's borders. These recommendations were incorporated into a counterinsurgency plan produced in November 2004. Some local commanders, from reading and leading troops in the field, were already adhering to the plan's prescriptions; others had to be told to follow the plan, and even then not all of them complied. Expectations that the new concepts would promptly produce major changes proved to be overly optimistic, for, once again, identifying what to do proved to be easier than doing it.[46]

On June 28, 2004, the United States dissolved CPA and transferred sovereignty to an interim government led by Iyad Allawi, a secular Shiite and former Baath Party member. Allawi warmed American hearts with promises to get tough with the insurgents and the militias, but then cooled them by failing to improve the security forces or reduce insurgent violence. Much of this trouble could be traced to the new government's lack of success in raising the quality of its military and police commanders. Bing West, a perceptive observer of the war, notified General Casey in an August 2004 memo that the chief problem of the Iraqi security forces (ISF) was not insufficient training or equipment but poor leadership. "The ISF lacks leaders at all levels," West wrote. "Particularly, the ISF needs tough battalion and company commanders and city district police chiefs. . . . The ISF has not one hero, not one single battalion commander who has taken the fight offensively and persistently to the enemy."[47] West urged Casey to effect changes of Iraqi commanders. But Casey and Petraeus were sharply constrained by the White House's decision, simultaneous with the transfer of sovereignty on June 28, to give the Iraqi government complete authority over Iraqi military and police leadership selection. That decision was to haunt the Americans for years to come.

During the early days of Allawi's tenure, the very capable interior minister was replaced by an incompetent who had a larger political following. The ministry went into a tailspin. Other ministries were likewise enfeebled by the politically motivated appointments of useless or dangerous leaders. Rampant corruption and ineptitude inhibited efforts to provide electricity and water, distribute food, reduce unemployment, and everything else the government was supposed to do for its citizenry.[48]

The most dangerous problem confronting the Iraqi and American governments in 2004 was the city of Fallujah in Anbar province, long the most troublesome city in Iraq, famous for its contempt for outsiders, its religious fanaticism, and its rough-and-tumble men. Major General James Mattis's 1st

Marine Division had arrived in Anbar province in the spring with hopes of defusing insurgent violence through a benevolent approach similar to the one it had used in the south in 2003. The Marines intended to employ armed force sparingly, treat the populace with respect, and convince locals to assist the counterinsurgency. But the Sunnis in Anbar province were much more hostile to Americans than were the Shiites in the south, so hostile that the benevolent approach was doomed from the start.[49]

In Ramadi, the capital of Anbar province, insurgents greeted the newly arrived Marines with large, well-coordinated attacks that compelled Marine commanders to sideline their civic action programs and employ powerful weapons like 25mm chain guns and AT-4 rockets, setting a trend of destructive combat between American troops and popularly supported insurgents that lasted in Ramadi for three years.[50] The Marines did not even have a chance to try benevolence in Fallujah, but it undoubtedly would have met the same fate that it met in Ramadi. Just one week after the Marines assumed responsibility for Fallujah, insurgents ambushed four American security contractors and then butchered, burned, and dragged their bodies through the streets, finally hanging them from a trestle bridge for the world to see on television. Convinced that a large American response would merely intensify anti-American sentiment in the city, Mattis and his boss, I Marine Expeditionary Force commander Lieutenant General James T. Conway, advocated patience. They would work on developing Iraqi security forces and gradually gaining support in the city and would nab the perpetrators in due course. But Rumsfeld, Bremer, and Sanchez believed that inaction would ruin America's international prestige and encourage rebellion in other Iraqi cities, so they called for an immediate and forceful response. President Bush decided to send the Marines into the city with overwhelming force.[51]

Mattis ordered Regimental Combat Team 1, commanded by Colonel John A. Toolan, to take control of the city and remove the insurgents and heavy weapons. Advancing on April 5, the Marines encountered fierce and intermittently skillful resistance from hundreds of insurgents. Over the next five days, they methodically fought their way into the city, building by building. Before they could finish sweeping the insurgents from the city, however, they were ordered to halt by President Bush, who had been chastened by Iraqi and foreign leaders upset at reports of civilian casualties in the Arab media, which had wildly exaggerated the loss of life.

The Marines came up with a solution to the impasse—give Saddam-era officers responsibility for security in the city. A few such officers had offered to do exactly that. With no decent alternatives, the Bush administration accepted a plan to organize a militia of Fallujans under the leadership of veteran Iraqi military officers. Pulling back from the city, the Marines armed a force of 2,000 Iraqis, put it under the command of Major General Latif Mahal Hamoud Sabawi, called it the Fallujah Brigade, and assigned it the missions of confiscating heavy weapons, evicting foreign fighters, and stopping attacks on coalition forces.

A former intelligence officer who had been ousted by Saddam for unknown reasons, General Latif was a man of mysterious motives and abilities who made inconsistent statements to different audiences. He was chosen mainly on the recommendation of other Iraqi officers, who themselves were difficult to read. In finding leadership for the Fallujah Brigade, Colonel Toolan recalled, "We didn't know who to trust, and we had to rely on people we knew little about."

Although the Fallujah Brigade fulfilled some of the promises it had made to the Americans, it did not remove heavy weapons or foreign fighters from the city or prevent kidnappings and murders by the Islamist insurgent factions now dominating the city. Latif alienated the men under his command with his open homosexuality and his habit of reacting to insurgent depredations by seeking peaceful compromises that verged on capitulation. When Latif failed to organize a forceful response to the mortaring of the brigade's compound, the brigade's other officers began ignoring him and taking orders from Major General Abdullah Muhamdi, his second-in-command. Muhamdi was no better at restoring order in the city, and he refused to talk to the Marines at all. Colonel Toolan decided to dissolve the ill-fated brigade when he learned that some of its members were accomplices to the torture and murder of Lieutenant Colonel Suleiman Al Marawi, whose National Guard battalion had been the one viable Iraqi unit in the area.[52]

By the end of the summer, Fallujah had become a safe haven for the most vicious strain of insurgents, men who cut off limbs and heads with glee. The American and Iraqi governments ultimately found that situation intolerable. In early November, after convincing all but a few hundred of the city's quarter-million civilians to leave, nine U.S. Marine and Army battalions and six Iraqi battalions went into the city to eradicate the insurgents. American infantrymen did most of the house-to-house fighting, calling upon air power when necessary to destroy entrenched urban guerrillas. By the time the insurgents had been cleared out of the city, 18,000 of the city's 39,000 buildings were destroyed or damaged.

One of the few capable Iraqi units assigned to the Fallujah battle was Combined Action Platoon India, which consisted of U.S. Marines and Iraqi National Guard soldiers. It was named after the Vietnam-era CAPs, but differed from its namesake in that it had an indigenous commander. One Marine observed that the Iraqis in Combined Action Platoon India functioned well and did not desert like other Iraqis because their Iraqi commander was an outstanding officer.[53] In some of the other Iraqi units, the designated Iraqi leaders were so worthless that the American advisers ended up serving as commanders.[54]

In 2005, General Casey directed U.S. and Iraqi forces to adhere to a "clear and hold" strategy, whereby U.S. forces cleared an area of insurgents and then moved on to the next area while Iraqi forces held the cleared area to prevent the insurgents from returning. As Casey and many other American military officers saw it, avoiding a sustained U.S. presence in a given locale would prevent the insurgents from fostering and exploiting anti-Americanism among discontented Iraqi citizens. Iraqi soldiers and policemen could, under proper leadership, keep insurgents out much more effectively than the Americans could, because they had local knowledge and numerous intelligence sources. This division of labor would also bolster the Iraqi security forces by compelling them to leave the nest of American protection and fly on their own, which ultimately would permit the United States to reduce its troop levels, as President Bush and the majority in the U.S. Congress favored. Last, this approach would enable U.S. forces to concentrate in a few large forward operating bases, which would be easier to protect and supply than numerous small bases.[55]

The Americans mostly did their part, bashing the insurgents and forcing them out of town after town, city district after city district. American commanders abided by restrictive rules of engagement to minimize the killing of innocent civilians, and they obtained some assistance from locals in identifying the insurgents. Kalev Sepp, who toured the country in the summer of 2005, reported that many of the captains and lieutenants that he encountered "showed resilience, flexibility and inventiveness."[56]

Too few Iraqi forces, however, had what it took to prevail in the "hold" phase. Although the Iraqi security forces increased from 114,000 to 214,000 during the year, their power grew little, if at all, because of the sluggish growth in the number of competent leaders. Casey had declared the improvement of Iraqi security forces his top priority and assigned more advisers to the mission, and Petraeus was working hard on personnel changes and development, but progress in the Iraqi army was slow. In the Iraqi police, progress was nonexistent. Controlled by an incompetent Ministry of the Interior, the leadership of the Iraqi police remained ineffective at best, the exceptions being a handful of Iraqi commanders and a small number of foreign advisers who had become de facto commanders of Iraqi police units. The inspectors general of the U.S. State and Defense Departments reported in mid-2005 that "in instances where good leadership is present (often provided by Coalition military personnel or International Police Liaison Officers), Iraqi Police perform satisfactorily and stand their ground in the face of attacks. The absence of such leaders correlates closely with instances in which Iraqi Police stations have been overrun, often with shocking casualties among ill-prepared and ill-led policemen."[57]

Compounding these problems was the inauguration of Ibrahim Al Jaafari as prime minister in April 2005. The leader of the Shiite Dawa Party, Jaafari was brought to power in the first national elections, in which the country's Shiite majority had voted along sectarian lines and yielded a government dominated by Shiites. Top American officials had presumed that Iraqi Shiites had come to despise oppression and love liberty because they had been oppression's victims in the past, and from this premise they deduced that the Shiites would not oppress the Sunni minority in the new democratic Iraq. It was the same logic that had informed American policy in other places with historic oppression — Cuba and Zimbabwe and Kosovo—and proved to be as wrong here as it had been there.

Prime Minister Jaafari's office was controlled by militant Shiites who were fixated on trampling the Sunni population until the faintest possibility of a Sunni return to political dominance was extinguished. Taking control of the Ministry of the Interior and other ministries, they replaced competent Sunnis with Shiite militia members who used the police and other arms of the government to harass and rob fellow Shiites and to round up and massacre Sunni civilians, severely damaging the government's image. Among the most telling events in this chapter of the war was the American discovery, in November 2005, of a secret Interior Ministry prison whose 170 emaciated Sunni prisoners were spotted with welts from frequent beatings. Casey demanded that Interior Minister Bayan Jabar fire those responsible for the prison, but Jabar refused, saying, "Uh, that's how Iraqis are." Casey took the matter up with Prime Minister Jaafari, who likewise did nothing.[58]

Jaafari appears to have merely allowed his allies to carry out these criminal acts, for he was probably too disorganized and passive to have perpetrated them himself. Babak Dehghanpisheh and Michael Hirsh reported in *Newsweek* that Jaafari "has come across almost as an anti-Saddam—a mild-mannered and well-meaning Iraqi who is utterly without charisma. Jaafari speaks in an undertone and mumbles during speeches; even some translators have trouble understanding him." At one meeting right before the deadline for approval of the Iraqi constitution, with many important matters in need of urgent resolution, he brought his cabinet together and spent three hours talking about whether tomato paste should be included in the rations issued for Ramadan, the Muslim month of fasting.[59]

For spectators rooting for the new Iraq, there were some moments of excitement in the otherwise dreary year of 2005. Such occurrences often involved collaboration between excellent American leaders and good Iraqi leaders in the "hold" phase of "clear and hold." In the spring, the 3rd Armored Cavalry Regiment arrived in Tal Afar, a craggy stone city of 250,000 in Iraq's northwestern desert, halfway between Mosul and the Syrian border. The regiment had a different commander than in 2003, and its conduct differed accordingly. The new commander, Colonel H. R. McMaster, had gained renown during the 1991 Gulf War for overrunning a bevy of Iraqi Republican Guard tanks in the Battle of 73 Easting, a feat subsequently studied at military schools as a tactical masterpiece. In 1997, he had published a penetrating book on the Vietnam War entitled *Dereliction of Duty*, bringing him fame inside and outside the military. During the regiment's pre-deployment training at Fort Carson, Colorado, McMaster devised new training methods based on the regiment's previous experiences. Dressing Arab-Americans in dishdashas, he simulated scenarios that his soldiers were likely to encounter in Iraq. It was "training in empathy," according to one of McMaster's officers. "If I was in a situation where my neighbor had gotten his head cut off, how would I react? If it was my kid that had gotten killed by mortars, how would I react?" McMaster put some of his soldiers into short courses on Arabic language and culture and issued everyone in the regiment a list of recommended counterinsurgency books.

The U.S. Army had been to Tal Afar several times before to deal with the city's hodgepodge of urban guerrillas and terrorists. Each time the Americans had come, they had chased the insurgents out and turned the city over to new police forces. Each time, the insurgents had returned and intimidated the populace, government, and most of the police into submission. Fearing yet another miserable round, very few locals were interested in helping the 3rd ACR when it showed up in Tal Afar.

Although the regiment had undergone extensive training in the delicate nuances of personal interaction, its main interaction with Iraqis at first was the exchange of bullets. From May to September, the American regiment and two Iraqi army brigades traded fire with insurgents on a daily basis while inching into the city. At times, McMaster's soldiers engaged in intense block-by-block fighting, calling on the firepower of Apache helicopters and, when the risk of civilian casualties was low, the blunt instrument of artillery.

In September, once most insurgents had been cleared out, the American and Iraqi forces established twenty-nine small outposts in the city and lived in them side by side. These outposts provided easy access to the population and enabled rapid response to insurgent incidents anywhere in the city. McMaster charged Lieutenant Colonel Chris Hickey, a highly regarded squadron commander, with the courting of Tal Afar's tribal leaders. Spending forty to fifty hours per week meeting with Shiite and Sunni sheiks, Hickey attained little from his initial overtures, but he persisted, and over time he won over many sheiks with persuasive entreaties emphasizing the need for Iraqi unity against the foreign terrorists. These sheiks eventually recruited 1,400 men into the police. Conscious of the failures to hold the city that had followed past American withdrawals from Tal Afar, McMaster secured permission to keep 1,000 of his soldiers in the city for the long term.[60]

In Mosul, Lieutenant Colonel Erik Kurilla's 1-24 Infantry battalion spent 2005 nullifying gains made by the insurgents after a major downsizing of the U.S. presence the previous year. A highly regarded U.S. battalion commander, Kurilla projected charisma through unstinting aggressiveness and indifference to danger, qualities especially prized by Iraqi soldiers and policemen, among whom Kurilla became something of a legend. Michael Yon, whose online chronicling of the 1-24 Infantry was eventually incorporated into a best-selling book, explained that Kurilla enjoyed such respect because "Iraqis respond very favorably to strong and just leadership. They respond very favorably to total hard-core soldiers, killers, who can take hits and keep on going, but who treat the people with justice and dignity." After firefights, Kurilla strolled through markets to buy sheep for Iraqi soldiers or policemen who had fought well, while everyone else stayed close to concrete walls or armored vehicles for fear of lingering enemies.

Kurilla excelled in social settings, which helped him win the cooperation of Iraqis and gain the counterinsurgents favorable coverage from the media, whom he actively cultivated. On top of everything else, Kurilla displayed uncommon ingenuity in combating the enemy. Making extensive use of captured cell phones, he deceived and disrupted the enemy's operations and tracked down insurgents. On one occasion, he had his soldiers stage a fake IED attack on an Iraqi security force truck to lure insurgents, who were accustomed to preying on vehicles in distress. When insurgents tried to pounce on the seemingly disabled truck, American snipers in surrounding buildings shot them to pieces.[61]

Another arena where American cheers could be heard in 2005 was Al Qaim, a district of Anbar province located along the Euphrates River just east of the Syrian border. Al Qaim served as the first way station in Iraq for foreign Muslim extremists traveling from Syria through the Euphrates River Valley to insurgent hotbeds in Iraq's interior. In early 2005, Al Qaim was also becoming a major logistical hub for the insurgents. For those reasons, the district became a matter of much interest to General Casey.

Insurgent operations in Al Qaim were managed by Al Qaeda in Iraq (AQI), an organization of Sunni religious fanatics with a large presence in Anbar province. Al Qaim's tribes, which were initially hostile to the Americans, became so disenchanted with AQI's extremism and bad behavior in the spring of 2005 that they decided to seek help from the nearest U.S. Marines. The Marines, however, did not strike a deal with the tribes and instead continued to rely on their own firepower in combating AQI and the foreign fighters, inflicting casualties but not loosening the enemy's grip on the population.

As the sizzling heat subsided in the late summer, a new Marine battalion arrived in Al Qaim under the command of Lieutenant Colonel Dale Alford, an Atlanta native of whom General Casey said afterward, "Alford was the best battalion commander I had." Sensing an opportunity, Casey transferred additional U.S. and Iraqi forces to Al Qaim to facilitate implementation of clear and hold. During the first week of October, in an operation called Iron Fist, Alford's 3/6 Marine battalion fought its way, building by building, to a dry streamed that bisected Al Qaim. On its banks, they established combat outposts. The battalion's snipers spent the next three weeks picking off insurgents who attempted to dislodge the Marines, while an Iraqi army battalion joined them in preparation for the next phase.

At the beginning of November, Alford's Marines and the Iraqi battalion spread out across Al Qaim, dispersed into smaller groups than had ever been employed there, to control the population and increase pressure on the enemy. Alford was taking big risks—one of the detachments could get overrun, and the detachments would be very difficult to keep supplied. These problems had, in fact, discouraged previous commanders from taking this course of action. But the insurgents were not able to overrun Alford's troops, because of the ability of Alford and his company commanders to improvise and to work with Iraqis. Alford was able to keep the troops supplied through what he called "sheer will power," together with tanks and armored trucks. After one week of house-to-house fighting that left many insurgents dead, the remaining insurgents went into hiding or left the area.

What followed next were holding operations that the U.S. military later taught in counterinsurgency courses as models of excellence. Marines and Iraqi soldiers established a galaxy of small outposts in the district's towns and along its roads, which they used as living quarters and bases for combined patrolling. The sociable Alford and his Marines engaged the Iraqi population with such success that they were invited into Iraqi homes for tea or food on a daily basis. Meeting regularly with sheiks, imams, and city councilmen, the battalion's officers convinced 1,300 local men to join the local police force, which until that time had possessed a total strength of zero. Iraqi soldiers and policemen and the Marines painstakingly collected intelligence from the population, facilitating the arrest or killing of insurgents who were passing through the district or attempting to operate covertly within it. With financial assistance from the Marines, the Iraqis restored water and electrical service, brought hospitals back into operation, and repaired roads. Iraqi entrepreneurs took out small loans from American civil-affairs officers and started new businesses that helped rejuvenate the local economy.[62]

Colonel Stephen W. Davis, Alford's commanding officer, considered the most important reason for Alford's success to be what he termed his "intelligent aggressiveness." Alford was constantly undertaking new initiatives and improvising solutions to immediate problems, all the while seeking permission to enter new territory. He also exceeded other officers in experience in irregular conflicts, willingness to work with Iraqis, and humility. As Davis noted, Alford was not the first Marine commander in Anbar province to conduct population security operations in concert with Iraqis, nor the first to do it successfully. Alford, however, achieved larger and more durable gains because of his exceptional leadership abilities and the willingness of General Casey to send large numbers of forces to Al Qaim.[63]

Near the end of 2005, after many months of effort, Casey secured the transfer of the entire police advisory program from the U.S. State Department to the U.S. military. The transfer meant more and better advisers for the Iraqi police and a sharp increase in the removal of bad Iraqi police chiefs. Casey was much more willing to press for the removal of bad leaders than the State Department had been, because the State Department, by tradition and position, was interested first and foremost in maintaining good relations with the host government, and it did not have the knowledge or experience to make shrewd assessments of counterinsurgency leadership capabilities. But Casey could not fire Iraqi police commanders himself, any more than he could sack Iraqi army commanders. He had to depend on cooperation from Iraq's officials, who were not always amenable to change, especially when it involved removing commanders who shared their sectarian or political agendas. "Two factors controlled all we did in Iraq," Casey said. "First, giving back sovereignty limited us in selecting good leaders. Second, deep sectarianism lurked beneath the surface. This was a compound problem, with the one affecting the other."[64]

The counterinsurgent cause suffered a huge setback on February 22, 2006, with the bombing of the Askariya Mosque in Samarra. Using high explosives, Sunni extremists caved in the golden dome of the mosque, one of Shiite Islam's holiest sites. The deed accomplished its strategic objective of generating strife and disorder that could be exploited by subversives. Shiites responded to the bombing with massive violence against Sunnis, which heightened Sunni violence against Shiites. The country seemed to be lurching toward civil war, if it was not already there.

Saving Iraq from a sectarian civil war demanded punishment of malefactors of all affiliations. But the Interior Ministry and the National Police, infested as they were with Shiite militiamen, averted their eyes when Shiite death squads murdered Sunnis, and even perpetrated murders of Sunnis themselves. Iraqi military and police officers who attempted to combat the Shiite militias were fired by the Interior Ministry or assassinated by militia members or policemen. In Baghdad, where the sectarian brutality was worst, Shiite militiamen and policemen removed all Sunnis from mixed Sunni-Shiite neighborhoods through intimidation and murder.[65]

Jaafari plainly had neither the fortitude nor the integrity to lift Iraq out of this morass. Sunnis and Kurds demanded that he be replaced with a capable and impartial leader, and the United States soon concurred. Behind the scenes, the Americans applied intense pressure on the Shiite parliamentary majority to oust the prime minister, who was very popular among Shiite political parties for having facilitated the oppression of the Sunnis. In the end, American pressure compelled the Shiite parties to oust Jaafari, the country's first democratically elected chief of state. To take Jaafari's place, the Shiite majority chose Nouri Al Maliki, another Shiite from the Dawa Party.[66]

Maliki had been in politics for many years, mostly as an exile in Iran and Syria, but he lacked executive experience. During his first months in power, he showed little more promise than Jaafari on the issue of sectarianism. He disregarded American exhortations to purge the Shiite militia elements from the police and the Interior Ministry and institute merit-based leadership selection. Likewise did he rebuff pleas from Sunni and Kurdish army officers for permission to crack down on the militias. Shiite policemen and militiamen continued to kill Sunnis and chase them from their homes with alarming frequency.[67]

In accordance with the strategic aim of gradually turning the war over to the Iraqis, Casey had planned to continue increasing Iraqi responsibility for population security once Maliki took power, but the new government's weakness and its toleration of sectarian violence convinced him to postpone his plans. In mid-2006, Casey started reinserting American forces into insecure areas, a move that he viewed not as a reversal of strategy but as a temporary measure to stabilize the situation.[68] In the summer and fall of 2006, he ordered large numbers of American troops to join the Iraqis for Operation Together Forward and Operation Together Forward II, which were aimed at quelling the violence in Baghdad. Both operations were crippled by the inactivity of Iraqi leaders who had little talent or were allied with sectarian militias, or both. Iraqi units did not show up for duty, failed to perform their assigned tasks, or tipped off the insurgents about imminent counterinsurgent operations. Although the Iraqis were originally in charge, they made such a mess of things that the Americans took control. American forces reduced the violence in a few areas of Baghdad, but violence then increased in the areas where they were not present, and total violence in Baghdad increased. According to James Kitfield of the *National Journal,* American leaders concluded from these operations that "good field leaders make all the difference in combat performance, and that [Iraq] has too few of them."[69]

As in the preceding year, a few bright rays did break through the clouds in 2006. The brightest ray shone on Ramadi, the Grand Central Station of the Sunni insurgency. After the recapture of Fallujah in 2004, the Americans had tried to quell the insurgents in Ramadi by co-opting tribal leaders and recruiting police, but insurgents assassinated those who cooperated with the Americans. Al Qaeda in Iraq, which had declared Ramadi the capital of its new caliphate, imposed its will on the city's 400,000 residents. In the middle of 2006, an internal U.S. Marine Corps report concluded that the United States had lost Ramadi and the rest of Anbar province politically and would be unable to retrieve them.[70]

Colonel Sean MacFarland's 1st Brigade Combat Team of the 1st Armored Division, composed of three Army battalions and one Marine battalion, showed up in Ramadi in June 2006. Everything they saw in the city was covered in a layer of gray dust, which seemed to symbolize the despair gripping the populace. MacFarland's superiors told him to rid the city of insurgents, but they let him decide how to do it. Convinced that the tribal sheiks remained highly influential, and unwilling to accept the contention that they could never be won back, MacFarland set out to bring the sheiks over to his side.

Most of the sheiks were already disillusioned with AQI because it had foisted its extreme rules and punishments on them, encroached on their political and economic power, and forced their young women to marry AQI fanatics. They would not side with the Americans, however, unless they could be convinced that they would be safe from AQI torturers and murderers. The American and Iraqi army troops would have to win a series of military successes to show that they had the martial prowess and stamina to knock the insurgents to the floor and keep them from getting back up.

MacFarland built combat outposts in Ramadi's neighborhoods to establish control over the population and lure the insurgents into making attacks that exposed them to counterinsurgent firepower. As AQI casualties piled up, Mac-Farland approached the sheiks through Captain Travis Patriquin, a personable Arabic-speaking American. Over innumerable cigarettes and cups of chai, Patriquin gained the confidence of key sheiks in the Ramadi area. Aware that the men of Ramadi wanted to stay in their own neighborhoods to protect their relatives, and not be shipped off to distant parts of Iraq to fight in the midst of hostile Shiites, the Americans offered to hire policemen who would work in their home neighborhoods, led by their own tribal sheiks, at police stations built and protected by American forces. The Americans also dangled lucrative reconstruction contracts and other prizes before the sheiks.

The sheik who wielded the most clout in Ramadi at this time was Abdul Sattar Abu Risha. Though hailing from a minor tribe, Sattar had in recent months gained in stature owing to his charisma, courage, and military skill, to the point that he was becoming a "sheik of sheiks." Sattar had already begun forming an alliance of sheiks against AQI when the Americans approached him. A degree of uncertainty enshrouds the reasons for his conversion into a zealous opponent of Al Qaeda in Iraq, but the principal reasons undoubtedly included confidence that the Americans were going to persist and a desire to avenge AQI's murders of his brothers and other fellow tribesmen. Sattar's inspired political and military leadership proved critical to "the Awakening," the turning of the Anbar tribes against AQI.

Once Sattar and his allies agreed to terms with the Americans, police recruitment in Ramadi soared, reaching 300 in the month of July 2006 and rising to 400 per month in the fall. Among those who stood in line to join the police were droves of former Baathists and former insurgents. Because they served in their own neighborhoods, the new policemen had plenty of intelligence sources and could easily discern the Al Qaeda members in their midst. The weakness of Iraqi police elsewhere was often attributed to inadequate training, but these policemen received little formal training, yet they were able to drive AQI from their neighborhoods, with some support from U.S. forces and the Iraqi army, because they had good leaders—namely, tribal sheiks with natural leadership ability and varying amounts of leadership experience. AQI and other insurgents assassinated some of the best Awakening leaders, eventually killing Sattar himself with a roadside bomb, but other sheiks took their places and finished off the extremists.

In the center of Ramadi, the situation did not turn as quickly as it did in the surrounding neighborhoods, for the dominant tribe there, the Alwani tribe, had no affection for Sattar's tribe and paid him no heed. The Marine battalion in central Ramadi during MacFarland's first months did not establish a strong rapport with this tribe or with other Iraqis in the area, concentrating instead on protecting the main street and the government center. The battalion's outposts faced incessant attacks, and the Marines could not go anywhere in the city without hitting IEDs or hostile fire.

In August, this battalion departed, and in came the 1st Battalion 6th Marines, commanded by Lieutenant Colonel William Jurney, who had a reputation as one of the finest officers in the Marine Corps. Jurney happened to be a close personal friend of Lieutenant Colonel Dale Alford, whom he had met shortly after the 1991 Gulf War. A couple of months before Jurney's arrival in Ramadi, the two lieutenant colonels had sat on Alford's porch in Camp Lejeune, North Carolina, and imbibed Jack Daniels while Alford explained to Jurney how he had defeated Al Qaim's insurgents. Jurney employed many of the methods that had been used in Al Qaim, as well as methods he himself had used during a previous tour in Fallujah. As usual, however, the principal challenge would not be knowing what should be done, but actually getting it done. In the inferno of central Ramadi, many good officers had come up short; success demanded an outstanding leader, unfettered.

MacFarland gave Jurney complete freedom to select his methods. He also let Jurney take whatever he wanted from the U.S. military's goodie bag, be it unmanned aerial vehicles, psychological operations teams, or Navy Seabees. To kick off his offensive, Jurney poured troops into the areas of Ramadi where the insurgents had been strongest and had hitherto been left alone. Demonstrating skill and perseverance in fiercely contested street battles, Jurney's companies let no insurgents stop their advances. They seized the most tactically important points in the city and guarded them while engineers built combat outposts, which Jurney's Marines and elements of an Iraqi army battalion occupied. Marines blocked streets with barricades, restricting entry into neighborhoods to a small number of checkpoints, where all entrants were inspected and monitored. Through incessant patrolling, Marine and Iraqi forces got to know the local people and turned them into intelligence sources. Recognizing the threat that the outposts posed, AQI's urban guerrillas attacked them head-on, which negated the insurgents' usual advantages in mobility and made them easy targets for the defenders.

After AQI had suffered large numbers of deaths and lost military control of most of the city center, the Alwani tribe chose to side with the Americans and the Iraqi army. Hundreds of men suddenly offered to join the police, and they were soon serving alongside the U.S. Marines and Iraqi soldiers at the combat outposts. The new policemen guided the Marines and soldiers to insurgents who remained within central Ramadi, and apprehended some on their own. AQI sped toward its demise.

By mid-2007 extremist attacks in Ramadi were down to one per day, a tiny fraction of what they had been one year earlier. Soldiers and reporters who had seen Ramadi in the throes of insurgency during the summer of 2006 were astounded to discover that they could now walk through the city without body armor, talk to Iraqis on the street, eat at outdoor restaurants, and shop at hundreds of reopened stores. Garbage collection and bus service were back, and the populace engaged freely in practices that had been banned by AQI, like smoking hookahs and listening to music.[71]

In 2006, General Petraeus and General Mattis led a group of current and former officers in producing a new joint counterinsurgency field manual, called Field Manual 3-24 / Marine Corps Warfighting Publication 3-33.5. Written by committee, the manual reflected many of the views of Petraeus and Mattis but did not fully capture their accumulated wisdom. With respect to leadership, the manual attached the greatest weight to adaptation, calling upon leaders to be flexible and to use judgment and creativity to identify solutions. In this way, it de-emphasized what is often perceived as the primary purpose of doctrine—providing specific solutions to specific types of problems. In another positive development, the counterinsurgency field manual advocated decentralized command. To the Marines, these principles were nothing new, but they represented major change for much of the Army, which had traditionally adhered more closely to doctrinal solutions than the Marines had, and had centralized authority to a greater degree.

The counterinsurgency manual also called for greater risk tolerance in the interest of promoting initiative. The manual's authors, like numerous other American veterans of the Iraq War, found fault with senior American commanders for compelling all units to abide by a laundry list of "force protection" measures designed to minimize American casualties, for many of these measures discouraged risk-taking and aggressiveness.[72] Commanders in Iraq were required, for instance, to dress all of their troops in thirty pounds of body armor, which reduced their speed, and were prohibited from conducting patrols with fewer than eight Americans, which reduced their stealth. Force-protection concerns encouraged commanders to keep troops inside a few large bases instead of numerous small bases, cramping their ability to influence the Iraqi people around them.[73]

For General Petraeus, who was now the commander of the U.S. Army

Combined Arms Center at Fort Leavenworth, the counterinsurgency manual meshed with other changes that he and the commanders of the U.S. Army Training and Doctrine Command were making in training, education, and doctrine to inculcate adaptive leadership and decentralized command in the officer corps. Petraeus considered adaptive leaders essential because of the demand in counterinsurgency for complex stability and support operations, as well as offensive and defensive military operations, and because of the variations in counterinsurgency environments over time and space. "Our focus in the Army, certainly through the Cold War era and really even beyond, was on the major combat operations piece, which is mostly offensive and defensive," said Petraeus. "Counterinsurgency of course requires more in the realm of stability and support, although you literally do go back and forth. So you need a leader who is capable in those different types of operations, who is adaptive, who learns and makes adjustments, who can lead in the toughest of combat and yet also succeed in the toughest of stability and support operations."[74]

Petraeus altered the Army's training and education to require soldiers to deal with uncertainty and problems for which no textbook solution existed, in order to test and improve their flexibility and creativity. The Army also created Adaptive Leaders Courses, in which instructors confronted officers with a multiplicity of complex problems requiring rapid solutions.[75] Whether those courses made leaders more adaptive than the courses Petraeus modified is not clear.

When work began on the counterinsurgency field manual, Mattis was commanding the Marine Corps Combat Development Command, which gave him dominion over all Marine Corps doctrine. Within the Marine Corps, Mattis's responsibility for doctrine occasioned more than a few guffaws, as he was famous for having once pronounced that "doctrine is the refuge of the unimaginative." But if it was peculiar, it was also fitting, since his skepticism about doctrine enjoyed wide currency among Marine officers. As Mattis saw it, doctrine that went beyond general principles tended to discourage leaders from taking the initiative and exercising their creativity, and he deemed both of those activities essential for commanders in counterinsurgency, and indeed in all forms of warfare.

The new counterinsurgency manual's elevation of adaptive leadership and decentralized command was, for Marines like Mattis, an encouraging indication that the Army was moving toward the Marine view of doctrine. Mattis also found the manual useful as a means of helping novice officers prepare their troops for war. But he noted that it would not solve most of the problems faced by experienced officers already steeped in counterinsurgency principles and methods, the officers who occupied the critical command slots. Doctrine, Mattis said, "cannot replace brilliance. It cannot replace commitment. It cannot replace open-mindedness." In mid-2008, by which time he had become the commander of U.S. Joint Forces Command and NATO's Supreme Allied Commander for Transformation, Mattis was saying that counterinsurgency doctrine was increasingly a hindrance to U.S. forces.[76]

As mentioned at the beginning of this book, the counterinsurgency manual did not give adequate attention to vital leadership issues. It understated the importance of leadership selection, although an appendix did contain the assertion that the military should "ruthlessly replace ineffective leaders."[77] The manual also ran into trouble in its attempts to formulate universally applicable principles and methods. The principles enumerated in its pages included many of the timeless principles of counterinsurgency, such as those advocating collection of information from the population, organization of indigenous security forces, and disruption of insurgent logistics, but others were viable only under certain conditions, and could in fact be counterproductive if employed under different conditions.

The manual repeatedly warned of the danger of alienating the populace through the use of lethal force and insisted that counterinsurgents minimize the use of force, even if in some instances it meant letting enemy combatants escape.[78] In one place, it went so far as to warn against aggressive pursuit of insurgents, contending that the counterinsurgents should "only attack insurgents when they get in the way," because "provoking combat usually plays into the enemy's hands by undermining the population's confidence."[79] As operations in Iraq and elsewhere have shown, aggressive and well-led offensive operations to chase down insurgents have frequently aided the counterinsurgent cause by robbing the insurgents of the initiative, disrupting their activities, and putting them in prison or in the grave. The lack of such operations has often permitted insurgents to concentrate military power and overwhelm counterinsurgent forces and installations.

Although the use of force alienated Iraqis in some cases, in many others it went a long way toward winning over the elites, and consequently the people, even when it was employed in a less than surgical manner and even in the absence of major social, political, or economic reforms. Few Iraqi elites were willing to cooperate with the Americans as long as armed insurgents roamed their neighborhoods and assassinated at will. Civil authorities could not re-store governance or stimulate the economy until the insurgents were subdued, and benevolence would not subdue hard-core insurgents—only force would. Not until U.S. troops showed themselves to be the dominant military power, capable of protecting their friends and destroying insurgents whenever they appeared, did the elites gravitate toward the American side. At Tal Afar, Al Qaim, Ramadi, and most other sites of major counterinsurgent success, the conversion of elites into counterinsurgents required at least a month of fierce offensive military action by counterinsurgent armed forces.

Major Todd S. Brown, who served as a company commander in several areas of Iraq during 2003 and 2004, wrote in a U.S. Army Center of Military History book that winning over a hostile population required stern displays of strength and the use of overwhelming force against insurgents that attacked the counterinsurgents, even if it entailed some damage to the civilian popu-lation. "The more violent you seem and the more scared they are, the more they cooperate," he said. After a short time, the population would turn on the insurgents, since they seemed to be losing, and at that point the counterinsur-gents could reduce the amount of force and concentrate on developing local security forces. Brown wrote of the Iraqis, "Don't in a million years think that they will love you, respect you, and cooperate with you because you rebuild the hospital and schools and fully equip the ICDC [Iraqi Civil Defense Corps] and police force. You are smoking crack if you think that money and projects can buy you these things. You have to interact with the people daily and convinc-ingly demonstrate your ability to destroy the bad guys opposing stability."[80] Similar observations about the value of force and toughness have been made by many other observers in Iraq, both American and Iraqi.[81]

The manual, it should be said, was not entirely consistent on the employ-ment of armed force. In one passage, it acknowledged that "true extremists are unlikely to be reconciled to any other outcome than the one they seek; therefore, they must be killed or captured."[82] As commanders in Iraq, Petraeus and Mattis reached the conclusion that the most committed insurgents were "irreconcilable" and had to be killed or captured, while the other insurgents were "reconcilable" and hence could be detached from the insurgency by other means. They believed, in addition, that insurgents should not only be elimi-nated when they attacked, but hunted down aggressively. When Petraeus subsequently returned to Iraq, he instructed his subordinates to "identify and pursue AQI and other extremist elements tenaciously," and he made sure that they did.[83]

Despite the new manual's emphasis on adaptation and its assertions that no one method works in all cases, certain passages stated or implied that particular methods were universally applicable, including some methods with track records that clearly did not warrant such claims of universality. For instance, the manual recommended that indigenous governments adopt Western political practices, such as holding democratic elections and empowering women through social and economic programs.[84] Yet elections have weakened some counterinsurgencies by giving power to inept or abusive or disloyal individuals. Muqtada Al Sadr, instigator of sectarian killings and hater of Americans, gained considerable influence in the Iraqi government by way of elections. The highly successful Anbar Awakening, on the other hand, achieved success by rejecting democracy in favor of the birthright authority inherent in the tribes. As for transferring power and wealth to women, Western efforts have, in Iraq and other countries, alienated large numbers of men who viewed the initiatives as affronts to their religion or culture.

The publication of the new counterinsurgency manual in December 2006 received extraordinary attention from the media, making it a rarity of rarities—military doctrine that sold well to the public. Journalists and many others became convinced that the manual was a critical step forward in Iraq and, more generally, in counterinsurgency. After Petraeus replaced General Casey in February 2007, his actions seemed to be guided by the counterinsurgency manual. He assigned large numbers of U.S. troops to small U.S.-Iraqi outposts, similar to those in Tal Afar and Al Qaim and Ramadi, and emphasized the need for population security and nonmilitary programs. To stop the violence in Baghdad, Petraeus allocated an American battalion to each of Baghdad's ten districts, which was possible only because President Bush, in defiance of widespread domestic demands to downsize the U.S. presence, had just decided to implement a "surge" that raised the U.S. troop strength in Iraq by 30,000, to a total of 150,000. Rather than rotating American troops once the situation had improved, as in the past, Petraeus left them in the same place to help keep the enemy out and to help rebuild.

Petraeus himself, however, knew the manual's usefulness to be more limited than was commonly thought. He believed adaptive leadership to be more important than adherence to specific approaches, and he knew from experience and study that the most difficult challenges of command lay not in identifying principles and methods but in putting them into practice. "It is, as with many things in life, much easier to explain than to do," Petraeus said with respect to the manual. "The basic concepts and principles are not rocket science or brain surgery, but they can be very hard to apply."[85]

Although Petraeus's dispersion of large numbers of additional U.S. troops was hailed far and wide as the actualization of timeless counterinsurgency principles, it really represented a triumph of judgment and creativity over doctrine. It was consistent with two principles that apply to most counterinsurgencies—that forces should be dispersed across the population and that they should maintain a permanent presence—but it ran contrary to a third: that foreign participation should be minimized in order to promote host-nation self-reliance and forestall xenophobia.[86]

Another reason why the manual was not vital, Petraeus knew, was that by the date of publication the majority of U.S. commanders were already adhering to many of the manual's core principles and employing many of its methods because of experience, the circulation of lessons learned, and training and education. On returning to Iraq in February 2007, Petraeus was particularly struck by the fact that nearly all U.S. brigade and battalion commanders appreciated the nonmilitary aspects of counterinsurgency. It was, he noted, a dramatic change from his earlier tours in Iraq.[87]

By the beginning of 2007 many Marine and some Army units were living among the people, patrolling on foot, and engaging in numerous nonmilitary activities, as the manual advocated. Others operated mainly by vehicle out of large bases and spent more time on offensive military operations, which was consistent with General Casey's strategy of gradual disengagement. Upon taking command, Petraeus directed some of those units to change their tactics in order to control the population in areas where the Iraqi security forces had failed at that mission. Petraeus was not introducing a fundamentally new approach to counterinsurgency—Iraqi security forces and their American advisers had been trying to secure the population in those areas with sound counterinsurgency methods for several years. He was, instead, changing the allocation of forces to that mission. He wanted American units involved more heavily in population security because they outclassed most Iraqi units in initiative, resilience, and respect for the population, primarily on account of differences between American and Iraqi leaders.

Petraeus did not devote as many of his forces to population security as was widely believed. Seeking to maintain the initiative and deny the enemy sanctuary, he and his subordinate commanders assigned a substantial number of American troops, including many of the surge forces, to raids and sweeps against Al Qaeda hideouts and staging areas. Some of these operations were very large, involving multiple battalions or brigades, in contravention of popular counterinsurgency theories that viewed large military operations as invariably futile. Petraeus and the corps commander, Lieutenant General Raymond Odierno, ordered some of the offensive operations themselves and, abiding by the principle of decentralized command, allowed subordinate commanders to order offensive operations as they saw fit.[88] Colonel Peter Mansoor, Petraeus's executive officer in 2007 and the first months of 2008, recounted that determining the mix of offensive, defensive, and stability and support operations "was a call for commanders at battalion and brigade level for the most part, although higher-level commanders could intervene if they felt more centralized direction was needed." Division headquarters became involved when there was a need for multibrigade clearing operations.[89]

Petraeus and the counterinsurgency manual made their greatest impact in Iraq through their clarion call for adaptive leadership. When Conrad Crane, the manual's lead author, visited Iraq in November 2007 and questioned American officers about the manual's influence, he was consistently told that the exhortation to adapt was the one element that had gained widespread acceptance.[90] The impact was greatest among Army officers. In the Counterinsurgency Leadership Survey, which was taken shortly after Crane's visit, 75 percent of Army respondents agreed that their service encouraged innovation and improvisation at the company and battalion levels. That figure was still well below the ninety-four percent for Marine respondents, but the disparity was narrower than in the past, as most Marines had believed all along that their service encouraged adaptation.[91] Reflecting the difference in the manual's impact on the two services was the fact that 45 percent of Army survey respondents described the counterinsurgency manual as "extremely influential" or "very influential," while only 23 percent of the Marines did.[92] Although some commanders were still much better at adapting than others, the heightened emphasis on adaptation served to unleash the creative powers of some commanders and helped others by unleashing the creativity of subordinates who could feed ideas to them.

The manual did not do as much to promote risk-taking in the Army, leaving in place a huge impediment to the exercise of initiative. Fifty-eight percent of

Marine respondents in the Counterinsurgency Leadership Survey said that their service encouraged risk-taking by company and battalion commanders, while 30 percent said that it discouraged risk-taking. By contrast, only 28 percent of Army respondents said that their service encouraged commanders to take risks, and 41 percent stated that the Army discouraged it.[93] One reason cited for this problem was the tendency of senior Army commanders to order investigations into anything with a hint of impropriety, either because of their fear of scandal or because of their desire for tight control.[94] General Casey attributed the problem to the lingering effects of the standardization of Army training and operations prior to 2003. Referring to the period preceding Iraq, Casey said, "Our combat training centers started evolving towards a process orientation, rather than an output orientation. When you go to a process orientation, you drive people to a mentality that says, 'I don't want to make a mistake here,' even though in the course of making a mistake you might accomplish something larger than that. I saw this in Iraq among a lot of officers at different levels." As the senior commander in Iraq, Casey urged commanders to seek bigger rewards by taking bigger risks and assured them that mistakes and setbacks resulting from sensible risk-taking would not be punished, a message that Petraeus also sent out when he took over from Casey.[95]

When Petraeus assumed command of U.S. forces in Iraq in early 2007, he did not relieve significant numbers of commanders on the American side, convinced that most of them were up to the tasks at hand. But in December 2007, at the direction of Secretary of Defense Robert Gates, he returned to the United States to preside over the U.S. Army's brigadier general promotion board, an extraordinary act for a wartime commander. Gates, and presumably also General Petraeus, believed that the U.S. Army was still not putting adequate emphasis on developing and promoting officers with the flexibility and creativity demanded by counterinsurgency, and Petraeus was there to see that it did.[96] The board promoted H. R. McMaster and several other noted innovators.

Petraeus's impact on the Iraqi leadership received much less media coverage than his impact on the U.S. Army's leadership and U.S. strategy, yet it was more important as far as making headway in the war was concerned. Petraeus spent 30 percent of his very long workday with Iraqi leaders and 30 percent in the field, with another 10 percent at headquarters and the other 30 percent on matters relating to Congress and the executive branch in Washington.[97] Combining his personal observations with assessments from American advisers, commanders, and intelligence officers, Petraeus urged President Maliki and his ministers to remove commanders for incompetence, corruption, or ties to insurgent groups. Petraeus also worked hard to block Maliki's repeated attempts to fire talented and impartial officers for vigorously attacking the Shiite militias.[98] He instructed his staff and subordinate commanders to work with their Iraqi counterparts to remove inferior commanders and protect the good ones. Colonel J. B. Burton, a U.S. Army brigade commander, remarked in the spring of 2007, "I constantly take up the issue of bad apples with trustworthy Iraqi commanders, letting them know that we know these guys are corrupt and that we can't work with them effectively."[99]

Demonstrating considerable tenacity and guile, top Iraqi officials resisted American requests for the removal of commanders who had strong political connections, for fear that fragile political alliances would buckle, sectarian agendas would be compromised, or the bloated presence of Maliki's Dawa Party would be constricted. As in Afghanistan, the United States had reduced its ability to twist the arm of the Iraqi government by professing respect for democracy and national sovereignty. But Petraeus and U.S. Ambassador Ryan Crocker were sufficiently skilled that their cajoling and pressure—in extreme cases involving threats to withhold military aid to particular units—overcame much of this resistance. Iraqi army officers as high as division commanders were relieved in 2007. Most of them were reassigned to desk jobs rather than being fired outright so as not to taint the honor of their family or their tribe.[100]

In ousting bad police commanders, Petraeus and Crocker found an ally in Major General Ahmed Taha Hashim Mohammed Abu Ragheef, the Interior Ministry's head of internal affairs. With the Americans providing political support and detailed intelligence on individual police commanders, he relieved seven of nine National Police brigade commanders and more than 2,000 Interior Ministry personnel in 2007. One of Iraq's most resolute leaders, he was cowed by neither the dozen attempts on his life nor the relentless efforts by Maliki and his ministers to fill jobs with cronies and political supporters, including militia members. Maliki and Interior Minister Jawad Al Bolani erected enough obstacles, however, to maintain significant levels of sectarianism and criminality in the police and the rest of the Interior Ministry.[101]

Finding capable officers to replace those who had been fired remained the most difficult task, primarily because of the dearth of officers with adequate leadership experience. Petraeus noted later that there were not enough good officers with more than a few years of experience to command the new security forces that were materializing with great rapidity—total security force strength rose by 140,000 men between the beginning of 2007 and the middle of 2008—let alone replace commanders who had been fired. "You cannot generate that many additional forces and also fill them up completely with the commissioned and non-commissioned officer leadership that you'd like to see," Petraeus commented.[102] General Martin Dempsey, head of the Multi-National Security Transition Command, remarked in June 2007, "We've been growing young second lieutenants through the military academies for about three years, but it's really difficult to grow majors, lieutenant colonels and brigadier generals. It simply can't be done overnight. So we've had to rely heavily on officer recalls and retraining programs. However, the pool of qualified recalls is beginning to thin out. Several generations of Iraqi leaders were culled out by the Saddam regime and the Iran-Iraq war, and many fine Iraqi military and police leaders have been killed and wounded in the ongoing fight."[103]

Despite much public rhetoric from the U.S. military about the importance of advisers, the investment of personnel in the advisory mission still left much to be desired in 2007. The Marines were assigning some of their best officers to head advisory teams, officers who had been or would subsequently become commanders, operations officers, or executive officers at the battalion level. Marine advisers often had the same occupational specializations as the Iraqis they were advising. The Army, on the other hand, continued to give advisory team commands to officers who were rated well below the officers selected to command American forces. A fair number of them lacked relevant command experience or had occupational specializations unrelated to those of their Iraqi counterparts. Gates expressed interest in compelling the Army to select advisers from the same pools of officers that provided combat commanders and to promote them at the same rate, but as of this writing, the Army had still not taken action in that direction.[104]

In Baghdad, scene of the most critical fighting, the Iraqi government chose Lieutenant General Abboud Gambar to lead the counterinsurgency campaign of early 2007. The Americans had objected to Gambar's appointment, fearing that he would obstruct efforts to arrest Shiite militiamen, but the Iraqi government ignored their protests.[105] Gambar's leadership and that of his subordinates during the first half of the year did little to improve his image in American eyes. Most Iraqi policemen and some Iraqi soldiers in Baghdad did not even attempt to perform their assigned duties, and a smaller number secretly abetted the insurgents. Iraqi forces failed to catch insurgents in substantial quantities or disrupt their activities.[106] Brigadier General Terry Wolff, commander of the coalition military training and assistance mission, remarked in mid-2007, "What we've learned from recent Baghdad operations is that the quality and readiness of Iraqi army units varies widely, and the difference usually comes down to leadership. . . . We've seen that good Iraqi leaders have good units and bad ones don't, and we shouldn't kid ourselves about the fact that the Iraqi army is short of midcareer officers and NCOs."[107]

Although the Americans bolstered their permanent troop presence in Shiite districts of Baghdad, most Shiite communities were too sympathetic to the Shiite militias to betray them to the Americans. Small American special operations forces—which pursued Mahdi Army leaders across geographic boundaries using powerful and highly classified intelligence collection methods—accounted for the arrest of more than twice as many Mahdi Army members as the American forces sent to occupy the Shiite districts. Some of the militias continued the systematic slaughter and ethnic cleansing of Sunnis in the first half of 2007.[108] U.S. forces had more success apprehending and killing members of Al Qaeda in Iraq, whom Petraeus had designated the targets of highest priority. But large numbers of AQI fighters simply left Baghdad for areas with lower American and Iraqi troop densities, where they could organize and kill with greater ease, albeit with much less international press coverage. Nationwide, American and Iraqi government casualties increased during the first six months of 2007.[109]

In the middle of the year, as politicians and pundits in the United States were declaring the war lost, the momentum shifted, although some time would pass before this reality became apparent to the outside world. Insurgent attacks entered into a steep decline, falling from 180 per day in June 2007 to 60 per day in November 2007, with Baghdad and Anbar province experiencing the largest decreases.[110] One reason for this dramatic change was an increase in initiative and determination among Iraqi security force leaders, which was largely the result of command changes championed by the Americans. Another was the American troop surge, completed in June, which enabled the Americans to conduct more offensive operations and population security operations. A third was the extension of the Awakening across Anbar province, three other predominantly Sunni provinces, and some of Baghdad's Sunni neighborhoods.[111]

Under assault from many directions, AQI contracted rapidly in the second half of the year, allowing the Americans and some Iraqi army forces to spend more time combating the Shiite militias than they had before. The arrest and killing of great numbers of Mahdi Army militiamen in the summer of 2007 was one of the main causes of the fourth factor in the sharp decline in violence, Muqtada Al Sadr's order to Mahdi Army units to stop fighting, issued in August 2007. Sadr was also influenced in this decision by Maliki's repudiation of the Mahdi Army in August, a complicated decision based upon gross Mahdi Army misconduct, revelations of Iranian support for the Shiite militias, and the shifting balance of power in Baghdad. Many, though not all, Mahdi Army units obeyed Sadr's directive. During the last months of 2007, the Shiite militias lost control of much of Baghdad to U.S. and Iraqi government forces.[112]

Security continued to improve in early 2008. In March the Maliki government and its armed forces faced a critical test in the southern city of Basra, where armed criminals and militiamen were running amok, having destroyed the local police through threats and murder. Maliki sent Iraqi army and police units from other parts of the country to reestablish governmental control, sparking intense fighting, especially in neighborhoods dominated by the Mahdi Army. Some of the first forces sent by Maliki fought poorly or refused to fight at all because their leaders were weak or had sympathies for the groups whom they had been dispatched to suppress. Resolved to hold the wrongdoers accountable, Maliki fired 1,300 soldiers and policemen, including thirty-seven senior police officers, for their unwillingness to enter the fray. The Americans helped identify those deserving of removal, drawing upon reports from U.S. intelligence agencies and advisory teams.[113] Said Petraeus of the Basra operation, "We worked very closely with our Iraqi partners at all levels to agree on those who did not measure up and then discussed what should be done in each case. There was not always full agreement, but by and large there very much was."[114]

Maliki, with extensive American advice and logistical and intelligence support, saved the day at Basra by installing commanders of superior quality and summoning the best-led Iraqi units from around the country. The Iraqi commanders did not show much regard for doctrine or planning, preferring to rely on their intuition for tactics and on the Americans for logistics, but they were effective. Braving enemy automatic weapons fire and IEDs, they pushed into the city and killed enough insurgents to convince the remainder to negotiate an end to the fighting. Although Maliki committed serious errors during the battle, he obtained much favorable coverage in the Arab media and, as a result, gained the status of a strong leader, an asset that he had been sorely missing. Sunnis applauded his willingness to combat the Shiite militias, and the Americans toned down their criticisms of his leadership.[115]

Another flashpoint at this time was Mosul. The counterinsurgency effort was bogged down there because of Iraqi commanders who were unwilling to lead their troops into combat. As in Basra, Maliki moved crack units to Mosul from other parts of the country. In May, with minimal help from U.S. combat troops, the Iraqi security forces launched a new wave of operations that swept most of the insurgents from the city.[116]

In 2008, Petraeus repeatedly intervened when the Iraqi Ministry of the Interior tried to expel Sunni officers in the security forces whose only transgression was combating the Shiite militias, and he often succeeded. He also convinced Maliki to purge more of the sectarian and ineffectual police and military commanders. Murders of Sunni military officers and Sunni civilians dropped sharply. The number of Iraqi units that could conduct counterinsurgency operations without major external support increased, although numerous Iraqi units remained heavily dependent on American logistics and maintenance because of cultural inattentiveness to these functions and the pilfering of supplies by corrupt officers.[117]

The American occupation of Iraq is a story of leadership opportunities exploited and squandered. The first scenes of the drama were filled mostly with squandering. Douglas Feith, despite his creativity and intelligence, committed grievous mistakes during the preparation for war and in the first months of occupation because of deficiencies in judgment, organization, and sociability. Many of the early failures in Iraq can be attributed to the ineffective leadership of Jay Garner, a retired Army lieutenant general; Tommy Franks, an Army general; and Ricardo Sanchez, an Army lieutenant general. All three were short on creativity, flexibility, and organizational ability, which kept them from taking actions early on that would have increased popular support for the Americans and undermined would-be insurgents, such as stopping looters and restoring electrical service and basic governance. The appointment of these three officers to positions of high authority is indicative of the incongruity between the demands of counterinsurgency and the priorities of the U.S. Army personnel system in the years leading up to 2003.

The diplomat L. Paul Bremer and the other Americans who masterminded de-Baathification and the disbanding of the Iraqi army did not anticipate the disastrous consequences of those decisions because they lacked empathy and judgment, as well as historical knowledge. Had they studied the American South after the Civil War, a much better analogue to Iraq than Germany after World War II, they might have foreseen that disfranchising entrenched elites and transferring political power to a new group of uncertain character via elections would drive the old elites into rebellion. Bremer exacerbated the animosity of the old elites, as well as the rest of the population, with his choices of Iraqi leaders; he empowered individuals who, like the new elites of Reconstruction, were inexperienced, inept, corrupt, and disdainful of large segments of the populace. CPA and other civilian U.S. governmental agencies could have assuaged some of the resentment by implementing large political and economic programs, but they were too small and too averse to risking casualties. Although adaptive U.S. military commanders stepped into the void and found ways to run the country, they would have been more successful with the help of experienced and skilled American civilians and Iraqis.

In the first years of the war, the performance of U.S. military commanders varied widely because of differences in prewar training and education and, more important, leadership traits. Frequent brushes with counterinsurgents and leadership cultures that exalted certain traits meant that the Marine Corps and the Army Special Forces exceeded the regular Army in preparation for counterinsurgency and in the attributes of counterinsurgency leadership. Talented officers unfamiliar with counterinsurgency often succeeded nonetheless by improvising, experimenting, and inspiring, while officers who knew a good deal about counterinsurgency sometimes failed because they did not produce solutions tailored to local dynamics, did not cultivate Iraqis who could help them, or did not control their troops.

Serious as the leadership problems were on the American side, those on the Iraqi side were far worse. Large numbers of Iraqi commanders lacked initiative and determination, and therefore they and their troops were likely to die or flee when the insurgents began attacking in force. In the initial development of Iraq's security forces, CPA repeated the error, by now familiar to readers of this book, of paying much more attention to mass-training of recruits than to leadership development and selection. Putting civilian contractors and the State Department in charge of force development yielded dreadfully incapable forces, eventually compelling the White House to turn over complete responsibility for Iraqi security forces to the U.S. military, which performed much better by virtue of its superior appreciation for leadership problems and its greater willingness to urge command changes on the Iraqi government. The military also benefited from Bremer's belated recognition that the Iraqi security forces needed competent and experienced leaders, which caused him, in April 2004, to allow former Iraqi army officers back in. That policy shift led to considerable improvement in the new army, although it did not bring back into the fold large numbers of disaffected elites who had already become insurgents.

When the United States handed the new Iraqi government authority to select security force commanders in June 2004, it deferred nobly to national independence, but the transfer set the Iraqi security forces back at least several years and caused the loss of much Iraqi and American blood. The Shiite-dominated government used this authority to put unqualified friends and political cronies into commands and to keep able Sunnis out. The government made commanders out of men who instigated or condoned the butchering of Sunnis, and it removed commanders who tried to stop the slaughter.

General George Casey's strategy of employing American forces to clear areas of insurgents and then dispatching Iraqi forces to hold those areas made much sense in theory, for it played to the strengths of each group and encouraged Iraqis to shift into a higher gear. It failed on Iraq's streets, however, because the Iraqi forces did not have the leaders to carry out the hold phase successfully. Even where U.S. special operations forces eliminated insurgents in significant numbers, as they sometimes did, insurgents could not be kept out of an area permanently without well-led Iraqi forces. American advisers could impart valuable knowledge, provide sound recommendations, and inspire their counterparts, but they could not turn Iraqis of modest abilities into strong commanders. Short of having their counterparts replaced, these advisers could transform the Iraqi units only by taking command themselves, an arrangement that neither the U.S. government nor the Iraqi government was willing to accept on a sustained basis.

In Anbar province, home to the most formidable Sunni rebels, the Americans eventually became so frustrated by the superiority of the Iraqi insurgents to the Iraqi counterinsurgents that they scaled back their ambitions for a democratic Iraq and courted tribal leaders who derived their authority from bloodlines instead of the ballot box. American offers of power and funding for tribal militias helped encourage sheiks to switch sides, but it took gifted American commanders, capable of establishing military dominance and developing personal relationships, to cement alliances. On the Iraqi side, it took charismatic and dedicated tribal leaders to stand up to AQI and destroy it.

Once the right elites were allied with the Americans in a given area, violence came to an end within a few months, even in places where peace had eluded American forces for several years. This result was a reminder of the power of traditional elites and common identity between elites and followers, and hence of the tragic costs of tossing aside Iraq's traditional elites in 2003. Although the Awakening and similar initiatives undid some of the damage caused by the upending of Iraq's elites in 2003, large elements of the Shiite and Sunni elites remained hostile to one another, which has continued to frustrate the integration of Sunni elites into the government, an essential ingredient for long-term peace and stability.

During General Petraeus's time as commander in Iraq, his emphasis on adaptation did much to promote adaptive leadership within the U.S. Army, for whom it was a more pressing issue than for the Marine Corps. Petraeus issued guidance and doctrine that advocated adaptation, and he produced a conducive command climate. But the new counterinsurgency field manual impeded innovation to a degree by advancing as universal certain principles and methods that were not actually viable in all or even most counterinsurgency settings, most notably the principles that force must be kept to an absolute minimum and that counterinsurgents must always focus on obtaining popular support, rather than on destroying the enemy. The better commanders knew to treat such principles and methods as less than sacrosanct.

Petraeus, like Creighton Abrams in Vietnam, increased the involvement of U.S. forces in population security and nonmilitary programs but did not abandon offensive operations against the enemy. He called for some large offensive operations himself, because he believed them essential to defeating the insurgents. In accordance with the principle of decentralized command, Petraeus allowed subordinate commanders to order offensive operations when they deemed them necessary, and those commanders, including the most astute and flexible of them, often deemed such offensive operations necessary. Only when offensive operations were conducted so intensively that they squeezed out civil operations and other military operations was Petraeus inclined to chastise a commander for overusing them.

Like Abrams, too, Petraeus bolstered the counterinsurgency by effecting leadership changes within the indigenous government. Perceiving that Iraqi commanders were too feeble to defeat the insurgents in Baghdad and many other locales, Petraeus used persuasion and the threat of withholding aid to secure major changes in the Iraqi army leadership and wholesale changes in the Iraqi police leadership. Finding adequate replacements was a greater challenge in Iraq than in Vietnam during Abrams's tenure, for there were far too few experienced officers to plug holes in existing units while also supplying new units. Although the Iraqi government had begun to generate new lieutenants, it had an acute shortage of field-grade officers with enough experience and talent to hold the critical jobs at the apex of local security forces—particularly the jobs of battalion commander and district police chief. The leaders of Iraq's security forces, like their predecessors in El Salvador and Vietnam, need time and American help to build an officer corps that is both large and capable. A big fraction of that time and help lies in the future.

CHAPTER 11

How to Win

The nine cases presented in this book offer a multitude of lessons for those seeking to improve counterinsurgency leadership today and tomorrow. Although a few of the lessons apply to all counterinsurgencies, most apply only under certain conditions. The commander must become intimately familiar with the dynamics of the particular insurgent environment and use judgment and creativity to determine when and how the lessons of the past can be applied profitably.

Improving Leadership Attributes

Many of the ten critical attributes of good counterinsurgency leadership—initiative, flexibility, creativity, judgment, empathy, charisma, sociability, dedication, integrity, and organization—can be enhanced, to varying degrees, through self-improvement, experience, and guidance from superiors. By studying the history and theory of counterinsurgency leadership, commanders can identify their own deficiencies in key attributes and strive to improve in those areas. They likewise can identify deficiencies in subordinate commanders and take corrective action, whether by serving as mentors or by providing appropriate training and education.

Initiative, dedication, and integrity are the attributes most subject to free will and therefore have the greatest potential for enhancement. Improvements may result from a moment's realization or an emotional spark, from attachment to ideals like nationalism or religion, or from external stimuli such as insurgent atrocities or the deaths of comrades. Like Ramon Magsaysay and Gerald Templer, leaders can use their charisma and their personal example to inspire subordinate commanders to heightened initiative, dedication, and integrity — to such an extent that they can make the difference between victory and defeat.

Judgment and organization involve the exercise of mental faculties with which commanders are not all equally endowed, but these two attributes can nonetheless be augmented. Because every commander employs judgment and organization regularly, a leader's levels of these attributes usually increase over time. They can be enhanced further through training and education and through the extra practice provided by delegating authority to lower levels of command.

Some of the characteristics that confer charisma are plainly the result of nature, such as height, physique, facial features, and voice. Others, however, are at least in part the result of nurture — self-confidence, bearing, devotion, and asceticism, for example. Although many academics remain badly confused on the subject of charisma, or deny its existence altogether, professional armed forces have long understood how to bolster the charisma of officers, from the lowliest lieutenants on up, through training and coaching.

The military has much less experience in enhancing sociability and empathy, the latter being the only one of the ten key attributes that is absent from the personality types most closely matched to the needs of counterinsurgency leadership. Both sociability and empathy can be increased through the efforts of leaders and those who oversee them. Colonel H. R. McMaster, it may be recalled, prepared his troops during training by having them imagine how Iraqis would view their actions. Education on foreign cultures demonstrates the real-world value of empathy and illuminates the differences between cultures in how they view the world.

Of the ten attributes, the most difficult for humans to improve are flexibility and creativity, the cornerstones of adaptive leadership. But those attributes can be enhanced to some degree through training, education, and experiences, if those activities demand reliance on adaptation and complex problem solving. Recently, some reformers have advocated making the U.S. Army an "adaptive organization" by transforming the organizational culture through new policies, incentives, educational programs, and organizational structures.[1] The desired final product — an adaptive organization — is the correct one, but the instruments proposed for creating it are inadequate; they cannot reshape an organization by themselves any more than chisels and rasps alone can change the shape of marble. Sweeping change requires senior leaders with change-oriented personalities who, like sculptors, use their tools creatively to make the organization and its culture adaptive.[2]

In this book's nine cases, top leaders occasionally devised innovative strategies or methods that helped local commanders across the theater of war, such as the Briggs plan in Malaya and the strategic hamlet program in Vietnam. The main function of senior leaders in achieving adaptation, however, was to encourage innovation and risk-taking at lower levels through guidance, training, education, and doctrine. Creative leaders like Gerald Templer, James Mattis, and David Petraeus all promoted adaptive leadership in this way. Most adaptation took place when local commanders had the attributes to comprehend the dynamics of the environment and to craft viable new methods. Contrary to much theorizing about the stifling of creativity inherent in the conventional organization of armed forces, conventional forces adapted very well when they had adaptive commanders, even when they had not been exposed to counterinsurgency doctrine or specialized counterinsurgency training beforehand.

In a preponderance of the cases, indigenous culture seriously impeded Western efforts to boost certain key attributes in host-nation leaders. In some cultures—such as those of South Vietnam and Afghanistan—dedication to a political cause was often viewed as less important than dedication to family, so the elites generally tolerated flagrant nepotism and corruption. In countries with traditions of highly centralized authority, like El Salvador and Iraq, officers at lower levels were reluctant to take the initiative or make decisions, no matter how often the Americans preached the virtues of decentralized command. Breaking through this sort of cultural resistance usually took a high-level indigenous leader who was extraordinarily flexible and committed to change, someone like Ramon Magsaysay or Carlos Eugenio Vides Casanova.

Recruiting

Because many of the key attributes are influenced by heredity, upbringing, or ingrained culture, counterinsurgents should adjust their screening of officer candidates to give preference to individuals already rich in those attributes. One objection that might be raised to such an adjustment is that focusing on readiness for counterinsurgency is inappropriate for armed forces that must be prepared for conventional warfare as well as counterinsurgency. But a good counterinsurgency leader will also be a good conventional leader, while a good conventional leader will not always make a good counterinsurgency leader. Counterinsurgency leadership requires all the attributes of conventional leadership plus additional ones—empathy and sociability—and it requires higher degrees of flexibility and creativity. In the nine conflicts contained herein, counterinsurgency commanders had to conduct a wide range of activities that required those extra and amplified traits, such as leading complex nonmilitary programs, gaining cooperation from civilians and allies, and obtaining intelligence on elusive guerrillas. In the Civil War and during Reconstruction, officers like Ulysses S. Grant, William T. Sherman, and Philip Sheridan showed that highly successful conventional commanders could be highly unsuccessful counterinsurgency commanders. Because of inadequate empathy, judgment, or integrity, they used the tools of destruction without discriminating adequately between friend, neutral, and enemy, thereby increasing civilian hostility toward the counterinsurgency. They were too inflexible to grapple effectively with moral ambiguities and make the sorts of compromises that would have enabled them to gain the support of Southerners.

For leadership candidates who have not been monitored and assessed in leadership situations, testing for the ten key attributes of counterinsurgency leadership is the best way to predict success in counterinsurgency command. Psychologists have developed tests that pinpoint some of these traits but not others. Until more tests are readily available, the best alternative is to use existing personality tests to identify individuals whose personality types align most closely with the ten attributes.

In the United States the personality test used most commonly by the military, government, and business, and hence the one easiest to apply to this task, is the Myers-Briggs Type Indicator (MBTI). Derived from the theories of the Swiss psychiatrist Carl Jung, this testing instrument places individuals into one of two categories along each of four personality dimensions: extraverted (E) versus introverted (I), sensing (S) versus intuitive (I), thinking (T) versus feeling (F), and judging (J) versus perceiving (P). For the purposes of this book, the pair that is most important is sensing versus intuitive. Sensing individuals rely primarily on the five senses to tell them about the world, which causes them to focus on concrete facts, details, and the present. They prefer their information in structured form and are most comfortable when it is presented in 100-slide PowerPoint presentations with multicolor charts and exhaustive statistics. Intuitive individuals rely primarily on insight, which causes them to focus on abstract ideas, the big picture, and the future. They find rigid structures unnecessarily constraining and like their information served up in short memoranda that convey the most important insights and information.

Each of the sixteen possible combinations of the MBTI categories constitutes a distinct personality type. Two of the sixteen types stand above the others in matching the attributes of effective counterinsurgency leaders—INTJ and ENTJ, commonly nicknamed Mastermind and Field Marshal. Both are high in initiative, judgment, creativity, and dedication. The Mastermind type is also high in flexibility, while the Field Marshal type has high levels of charisma, organization, and sociability. Masterminds are considered the best of all the personality types at finding creative solutions to complex problems; Field Marshals are considered the best at leading.[3] People of these two types are especially valuable recruits for leadership positions in counterinsurgency because they are loaded with important attributes that are heavily influenced by heredity. It is no surprise that INTJs and ENTJs are plentiful in the leadership ranks of all sorts of organizations.

Two other personality types, Architect (INTP) and Inventor (ENTP), join Mastermind and Field Marshal to form the "intuitive-thinking" group, which is generally characterized by innovation, rationality, and strategic insight. Organizations dominated by intuitive-thinking personalities are known for their ability to adapt to changing circumstances and their commitment to continuous self-examination and self-improvement. Hence, they tend to thrive in fields that involve frequent and rapid change—such as counterinsurgency. They are the second most common types of organizations.[4]

The most common types of organizations are dominated by "sensing-judging" personality types, Inspector (ISTJ) and Supervisor (ESTJ) in particular. Most organs of the U.S. military fit into this category.[5] Studies by leadership experts and psychologists have found that sensing-judging organizations cherish structure, control, and standard operating procedures. Inclined to develop detailed plans based on past experiences, they are reluctant to deviate from plans or try new approaches. They do not generate major innovations, although they may excel at making incremental changes to the existing system or quick fixes to tactical problems. Sensing-judging organizations thrive in environments that change little. They also predominate among very large organizations because size creates a need for standardization—which helps explain, for example, why the U.S. Army has stronger sensing-judging tendencies than do the U.S. Marine Corps and most special operations forces.[6]

In the decades preceding the wars in Iraq and Afghanistan, recruitment and promotion in the U.S. Army and, to a lesser extent, the U.S. Marine Corps, favored those best suited to conventional warfare, which in practice often meant those with sensing-judging personalities. Two counterinsurgent wars have not resulted in dramatic changes to recruitment and promotion. In the Counterinsurgency Leadership Survey conducted for this book in 2008, only 10 percent of Army respondents and 3 percent of Marine respondents stated that their service had made major changes to how it recruited and promoted officers since the beginning of counterinsurgency operations in Afghanistan and Iraq. Seventy-six percent of Army respondents and 46 percent of the Marines believed that their service needed to make further substantial changes to yield commanders highly capable of leading in an insurgent environment.[7]

As a general principle, recruiters from the armed forces and other organizations involved in counterinsurgency should target individuals with intuitive-thinking personality types. Recruiting them in large numbers may require a special effort, particularly in a conscripted armed force, for intuitive-thinkers comprise only 6 percent of the general population.[8] For the U.S. military, however, focused recruiting is not a viable option at present, because the heavy demands of the wars in Iraq and Afghanistan prevent the armed services from being so selective in whom they admit into the ranks of officers. Fortunately, the young men and women who enter as officers include a disproportionately high share of intuitive-thinkers.[9] No doubt the natural leadership abilities of these individuals draws them to the military, and draws the military to them. The officer corps, moreover, does not have to bulge with prototypical counterinsurgency leaders. A large percentage of officers will go into support areas or aviation, where they are not likely to lead counterinsurgents in the field. And the number of commanders who do lead troops in the midst of the insurgency-afflicted population is relatively small, especially at the middle and upper levels of command. The principal challenge, then, lies in finding that minority of officers best suited for the key counterinsurgency commands.

While the U.S. military is right to give special attention to the pursuit of creative and flexible officers, other organizations seeking good counterinsurgency leaders should beware of placing too much emphasis on those attributes, for they are insufficient without the other eight. The leadership of the U.S. military is suffused with most of those other eight because people who are deficient in many of them are systematically weeded out. Many other civil and military organizations around the world do not have such bounty, because of the lack of rigorous hiring and promotion systems or because of cultural and political factors, and can ill afford to disregard individuals who are strong in those eight traits but not very creative or flexible. During the Iraq War and other counterinsurgencies, the civilian side of the U.S. government suffered from the presence of leaders who were creative but were wanting in other areas, such as organization, initiative, charisma, dedication, judgment, or sociability. Such creative people can be very useful in dreaming up new counterinsurgency technologies or envisioning the future of warfare, but they cannot cope with the human dimensions of counterinsurgency leadership or its day-to-day practical challenges.

Leadership Development

In the cases examined here, the counterinsurgents typically responded to the mushrooming of the insurgency with a rapid expansion of their security forces but were, in many instances, stymied by their inability to provide those forces with leaders of adequate experience and talent. Time and again, counterinsurgent planners assumed that training and equipping large numbers of forces would suffice, and gave scant attention to leadership quality. The resultant forces were invariably distinguished by inertia, ineptitude, and degeneracy. At times, force expansion occurred with such swiftness that it actually diminished overall capability, for the good leaders were spread too thinly and the ratio of good leaders to weak leaders sank too far. Avoiding this pitfall requires screening potential leaders carefully and limiting the force expansion rate based on the availability of competent leaders. It may even call for shrinking the size of forces that have grown too quickly, as Gerald Templer did with the Malayan police.

When the counterinsurgents tried to mass-produce officers by putting inexperienced recruits through very short officer-training programs, as in Afghanistan and Iraq, they rolled out woefully defective products. In Malaya, El Salvador, and Vietnam, the counterinsurgents had a larger pool of experienced leaders to tap when creating new units, but too many of them were of low caliber. The British were able to fix the leadership problems in the Malayan security forces by importing officers from other parts of their empire. In El Salvador, good leaders were developed slowly and were still too few in number when the war ended. South Vietnam took seven years to produce the leaders required for top local-level commands, and many of those were not molded from completely raw material but were young men with a few years of experience fighting in the Franco–Viet Minh War. In countries without such a base of experience, developing a new generation of leaders is likely to take ten years at the very least.

Effective leadership did not develop automatically with the accumulation of experience. Effectiveness depended upon the leaders at the national level who set the standards for recruitment and advancement and determined the rigor and nature of development programs. Without Ngo Dinh Diem's leadership, the South Vietnamese leaders who were produced between 1954 and 1961 would have been no better than their predecessors. In El Salvador, Afghanistan, and Iraq, efforts to develop leaders were hindered by the national leadership's inactivity and its toleration of abuses of power. El Salvador eventually attained national leaders, in the form of the minister of defense and the chief of state, who guided effective leadership development. Afghanistan and Iraq had decent leaders at the top of their defense ministries but poor leaders in the Interior and other ministries and in the chief of state's office, with the result that leadership development progressed much more quickly in the military than in the rest of the government.

Doctrine, training, and education contributed to leadership development by familiarizing leaders with counterinsurgency basics before they were thrust into a counterinsurgency situation for the first time. The U.S. Marine officers and U.S. Army Special Forces officers who assumed occupation duty in Afghanistan and Iraq in 2002 and 2003 had been familiarized with counterinsurgency in advance, whereas most U.S. Army officers had not, a result of the Army's gutting of counterinsurgency from its training and education programs after the Vietnam War. This difference helped account for the ability of the Marine Corps and the Special Forces to become effective more quickly than the regular Army. The Army's officers often had to spend much of their initial tours learning the basics, and some never fully comprehended the basics. After the insurgencies in Afghanistan and Iraq are over, the United States must at all costs avoid the mistake of expunging counterinsurgency from training and education.

Doctrine, training, and education could get an officer off the ground more quickly than on-the-job training, but they did not determine how high that officer could fly. The counterinsurgency commanders most abundant in the ten leadership attributes soared the highest, miles above those not well endowed with the attributes. Experience, self-improvement, guidance from commanders, and advanced study of counterinsurgency history and theory brought them toward maximum altitude.

Foreign Influence on Leadership Development

When attempting to build the counterinsurgency capabilities of third world allies, Western countries were often slow to grasp the importance of leadership development, even though their allies' leadership problems were usually much worse than any seen in the West. In Afghanistan and Iraq, the task of developing indigenous security forces belonged at first to civilian agencies of the U.S. government and to private American contractors. Both groups performed miserably, owing to the inadequate experience and numerical strength of their personnel. The U.S. government eventually relieved them of these duties and handed the U.S. military responsibility for all indigenous security forces, to include the police, disregarding objections from American civilians that the police had to remain under civilian control to prevent militarization of the state. The U.S. military performed much better in security force development than the civilian and private organizations had, primarily because of its superiority in improving leadership quality through advising, training, and the influencing of command selection. These experiences suggest that the United States should, in future conflicts, charge the U.S. military with developing all indigenous security forces, rather than conducting further experiments with civilian control. As a corollary, the military should continue to prepare numerous officers for security assistance, even during periods of peace. In times of war, the military should assign some of its finest officers to indigenous security force development, as it did when it put General David Petraeus in charge of Iraq's security forces in 2004.

During the Salvadoran Insurgency, the United States assigned advisers to work with Salvadoran officers, and it sent Salvadorans through officer training programs in the United States. In addition to inculcating basic skills and methods, the Americans preached the importance of respecting human rights. Acts of persuasion did not always suffice to halt human rights abuses, so on occasion the Americans used the threat of aid termination to compel compliance with international norms. In principle, threats to terminate aid would have been better used to demand the replacement of poor leaders, but U.S.

politics were such that essential aid to El Salvador was conditioned on respect for human rights, and therefore American leverage had to be devoted to the human rights issue.

American advisers spent countless hours counseling non-Western allies to develop good staff officers and noncommissioned officers who could take up some of the slack if a commander was weak or incapacitated. This advice rarely sank in. For Salvadorans, Afghans, and Iraqis, it ran contrary to the traditional centralization of authority and status. Whatever progress was made in this area was very gradual and was usually the result of persistent American action or pressure. The continued lack of strong staff officers and noncommissioned officers meant that the quality of host-nation commanders remained even more important to unit effectiveness for their forces than it was for U.S. units.

Because of differing personalities and occupational specializations, foreign advisers varied greatly in their effectiveness. In the cases studied here, sociable and empathetic officers generally made better advisers than others. The same could be said of officers who had experience in the type of work that their counterparts were performing. An American with past experience leading an infantry battalion made a much better adviser to an infantry battalion commander than did an American whose past experiences had all been in aircraft maintenance. In recent conflicts, the Marines have tried harder than the Army to find officers with the optimal personality traits and expertise. No matter how compatible they were with their counterparts, however, advisers could not transform poor officers into successful commanders.

Command Selection and Deselection

In all of the case studies, some senior leaders dedicated more attention to leadership appointments than others, and hence made better choices of commanders and more often replaced poor commanders. Some of the most effective leaders at the national level made leadership selection a top priority. Leaving their staffs in charge of administrative matters, they devoted long stretches of time to touring the country in order, among other things, to assess leaders and fire or promote them as necessary. One of the most important lessons, therefore, is also one of the simplest: senior commanders should make leadership selection and deselection one of their top priorities. If possible, counterinsurgency leaders should also dedicate some of their best officers to the task of assessing commanders and potential commanders.

Leaders and organizational personnel systems varied greatly in their success in appointing commanders with the attributes required in counterinsurgency. Empathy and sociability, for instance, were often given short shrift by military organizations. Sensing-judging organizations like the U.S. Army underemphasized flexibility and creativity.

The U.S. Army, owing to its size and the entrenchment of personalities, will no doubt remain a sensing-judging organization, but it can become closer to an intuitive-thinking organization by putting more intuitive-thinking officers into important leadership slots. The first step is to steer young officers with those personality types into the military occupational specialties that have a high probability of leading to counterinsurgency command—mainly the ground combat arms, civil affairs, and special operations. These are also the Army specializations that have the greatest need for adaptive leaders in conventional warfare. Officers with sensing-judging personalities can be shepherded toward specialties where structure and standard procedures remain the norm, such as air traffic control, supply, and acquisition. This approach ensures the assignment of intuitive-thinking leaders at the lowest levels of counterinsurgency command and increases the likelihood that they will become battalion commanders, often the most valuable commanders in counterinsurgency.

When sensing-judging officers dominate military-promotion and command-selection boards, as they often do, the boards are less likely to advance intuitive-thinking officers than other types, because intuitive-thinkers do not fit the standard mold. Sensing-judging commanding officers are likely to have a similar bias in writing officer efficiency reports, which those boards use in making choices. The intuitive-thinking officers under evaluation may seem less qualified to sensing-judgers because, for example, they may have spent more of their career than the average officer in academic study or in unusual jobs, or because they may have demonstrated less attention to minor details or less deference to standard operating procedures. On the plus side, numerous U.S. Army officers have come to appreciate the importance of creativity and complex problem solving in the streets of Iraq or the fields of Afghanistan, and they assess other officers accordingly. The same does not hold true, however, for the majority of officers, for they have not had those experiences, and they continue to follow the procedures that were followed ten or twenty years ago; they may operate in logistics, finance, engineering, or any of a number of other fields where standard methods still work most of the time.[10]

Officers who seek to increase innovation in the U.S. Army view ongoing favoritism toward sensing-judging behavior within the officer corps as the principal impediment to progress. Lieutenant General David Barno, commander of coalition forces in Afghanistan from 2003 to 2005, said in 2008, "I still tend to see, especially at the most senior level, more rewards for teamwork, conformance, and aggressiveness than I see for creativity, adaptability, outside-the-box solutions. I don't see a pattern of rewarding those behaviors."[11] Colonel Peter Mansoor, who retired after serving as General David Petraeus's executive officer in Iraq in 2007 and 2008, faults the U.S. Army's personnel system for "rewarding technical and tactical competence at the expense of intellectual understanding and a broader, deeper grasp of the world in which we live." The system must be changed, he believes, to reward "those who can think creatively, lead change, and understand information warfare and the asymmetric battlefield—those who are flexible and adaptive."[12]

Top leaders must ensure that intuitive-thinking officers receive fair treatment in promotion and command selection decisions. The senior leadership may even wish to promote intuitive-thinkers above others with similar levels of experience and records of achievement. General Charles Krulak, during his time as Marine Corps commandant, met with all of the Marine promotion and command selection boards to ensure that they did not overlook intuitive-thinking officers who did not fit into the sensing-judging box.[13] General David Petraeus's participation in the U.S. Army's brigadier general selection process was likewise an attempt to promote intuitive-thinking individuals within a sensing-judging organization. As Army chief of staff, General George Casey recently instructed Army promotion and command selection boards to reward adaptive leadership because he believed that senior officers without counterinsurgency experience did not fully appreciate the special need for adaptiveness and other high intellectual abilities in counterinsurgency.[14] Whether the proponents of intuitive-thinking leadership will prevail is one of the most important questions for the U.S. Army in the early twenty-first century.

Although personality type should be a key criterion when recruiting officers and determining their occupational specialties, actual demonstration of leadership attributes during assignments must be accorded much weight in promotion and command selection. Some intuitive-thinkers will be too weak in essential areas to make strong leaders in practice, and some non-intuitive-thinkers may be blessed with plentiful creativity and flexibility. Nor should the other eight traits besides creativity and flexibility be discounted, even in highly professional military organizations that habitually screen for those traits, and officers with a variety of personality types are well supplied with those eight.

While some counterinsurgency organizations ignored beneficial attributes in selecting commanders, others just as frequently favored attributes that were irrelevant or even harmful. Commanders in the upper echelons of the U.S. occupation forces during the Philippine Insurrection were appointed based strictly upon seniority. Salvadoran officers earned appointments based upon the year they graduated from the military academy. During the first years of the Huk Rebellion and the wars in Afghanistan and Iraq, indigenous leaders routinely gave commands to friends and family.

In most of the nine cases, political considerations frequently outweighed merit in the appointment of commanders. War, however, is ultimately a political enterprise, so politics at times deserved precedence over merit. When the indigenous government or the general population was plagued by internal dissension, selecting the leader of a political faction could garner badly needed support for the government. Abraham Lincoln's appointment of political generals gained the votes and recruits required to continue prosecution of the war. Hamid Karzai obtained support from Afghanistan's disparate ethnic groups by appointing officers in proportion to each group's representation in the population. In South Vietnam, Ngo Dinh Diem had to appoint some officers on the basis of personal loyalty in order to prevent a coup by military officers who were entirely unfit to lead the nation, a never-ending threat because of the fractious character of the country's elites. National leaders had to strike a balance between political considerations and merit when selecting leaders; if politics trumped merit too often, the counterinsurgents did not have enough leaders to conduct the necessary counterinsurgency operations. Afghanistan and Iraq provided prime examples of governments rendered ineffective by the excessive politicization of appointments.

One useful method of discouraging non-merit appointments was the use of centralized selection boards. Depending on the size of the organization, a certain number of board members would not know the officers in question and thus could be objective in appraising them. Factionalism could be discouraged by selecting board members at random or by making a conscious effort to prevent one faction from dominating. Centralized selection has generally been a success in the U.S. armed forces since its implementation after Vietnam. In the Counterinsurgency Leadership Survey, only 24 percent of Army respondents and 10 percent of Marine respondents stated that their service often chose company or battalion commanders for Iraq or Afghanistan who were less likely to succeed in counterinsurgency than officers not selected.[15] Centralized selection boards have worked less well for the Afghan government simply because President Karzai has repeatedly overridden them.

The other principal method of promoting merit-based command was to put command selection directly in the hands of a senior leader committed to voiding inappropriate criteria. Oftentimes it was a chief of state or a cabinet minister with broad powers. Ramon Magsaysay replaced large numbers of incompetent commanders, including cronies of President Elpidio Quirino, with able officers, having insisted at the time of his appointment as secretary of national defense that he have a free hand in personnel matters. General Carlos Eugenio Vides Casanova, upon becoming Salvadoran defense minister in 1983, took vigorous and firm actions that pushed merit ahead of graduation class in command selection.

In other instances, particularly those involving foreign powers, the senior military or political commander in the theater was best suited to hiring and firing commanders. As with cabinet ministers, the first challenge was convincing superiors to grant them complete authority to make leadership changes. Sir Harold Briggs failed to see his plan through in Malaya because he lacked this authority. His successor, Gerald Templer, secured that authority and used it to replace droves of weak leaders with better officers, which enabled him to make great progress in the war using the same methods that Briggs had tried.

Relieving weak commanders was not as easy as it might appear to the casual observer, even for senior leaders who had full authority to hire and fire. In many organizations reviewed here, the process required such burdensome tasks or involved such large obstacles that it discouraged authorities from relieving all but the very worst commanders. Firing a subordinate leader demanded a strong commitment to the greater cause, not to mention a considerable degree of emotional detachment, if not ruthlessness, for it often meant relieving a friend or a relative or a protégé whom the commander had nurtured. And relief often meant not merely humiliation for the relieved commander but career ruin. Adna Chaffee, along with Magsaysay and Templer, had the necessary dispassion. General William Westmoreland and many others did not, and therefore their subordinate commanders were of lower quality than they could have been.

Within both the U.S. Army and U.S. Marine Corps, many of today's officers believe that senior commanders are too reluctant to remove poor counterinsurgency leaders at the crucial upper levels of local command. In the Counter-insurgency Leadership Survey, 59 percent of Army survey respondents and 49 percent of Marine respondents said that American company and battalion commanders ought to be relieved for poor performance more often.[16] Furthermore, 51 percent of soldiers and 45 percent of Marines said that onerous procedures for relieving commanders discouraged the removal of poor commanders in their service.[17] These results suggest that the U.S. armed forces should act promptly and powerfully to remove the barriers to relief of under-performing commanders. Lives are at stake.

Although leaders like Magsaysay and Templer achieved great success through wholesale changes in commanders, that method was far from universally applicable. Highly professional Western armed forces did not normally have leadership problems of sufficient magnitude to justify major purges. At certain points in time during the wars in Vietnam, Afghanistan, and Iraq, the relief of weak indigenous leaders ended in failure because the replacements were as bad or even worse. Mass relief of commanders also ran the risk of creating such a fear of mistakes in other commanders that they would become less aggressive or stop trying innovative methods, as occasionally occurred in the Vietnam War. Some mistakes had to be tolerated in order to preserve the initiative and creativity that are vital in counterinsurgency. Commanders needed to supervise subordinate commanders closely to determine whether mistakes resulted from sensible risk-taking or poor leadership, and whether the successes outweighed the failures. When they decided to relieve a commander, they had to make clear throughout the command that the relief resulted from inadequate leadership rather than audacity or independence of mind.

Overseers of counterinsurgencies also faced difficult choices concerning retention of good commanders. With some organizations, like the U.S. Army during the Philippine Insurrection, counterinsurgent leaders who distinguished themselves were often kept in the field, sometimes for the duration of the war if they agreed to stay. With others, all commanders, good and bad, regularly rotated out of the war, and even the best commanders could be kept out for several years or more. Frequent turnover was a serious problem not only because it gave the most effective leaders no more time in the field than any others but also because commanders typically spent the first months of their tours taking in the environment and developing relationships with local leaders, during which time their effectiveness was substantially below its maximum potential. In lengthy wars, this problem could be mitigated by sending commanders or units to the same areas where they had served on previous tours.

In the U.S. military today, and especially in the Marine Corps, there exists significant sentiment for reducing the time between tours for the most successful commanders. In the Counterinsurgency Leadership Survey, 58 percent of the Marines and 33 percent of the soldiers responded that American commanders who performed well in Iraq or Afghanistan ought to be given another command in one of those countries sooner than is currently the case.[18] Marines, whose tours have been only seven months in length, were also much more open to the idea of longer tours than their Army counterparts, who initially had twelve-month rotations, later extended to fifteen months. Forty-eight percent of Marine respondents, versus 25 percent of Army respondents, said that counterinsurgency tours were too short in their service.[19] But the large majority of military officers today, both senior and junior, oppose tours exceeding one year, on the grounds that longer tours would burn out officers or cause them to leave the military for family reasons.[20] Those concerns must be taken seriously, especially given the long duration of the wars in Iraq and Afghanistan. Open-ended deployment of officers in wars of such length is unrealistic, but past experiences indicate that longer deployments are worth serious consideration. To facilitate extended deployments, it may be worthwhile to reduce the intensity of operations or provide commanders more rest and recuperation during their tours in order to prevent burnout, as has been done in past conflicts.

In the nine cases, the counterinsurgents usually put their best leaders into centrally commanded reserve forces or into local commands in areas where either the insurgents were strongest or the counterinsurgents stood the most to lose in terms of resources, media exposure, or key terrain. As matters of general practice, these personnel policies were sound. But counterinsurgents also needed decent leaders and sizable security forces in areas where the insurgents were less active. If the counterinsurgents inflicted too much damage on the insurgents in one area, the insurgents were liable to flee to other areas, as the Salvadoran insurgents did when the Salvadoran government concentrated forces in one province. The insurgents in Iraq evaded American forces in the same manner until the growth of local Iraqi security forces and the arrival of U.S. surge forces provided enough fighting power to control most of the cities simultaneously.

Foreign Influence on Command Selection and Deselection

A surprisingly large number of high-level foreign allies did not press host nations to replace poor commanders, either because of inattention or because of deference to national sovereignty. The absence of such pressure was, without exception, detrimental to the counterinsurgency. Concerns about infringing on national sovereignty were almost always overblown, for persuasion and pressure could have been applied out of sight of the media. No injury to national pride could have hurt the host nation as much as the continued presence of weak counterinsurgency leaders hurt it.

If and when a foreign patron recognized the need to influence the host nation's leadership selections, it typically had an array of levers to pull, although none of them was easy to operate. Of all the levers, those with the highest risks and the highest potential rewards involved covert action to replace the chief of state. In South Vietnam in 1963, a badly divided U.S. government fomented a military coup based on grossly inaccurate perceptions of South Vietnamese president Ngo Dinh Diem and the generals who overthrew him. It proved to be the worst blunder of the entire Vietnam War, for Diem's successors were far weaker leaders than he had been, and the coup was followed by a succession of new coups, each resulting in devastating purges of officers loyal to the preceding regime. A future coup in some other insurgent-plagued country will not necessarily have the same outcome, but it very well might if the country's governing elites are not highly cohesive.

In El Salvador, covert CIA assistance helped José Napoleón Duarte win the presidential election of 1984 over Roberto D'Aubuisson. The outcome proved to be a boon for El Salvador, though less because of Duarte's talents than because of his palatability to American liberals. Duarte's election did not lead to the sort of turbulence inside the government that followed Diem's downfall. For one thing, Duarte did not wreck the government and display complete incompetence, as Diem's successors did. For another, El Salvador's officer corps was much more unified than South Vietnam's and did not break into competing factions under stress.

In several of the conflicts, the United States threatened to withdraw aid in an effort to compel a recalcitrant ally to replace bad leaders. The efficacy of that approach depended heavily on the credibility of the threat. With El Salvador, the small size of the U.S. counterinsurgency commitment and the widespread American public opposition to the war convinced Salvadorans that U.S.

threats to cut off aid were not bluffs, so the Salvadoran government yielded to American demands at critical junctures. In countries where the United States had a large presence and a vocal public commitment, threats carried a good deal less weight. American commanders in such conflicts did, however, come up with effective threats that fell short of slashing the government's entire aid budget, such as General Petraeus's threats to withhold aid to particular Iraqi units.

When subjected to foreign pressure, some allies became obstinate, taking it as an insult and fearing that succumbing would show them to be pawns of foreign interests. The carrot, in the form of additional aid, was generally more effective in obtaining cooperation than the stick of threatened aid reduction. During the Huk Rebellion, the United States convinced President Quirino to relieve the Philippine secretary of national defense and replace him with Ramon Magsaysay in return for more aid. It proved to be the most important action of the entire war, for Magsaysay transformed the Philippine armed forces and stole the momentum from the insurgents.

Some foreign allies, seeking to zap leadership problems in their incipient stage, tried to change a host nation's very command selection processes. The World Bank and the countries of NATO compelled Karzai to institute merit-based personnel practices in the Afghan government to halt nepotism and cronyism. Karzai and other senior Afghan leaders, however, tolerated circumvention of the merit-based regulations on a regular basis, and themselves continued hiring their own friends and relatives. Without a high-level commitment from the host-nation government, merit-based hiring was an illusion.

A more intrusive, and much more effective, means of foreign influence was direct foreign control of the host nation's command selection. The United States used this model on a small scale with the Provincial Reconnaissance Units in Vietnam. The American prerogative to hire and fire the organization's South Vietnamese leaders eliminated the influence of politics and other non-merit factors, which made the Provincial Reconnaissance Units South Vietnam's most capable counterinsurgency forces. Between the fall of Saddam Hussein in March 2003 and the transfer of sovereignty to the Allawi government in June 2004, the United States controlled the leadership of the new Iraqi security forces, but it lacked the information necessary to make good choices. Although foreign control of leadership appointments could be inconspicuous with small forces, it was readily apparent when applied to an entire country and could arouse opposition in a variety of quarters. Another drawback was the inferiority of foreign patrons in juggling the political factors that needed to be considered in indigenous command selection—very few foreigners could grasp a country's internal politics as well as that country's elites.

The method most commonly used by the United States to improve allied leadership was also the least risky: persuasion. More often than not, the ability to persuade hinged upon the quality of personal relationships between the top U.S. leaders and the top host-government leaders. In Vietnam, senior Americans like General Paul Harkins and General Creighton Abrams who built strong relationships with the South Vietnamese president were able to effect the removal of dozens of ineffectual South Vietnamese leaders, far more than Americans who chose not to forge such relationships, like Ambassadors Elbridge Durbrow and Henry Cabot Lodge. Identifying host-nation commanders deserving of replacement required reliable information on their performance, which was much easier to obtain when foreign advisers worked alongside the commanders. Where the host-nation commanders did not need extensive guidance from advisers, as during the latter part of the Vietnam War, the monitoring of a counterpart's performance became an adviser's most important function. If an advisory presence was lacking, a good alternative was to hire secret informants within the organization. The most astute foreign counterinsurgents also assigned good officers to the task of pulling together and analyzing all available information on indigenous commanders. That method had the added benefit of producing more objective appraisals than the advisers', since advisers sometimes exaggerated the strength of their counterparts in order to show how splendid their own advice was.

To compensate for the scarcity of capable indigenous leaders, foreign allies at times put their own officers in command of indigenous units. This arrangement usually succeeded if those officers had the right attributes, even if they had to converse through an interpreter, although it was of course beneficial to know the local tongue. Philippine units that were led by American officers thrived during the Philippine Insurrection. Numerous British officers ably led Malayan forces during the Emergency, even after Malaya gained its independence. In Vietnam, U.S. Marine officers and noncommissioned officers commanded Combined Action Platoons, composed of a mixture of South Vietnamese militiamen and U.S. Marines, which became some of the most effective counterinsurgency forces of the war. A number of Americans, indeed, advocated putting the entire South Vietnamese armed forces under the command of U.S. officers but found no receptivity among top American and South Vietnamese leaders, who consistently rejected the concept out of respect for national independence and concern that it would retard indigenous leadership development.

In Afghanistan and Iraq, some of the American advisers to indigenous units became the de facto commanders because of the incompetence of their indigenous counterparts. The United States could have put Americans in command of Afghan or Iraqi units on a large scale, but it did not do so for the same basic reasons as in Vietnam. In 2002 and 2003, when top U.S. leaders decided to rely on indigenous leaders in Afghanistan and Iraq, the Americans did not anticipate the magnitude of the problems that would be caused by poor indigenous leadership. In hindsight, putting U.S. officers in charge of Afghan or Iraqi security forces at the outset seems an attractive choice. The attraction has decreased over time, for Iraqi and Afghan leaders have gained much counterinsurgency experience, and in Iraq the security situation is much improved. But some attraction remains, especially in Afghanistan.

One other means by which foreign powers improved indigenous leadership was disengagement from the war. This method held obvious appeal for foreign patrons, who typically were eager to reduce their investments in the costly business of counterinsurgency. In Vietnam, the gradual withdrawal of American forces after the Tet Offensive increased the willingness of South Vietnam's leaders to fight by forcing them to stand without the crutches of American ground forces. But this method also ran the risk of giving the indigenous forces more than they could handle, possibly resulting in major setbacks, if not total defeat. When General George Casey and General John Abizaid decreased American participation in counterinsurgency operations, the Iraqis did not improve rapidly enough to prevent a dramatic deterioration of the security situation, one that ultimately compelled the U.S. forces to return to an environment less favorable than the one they had left. In addition, by manifestly removing some of the most formidable forces standing between the insurgents and victory, disengagement heightened the aggressiveness and resolve of the insurgents.

Lines of Authority

The lines of authority connecting commanders to civil and military organizations empowered counterinsurgency leaders at some times and shackled them at others. In the nine conflicts, superior counterinsurgency leaders performed best when given dominion over all civil and military organizations in their jurisdictions because they could integrate and drive all activities in unison and fix leadership problems in all of the organizations. In several cases, the establishment of unity of command at the local level made it possible to coordinate organizations quickly and efficiently without dragging in higher levels of authority. Disunity of command, by contrast, meant duplication of effort and missed opportunities for collaboration, and it allowed weak commanders to retain their jobs.

When civil and military authorities were vested in one commander, leaders with extensive military experience, like Templer, Magsaysay, and South Vietnam's provincial chiefs, usually outperformed those lacking military experience, like Nathaniel Banks, L. Paul Bremer, and the civilian Provincial Reconstruction Team commanders in Afghanistan and Iraq. Familiarity with military affairs was invaluable in organizing the military activities fundamental to counterinsurgency. The superiority of military organizations over civilian organizations in rooting out weak leaders also contributed to this trend. In a large number of the conflicts, civilians forecast dire consequences if military officers were put in charge of civilian agencies, ranging from the misdirection of civilian programs because of the military's ignorance to the overthrow of a civilian government by sinister military officers, but such fears were almost always unwarranted. In the future, the optimal organizational architecture is likely to remain one in which civil and military authorities operate under the unified command of a talented, militarily experienced leader.

The civil and military sides were not unified in some of the cases for the simple reason that the civil side was absent, owing to lack of personnel and resources, or to aversion to the dangers of counterinsurgency. During the Philippine Insurrection, the local U.S. military leaders commanded all counterinsurgency enterprises. In Iraq, despite vast improvements in the U.S. government's capacity for transporting civilians to the theater of operations, American civilians have seldom been seen in much of the country, requiring U.S. military commanders to lead virtually all civil and military operations in practice, even if they were not the designated leaders on paper. From 2003 on, much effort has been spent in the United States to step up the involvement of civilian governmental agencies in Afghanistan and Iraq so that their expertise in civil activities can be put to use. To date, the exertions have borne little fruit, on account of the resistance of agencies to surrendering authorities and sending personnel on long tours to places where they could get shot or blown up. Whether the civilian agencies will be forced to become more involved is an open question. In the meantime, the U.S. government must continue to assign leadership in civil affairs to adaptive military commanders who draw on the expertise of military Civil Affairs, Reserve, and National Guard personnel.

Delegation of Authority

Effective upper-level leaders relied primarily on decentralized command, giving local commanders only a mission and a short list of constraints, most of them designed to prevent actions inconsistent with national policy, strategy, or ethics. As Creighton Abrams and David Petraeus experienced, decentralization impeded efforts to impose new tactics across a theater. But it beat forcing all subordinates to employ specific methods, which discouraged adaptation and compelled some commanders to use methods ill suited to conditions in their areas.

High-level commanders did have some powerful tools for directing the war, in addition to influencing and replacing commanders. They determined the allocation of troops, leaders, and material resources to different areas and missions. Such decisions could be crucial in conflicts where the security forces varied widely in capability or identity and where the counterinsurgents faced a multiplicity of necessary tasks, such as population security, offensive counterguerrilla operations, border control, and defense of cities. In the Civil War, senior Union commanders influenced the efficacy of counterinsurgency through their division of forces among population security, conventional warfare, protection of logistics, and homeland defense. General Sir Neil Ritchie in Malaya and General William Westmoreland in Vietnam assigned a variety of foreign and indigenous security forces to offensive operations against a mixture of irregulars and regulars, which reduced the troops available for population security but disrupted the enemy's offensive operations. Gerald Templer, Creighton Abrams, David W. Barno, and David Petraeus made major gains in population security by increasing or altering the involvement of foreign officers and troops in that activity.

Both Abrams and Petraeus centralized command for the large offensive military operations that they believed essential to success. In addition, when insurgents had appreciable conventional strength, as they did in Vietnam, the counterinsurgents needed centrally commanded reserve forces that could chase enemy forces as they traveled from one area of the country to another. Similarly, centralized special operations forces were needed when insurgent leaders, terrorists, arms suppliers, or other important subversives crisscrossed jurisdictions. Even in the absence of such threats, centrally directed forces could be highly useful as strategic reserve units; they could be transported swiftly to the sites of significant enemy attacks and other crises anywhere in the country. In Vietnam, El Salvador, and Iraq, centralized reserve forces saw more combat than any other units did, and participated in many of the most important battles, justifying the decisions of senior leaders to put some of their finest leaders in command of those units.

Methods of Command

With very few exceptions, effective counterinsurgency leaders regularly paid announced and unannounced visits to subordinates in the field, and some had their assistants make additional visits on their behalf. Such trips facilitated assessment and guidance of subordinate commanders, as well as comprehension of the war's dynamics. Through on-the-spot coaching, commanders helped bring along the leadership abilities of their subordinates—for instance, by steering them through the process of analyzing the environment or by suggesting ways to improve their charisma. They encouraged initiative and creativity and provided inspiration. Unannounced inspections also energized subordinate commanders elsewhere, for word spread, and no one wanted to be caught pedaling at half speed. Wise counterinsurgents undertook thorough security measures during such trips, aware that insurgents were constantly striving to kill talented counterinsurgent commanders.

High-level commanders who remained cooped up in their headquarters, like Ricardo Sanchez in Iraq, could neither assess nor coach subordinate commanders. They formed their mental picture of the war from written reports and statistical measures of effectiveness, neither of which conveyed reality as fully as field inspections could. Voracious in their appetite for more reports and statistics, they generated huge demands for paperwork, squandering the time of those responsible for the actual work of counterinsurgency. Some officers who seldom ventured far from their offices, such as Sir Henry Gurney in Malaya, attempted to micromanage the war, which was almost invariably counterproductive, and was doubly so when the micromanager had a poor understanding of conditions on the ground.

Three other principal activities absorbed the time of effective counterinsurgency leaders, each involving lengthy interactions with a particular group of people. The first group with whom the counterinsurgency leader needed to spend time was the leadership of the allied government. As case after case showed, cooperation usually hinged on personal relationships with allied leaders. The second group was the media, the importance of which has been ascending almost continuously for the past 150 years. With few exceptions, commanders who spoke frequently with the press obtained more favorable coverage of themselves and the war they were fighting than did commanders who spared themselves the trouble. The third group consisted of local civilian elites, whose support was essential for gaining assistance from the general populace. How to influence those elites is a topic unto itself.

Co-opting of Elites

Because leaders were the centers of power in the insurgent environment and because the population generally preferred elites who shared their group identities, savvy counterinsurgents went to great lengths to win over indigenous elites. In some of the conflicts, their efforts approached the toils of Sisyphus, for counterinsurgent policy was so odious to the local elites that they refused to side with the counterinsurgents under any circumstances. In much of the Confederacy during the Civil War, the elites were alienated to that degree by Lincoln's policy of restoring the Union by force. In Iraq, de-Baathification and the empowerment of Shiites made most of the Sunni elites into implacable insurgents. At times, stubborn insurgent elites caused so much harm that the counterinsurgents had to reconsider whether their initial policy objectives were worth the costs of alienating the elites. The Union chose not to revise its objective and thus remained unable to co-opt the elites in most of the South. In Iraq, the United States eventually backed away from de-Baathification and liberal democracy and thereby succeeded in recruiting former Baathists and other Sunni elites to lead tribal security forces, which quickly robbed the insurgents of leaders and turned the war around. When appraising policy options, therefore, policymakers must carefully weigh the effects on local elites against other projected effects.

Counterinsurgent leaders won elites over to their side with a wide assortment of tools, most often using multiple tools at the same time. Virtuous leaders employed good governance and their personal charisma and sociability. They influenced the less ideologically committed elites by offering money or power, or by destroying property belonging to supporters of the insurgency. Opportunistic elites could also be swayed through the establishment of security by means of a persistent armed presence and the capturing or killing of insurgents. When counterinsurgent leaders directed violence at their enemies, not at innocent civilians, and when they delivered it in sufficient potency to gain the upper hand militarily, most citizens did not blame them for the harm to bystanders and property caught in the crossfire, instead blaming the insurgents for provoking battles they could not win. Of the most commonly used counterinsurgency tools, those that had the most modest effects were large social and economic programs, which indicates that such programs should receive a lower priority in resource allocation than security forces, civil administration, and leadership development.

In the Philippine Insurrection, the initial American approach of providing good government and social and economic development programs failed to weaken elite support for the insurgents, but once the Americans started arresting and killing insurgents and punishing their supporters, large numbers of elites broke away from the insurgents, and some joined the American side, carrying the peasants with them. In Vietnam, Afghanistan, and Iraq, the use of military force similarly caused local elites to gravitate toward the counterinsurgent side, converting them into either passive supporters or active participants. Coercion and force were not universally successful, however, as shown by the Civil War, in which Southern elites so hated Union policy that they refused to switch from the insurgent to the counterinsurgent side despite the threats, punishments, and military successes of the Union occupation forces.

In certain countries, cities, provinces, and villages, bringing one group of elites into the counterinsurgency was guaranteed to alienate another, forcing the counterinsurgents to make difficult choices between elites. The choices sometimes decided the outcome of the entire war, and yet they were often made without serious deliberation. Instead, the decision was based on the assumption that leadership abilities varied little from one group to another. The U.S. government doomed Radical Reconstruction by casting its lot with Carpetbaggers, Scalawags, and freedmen who lacked integrity, initiative, dedication, and experience, a decision that alienated the traditional white elites, many of them veterans of the Confederate armed forces and government who were capable and popular leaders. In Iraq, the United States was similarly careless in its choice of elites when it sided with the Shiites, whose elites were replete with all of the weaknesses and few of the strengths of the Baathist elites they replaced. The Americans who made that choice paid too much attention to cosmopolitan, English-speaking, power-seeking Iraqis, and too little to experts with a more dispassionate view of Iraq's elites.

Reconstruction and Iraq also illustrated the perils of substituting new groups for traditional elites. In these cases, as in many others, the traditional elites outmatched the new elites in experience and knowledge, and they shared powerful group identities with the masses. As a consequence, controlling the population was usually much easier when the counterinsurgents allied with long-standing elites, even if not of especially high caliber, as occurred, for instance, in the Philippine Insurrection and the Salvadoran Insurgency. Of course, if the traditional elite was very weak, then seeking a new elite was necessary. The general importance of experience for counterinsurgent leaders, as well as the results of Reconstruction and Iraq, indicate that introducing a new elite on a crash basis is unlikely to produce success. The most fruitful effort to build a new elite, in Vietnam during the rule of Ngo Dinh Diem, took seven years to yield results, and it did not start entirely from scratch, for some of the new leaders had already possessed experience as junior officers when Diem came to power.

In the future, to escape entanglement in an inordinately costly war or to avoid partnership with the wrong elites once a war has begun, the leaders of great powers must increase their comprehension of foreign elites. They can seek out experts in their own governments who have spent years or decades covering the country in question. They can seek out expatriates and academic experts, while bearing in mind that both of those groups tend to be biased in favor of indigenous elites who share their cosmopolitan worldviews and who may not be representative of the country's elites as a whole. Diplomats and military officers can build up knowledge of a society's leaders by learning the local tongue, immersing themselves in the local culture, and developing relationships with local elites. In addition, intelligence personnel can recruit sources within the various elite groups to gain inside perspectives, something the United States did in Vietnam and, only belatedly, in Afghanistan and Iraq. In the longer term, much can be gained by building up governmental and academic research centers dedicated to exploring politics and culture in specific countries or regions.

During Reconstruction, the war in El Salvador, and the present conflicts in Afghanistan and Iraq, the United States supported elections that transferred power to new elites. According to population-centric theories, the elections should have produced dramatic gains in the effectiveness of counterinsurgency initiatives because the majority that voted the government into power would support it once it took office. But no such improvement materialized in three of these four cases, because the quality of the country's leaders was much more important to success than how they were chosen. In El Salvador, elections bolstered the capabilities of the counterinsurgents because reasonably good elites won. In the other three conflicts, elections did not have such an effect because the election winners were weak, corrupt, disorganized, or otherwise unendowed with leadership abilities. The electorate in each case lacked the experience in democracy that helps individuals differentiate the good candidates from the poor, a recurring problem in countries beleaguered by insurgents.

In the elections held during Reconstruction and the Iraq War, the traditional elites—former Confederates and former Baathists, respectively—were barred from holding office and, in the first case, from voting, which shrank the pool of good candidates and helped drive the traditional elites into insurgency. Elections also provided the means for parties hostile to the counterinsurgency's objectives to enter the government. In much of the South during the early and mid 1870s, incumbents lost elections to whites who opposed the basic counterinsurgent objectives of racial equality and federal oversight. These whites eventually won at the ballot box what they had failed to win as armed insurgents. In Iraq, the anti-American zealot Muqtada Al Sadr gained tremendous influence in the government through elections, and he used that influence to promote sectarian violence that was inimical to the counterinsurgent goal of a peaceful and multiethnic Iraq. Democracy in counterinsurgency is like dynamite in a coal mine, capable of reshaping the environment to the user's advantage or of destroying everything, the user included.

At the start of the insurgencies in Afghanistan and Iraq, precious few American civilian or military leaders understood the leader-centric nature of counterinsurgency. As a consequence, the U.S. government made a plethora of bad decisions on leadership matters, some of such import that they still haunt the United States. Over time, through experience and the labors of gifted leaders, the United States has been able to use leader-centric policies and actions to correct many of those misjudgments. It invested many of its assets in the improvement of Afghan and Iraqi leadership quality, and it started cultivating traditional elites who initially had been shunned. It promoted creativity and flexibility among its military officers. Still, much room for improvement remains.

The odds are good that the future has additional counterinsurgencies in store for the United States. Enemies of the United States have inferred from the wars in Afghanistan and Iraq that insurgency is a far more effective weapon than conventional warfare in fighting Americans, and hence they will confront the United States with more decisions on whether and how to intervene in insurgent environments. If the United States is to steer clear of inordinately costly wars, if it is to avoid falling behind in the first act of the next war, it must heed the principles of leader-centric warfare and the lessons offered by the history of past leaders. The choice for or against war must be based upon accurate appraisals of the elites that will provide the insurgent and the counterinsurgent leaders. The United States must develop its most talented counterinsurgency leaders and those of its allies and place them into positions where they can wage war without fetters, their unshakable initiative and creative brilliance streaming across the plains and mountains.

Counterinsurgency Leadership Survey

The respondents consisted of 131 veterans of Iraq and Afghanistan who were surveyed in the first half of 2008. Most were U.S. Army (USA) or U.S. Marine Corps (USMC) officers ranging in rank from captain to colonel.

Because of rounding, the columns do not always total 100 percent.

Host-Nation Leadership

1. Do you agree with this statement: The primary determinant of success for an Iraqi/Afghan unit is the quality of its commanding officer.

	Iraq	Afghanistan
Strongly agree	41%	39%
Agree	50%	43%
Neither agree nor disagree	3%	11%
Disagree	3%	0%
Strongly disagree	0%	0%
Don't know / not applicable	4%	7%

2. When Iraqi/Afghan military battalion and company commanders led counterinsurgency operations, what percentage were:

	Iraq	*Afghanistan*
Outstanding	7%	21%
Good	19%	19%
Mediocre	37%	33%
Weak	24%	21%
Awful	12%	6%

3. When Iraqi/Afghan police commanders led counterinsurgency operations, what percentage were:

	Iraq	*Afghanistan*
Outstanding	7%	19%
Good	16%	14%
Mediocre	30%	33%
Weak	28%	23%
Awful	19%	11%

4. How often did Iraqi/Afghan commanders at higher echelons visit companies and battalions to see how well subordinate commanders were performing?

	Iraq	*Afghanistan*
Constantly	0%	0%
Very often	17%	11%
Sometimes	31%	36%
Rarely	26%	29%
Never	2%	4%
Don't know / not applicable	23%	21%

5. Do you agree with this statement: In general, Iraqi/Afghan leaders who perform well against the insurgents are promoted to positions of higher authority.

	Iraq	Afghanistan
Strongly agree	1%	4%
Agree	19%	14%
Neither agree nor disagree	25%	14%
Disagree	17%	39%
Strongly disagree	5%	0%
Don't know / not applicable	32%	29%

6. Iraqi/Afghan leaders who perform well against the insurgents have _____ been demoted or fired without cause.

	Iraq	Afghanistan
Invariably	0%	0%
Frequently	6%	4%
Occasionally	22%	25%
Rarely	16%	14%
Never	6%	7%
Don't know / not applicable	50%	50%

7. Do you agree with this statement: Iraqi/Afghan corruption has led to serious shortages of equipment for indigenous forces.

	Iraq	Afghanistan
Strongly agree	25%	25%
Agree	39%	36%
Neither agree nor disagree	9%	11%
Disagree	7%	7%
Strongly disagree	0%	0%
Don't know / not applicable	20%	21%

8. Do you agree with this statement: Among Iraqi/Afghan forces, desertion and unauthorized absences are considerably higher in units with poor leaders than in units with strong leaders.

	Iraq	Afghanistan
Strongly agree	33%	32%
Agree	42%	39%
Neither agree nor disagree	4%	4%
Disagree	3%	7%
Strongly disagree	1%	0%
Don't know / not applicable	17%	18%

Indigenous Support

9. Do you agree with this statement: Many of the Iraqis/Afghans who possess the attributes of an excellent leader are not currently serving in the Iraqi/Afghan government or security forces.

	Iraq	Afghanistan
Strongly agree	6%	7%
Agree	39%	46%
Neither agree nor disagree	17%	21%
Disagree	9%	11%
Strongly disagree	2%	0%
Don't know / not applicable	27%	14%

10. Do you agree with this statement: Some of Iraq's/Afghanistan's most talented leaders are serving on the side of the enemy.

	Iraq	Afghanistan
Strongly agree	3%	4%
Agree	35%	25%
Neither agree nor disagree	17%	29%
Disagree	20%	32%
Strongly disagree	4%	4%
Don't know / not applicable	21%	7%

11. Do you agree with this statement: The Iraqi/Afghan security forces would be much better today had the United States not removed supporters of the former regime from the military and the government.

	Iraq	Afghanistan
Strongly agree	31%	4%
Agree	42%	29%
Neither agree nor disagree	7%	14%
Disagree	3%	18%
Strongly disagree	5%	14%
Don't know / not applicable	13%	21%

Advice

12. Do you agree with this statement: The U.S. knows enough about the quality of the Iraqi/Afghan commanders to make judgments about which ones should be removed.

	Iraq	Afghanistan
Strongly agree	6%	7%
Agree	49%	50%
Neither agree nor disagree	19%	21%
Disagree	17%	14%
Strongly disagree	4%	0%
Don't know / not applicable	5%	7%

13. In _____ cases, the U.S. needs to do more to get the right Iraqis/ Afghans into leadership positions.

	Iraq	Afghanistan
All	19%	25%
Most	40%	39%
Some	30%	32%
A few	6%	0%
No	3%	4%
Don't know / not applicable	2%	0%

14. Do you agree with this statement: The United States and its allies need to provide more advisers to Iraqi/Afghan security forces.

	Iraq	Afghanistan
Strongly agree	36%	32%
Agree	30%	39%
Neither agree nor disagree	16%	11%
Disagree	10%	18%
Strongly disagree	4%	0%
Don't know / not applicable	5%	0%

15. Do you agree with this statement: My service needs to assign better officers to advisory duty in Iraq/Afghanistan.

	USA	USMC
Strongly agree	53%	33%
Agree	22%	28%
Neither agree nor disagree	16%	13%
Disagree	6%	18%
Strongly disagree	2%	3%
Don't know / not applicable	2%	4%

U.S. Leadership Quality

16. Do you agree with this statement: The primary determinant of success for an American unit is the quality of its commanding officer.

	USA	USMC
Strongly agree	20%	25%
Agree	37%	45%
Neither agree nor disagree	24%	9%
Disagree	14%	18%
Strongly disagree	2%	1%
Don't know / not applicable	4%	1%

17. When American battalion and company commanders led counterinsurgency operations, what percentage were:

	USA	USMC
Outstanding	18%	27%
Good	35%	33%
Mediocre	25%	23%
Weak	12%	12%
Awful	10%	4%

18. How many U.S. company and battalion commanders are overly concerned with kinetic operations?

	USA	USMC
All	6%	3%
Most	47%	24%
Some	31%	48%
Few	8%	16%
None	0%	1%
Don't know / not applicable	8%	7%

19. Do you agree with this statement: Some commanders who excel in conventional operations are ineffective in counterinsurgency operations.

	USA	USMC
Strongly agree	37%	22%
Agree	49%	49%
Neither agree nor disagree	4%	15%
Disagree	6%	4%
Strongly disagree	0%	4%
Don't know / not applicable	4%	4%

20. Do you agree with this statement: Good officers can switch easily and quickly between conventional operations and counterinsurgency operations.

	USA	USMC
Strongly agree	20%	37%
Agree	37%	46%
Neither agree nor disagree	16%	7%
Disagree	24%	9%
Strongly disagree	2%	0%
Don't know / not applicable	2%	0%

21. Do you agree with this statement: Most mistreatment of indigenous civilians by U.S. troops in Iraq/Afghanistan is the result of poor leadership.

	USA	USMC
Strongly agree	41%	46%
Agree	24%	37%
Neither agree nor disagree	8%	7%
Disagree	2%	1%
Strongly disagree	2%	3%
Don't know / not applicable	24%	4%

22. Success in obtaining information on the insurgents depends _____ on the quality of the officers in charge of intelligence collection.

	Iraq	Afghanistan
Entirely	3%	0%
Heavily	41%	46%
Somewhat	39%	36%
Slightly	11%	4%
Not at all	1%	4%
Don't know / not applicable	6%	11%

U.S. Leadership Methods

23. How often did American commanders at higher echelons visit units in the field to see how well subordinate commanders were performing?

	USA	USMC
Constantly	8%	15%
Very often	24%	43%
Sometimes	33%	27%
Rarely	25%	10%
Never	4%	0%
Don't know / not applicable	6%	4%

24. How often did American commanders at higher echelons attempt to micromanage operations in the field?

	USA	USMC
Constantly	4%	7%
Very often	18%	12%
Sometimes	45%	54%
Rarely	27%	19%
Never	2%	3%
Don't know / not applicable	4%	4%

25. How would you describe the effects of micromanagement on counterinsurgency efforts?

	USA	USMC
Very helpful	0%	1%
Helpful	0%	6%
Neither helpful nor harmful	14%	13%
Harmful	55%	36%
Very harmful	24%	34%
Don't know / not applicable	8%	9%

26. Do you agree with this statement: Higher headquarters have put too many restrictions on the use of information operations.

	Iraq	*Afghanistan*
Strongly agree	24%	4%
Agree	24%	25%
Neither agree nor disagree	15%	29%
Disagree	17%	29%
Strongly disagree	4%	4%
Don't know / not applicable	16%	11%

27. Do you agree with this statement: Emphasis from higher headquarters on force protection has unnecessarily reduced the ability of security forces to accomplish their mission.

	USA	*USMC*	*Iraq*	*Afghanistan*
Strongly agree	18%	22%	17%	21%
Agree	45%	39%	43%	39%
Neither agree nor disagree	14%	16%	16%	18%
Disagree	24%	16%	18%	18%
Strongly disagree	0%	3%	2%	0%
Don't know / not applicable	0%	3%	3%	4%

28. Do you agree with this statement: Higher headquarters have put too many restrictions on the use of force.

	USA	*USMC*	*Iraq*	*Afghanistan*
Strongly agree	6%	10%	8%	7%
Agree	12%	13%	11%	21%
Neither agree nor disagree	27%	13%	19%	18%
Disagree	51%	51%	49%	39%
Strongly disagree	0%	9%	9%	7%
Don't know / not applicable	4%	3%	4%	7%

29. American forces in Iraq/Afghanistan spend _____ of their time completing paperwork.

	USA	USMC	Iraq	Afghanistan
Far too much	24%	10%	13%	18%
Too much	41%	45%	45%	39%
The right amount	20%	31%	26%	25%
Too little	4%	3%	3%	4%
Far too little	0%	0%	0%	0%
Don't know / not applicable	12%	10%	14%	14%

U.S. Personnel Practices

30. My service _____ selects officers for company or battalion commands in Iraq/Afghanistan who are less likely to succeed in leading counterinsurgency operations than officers who were not selected.

	USA	USMC
Invariably	2%	1%
Frequently	22%	9%
Occasionally	25%	25%
Rarely	12%	33%
Never	0%	0%
Don't know / not applicable	39%	31%

31. The current tour length of company and battalion commanders in my service is _____.

	USA	USMC
Much too long	6%	0%
Too long	10%	0%
Just right	53%	49%
Too short	25%	45%
Much too short	0%	3%
Don't know / not applicable	6%	3%

32. Do you agree with this statement: U.S. commanders who perform well in Iraq/Afghanistan should be given a subsequent command in Iraq/Afghanistan sooner than is currently the case.

	USA	USMC
Strongly agree	4%	13%
Agree	29%	45%
Neither agree nor disagree	29%	24%
Disagree	25%	9%
Strongly disagree	4%	4%
Don't know / not applicable	8%	4%

33. U.S. company and battalion commanders should be removed for poor performance _____.

	USA	USMC
Much more often than now	14%	12%
More often than now	45%	37%
As often as now	31%	42%
Less often than now	8%	0%
Much less often than now	0%	0%
Don't know / not applicable	2%	9%

34. Do you agree with this statement: In Iraq/Afghanistan, my service is reluctant to relieve its commanders for poor performance because the bureaucratic procedures for relief are onerous.

	USA	USMC
Strongly agree	14%	18%
Agree	37%	27%
Neither agree nor disagree	12%	15%
Disagree	16%	27%
Strongly disagree	4%	4%
Don't know / not applicable	18%	9%

35. My service _____ innovation and improvisation by company and battalion commanders.

	USA	USMC
Strongly encourages	12%	33%
Encourages	63%	61%
Neither encourages nor discourages	14%	1%
Discourages	12%	0%
Strongly discourages	0%	3%
Don't know / not applicable	0%	1%

36. My service _____ risk-taking by company and battalion commanders.

	USA	USMC
Strongly encourages	4%	6%
Encourages	24%	52%
Neither encourages nor discourages	31%	9%
Discourages	33%	27%
Strongly discourages	8%	3%
Don't know / not applicable	0%	3%

37. Since the beginning of counterinsurgency operations in Afghanistan and Iraq, my service has made _____ changes to how it recruits and promotes officers.

	USA	USMC
Sweeping	2%	0%
Major	8%	3%
Moderate	27%	13%
Minor	24%	15%
No	35%	37%
Don't know / not applicable	4%	31%

38. My service now needs to make _____ changes to how it recruits and promotes officers in order to get officers who are highly capable of leading in a counterinsurgency environment.

	USA	USMC
Sweeping	12%	3%
Major	29%	15%
Moderate	35%	28%
Minor	4%	18%
No	8%	25%
Don't know / not applicable	12%	10%

Doctrine

39. In counterinsurgency operations in Iraq/Afghanistan, the quality of local U.S. and indigenous leadership is _____ the quality of doctrine.

	USA	USMC
Much more important than	53%	46%
Somewhat more important than	22%	33%
As important as	22%	18%
Somewhat less important than	2%	0%
Much less important than	0%	0%
Don't know / not applicable	2%	3%

40. How much influence has the Army–Marine Corps counterinsurgency manual (Field Manual 3-24 / Marine Corps Warfighting Publication 3-33.5) exerted upon the conduct of counterinsurgency operations since it was published?

	USA	USMC
Extremely influential	6%	7%
Very influential	39%	16%
Somewhat influential	24%	46%
Slightly influential	18%	6%
Not at all influential	2%	3%
Don't know / not applicable	12%	21%

41. If there were no official counterinsurgency doctrine, American conduct of the war would be _____.

	USA	USMC
Entirely different	12%	3%
Somewhat different	45%	31%
Slightly different	20%	27%
Almost the same	20%	33%
Exactly the same	2%	4%
Don't know / not applicable	2%	1%

42. Do you agree with this statement: A unit that is well led will thrive in Iraq/Afghanistan even if it did not receive extensive training and education focused on counterinsurgency prior to deployment.

	USA	USMC
Strongly agree	20%	18%
Agree	33%	52%
Neither agree nor disagree	6%	7%
Disagree	25%	13%
Strongly disagree	16%	6%
Don't know / not applicable	0%	3%

Notes

Chapter 1. Leader-Centric Warfare

1. The White House, "A National Security Strategy for a New Century," December 1999, http://www.dtic.mil/doctrine/jel/other_pubs/nssr99.pdf.

2. For studies of individual counterinsurgencies, see, for example, Todd Greentree, *Crossroads of Intervention: Insurgency and Counterinsurgency Lessons from Central America* (Westport, Conn.: Praeger, 2008); Robert D. Crews and Amin Tarzi, eds., *The Taliban and the Crisis of Afghanistan* (Cambridge: Harvard University Press, 2008); Cyrus Hodes and Mark Sedra, *The Search for Security in Post-Taliban Afghanistan* (New York: Routledge, 2007); International Crisis Group, "Countering Afghanistan's Insurgency: No Quick Fixes," November 2, 2006, http://www.crisis group.org; Anthony H. Cordesman and Adam Mausner, *Iraqi Force Development: Conditions for Success, Consequences of Failure* (Washington, D.C.: CSIS Press, 2007); Daniel Marston and Carter Malkasian, eds., *Counterinsurgency in Modern Warfare* (Oxford, England: Osprey, 2008); Bing West, *The Strongest Tribe: War, Politics, and the Endgame in Iraq* (New York: Random House, 2008). Topical studies include Michael Bhatia and Mark Sedra, *Afghanistan, Arms and Conflict: Armed Groups, Disarmament and Security in a Post-War Society* (London: Routledge, 2008); Andrew J. Birtle, *U.S. Army Counterinsurgency and Contingency Operations Doctrine, 1942–1976* (Washington, D.C.: U.S. Army Center of Military History, 2006); Robert D. Ramsey, *Advising Indigenous Forces: American Advisors in Korea, Vietnam, and El Salvador* (Fort Leavenworth, Kans.: Combat Studies Institute Press, 2006).

3. In this book, insurgency and related terms are defined according to the Department of Defense Dictionary of Military and Associated Terms (Joint Publication 1–02). Thus, an insurgency is "an organized movement aimed at the overthrow of a constituted government through use of subversion and armed conflict." Among the forms of armed conflict are conventional warfare; guerrilla warfare, which is defined as "military and paramilitary operations conducted in enemy-held or hostile territory by irregular, predominantly indigenous forces"; and terrorism, which is defined as "the calculated use of unlawful violence or threat of unlawful violence to inculcate fear; intended to coerce or to intimidate governments or societies in the pursuit of goals that are generally political, religious, or ideological." Counterinsurgency is "those military, paramilitary, political, economic, psychological, and civic actions taken by a government to defeat insurgency."

4. Thomas X. Hammes, *The Sling and the Stone: On War in the 21st Century* (St. Paul, Minn.: Zenith, 2006).

5. Gil Merom, *How Democracies Lose Small Wars: State, Society, and the Failures of France in Algeria, Israel in Lebanon, and the United States in Vietnam* (Cambridge: Cambridge University Press, 2003).

6. Among the most influential of the hearts-and-minds books are Robert B. Asprey, *War in the Shadows: The Guerrilla in History*, 2 vols. (New York: Doubleday, 1975); Andrew Krepinevich, *The Army in Vietnam* (Baltimore: Johns Hopkins University Press, 1986); Timothy J. Lomperis, *From People's War to People's Rule: Insurgency, Intervention, and the Lessons of Vietnam* (Chapel Hill: University of North Carolina Press, 1996); Anthony James Joes, *Resisting Rebellion: The History and Politics of Counterinsurgency* (Lexington: University Press of Kentucky, 2004); John A. Nagl, *Counterinsurgency Lessons from Malaya and Vietnam: Learning to Eat Soup with a Knife* (Westport, Conn.: Praeger, 2002); John T. Fishel and Max G. Manwaring, *Uncomfortable Wars Revisited* (Norman: University of Oklahoma Press, 2006); Robert M. Cassidy, *Counterinsurgency and the Global War on Terror: Military Culture and Irregular War* (Westport, Conn.: Praeger, 2006); Rupert Smith, *The Utility of Force: The Art of War in the Modern World* (New York: Knopf, 2007).

7. For comparison of the population-centric and enemy-centric schools, see Austin Long, *On "Other War": Lessons from Five Decades of RAND Counterinsurgency Research* (Santa Monica: Rand, 2006); Colin H. Kahl, "COIN of the Realm: Is There a Future for Counterinsurgency?" *Foreign Affairs* 86 (November–December 2007), 169–176; Nagl, *Counterinsurgency Lessons from Malaya and Vietnam*, 26–29; Andrew F. Krepinevich, Jr., "How to Win in Iraq," *Foreign Affairs* 84 (September–October 2005), 87–104.

8. A recent exposition of this view is Edward Luttwak, "Dead End: Counterinsurgency Warfare as Military Malpractice," *Harper's*, February 2007, 33–42.

9. Ralph Peters, *Wars of Blood and Faith: The Conflicts That Will Shape the Twenty-first Century* (Mechanicsburg, Pa.: Stackpole Books, 2007); Nathan Leites and Charles Wolf, Jr., *Rebellion and Authority: An Analytic Essay on Insurgent Conflicts* (Chicago: Markham, 1970).

10. For historians, see Richard L. Clutterbuck, *The Long, Long War: Counterinsurgency in Malaya and Vietnam* (New York: Praeger, 1966); Brian McAllister Linn, *The U.S. Army and Counterinsurgency in the Philippine War, 1899–1902* (Lawrence: University Press of Kansas, 1989); Andrew J. Birtle, *U.S. Army Counterinsurgency and Contingency Operations Doctrine, 1860–1941* (Washington, D.C.: U.S. Army Center of Military History, 1998); Brian McAllister Linn, *The Philippine War, 1899–1902* (Lawrence: University Press of Kansas, 2000); Linn, "The Philippines: Nation-building and Pacification," *Military Review* 85 (March–April 2005); Thomas A. Marks, "A Model Counterinsurgency: Uribe's Colombia (2002–2006) vs. FARC," *Military Review* 87 (March–April 2007), 41–56. Present commentators include Barnett R. Rubin, "Saving Afghanistan," *Foreign Affairs* 86 (January–February 2007), 57–78; West, *Strongest Tribe*; Bing West and Owen West, "Iraq's Real 'Civil War,'" *Wall Street Journal*, April 5, 2007; Bing West, "Start of the Surge," *National Review*, May 28, 2007; Huba Wass de Czege, "Of 'Intellectual and Moral' Failures," *Army*, July 2007. Classic treatises are C. E. Callwell, *Small Wars: Their Principles and Practice* (Lincoln: University of Nebraska Press, 1996), 71–84, 125–131; U.S. Marine Corps, *Small Wars Manual* (Washington, D.C.: U.S. Government Printing Office, 1940), chaps. 1, 9, 21; David Galula, *Counterinsurgency Warfare: Theory and Practice* (New York: Praeger, 1964), 26, 67, 75–77, 96, 129–132.

11. Much more research has been done on the effects of leadership in conventional warfare and in the business world than in counterinsurgency. Researchers have consistently found leadership to be a highly important factor in the behaviors and achievements of armies and corporations, although they disagree as to whether it is the most important factor. See, for instance, Bruce J. Avolio and Fred Luthans, *The High Impact Leader* (New York: McGraw-Hill, 2005); William A. Cohen, *The New Art of the Leader* (Paramus, N.J.: Prentice Hall, 2000); Christopher Kolenda, ed., *Leadership: The Warrior's Art* (Carlisle, Pa.: Army War College Foundation Press, 2001); Kenneth E. Clark et al., eds., *Impact of Leadership* (Greensboro, N.C.: Center for Creative Leadership, 1992); David Ulrich et al., *Results-Based Leadership* (Boston: Harvard Business School Press, 1999); Joseph J. Thomas, ed., *Leadership Embodied: The Secrets to Success of the Most Effective Navy and Marine Corps Leaders* (Annapolis, Md.: Naval Institute Press, 2005); Harry S. Laver and Jeffrey J. Matthews, *The Art of Command: Military Leadership from George Washington to Colin Powell* (Lexington: University Press of Kentucky, 2008).

12. A wide variety of counterinsurgency books examine methods in great detail, from single and multiwar histories to doctrinal and theoretical publications. Among the most useful histories are Uldarico S. Baclagon, *Lessons from the Huk Campaign in the Philippines* (Manila: M. Colcol,

1956); Clutterbuck, *Long, Long War;* Mark Moyar, *Phoenix and the Birds of Prey: Counterinsurgency and Counterterrorism in Vietnam,* new ed. (Lincoln: University of Nebraska Press, 2007), 164–173; Robert Thompson, *Defeating Communist Insurgency: The Lessons of Malaya and Vietnam* (New York: Praeger, 1966). Useful theoretical and doctrinal works include Callwell, *Small Wars;* U.S. Marine Corps, *Small Wars Manual;* Galula, *Counterinsurgency Warfare;* Director of Operations, Malaya, *The Conduct of Anti-Terrorist Operations in Malaya,* 3rd ed. (London: Her Britannic Majesty's Stationery Office, 1958); Roger Trinquier, *Modern Warfare: A French View of Counterinsurgency,* trans. Daniel Lee (New York: Praeger, 1964).

13. Many, though not all, leadership theorists believe that leadership effectiveness in a given type of setting depends primarily upon possession of a set of traits. See, for instance, Peter G. Northouse, *Leadership: Theory and Practice,* 4th ed. (Thousand Oaks, Calif.: Sage, 2004); Ulrich et al., *Results-Based Leadership;* C. Brooklyn Derr et al., eds., *Cross-Cultural Approaches to Leadership Development* (Westport, Conn.: Quorum Books, 2002); Daniel Goleman et al., *Primal Leadership: Realizing the Power of Emotional Intelligence* (Boston: Harvard Business School Press, 2002); Donald E. Riggio, ed., *Multiple Intelligences and Leadership* (Mahwah, N.J.: Lawrence Earlbaum, 2002); Jon J. Fallesen and Rebecca J. Reichard, *Leadership Competencies: Building a Foundation for Army Leader Development* (Los Angeles: Society of Industrial and Organizational Psychologists, 2005). Other theories, which put greater emphasis on processes, subordinates, and other factors, have been assessed based on the data collected for this book and have been found to be incapable of accounting adequately for individual differences in leadership effectiveness.

14. *The U.S. Army/Marine Corps Counterinsurgency Field Manual* points out that the varied nature of counterinsurgency calls for commanders with the ability to adapt to local circumstances, and notes the importance of several traits that enable leaders to identify appropriate counterinsurgency methods. It does not, however, consider other traits that are essential to implementing counterinsurgency methods. Field Manual 3-24/Marine Corps Warfighting Publication 3-33.5, *Counterinsurgency,* ix, 1-26, 5-31, 7-3, 7-4. The Army also published new leadership doctrine in late 2006. It covers more, but not all, of the ten traits identified in this book as the key counterinsurgency leadership attributes. Like the counterinsurgency manual, the new leadership doctrine does not explain how to find the right officers for the key command slots. Field Manual 6-22, *Army Leadership* (Washington, D.C.: Department of the Army, October 2006). One must also avoid assuming, as is sometimes assumed in studies of military organizations, that organizations necessarily adhere to their doctrine. As later chapters show, promotion and command selection boards in the U.S. military do not always base their decisions on the attributes stressed in doctrine.

15. Numerous psychologists and leadership consultants have concluded that many personal attributes, including most of the ten key counterinsurgency attributes identified here, are partly or completely innate. Isabell Briggs Myers, *Gifts Differing: Understanding Personality Type* (Palo Alto, Calif.: Davies-Black, 1995); Richard L. Hughes et al., *Leadership: Enhancing the Lessons of Experience* (New York: McGraw-Hill/Irwin, 2005); David Keirsey, *Please Understand Me II: Temperament, Character, Intelligence* (Del Mar, Calif.: Prometheus Nemesis, 1998); Otto Kroeger et al., *Type Talk at Work: How the 16 Personality Types Determine Your Success on the Job* (New York: Dell, 2002); Lee Barr and Norma Barr, *The Leadership Equation: Leadership, Management, and the Myers-Briggs* (Austin, Tex.: Eakin, 1989). Military officers and military historians have long held that the traits of effective leaders in conventional warfare are heavily influenced by genetics. See Edgar F. Puryear, Jr., *Character Is Everything: The Art of Command* (Novato, Calif.: Presidio, 2000); Carol McCann and Ross Pigeau, *The Human in Command: Exploring the Modern Military Experience* (New York: Kluwer Academic/Plenum, 2000); James G. Hunt et al., eds., *Out-of-the-Box Leadership: Transforming the Twenty-first-Century Army and Other Top-Performing Organizations* (Stamford, Conn.: JAI, 1999).

Chapter 2. The Civil War

1. Darl L. Stephenson, *Headquarters in the Brush: Blazer's Independent Union Scouts* (Athens: Ohio University Press, 2001), 162–182; J. Marshall Crawford, *Mosby and His Men: A Record of the Adventures of That Renowned Partisan Ranger, John S. Mosby* (New York: G. W. Carleton, 1867), 285–304; John H. Alexander, *Mosby's Men* (New York: Neal, 1907), 116–128 (quotation on p. 116).

2. Grimsley, *Hard Hand of War;* Ash, *When the Yankees Came.*

3. Andrew J. Birtle, *U.S. Army Counterinsurgency and Contingency Operations Doctrine, 1860-1941* (Washington, D.C.: U.S. Army Center of Military History, 1998), 42.

4. George Crook, *General George Crook* (Norman: University of Oklahoma Press, 1946), 87-88.

5. Tom Chaffin, *Pathfinder: John Charles Frémont and the Course of American Empire* (New York: Hill and Wang, 2002), 455-457.

6. Goss, *War Within the Union High Command,* 51, 69-70; Chaffin, *Pathfinder,* 459-462.

7. Chaffin, *Pathfinder,* 460-461 (quotation), 466.

8. Goss, *War Within the Union High Command,* 70.

9. Castel, *Civil War Kansas,* 61-64.

10. Richard S. Brownlee, *Gray Ghosts of the Confederacy: Guerrilla Warfare in the West, 1861-1865* (Baton Rouge: Louisiana State University Press, 1958), 18, 36-37; Grimsley, *Hard Hand of War,* 48-49; Goss, *War Within the Union High Command,* 70; Chaffin, *Pathfinder,* 463-472.

11. Stephen E. Ambrose, *Halleck: Lincoln's Chief of Staff* (Baton Rouge: Louisiana State University Press, 1962), 5-10; Marszalek, *Commander of All Lincoln's Armies,* 15-108.

12. McClellan to Halleck, November 11, 1861, in U.S. War Department, *The War of the Rebellion: A Compilation of the Official Records of the Union and Confederate Armies,* ser. I, vol. 5, pp. 1120-1121.

13. Marszalek, *Commander of All Lincoln's Armies,* 109-110; Grimsley, *Hard Hand of War,* 49 (quotation); Goss, *War Within the Union High Command,* 71-72.

14. Grimsley, *Hard Hand of War,* 50.

15. Fellman, *Inside War,* 84, 122-126; Brownlee, *Gray Ghosts of the Confederacy,* 157-159, 175-176.

16. Fellman, *Inside War,* 81-82, 112-113, 117-123, 128-129, 157-158, 166, 169.

17. Castel, *Civil War Kansas,* 81-89.

18. Donald B. Connelly, *John M. Schofield and the Politics of Generalship* (Chapel Hill: University of North Carolina Press, 2006), 65-77.

19. Castel, *Civil War Kansas,* 121-122, 142-144, 152-153.

20. Ibid., 148, 150-151, 161-164 (quotations on pp. 148 and 150).

21. Stephen D. Engle, *Struggle for the Heartland: The Campaigns from Fort Henry to Corinth* (Lincoln: University of Nebraska Press, 2001), 196-205; B. Franklin Cooling, "A People's War: Partisan Conflict in Tennessee and Kentucky," in Sutherland, *Guerrillas, Unionists, and Violence;* Grimsley, *Hard Hand of War,* 113-118; John F. Marszalek, *Sherman: A Soldier's Passion for Order* (New York: Free Press, 1993), 194-196.

22. Rachel Sherman Thorndike, ed., *The Sherman Letters: Correspondence Between General and Senator Sherman from 1837 to 1891* (New York: Scribner's, 1894), 245-246.

23. Groce, *Mountain Rebels,* 123-126; Hans L. Trefousse, *Andrew Johnson: A Biography* (New York: Norton, 1989), 156-169; Cooling, "A People's War," 120-132.

24. Trefousse, *Andrew Johnson,* 162.

25. Fisher, *War at Every Door,* 81-82, 90 (quotation).

26. Ibid., 132-133, 153.

27. Ibid., 146-148 (quotations on p. 148).

28. Mackey, *Uncivil War,* 25-31.

29. Ibid., 36-41, 48.

30. Bussey to Levering, March 8, 1865, in U.S. War Department, *War of the Rebellion,* ser. I, vol. 48, part 1, pp. 1120-1121.

31. Mackey, *Uncivil War,* 32-33, 53-57.

32. Ibid., 61-71 (quotation on p. 71).

33. Joseph G. Dawson, *Army Generals and Reconstruction: Louisiana, 1862-1877* (Baton Rouge: Louisiana State University Press, 1982), 5-6; Goss, *War Within the Union High Command,* 25-26, 40-41, 228, 261.

34. Goss, *War Within the Union High Command,* 152-153.

35. Dick Nolan, *Benjamin Franklin Butler: The Damnedest Yankee* (Novato, Calif.: Presidio,

1991), 156–221; Howard P. Nash, Jr., *Stormy Petrel: The Life and Times of General Benjamin F. Butler, 1818–1893* (Rutherford, N.J.: Fairleigh Dickinson University Press, 1969), 145–177; Dawson, *Army Generals and Reconstruction*, 6–11; Joe Gray Taylor, *Louisiana Reconstructed, 1863–1877* (Baton Rouge: Louisiana State University Press, 1974), 2–18.

36. Goss, *War Within the Union High Command*, 29–30.

37. Brooks D. Simpson, *The Reconstruction Presidents* (Lawrence: University Press of Kansas, 1998), 38–45; Goss, *War Within the Union High Command*, 136–139; Taylor, *Louisiana Reconstructed*, 18–52.

Chapter 3. Reconstruction in the South

1. Thomas B. Alexander, *Political Reconstruction in Tennessee* (Nashville, Tenn.: Vanderbilt University Press, 1950), 51–54, 58–68; Noel C. Fisher, *War at Every Door: Partisan Politics and Guerrilla Violence in East Tennessee, 1860–1869* (Chapel Hill: University of North Carolina Press, 1997), 154–164; W. Todd Groce, *Mountain Rebels: East Tennessee Confederates and the Civil War, 1860–1870* (Knoxville: University of Tennessee Press, 1999), 127–151.

2. Groce, *Mountain Rebels*, 134.

3. Michael Fellman, *Inside War: The Guerrilla Conflict in Missouri during the American Civil War* (New York: Oxford University Press, 1989), 231–240.

4. Ibid., 238–242 (quotations on p. 241).

5. Hans L. Trefousse, *Andrew Johnson: A Biography* (New York: Norton, 1989), 214–233.

6. Sefton, *United States Army and Reconstruction*, 93.

7. Thomas J. Goss, *The War Within the Union High Command: Politics and Generalship during the Civil War* (Lawrence: University Press of Kansas, 2003), 196–198; Brooks D. Simpson, *Ulysses S. Grant: Triumph over Adversity, 1822–1865* (New York: Houghton Mifflin, 2000), 392.

8. Halleck to Grant, April 29, 1865, in U.S. War Department, *The War of the Rebellion: A Compilation of the Official Records of the Union and Confederate Armies*, ser. I, vol. 46, part 3, pp. 1005–1006.

9. Grant to Halleck, April 30, 1865, in U.S. War Department, *War of the Rebellion*, ser. I, vol. 46, part 3, p. 1016.

10. Walter L. Fleming, ed., *Documentary History of Reconstruction* (Gloucester, Mass.: Peter Smith, 1960), vol. 1, pp. 340–342.

11. Ibid., vol. 1, pp. 366–367.

12. Randy Finley, "The Personnel of the Freedmen's Bureau in Arkansas," in Cimbala and Miller, *Freedmen's Bureau and Reconstruction*, 97–99; Thomas Staples, *Reconstruction in Arkansas, 1862–1874* (New York: Columbia University Press, 1923), 168, 197.

13. James M. Smallwood et al., *Murder and Mayhem: The War of Reconstruction in Texas* (College Station: Texas A & M University Press, 2003), 30; Thompson, *Civil War to the Bloody End*, 324.

14. Eric J. Wittenberg, *Little Phil: A Reassessment of the Civil War Leadership of Gen. Philip H. Sheridan* (Washington, D.C.: Brassey's, 2002), xv.

15. Richter, *Army in Texas during Reconstruction*, 13.

16. Carl H. Moneyhon, *Texas after the Civil War* (College Station: Texas A & M University Press, 2004), 35–37, 66–68; Richter, *Army in Texas during Reconstruction*, 32–43, 82–83; Smallwood et al., *Murder and Mayhem*, 16–17, 27–30, 40–51; Thompson, *Civil War to the Bloody End*, 325.

17. Thompson, *Civil War to the Bloody End*, 337; Richter, *Army in Texas during Reconstruction*, 73–74.

18. Sefton, *United States Army and Reconstruction*, 158.

19. Ibid.

20. Roy Morris, Jr., *Sheridan: The Life and Wars of General Phil Sheridan* (New York: Crown, 1992), 280.

21. Ibid., 276–277.

22. Richter, *Army in Texas during Reconstruction*, 74.

23. Ibid., 73–74, 86–89.

24. Sefton, *United States Army and Reconstruction*, 140.

25. Thompson, *Civil War to the Bloody End*, 334–335; Morris, *Sheridan*, 278–281; Richter, *Army in Texas during Reconstruction*, 135; Moneyhon, *Texas after the Civil War*, 63–64.

26. William Blair, "The Use of Military Force to Protect the Gains of Reconstruction," *Civil War History* 51, no. 4 (December 2005), 394–396.

27. Dan T. Carter, *When the War Was Over: The Failure of Self-Reconstruction in the South, 1865–1867* (Baton Rouge: Louisiana State University Press, 1985), 61–95; Foner, *Reconstruction*, 185–197, 297–307; Randall and Donald, *Civil War and Reconstruction*, 626–629; Avery Craven, *Reconstruction: The Ending of the Civil War* (New York: Holt, Rinehart and Winston, 1969), 224–236; Randolph B. Campbell, *Grass-Roots Reconstruction in Texas, 1865–1880* (Baton Rouge: Louisiana State University Press, 1997), 220–227; Sefton, *United States Army and Reconstruction*, 102.

28. C. Vann Woodward, *The Strange Career of Jim Crow*, commemorative ed. (New York: Oxford University Press, 2001), 23–24, 106–107; William Cohen, "Negro Involuntary Servitude in the South, 1865–1940: A Preliminary Analysis," *Journal of Southern History* 42 (February 1976), 31–60; Randall and Donald, *Civil War and Reconstruction*, 571–574.

29. Donald B. Connelly, *John M. Schofield and the Politics of Generalship* (Chapel Hill: University of North Carolina Press, 2006), 192.

30. Richard Nelson Current, *Lincoln's Loyalists: Union Soldiers from the Confederacy* (Boston: Northeastern University Press, 1992), 206–210; Rable, *But There Was No Peace*, 81–86, 110–111; Randall and Donald, *Civil War and Reconstruction*, 680–685; Foner, *Reconstruction*, 547–550; Richard Zuczek, *State of Rebellion: Reconstruction in South Carolina* (Columbia: University of South Carolina Press, 1996), 75–82.

31. Martinez, *Carpetbaggers, Cavalry, and the Ku Klux Klan*, 115; Randall and Donald, *Civil War and Reconstruction*, 576–577, 680–681 (quotation on p. 680); Otis A. Singletary, *Negro Militia and Reconstruction* (Austin: University of Texas Press, 1957), 41–49, 107–108.

32. Steven Hahn, *A Nation Under Our Feet: Black Political Struggles in the Rural South from Slavery to the Great Migration* (Cambridge: Belknap Press of Harvard University Press, 2003), 285.

33. Singletary, *Negro Militia and Reconstruction*, 34–35, 107–108. See also Rable, *But There Was No Peace*, 24–25, 36–42.

34. Trelease, *White Terror*, 6–10; Rable, *But There Was No Peace*, 70–71, 92–94, 98; James Welch Patton, *Unionism and Reconstruction in Tennessee, 1860–1869* (Chapel Hill: University of North Carolina Press, 1934), 176–180.

35. Thomas H. O'Connor, *The Disunited States: The Era of Civil War and Reconstruction* (New York: Harper and Row, 1978), 246–251; Foner, *Reconstruction*, 382–389; Craven, *Reconstruction*, 227–231, 243–245, 275.

36. Martinez, *Carpetbaggers, Cavalry, and the Ku Klux Klan*, 115–119; Randall and Donald, *Civil War and Reconstruction*, 680–682; Craven, *Reconstruction*, 242–245.

37. Hahn, *Nation Under Our Feet*, 267–269; Jack Hurst, *Nathan Bedford Forrest: A Biography* (New York: Knopf, 1993), 294–317.

38. Alexander, *Political Reconstruction in Tennessee*, 203.

39. Ben H. Severance, *Tennessee's Radical Army: The State Guard and Its Role in Reconstruction* (Knoxville: University of Tennessee Press, 2005), 64–119, 146–172.

40. Trelease, *White Terror*, 6–17, 28; Alexander, *Political Reconstruction in Tennessee*, 149–203; Craven, *Reconstruction*, 232–233; Richter, *Army in Texas during Reconstruction*, 144. For more on the freedmen in the early postwar period, see Sefton, *United States Army and Reconstruction*, 42–50; Carter, *When the War Was Over*, 162–164; Richter, *Army in Texas during Reconstruction*, 34–35; Michael W. Fitzgerald, "Emancipation and Military Pacification: The Freedmen's Bureau and Social Control in Alabama," in Cimbala and Miller, *Freedmen's Bureau and Reconstruction*, 46–66; Finley, "Personnel of the Freedmen's Bureau," 93–118.

41. John Allan Wyeth, *That Devil Forrest: Life of General Nathan Bedford Forrest* (New York: Harper, 1959), 561.

42. Hurst, *Nathan Bedford Forrest*, 258.

43. Brian Steel Wills, *A Battle from the Start: The Life of Nathan Bedford Forrest* (New York: HarperCollins, 1992), 318–352 (quotation on p. 351); Martinez, *Carpetbaggers, Cavalry, and the Ku Klux Klan*, 18–21.

44. Severance, *Tennessee's Radical Army*, 197–198; Trelease, *White Terror*, 28–33; Hurst, *Nathan Bedford Forrest*, 294–368.

45. Trelease, *White Terror*, 384–385; Walter L. Fleming, *Civil War and Reconstruction in Alabama* (New York: Columbia University Press, 1905), 693–707; Richter, *Army in Texas during Reconstruction*, 145.

46. Singletary, *Negro Militia and Reconstruction*, 22–24.

47. Alexander, *Political Reconstruction in Tennessee*, 187–198; Severance, *Tennessee's Radical Army*, 185–228 (quotation on p. 185).

48. Powell Clayton, *The Aftermath of the Civil War in Arkansas* (New York: Neal, 1915), 63–67; Randy Finley, *From Slavery to Uncertain Freedom: The Freedmen's Bureau in Arkansas, 1865–1869* (Fayetteville: University of Arkansas Press, 1996), 159–160.

49. Trelease, *White Terror*, 161–162; Clayton, *Aftermath of the Civil War*, 111–113 (quotation on p. 113).

50. Clayton, *Aftermath of the Civil War*, 114–115; Trelease, *White Terror*, 162–163; Singletary, *Negro Militia and Reconstruction*, 44.

51. Staples, *Reconstruction in Arkansas*, 297–298; Trelease, *White Terror*, 163–164.

52. Trelease, *White Terror*, 164.

53. William Monks, *A History of Southern Missouri and Northern Arkansas* (West Plains, Mo.: West Plains Journal Company, 1907), 217–225 (quotation on p. 218); Staples, *Reconstruction in Arkansas*, 298–299; Trelease, *White Terror*, 165–167; Clayton, *Aftermath of the Civil War*, 119–126.

54. Singletary, *Negro Militia and Reconstruction*, 44; Trelease, *White Terror*, 167–169; Clayton, *Aftermath of the Civil War*, 126–136.

55. Jean Edward Smith, *Grant* (New York: Simon and Schuster, 2001), 543; Trelease, *White Terror*, 384.

56. John S. Reynolds, *Reconstruction in South Carolina* (Columbia, South Carolina: State Company, 1905), 182–191, 195–196; Trelease, *White Terror*, 349–380; Martinez, *Carpetbaggers, Cavalry, and the Ku Klux Klan*, 73–74, 115–126.

57. Martinez, *Carpetbaggers, Cavalry, and the Ku Klux Klan*, 68–71 (quotation on p. 69); Smith, *Grant*, 545–547.

58. Trelease, *White Terror*, 399–411.

59. Allan R. Millett and Peter Maslowski, *For the Common Defense: A Military History of the United States* (New York: Free Press, 1984), 244; Sefton, *United States Army and Reconstruction*, 222.

60. Martinez, *Carpetbaggers, Cavalry, and the Ku Klux Klan*, 76–102, 137; Budiansky, *Bloody Shirt*, 109–112 (quotation on p. 111).

61. Zuczek, *State of Rebellion*, 94; Martinez, *Carpetbaggers, Cavalry, and the Ku Klux Klan*, 139–141; Budiansky, *Bloody Shirt*, 122–129.

62. Trelease, *White Terror*, 403–406; Budiansky, *Bloody Shirt*, 135–138; Martinez, *Carpetbaggers, Cavalry, and the Ku Klux Klan*, 151, 154; Zuczek, *State of Rebellion*, 98–99.

63. Trelease, *White Terror*, 402–403 (quotation); Budiansky, *Bloody Shirt*, 136.

64. Martinez, *Carpetbaggers, Cavalry, and the Ku Klux Klan*, 155; Trelease, *White Terror*, 404.

65. Budiansky, *Bloody Shirt*, 142–145; Martinez, *Carpetbaggers, Cavalry, and the Ku Klux Klan*, 163–198; Zuczek, *State of Rebellion*, 100–103.

66. James K. Hogue, *Uncivil War: Five New Orleans Street Battles and the Rise and Fall of Radical Reconstruction* (Baton Rouge: Louisiana State University Press, 2006), 95–106; Taylor, *Louisiana Reconstructed*, 241–249, 253–256; Dawson, *Army Generals and Reconstruction*, 133–144.

67. Taylor, *Louisiana Reconstructed*, 253–273; Dawson, *Army Generals and Reconstruction*, 145–156.

68. Martinez, *Carpetbaggers, Cavalry, and the Ku Klux Klan*, 225.

69. Dawson, *Army Generals and Reconstruction*, 158–159; Taylor, *Louisiana Reconstructed*, 281–291.

70. Singletary, *Negro Militia and Reconstruction*, 77 (quotation); Budiansky, *Bloody Shirt*, 159–160.

71. Hogue, *Uncivil War*, 144–146; Budiansky, *Bloody Shirt*, 163–164; Dawson, *Army Generals and Reconstruction*, 173–176 (quotation on p. 173).

72. Dawson, *Army Generals and Reconstruction*, 177–179 (quotation on p. 177); Taylor, *Louisiana Reconstructed*, 295.

73. Budiansky, *Bloody Shirt*, 168–176; Dawson, *Army Generals and Reconstruction*, 187 (quotation); Martinez, *Carpetbaggers, Cavalry, and the Ku Klux Klan*, 225; Taylor, *Louisiana Reconstructed*, 296.

74. Martinez, *Carpetbaggers, Cavalry, and the Ku Klux Klan*, 226.

75. Sefton, *United States Army and Reconstruction*, 240.

76. Paul Andrew Hutton, *Phil Sheridan and His Army* (Lincoln: University of Nebraska Press, 1985), 263–264.

77. Taylor, *Louisiana Reconstructed*, 304–305; Hutton, *Phil Sheridan and His Army*, 265–266; Dawson, *Army Generals and Reconstruction*, 203–204.

78. Smith, *Grant*, 565.

79. Dawson, *Army Generals and Reconstruction*, 207–210.

80. Simpson, *Reconstruction Presidents*, 176.

81. Hutton, *Phil Sheridan and His Army*, 268.

82. Sefton, *United States Army and Reconstruction*, 245; Simpson, *Reconstruction Presidents*, 177–180; Taylor, *Louisiana Reconstructed*, 308–309; Dawson, *Army Generals and Reconstruction*, 207; Hutton, *Phil Sheridan and His Army*, 266–272; Hogue, *Uncivil War*, 154–157.

Chapter 4. The Philippine Insurrection

1. Ivan Musicant, *Empire by Default: The Spanish-American War and the Dawn of the American Century* (New York: Henry Holt, 1998), 191–234; A. B. Feuer, *America at War: The Philippines, 1898–1913* (Westport, Conn.: Praeger, 2002), 12–20; G. J. A. O'Toole, *The Spanish War: An American Epic—1898* (New York: Norton, 1984), 176–189; Michael Blow, *A Ship to Remember: The Maine and the Spanish-American War* (New York: William Morrow, 1992), 227–234.

2. Edmund Morris, *The Rise of Theodore Roosevelt* (New York: Modern Library, 2001), 638. The inquiry's conclusion later came under intense criticism; the cause of the explosion has never been determined conclusively.

3. For the origins of the Spanish-American War and American involvement in the Philippines, see Richard Welch, *Response to Imperialism: The United States and the Philippine-American War, 1899–1902* (Chapel Hill: University of North Carolina Press, 1979); H. W. Brands, *Bound to Empire: The United States and the Philippines* (New York: Oxford University Press, 1992); Musicant, *Empire by Default*; Miller, *"Benevolent Assimilation"*; Silbey, *War of Frontier and Empire*.

4. Warren Zimmerman, *First Great Triumph: How Five Americans Made Their Country a World Power* (New York: Farrar, Straus and Giroux, 2002), 387.

5. Linn, *Philippine War*, 187–191; Gates, *Schoolbooks and Krags*, 156–162; Birtle, *U.S. Army Doctrine, 1860–1941*, 110–112.

6. John R. M. Taylor, *The Philippine Insurrection against the United States, 1898–1903: A Compilation of Original Documents with Notes and Introductions*, 5 vols. (Washington, D.C.: U.S. Government Printing Office, 1906), vol. 2, p. 305; May, *A Past Recovered*, 102–116, 159–160; Birtle, *U.S. Army Doctrine, 1860–1941*, 111–112, 125–126; Linn, *Philippine War*, 78–80, 175.

7. Linn, *Philippine War*, 28–30; Brian McAllister Linn, E-mail to author, August 24, 2008.

8. Linn, *U.S. Army and Counterinsurgency*, 122; Linn, *Philippine War*, 277.

9. Linn, *U.S. Army and Counterinsurgency*, 33–35, 61.

10. Ibid., 76–86.

11. Allan R. Millett, *The General: Robert L. Bullard and Officership in the United States Army, 1881–1925* (Westport, Conn.: Greenwood Press, 1975), 111–115; James Parker, *The Old Army: Memories, 1872–1918* (Mechanicsburg, Pa.: Stackpole Books, 2003), 299, 369–371; Graham A. Cosmas, *An Army for Empire: The United States Army in the Spanish-American War* (Columbia: University of Missouri Press, 1971), 148–150, 296–308; Linn, *Philippine War*, 125–126, 327; Edward M. Coffman, *The Regulars: The American Army, 1898–1941* (Cambridge: Harvard University Press, 2004), 6, 50.

12. Silbey, *War of Frontier and Empire*, 105–107; Linn, *Philippine War*, 126.

13. Linn, "The Philippines," 50. Brian Linn remarks, "The Philippine War overwhelmingly confirms the absolute necessity of having officers of character, initiative, and humanity in counter-

insurgency operations." Ibid. See also Linn, *U.S. Army and Counterinsurgency*, 22; Linn, *Philippine War*, 327; Leon Wolff, *Little Brown Brother: How the United States Purchased and Pacified the Philippine Islands at the Century's Turn* (Garden City, N.Y.: Doubleday, 1961), 333.

14. May, *Battle for Batangas*, 136.

15. Silbey, *War of Frontier and Empire*, 216; Linn, "The Philippines," 52; Birtle, *U.S. Army Doctrine, 1860–1941*, 112–116.

16. Linn, *U.S. Army and Counterinsurgency*, 169.

17. Birtle, *U.S. Army Doctrine, 1860–1941*, 101–104; May, *Battle for Batangas*, 141–142.

18. Linn, "The Philippines," 47, 51–52 (quotation). See also Gates, *Schoolbooks and Krags*, 140–141; Birtle, *U.S. Army Doctrine, 1860–1941*, 121–122.

19. Gates, *Schoolbooks and Krags*, 198; Birtle, *U.S. Army Doctrine, 1860–1941*, 120–121.

20. Silbey, *War of Frontier and Empire*, 135–138; Gates, *Schoolbooks and Krags*, 133–141; Birtle, *U.S. Army Doctrine, 1860–1941*, 119–121.

21. Linn, *Philippine War*, 259, 200–202, 282–284, 289–290; Linn, *U.S. Army and Counterinsurgency*, 108–110, 124–128; Gates, *Schoolbooks and Krags*, 132–133.

22. Gates, *Schoolbooks and Krags*, 145–147 (quotation on p. 146).

23. Birtle, *U.S. Army Doctrine, 1860–1941*, 127–128; Gates, *Schoolbooks and Krags*, 174–175.

24. Linn, *Philippine War*, 235–240 (quotation on p. 240).

25. Heath Twichell, Jr., *Allen: The Biography of an Army Officer* (New Brunswick, N.J.: Rutgers University Press, 1974), 105–108; Linn, *Philippine War*, 233–234.

26. Young, *General's General*, 79 (quotation).

27. Frank H. Golay, *Face of Empire: United States–Philippine Relations* (Madison: University of Wisconsin-Madison Center for Southeast Asian Studies, 1998), 66; Young, *General's General*, 272–276; Linn, *Philippine War*, 208–218; Silbey, *War of Frontier and Empire*, 142–143; Sexton, *Soldiers in the Sun*, 248–249.

28. May, *Battle for Batangas*, 159–161; Birtle, *U.S. Army Doctrine, 1860–1941*, 124–128; Gates, *Schoolbooks and Krags*, 166–70.

29. Linn, *Philippine War*, 249–252, 290–293; Linn, *U.S. Army and Counterinsurgency*, 49–50, 129, 138–142.

30. Taylor, *Philippine Insurrection*, vol. 5, p. 106; Sexton, *Soldiers in the Sun*, 249–256; Birtle, "U.S. Army's Pacification of Marinduque," 260–262; Young, *General's General*, 279.

31. Gates, *Schoolbooks and Krags*, 188–189 (quotation on p. 189); May, *Battle for Batangas*, 161–162.

32. Young, *General's General*, 278–280; Wolff, *Little Brown Brother*, 334; Gates, *Schoolbooks and Krags*, 205–208, 216–217 (quotation on p. 206); Welch, *Response to Imperialism*, 36–37; Birtle, *U.S. Army Doctrine, 1860–1941*, 128.

33. Birtle, *U.S. Army Doctrine, 1860–1941*, 127–128; Gates, *Schoolbooks and Krags*, 214–216; Linn, *Philippine War*, 213–214.

34. Taylor, *Philippine Insurrection*, vol. 5, pp. 358–359; Linn, *Philippine War*, 229–230, 282–286, 293–296; Linn, *U.S. Army and Counterinsurgency*, 55–56, 95–118; Silbey, *War of Frontier and Empire*, 166–173.

35. Linn, *Philippine War*, 214–215, 220–221; Birtle, "U.S. Army's Pacification of Marinduque," 271–272; Gates, *Schoolbooks and Krags*, 210; Birtle, *U.S. Army Doctrine, 1860–1941*, 130–131.

36. Gates, *Schoolbooks and Krags*, 232 (quotation); Linn, *U.S. Army and Counterinsurgency*, 60.

37. Linn, *Philippine War*, 220–222; Twichell, *Allen*, 101–103; May, *Battle for Batangas*, 155–158; Sexton, *Soldiers in the Sun*, 240–242; Young, *The General's General*, 277–278.

38. Gates, *Schoolbooks and Krags*, 226–232; May, *Battle for Batangas*, 203; Linn, *Philippine War*, 279; Birtle, "U.S. Army's Pacification of Marinduque," 269, 282.

39. Linn, *U.S. Army and Counterinsurgency*, 76–86, 108–116; Linn, *Philippine War*, 282–286.

40. Taylor, *Philippine Insurrection*, vol. 2, pp. 280–285; Gates, *Schoolbooks and Krags*, 218–219, 228–232; Sexton, *Soldiers in the Sun*, 258–259; Linn, *U.S. Army and Counterinsurgency*, 54–55.

41. Twichell, *Allen*, 123 (quotation); Linn, *Philippine War*, 204, 210, 239–240, 260; Gates, *Schoolbooks and Krags*, 195–196, 213–214, 231; Linn, "The Philippines," 53; Linn, *U.S. Army and Counterinsurgency*, 109–118.

42. Gates, *Schoolbooks and Krags*, 230–231, 241–243; Linn, *Philippine War*, 214–215, 272–274, 322–327.

43. Linn, *Philippine War*, 34–36; May, *A Past Recovered*, 102–116, 156–159; Birtle, "U.S. Army's Pacification of Marinduque," 257; May, *Battle for Batangas*, 174–178.

44. Birtle, *U.S. Army Doctrine, 1860–1941*, 133; Roth, *Muddy Glory*, 24; Young, *The General's General*, 289.

45. Linn, *Philippine War*, 231; Gates, *Schoolbooks and Krags*, 253.

46. Fred R. Brown, *History of the Ninth U.S. Infantry, 1799–1909* (Chicago: R. R. Donnelley and Sons, 1909), 575–596; Taylor, *Philippine Insurrection*, vol. 5, pp. 703–705; James O. Taylor, ed., *The Massacre of Balangiga: Being an Authentic Account by Several of the Few Survivors* (Joplin, Mo.: McCarn Printing, 1931); Linn, *Philippine War*, 310–312; Joseph L. Schott, *The Ordeal of Samar* (Indianapolis: Bobbs-Merrill, 1964), 36–55; Sexton, *Soldiers in the Sun*, 268–272.

47. Miller, "Benevolent Assimilation," 200–206; Feuer, *America at War*, 204; Linn, *Philippine War*, 310–313; Silbey, *War of Frontier and Empire*, 190; Schott, *Ordeal of Samar*, 23–24.

48. Silbey, *War of Frontier and Empire*, 194–195; Linn, *Philippine War*, 311–313; Miller, "Benevolent Assimilation," 196–200, 219–220.

49. Linn, *Philippine War*, 313–315; Gates, *Schoolbooks and Krags*, 254–255 (quotation on p. 255); Sexton, *Soldiers in the Sun*, 273.

50. Sexton, *Soldiers in the Sun*, 273.

51. John H. Clifford, *History of the Pioneer Marine Battalion at Guam, L.I., 1899, and the Campaign in Samar, P.I., 1901* (Portsmouth, N.H.: Chronicle Job Print, 1914), 34–40; Feuer, *America at War*, 205–211; Schott, *Ordeal of Samar*, 68–278; Sexton, *Soldiers in the Sun*, 273–274; Roth, *Muddy Glory*, 24–25.

52. Linn, *Philippine War*, 320–321; Gates, *Schoolbooks and Krags*, 255–256; Silbey, *War of Frontier and Empire*, 196.

53. Silbey, *War of Frontier and Empire*, 201–203; Gates, *Schoolbooks and Krags*, 256; Schott, *Ordeal of Samar*, 278–279 (quotation); Miller, "Benevolent Assimilation," 227–252.

54. Ramsey, *Masterpiece of Counterguerrilla Warfare*, 50.

55. Roth, *Muddy Glory*, 93–94; Gates, *Schoolbooks and Krags*, 259–261 (quotation on p. 259).

56. Ramsey, *Masterpiece of Counterguerrilla Warfare*, 46.

57. Ibid., 35.

58. Sexton, *Soldiers in the Sun*, 279–281; Linn, *U.S. Army and Counterinsurgency*, 152–158; Roth, *Muddy Glory*, 83–85; May, *Battle for Batangas*, 251–252; Gates, *Schoolbooks and Krags*, 260.

59. Ramsey, *Masterpiece of Counterguerrilla Warfare*, 47.

60. May, *A Past Recovered*, 90–94; James H. Blount, *The American Occupation of the Philippines, 1898–1912* (New York: G. P. Putnam's Sons, 1913), 392–396; May, *Battle for Batangas*, 250–251, 262–267.

61. May, *Battle for Batangas*, 252–269, 280–284; Linn, *Philippine War*, 302–304; Linn, *U.S. Army and Counterinsurgency*, 154–160; Gates, *Schoolbooks and Krags*, 259–263.

Chapter 5. The Huk Rebellion

1. Kerkvliet, *Huk Rebellion*, 2–14.

2. Lachica, *Huks*, 59–61; Kerkvliet, *Huk Rebellion*, 15–25.

3. Taruc, *He Who Rides the Tiger*, 16–35, 50–53, 148–157, 166–172; Lachica, *Huks*, 88–102; Scaff, *Philippine Answer to Communism*, 7–21; Kerkvliet, *Huk Rebellion*, 232–233.

4. Smith, *Philippine Freedom*, 142–143; Kerkvliet, *Huk Rebellion*, 62–69, 87, 93–94, 108, 206; Scaff, *Philippine Answer to Communism*, 23, 117; U.S. Army, *Counter-Guerrilla Operations in the Philippines, 1946–1953: A Seminar on the Huk Campaign Held at Fort Bragg* (Fort Bragg, N.C.: U.S. Army Special Forces Center and School, 1961), chap. 2, pp. 14–15.

5. Kerkvliet, *Huk Rebellion*, 115.

6. William O. Douglas, *North from Malaya: Adventure on Five Fronts* (Garden City, N.Y.: Doubleday, 1953), 108; Kerkvliet, *Huk Rebellion*, 116–132; Baclagon, *Lessons from the Huk Campaign*, 194–198.

7. Kerkvliet, *Huk Rebellion*, 133, 139–142; Lachica, *Huks*, 119–120; Greenberg, *Hukbalahap Insurrection*, 38–39.

8. Greenberg, *Hukbalahap Insurrection*, 51–52; Kerkvliet, *Huk Rebellion*, 175, 179–188, 218–223; Taruc, *He Who Rides the Tiger*, 40–42, 54–56.

9. A. H. Peterson et al., eds., *Symposium on the Role of Airpower in Counterinsurgency and Unconventional Warfare: The Philippine Huk Campaign* (Santa Monica, Calif.: Rand, 1963), 14–15; Romulo, *Crusade in Asia*, 101–102, 124; Smith, *Philippine Freedom*, 144.

10. Valeriano and Bohannon, *Counter-Guerrilla Operations*, 114–115; Greenberg, *Hukbalahap Insurrection*, 56–57, 68–70, 75; Beth Day, *The Philippines: Shattered Showcase of Democracy in Asia* (New York: M. Evans, 1974), 128; Romulo, *Crusade in Asia*, 101–103; Renato Constantino and Letizia R. Constantino, *The Philippines: The Continuing Past* (Manila: Foundation for Nationalist Studies, 1978), 211–212, 221–222; Smith, *Philippine Freedom*, 144–146.

11. Valeriano and Bohannan, *Counter-Guerrilla Operations*, 236–237; Kerkvliet, *Huk Rebellion*, 196–199; Constantino and Constantino, *The Philippines*, 211–212.

12. Joes, *America and Guerrilla Warfare*, 192; Lachica, *Huks*, 38, 49–54; Kerkvliet, *Huk Rebellion*, 164–171, 177, 196, 227, 235–236; Scaff, *Philippine Answer to Communism*, 35.

13. Pomeroy, *Forest*, 43.

14. Lachica, *Huks*, 43–44; Day, *The Philippines*, 126–127; Scaff, *Philippine Answer to Communism*, 116–122.

15. Kerkvliet, *Huk Rebellion*, 227.

16. Taruc, *He Who Rides the Tiger*, 62; Lachica, *Huks*, 25–26 (quotation on p. 26).

17. Joes, *America and Guerrilla Warfare*, 204.

18. Valeriano and Bohannon, *Counter-Guerrilla Operations*, 53; Kerkvliet, *Huk Rebellion*, 210, 219–220; Taruc, *He Who Rides the Tiger*, 68–78.

19. Brands, *Bound to Empire*, 241; U.S. Army, *Counter-Guerrilla Operations in the Philippines*, chap. 2, pp. 18–19; Greenberg, *Hukbalahap Insurrection*, 65–67; Lachica, *Huks*, 128–130.

20. Romulo and Gray, *Magsaysay Story*; Smith, *Philippine Freedom*.

21. Stanley Karnow, *In Our Image: America's Empire in the Philippines* (New York: Random House, 1989), 345–346; Currey, *Edward Lansdale*, 56–73.

22. Smith, *Philippine Freedom*, 154–155; Brands, *Bound to Empire*, 242; Currey, *Edward Lansdale*, 71–73; Karnow, *In Our Image*, 345–346; Douglas, *North from Malaya*, 110; Romulo, *Crusade in Asia*, 123.

23. Edward Lansdale, *In The Midst of Wars: An American's Mission to Southeast Asia* (New York: Harper and Row, 1972), 37; Currey, *Edward Lansdale*, 85–91.

24. Currey, *Edward Lansdale*, 83.

25. Ibid., 45.

26. Baclagon, *Lessons from the Huk Campaign*, 6, 36; Smith, *Philippine Freedom*, 156–157; Romulo, *Crusade in Asia*, 125–126; Andrew J. Birtle, *U.S. Army Counterinsurgency and Contingency Operations Doctrine, 1942–1976* (Washington, D.C.: U.S. Army Center of Military History, 2006), 62; Currey, *Edward Lansdale*, 88–89; Brands, *Bound to Empire*, 243; Romulo and Gray, *Magsaysay Story*, 128–129.

27. Romulo and Gray, *Magsaysay Story*, 129–131, 150; Romulo, *Crusade in Asia*, 126 (quotation), 157; Joes, *America and Guerrilla Warfare*, 194; Lachica, *Huks*, 130; Peterson et al., *Symposium on the Role of Airpower*, 18; Smith, *Philippine Freedom*, 158; Robert Ross Smith, *The Hukbalahap Insurgency: Economic, Political, and Military Factors* (Washington, D.C.: Office of the Chief of Military History, 1963), 102.

28. Day, *The Philippines*, 133; Romulo and Gray, *Magsaysay Story*, 125–126; Smith, *Philippine Freedom*, 156; Romulo, *Crusade in Asia*, 130–131.

29. Valeriano and Bohannon, *Counter-Guerrilla Operations*, 139.

30. Greenberg, *Hukbalahap Insurrection*, 82–83, 93.

31. Smith, *Philippine Freedom*, 158–159; Valeriano and Bohannon, *Counter-Guerrilla Operations*, 67–68; Romulo, *Crusade in Asia*, 133–136; Kerkvliet, *Huk Rebellion*, 220.

32. Richard J. Kessler, *Rebellion and Repression in the Philippines* (New Haven: Yale University Press, 1989), 34; Greenberg, *Hukbalahap Insurrection*, 116; Valeriano and Bohannon, *Counter-Guerrilla Operations*, 125–131.

33. Baclagon, *Lessons from the Huk Campaign*, 112–113.

34. Pomeroy, *Forest*, 89–90.

35. Birtle, *U.S. Army Doctrine, 1942–1976*, 62–63; Baclagon, *Lessons from the Huk Campaign*, 24–25, 28, 133, 229–230.

36. Baclagon, *Lessons from the Huk Campaign*, 46–48, 52.

37. Taruc, *He Who Rides the Tiger*, 97; Kerkvliet, *Huk Rebellion*, 208.

38. Valeriano and Bohannon, *Counter-Guerrilla Operations*, 208; Smith, *Philippine Freedom*, 156.

39. Kessler, *Rebellion and Repression in the Philippines*, 34–35; Kerkvliet, *Huk Rebellion*, 238–240; Constantino and Constantino, *The Philippines*, 237–244.

40. Blitz, *Contested State*, 90; Valeriano and Bohannon, *Counter-Guerrilla Operations*, 222–226; Brands, *Bound to Empire*, 243–245; Scaff, *Philippine Answer to Communism*, 39–115.

41. Scaff, *Philippine Answer to Communism*, 123; Kerkvliet, *Huk Rebellion*, 208, 233–236, 241–242; Pomeroy, *Forest*, 156–215.

42. Pomeroy, *Forest*, 157; Kerkvliet, *Huk Rebellion*, 207, 233–234.

43. Kerkvliet, *Huk Rebellion*, 238.

44. Ibid., 207.

45. Taruc, *He Who Rides the Tiger*, 121–132; Kerkvliet, *Huk Rebellion*, 226–227, 247; Lachica, *Huks*, 14, 134–135.

46. Blitz, *Contested State*, 91–94; Sung Yong Kim, *United States–Philippine Relations, 1946–1956* (Washington, D.C.: Public Affairs Press, 1968), 17–22; Constantino and Constantino, *The Philippines*, 250–260; Currey, *Edward Lansdale*, 113–131; Brands, *Bound to Empire*, 252–254; Kerkvliet, *Huk Rebellion*, 238.

47. Romulo and Gray, *Magsaysay Story*, 235, 300 (quotation).

48. Valeriano and Bohannon, *Counter-Guerrilla Operations*, 99–100; Currey, *Edward Lansdale*, 131.

49. Gregg R. Jones, *Red Revolution: Inside the Philippine Guerrilla Movement* (Boulder, Colo.: Westview Press, 1989), 41–42; Day, *The Philippines*, 135–136; Smith, *Philippine Freedom*, 193.

50. Kerkvliet, *Huk Rebellion*, 234–235, 238; Joes, *America and Guerrilla Warfare*, 199.

Chapter 6. The Malayan Emergency

1. Chin, *My Side of History*, 57–59; Short, *Communist Insurrection in Malaya*, 20; J. H. Brimmell, *Communism in South East Asia: A Political Analysis* (London: Oxford University Press, 1959), 88–96, 146–149.

2. Barber, *War of the Running Dogs*, 28–33; Chin, *My Side of History*, 192–193, 201–208; Coates, *Suppressing Insurgency*, 7; Clutterbuck, *Long, Long War*, 44.

3. Short, *Communist Insurrection in Malaya*, 26–27, 43–59, 130–131; Clutterbuck, *Long, Long War*, 30–31; Christopher Bayly and Tim Harper, *Forgotten Wars: Freedom and Revolution in Southeast Asia* (Boston: Harvard University Press, 2007), 425–427.

4. Chin, *My Side of History*, 214–215; Barber, *War of the Running Dogs*, 19–21; Miller, *Communist Menace in Malaya*, 82–84.

5. Clutterbuck, *Long, Long War*, 35–41; Short, *Communist Insurrection in Malaya*, 59–96; Coates, *Suppressing Insurgency*, 18; Chin, *My Side of History*, 215–226; Bayly and Harper, *Forgotten Wars*, 429–433.

6. Lucian W. Pye, *Guerrilla Communism in Malaya: Its Social and Political Meaning* (Princeton, N.J.: Princeton University Press, 1956), 187–189; Short, *Communist Insurrection in Malaya*, 213; Clutterbuck, *Long, Long War*, 44–46; Walter C. Ladwig III, "Managing Counterinsurgency: Lessons from Malaya," *Military Review*, vol. 87 (May–June 2007): 57–59; Coates, *Suppressing Insurgency*, 12, 57–58, 86; Miller, *Communist Menace in Malaya*, 103–107.

7. Short, *Communist Insurrection in Malaya*, 26–27; Coates, *Suppressing Insurgency*, 28–29; Stubbs, *Hearts and Minds in Guerrilla Warfare*, 11–16, 32–36.

8. Miller, *Communist Menace in Malaya*, 89, 96; Clutterbuck, *Long, Long War*, 44, 56; Stubbs, *Hearts and Minds in Guerrilla Warfare*, 71–73; Coates, *Suppressing Insurgency*, 25, 203–204; Barber, *War of the Running Dogs*, 68; Henniker, *Red Shadow over Malaya*, 32–33 (quotation).

9. Stubbs, *Hearts and Minds in Guerrilla Warfare*, 135–136.

10. Ladwig, "Managing Counterinsurgency," 58; Clutterbuck, *Long, Long War*, 40; Short, *Communist Insurrection in Malaya*, 243–244; Stubbs, *Hearts and Minds in Guerrilla Warfare*, 77–81.

11. Clutterbuck, *Long, Long War*, 42–43; Coates, *Suppressing Insurgency*, 31–33; Short, *Communist Insurrection in Malaya*, 114–117, 229–230.

12. Stubbs, *Hearts and Minds in Guerrilla Warfare*, 71–77.

13. Newsinger, *British Counterinsurgency*, 43–45; Mockaitis, *British Counterinsurgency*, 162; Sunderland, *Army Operations in Malaya*, 30–31, 126–132, 198–199; Coates, *Suppressing Insurgency*, 49–52, 143; Clutterbuck, *Long, Long War*, 50–51.

14. Coates, *Suppressing Insurgency*, 36–37, 159–160; Short, *Communist Insurrection in Malaya*, 138–139; Clutterbuck, *Long, Long War*, 51–54.

15. Christopher Pugsley, *From Emergency to Confrontation: The New Zealand Armed Forces in Malaya and Borneo, 1949-1966* (South Melbourne: Oxford University Press, 2003), 152–153.

16. Short, *Communist Insurrection in Malaya*, 212; Clutterbuck, *Long, Long War*, 55–56; Coates, *Suppressing Insurgency*, 61–62.

17. Coates, *Suppressing Insurgency*, 80–81; Clutterbuck, *Long, Long War*, 56–57.

18. A. J. Stockwell, ed., *British Documents on the End of Empire: Malaya*, part II (London: Her Majesty's Stationery Office, 1995), 324.

19. Clutterbuck, *Long, Long War*, 57–60; Short, *Communist Insurrection in Malaya*, 237–238; Coates, *Suppressing Insurgency*, 82–85.

20. Riley Sunderland, *Organizing Counterinsurgency in Malaya, 1947-1960* (Santa Monica, Calif.: Rand, 1964), 55–59; Short, *Communist Insurrection in Malaya*, 242–243; Coates, *Suppressing Insurgency*, 94–95, 101, 151.

21. Stubbs, *Hearts and Minds in Guerrilla Warfare*, 102–107; Short, *Communist Insurrection in Malaya*, 242–243; Miller, *Communist Menace in Malaya*, 150–151; Clutterbuck, *Long, Long War*, 60–62.

22. Miller, *Communist Menace in Malaya*, 170–171; Chin, *My Side of History*, 268; Lennox A. Mills, *Malaya: A Political and Economic Appraisal* (Minneapolis: University of Minnesota Press, 1958), 56–57; Short, *Communist Insurrection in Malaya*, 282–288, 293–294; Coates, *Suppressing Insurgency*, 99–101, 110; Stockwell, *British Documents on the End of Empire*, 310–311; Stubbs, *Hearts and Minds in Guerrilla Warfare*, 120, 157–158.

23. Short, *Communist Insurrection in Malaya*, 283–284.

24. Coates, *Suppressing Insurgency*, 95–99; Short, *Communist Insurrection in Malaya*, 231, 299, 302–303.

25. Short, *Communist Insurrection in Malaya*, 295–296; Nagl, *Counterinsurgency Lessons from Malaya and Vietnam*, 78; Stockwell, *British Documents on the End of Empire*, 310–311 (quotation).

26. Chin, *My Side of History*, 280–286; Clutterbuck, *Long, Long War*, 63–64; Coates, *Suppressing Insurgency*, 66; Short, *Communist Insurrection in Malaya*, 319–321; Stubbs, *Hearts and Minds in Guerrilla Warfare*, 148–150.

27. Oliver Lyttelton Chandos, *The Memoirs of Lord Chandos: An Unexpected View from the Summit* (New York: New American Library, 1963), 352–354; Stockwell, *British Documents on the End of Empire*, 318–353 (quotation on p. 324); Short, *Communist Insurrection in Malaya*, 334–336; Coates, *Suppressing Insurgency*, 111; Cloake, *Templer*, 200–202.

28. Stockwell, *British Documents on the End of Empire*, 357–359.

29. Coates, *Suppressing Insurgency*, 113; Short, *Communist Insurrection in Malaya*, 325–329; Cloake, *Templer*, 201–205; Stockwell, *British Documents on the End of Empire*, 361 (quotation).

30. Cloake, *Templer*.

31. Chin, *My Side of History*, 294.

32. Mills, *Malaya*, 59.

33. Susan L. Carruthers, *Winning Hearts and Minds: British Governments, the Media and Colonial Counterinsurgency, 1944-1960* (London: Leicester University Press, 1995), 95; Cloake, *Templer*, 210–212, 236–237; Harry Miller, *Jungle War in Malaya: The Campaign against Communism, 1948-60* (London: Arthur Barker, 1972), 92–94; Chandos, *Memoirs*, 366.

34. Shennan, *Out in the Midday Sun*, 320–321; Coates, *Suppressing Insurgency*, 116–117, 130–131; Cloake, *Templer*, 212–213, 241, 267 (quotation), 270–271; Clutterbuck, *Long, Long War*, 83–84.

35. Stubbs, *Hearts and Minds in Guerrilla Warfare*, 161; Cloake, *Templer*, 246–247.

36. Miller, *Jungle War in Malaya*, 91–97; Coates, *Suppressing Insurgency*, 124–125; Stubbs, *Hearts and Minds in Guerrilla Warfare*, 156–157.

37. Peter Dennis and Jeffrey Gray, *Emergency and Confrontation: Australian Military Operations in Malaya and Borneo, 1950–1966* (St. Leonards, Australia: Allen and Unwin, 1996), 59–61; Cloake, *Templer*, 249–250 (quotation on p. 249); Short, *Communist Insurrection in Malaya*, 412–414; Coates, *Suppressing Insurgency*, 121.

38. Cloake, *Templer*, 213.

39. Shennan, *Out in the Midday Sun*, 319.

40. Barber, *War of the Running Dogs*, 180, 199; Cloake, *Templer*, 267; Stubbs, *Hearts and Minds in Guerrilla Warfare*, 143.

41. Miller, *Communist Menace in Malaya*, 212; Cloake, *Templer*, 219, 265–269; Coates, *Suppressing Insurgency*, 116.

42. Shennan, *Out in the Midday Sun*, 320.

43. Cloake, *Templer*, 263–268; Short, *Communist Insurrection in Malaya*, 342–343.

44. Director of Operations, Malaya, *The Conduct of Anti-Terrorist Operations in Malaya*, 3rd ed. (London: Her Britannic Majesty's Stationery Office, 1958).

45. Marston, "Lost and Found in the Jungle," 98–103; Gregorian, "'Jungle Bashing' in Malaya," 346–353; Tom Pocock, *Fighting General: The Public and Private Campaigns of General Sir Walter Walker* (London: Collins, 1973), 88–93; David A. Charters, "From Palestine to Northern Ireland: British Adaptation to Low-Intensity Operations," in David A. Charters and Maurice Tugwell, eds., *Armies in Low-Intensity Conflict: A Comparative Analysis* (London: Brassey's, 1989), 203–205; Mockaitis, *British Counterinsurgency*, 183–188; Hew Strachan, "British Counter-Insurgency from Malaya to Iraq," *RUSI Journal* 152 (December 2007), 8–11; Sunderland, *Army Operations in Malaya*, 27–30. Even the most celebrated of the manual's principles, such as the superiority of small-unit operations to large operations, had been widely circulated and accepted well before Templer showed up on the scene. Nagl, *Counterinsurgency Lessons from Malaya and Vietnam*, 96; Sunderland, *Organizing Counterinsurgency in Malaya*, 52; Coates, *Suppressing Insurgency*, 149; Sunderland, *Army Operations in Malaya*, 133–134.

46. Gregorian, "'Jungle Bashing' in Malaya," 341–353; Charters, "From Palestine to Northern Ireland," 203–205; Marston, "Lost and Found in the Jungle," 98–103; Mockaitis, *British Counterinsurgency*, 183–188; Sunderland, *Army Operations in Malaya*, 27–30. For the Marine Corps manual, see U.S. Marine Corps, *Small Wars Manual* (Washington, D.C.: U.S. Government Printing Office, 1940). For changes in Communist tactics, see Henniker, *Red Shadow over Malaya*, 117–119, 154.

47. Charters, "From Palestine to Northern Ireland," 204–205, 230–231.

48. Director of Operations, Malaya, *Conduct of Anti-Terrorist Operations in Malaya*, chap. XV, p. 6. See also Mockaitis, *British Counterinsurgency*, 166.

49. Newsinger, *British Counterinsurgency*, 52–53; Clutterbuck, *Long, Long War*, 80; Barber, *War of the Running Dogs*, 150–153; Henniker, *Red Shadow over Malaya*, 27–28; Mockaitis, *British Counterinsurgency*, 166–167; Cloake, *Templer*, 213–214, 243; Coates, *Suppressing Insurgency*, 114, 119; Sunderland, *Organizing Counterinsurgency in Malaya*, 65.

50. Sunderland, *Army Operations in Malaya*, 57–58; Dennis and Gray, *Emergency and Confrontation*, 93–155; Pugsley, *From Emergency to Confrontation*, 101–169; Clutterbuck, *Long, Long War*, 86–87; Nagl, *Counterinsurgency Lessons from Malaya and Vietnam*, 92.

51. Coates, *Suppressing Insurgency*, 161–163.

52. Henniker, *Red Shadow over Malaya*, 105.

53. Stubbs, *Hearts and Minds in Guerrilla Warfare*, 157, 167–168, 213–214; Cloake, *Templer*, 279; Short, *Communist Insurrection in Malaya*, 402–403; Chin, *My Side of History*, 268–270; Newsinger, *British Counterinsurgency*, 46–53.

54. Thompson, *Defeating Communist Insurgency*, 40; Coates, *Suppressing Insurgency*, 69, 89–91, 124, 132; Clutterbuck, *Long, Long War*, 80; Chin, *My Side of History*, 267–268.

55. Coates, *Suppressing Insurgency*, 131.

56. Short, *Communist Insurrection in Malaya*, 489.

57. Stubbs, *Hearts and Minds in Guerrilla Warfare*, 230–238; Clutterbuck, *Long, Long War*, 146–148; Chin, *My Side of History*, 397–412, 435; Short, *Communist Insurrection in Malaya*, 492; Dennis and Grey, *Emergency and Confrontation*, 155–166; Pugsley, *From Emergency to Confrontation*, 169–171.

Chapter 7. The Vietnam War

1. Moyar, *Triumph Forsaken*, 33–34.

2. Ibid., 39–53.

3. Ibid., 80.

4. Ibid., 67–71.

5. Ibid., 67–71, 81–82.

6. Ibid., 71–72.

7. Ibid., 99–100.

8. Ibid., 93–97.

9. Ibid., 98.

10. Ibid., 154–155.

11. Ibid., 153–159.

12. Ibid., 165–168.

13. Ibid., 168–169, 181–185 (quotation on p. 185).

14. Ibid., 206–211.

15. Ibid., 248, 256.

16. Ibid., 226–227, 235–241, 256, 262, 271.

17. Ibid., 281.

18. Ibid., 281–285 (quotation on p. 282).

19. Ibid., 295.

20. Ibid., 293–296.

21. Ibid., 303.

22. Ibid., 303–304; Moyar, *Phoenix and the Birds of Prey*, 164–173.

23. Moyar, *Triumph Forsaken*, 315–318 (quotation on p. 316).

24. Ibid., 318–328 (quotation on p. 319).

25. Ibid., 324–326, 332–333, 356–357, 363–365.

26. Ibid., 372, 394–395 (quotation on p. 394).

27. Ibid., 402–403.

28. Ibid., 403–416.

29. Zaffiri, *Westmoreland*; William C. Westmoreland, *A Soldier Reports* (Garden City, N.Y.: Doubleday, 1976); Jack Langguth, "Inheritor of a Wretched War," *New York Times Magazine*, November 15, 1964.

30. Zaffiri, *Westmoreland*, 118–119.

31. Ibid., 224–229 (quotation on p. 226).

32. The most famous case was that of Westmoreland's friend Major General William DePuy, commander of the 1st Infantry Division in 1966 and 1967. Gole, "DePuy's Relief of Subordinates in Combat," 35–47.

33. Draude, "When Should a Commander Be Relieved," 6.

34. Ibid., 29–32, 73.

35. Moyar, *Triumph Forsaken*, 335–336, 407–408.

36. Jack Shulimson, *U.S. Marines in Vietnam: An Expanding War, 1966* (Washington, D.C.: History and Museums Division, Headquarters, U.S. Marine Corps, 1982), 240.

37. Allnutt, *Marine Combined Action Capabilities*, 35.

38. Ibid., 48.

39. Moyar, *Phoenix and the Birds of Prey*, 44–45.

40. Ibid., 162–163.

41. Ibid., 47–50.

42. Ibid., 50–52, 60–61, 133–143, 225–227.

43. Ibid., 81–85, 119–124, 203–206.

44. Ibid., 65, 242–243.

45. Sorley, *Thunderbolt*.

46. Sorley, *A Better War*, 56.

47. Sorley, *Thunderbolt*, 95–96.

48. Davidson, *Vietnam at War*, 577.

49. Sorley, *Thunderbolt*, 247–249; Davidson, *Vietnam at War*, 580–583.

50. Sorley, *Thunderbolt*, 247.

51. Lewis Sorley, interview with author, July 14, 2008.

52. Ronald H. Spector, *After Tet: The Bloodiest Year in Vietnam* (New York: Free Press, 1993), 215–218; Birtle, *U.S. Army Doctrine, 1942–1976*, 367–368; Davidson, *Vietnam at War*, 571–572, 612–615; Moyar, *Phoenix and the Birds of Prey*, 200–201; Sorley, *A Better War*, 138–142, 175 (quotation); Hunt, *Pacification*, 221–233; Lewy, *America in Vietnam*, 139–153.

53. Kevin M. Boylan, "The Red Queen's Race: The 173rd Airborne Brigade and Pacification in Binh Dinh Province, 1969–1970" (Ph.D. diss., Temple University, 1994); Sorley, *A Better War*; Eric M. Bergerud, *The Dynamics of Defeat: The Vietnam War in Hau Nghia Province* (Boulder, Colo.: Westview Press, 1991), 223–308; Lewy, *America in Vietnam*, 134–136; Hunt, *Pacification*, 172–207, 221–233.

54. Lewy, *America in Vietnam*, 311; Boylan, "Red Queen's Race"; Birtle, *U.S. Army Doctrine, 1942–1976*, 402–405; Bergerud, *Dynamics of Defeat*, 274. For more information on the paucity of American involvement in atrocities, see B. G. Burkett and Glenna Whitley, *Stolen Valor: How the Vietnam Generation Was Robbed of Its Heroes and Its History* (Dallas: Verity, 1998); Eric M. Bergerud, *Red Thunder, Tropic Lightning: The World of a Combat Division in Vietnam* (Boulder, Colo.: Westview Press, 1993); Lewy, *America in Vietnam*; Sorley, *A Better War*; Moyar, *Phoenix and the Birds of Prey*; Michael Lind, *Vietnam, the Necessary War: A Reinterpretation of America's Most Disastrous Military Conflict* (New York: Free Press, 1999).

55. Moyar, *Phoenix and the Birds of Prey*, 71, 180 (quotation), 282, 317, 321–324.

56. Ibid., 50, 160–161, 179–181, 197, 327 (quotation).

57. Thomas C. Thayer, *War Without Fronts: The American Experience in Vietnam* (Boulder, Colo.: Westview Press, 1985), 62–66.

58. Sorley, *Vietnam Chronicles*, 294.

59. Moyar, *Phoenix and the Birds of Prey*, 181–188.

60. Ibid., 245–250.

Chapter 8. The Salvadoran Insurgency

1. Joes, *America and Guerrilla Warfare*, 259; Shirley Christian, "El Salvador's Divided Military," *Atlantic Monthly*, June 1983, 51; Schwarz, *American Counterinsurgency Doctrine and El Salvador*, 44.

2. Edelberto Torres-Rivas, "Insurrection and Civil War in El Salvador," in Doyle et al., *Keeping the Peace*, 214–218; Greentree, *Crossroads of Intervention*, 77–78.

3. LeoGrande, *Our Own Backyard*, 38.

4. Ibid., 40–42.

5. Meara, *Contra Cross*, 47–51, 60–63, 69–70; Yvon Grenier, *The Emergence of Insurgency in El Salvador: Ideology and Political Will* (Pittsburgh: University of Pittsburgh Press, 1999), 43–47.

6. Raymond Bonner, *Weakness and Deceit: U.S. Policy and El Salvador* (New York: Times Books, 1984), 47–51; Schwarz, *American Counterinsurgency Doctrine and El Salvador*, 2; Christian, "El Salvador's Divided Military," 50–53; Meara, *Contra Cross*, 48–50.

7. H. Joachim Maitre, "The Subsiding War in El Salvador," *Strategic Review*, Winter 1985, 23–24; John Waghelstein Oral History, 1985, p. 34, U.S. Army Military History Institute; LeoGrande, *Our Own Backyard*, 42–47, 166–168.

8. Joes, *America and Guerrilla Warfare*, 261–262; Schwarz, *American Counterinsurgency Doctrine and El Salvador*, 41–43; LeoGrande, *Our Own Backyard*, 50; Alan Riding, "Duarte's Strategy May Work Better in U.S. than in Salvador," *New York Times*, September 27, 1981.

9. Grenier, *Emergence of Insurgency in El Salvador*, 43–47, 69–90.

10. Greentree, *Crossroads of Intervention*, 90–91.

11. James LeMoyne, "El Salvador's Forgotten War," *Foreign Affairs* 68 (Summer 1989), 119; LeoGrande, *Our Own Backyard,* 68–69 (quotation on p. 69).

12. Joes, *America and Guerrilla Warfare,* 263; Bosch, *Salvadoran Officer Corps.*

13. LeoGrande, *Our Own Backyard,* 69–70.

14. Robert Pastor, *Not Condemned to Repetition: The United States and Nicaragua,* 2nd ed. (Boulder, Colo.: Westview Press, 2002), 42.

15. LeMoyne, "El Salvador's Forgotten War," 117–120; Greentree, *Crossroads of Intervention,* 89–90; Byrne, *El Salvador's Civil War,* 151–152.

16. Corum and Johnson, *Airpower in Small Wars,* 330; Waghelstein, "El Salvador," 39; Leo-Grande, *Our Own Backyard,* 135; Lungo Uclés, *El Salvador in the Eighties,* 54–55.

17. LeoGrande, *Our Own Backyard,* 81–95; Bacevich et al., *American Military Policy in Small Wars,* 10; Joes, *America and Guerrilla Warfare,* 263; Waghelstein Oral History, p. 119; Christian, "El Salvador's Divided Military," 52, 59–60.

18. Michael Childress, *The Effectiveness of U.S. Training Efforts in Internal Defense and Development: The Cases of El Salvador and Honduras* (Santa Monica, Calif.: Rand, 1995), 26–27; Manwaring and Prisk, *El Salvador at War,* 278–279; Waghelstein Oral History, p. 53; Waghelstein, "El Salvador," 39.

19. Ramsey, *Advising Indigenous Forces,* 86; Waghelstein Oral History, p, 53; Manwaring and Prisk, *El Salvador at War,* 302–304; Bacevich et al., *American Military Policy in Small Wars,* 27.

20. Waghelstein, "El Salvador," 35–36; Corum and Johnson, *Airpower in Small Wars,* 330; Manwaring and Prisk, *El Salvador at War,* 278–279; Lungo Uclés, *El Salvador in the Eighties,* 70–72.

21. Manwaring and Prisk, *El Salvador at War,* 398–399.

22. Sepp, "Evolution of United States Military Strategy," 95–96; Manwaring and Prisk, eds., *El Salvador at War,* 278–279.

23. Sepp, "Evolution of United States Military Strategy," 225. See also Ramsey, *Advising Indigenous Forces,* 94; Meara, *Contra Cross,* 54–55, 66.

24. Ramsey, *Advising Indigenous Forces,* 91–96; Manwaring and Prisk, *El Salvador at War,* 305; Sepp, "Evolution of United States Military Strategy," 108–109.

25. Lungo Uclés, *El Salvador in the Eighties,* 70–72; Bacevich et al., *American Military Policy in Small Wars,* 25; Waghelstein Oral History, p. 118.

26. Bacevich et al., *American Military Policy in Small Wars,* 27–28.

27. Byrne, *El Salvador's Civil War,* 84; Lungo Uclés, *El Salvador in the Eighties,* 55–57; Waghelstein Oral History, pp. 28–32 (quotation on p. 28).

28. Waghelstein Oral History, pp. 46–48.

29. Waghelstein Oral History, pp. 52 (quotation), 113.

30. LeoGrande, *Our Own Backyard,* 176–183; Corum and Johnson, *Airpower in Small Wars,* 342; Waghelstein Oral History, pp. 46–48.

31. Byrne, *El Salvador's Civil War,* 85–86; Lungo Uclés, *El Salvador in the Eighties,* 57; Leo-Grande, *Our Own Backyard,* 184.

32. Schwarz, *American Counterinsurgency Doctrine and El Salvador,* 51; LeoGrande, *Our Own Backyard,* 224–226; Bacevich et al., *American Military Policy in Small Wars,* 44.

33. LeoGrande, *Our Own Backyard,* 186; Manwaring and Prisk, *El Salvador at War,* 233.

34. Sepp, "Evolution of United States Military Strategy," 40–44.

35. LeoGrande, *Our Own Backyard,* 183–184.

36. Manwaring and Prisk, *El Salvador at War,* 212–214, 274–275.

37. H. Joachim Maitre, "El Salvador's Worst Enemy: Washington's No-Win Attitude," *Wall Street Journal,* February 24, 1984; Maitre, "Subsiding War in El Salvador," 26; LeoGrande, *Our Own Backyard,* 226.

38. Maitre, "Subsiding War in El Salvador," 26–27; Rosello, "Lessons from El Salvador," 104–108; Waghelstein Oral History, pp. 37, 44–45; Manwaring and Prisk, *El Salvador at War,* 145–146, 274–275, 300–301.

39. LeoGrande, *Our Own Backyard,* 230–231; Bacevich et al., *American Military Policy in Small Wars,* 25.

40. Manwaring and Prisk, *El Salvador at War*, 213–215, 271; LeoGrande, *Our Own Backyard*, 230–231.

41. Philip Taubman, "U.S. Aides Say Salvador Army Is Now on Top," *New York Times*, October 7, 1984.

42. Manwaring and Prisk, *El Salvador at War*, 408–410.

43. Ibid.

44. Ibid., 302–304.

45. LeoGrande, *Our Own Backyard*, 267–268; Bacevich et al., *American Military Policy in Small Wars*, 32–33; Byrne, *El Salvador's Civil War*, 88.

46. Schwarz, *American Counterinsurgency Doctrine and El Salvador*, 72–73; LeoGrande, *Our Own Backyard*, 248–250.

47. Bacevich et al., *American Military Policy in Small Wars*, 35; LeoGrande, *Our Own Backyard*, 256–259.

48. LeoGrande, *Our Own Backyard*, 261.

49. Ibid., 261, 264–265, 564–566.

50. Bacevich et al., *American Military Policy in Small Wars*, 26; Bosch, *Salvadoran Officer Corps*, 117–120; Byrne, *El Salvador's Civil War*, 147–150, 170; Manwaring and Prisk, *El Salvador at War*, 306–308, 409–410, 435.

51. Rosello, "Lessons from El Salvador," 104; LeoGrande, *Our Own Backyard*, 565–566; LeMoyne, "El Salvador's Forgotten War," 109–114.

52. LeoGrande, *Our Own Backyard*, 264, 565–568; Joes, *America and Guerrilla Warfare*, 268–269; Rosello, "Lessons from El Salvador," 102.

53. Byrne, *El Salvador's Civil War*, 152, 161.

54. Childress, *Effectiveness of U.S. Training Efforts*, 37; Byrne, *El Salvador's Civil War*, 152–153; Corum and Johnson, *Airpower in Small Wars*, 340.

55. LeoGrande, *Our Own Backyard*, 569–571; Schwarz, *American Counterinsurgency Doctrine and El Salvador*, 65.

56. Meara, *Contra Cross*, 56; LeoGrande, *Our Own Backyard*, 569–570, 576; Sepp, "Evolution of United States Military Strategy," 184, 187–191, 206–210, 222–223.

57. Bosch, *Salvadoran Officer Corps*, 121–124; Byrne, *El Salvador's Civil War*, 171–176, 185; LeoGrande, *Our Own Backyard*, 572–577; Mark Levine, "Peacemaking in El Salvador," in Doyle et al., *Keeping the Peace*, 227–244.

58. James LeMoyne, "Out of the Jungle—in El Salvador, Rebels with a New Cause," *New York Times*, February 9, 1992 (quotation); David H. McCormick, "From Peacekeeping to Peacebuilding: Restructuring Military and Police Institutions in El Salvador," in Doyle et al., *Keeping the Peace*, 297.

59. Ian Johnstone, "Rights and Reconciliation in El Salvador," in Doyle et al., *Keeping the Peace*, 323–325; McCormick, "From Peacekeeping to Peacebuilding," 292–294.

60. James Dobbins et al., *The UN's Role in Nation-Building: From the Congo to Iraq* (Santa Monica, Calif.: Rand, 2005), 56–58; McCormick, "From Peacekeeping to Peacebuilding," 302–305 (quotation on p. 305).

61. Joes, *America and Guerrilla Warfare*, 269–270; Dobbins et al., *UN's Role in Nation-Building*, 61–62.

Chapter 9. The War in Afghanistan

1. Ahmed Rashid, *Taliban: Militant Islam, Oil and Fundamentalism in Central Asia* (New Haven: Yale University Press, 2000); Hodes and Sedra, *Search for Security*, 11–18.

2. Maloney, *Enduring the Freedom*, 38–45; Jones, "Rise of Afghanistan's Insurgency," 7.

3. Nick B. Mills, *Karzai: The Failing American Intervention and the Struggle for Afghanistan* (Hoboken: John Wiley, 2007); Amin Tarzi, "The Neo-Taliban," in Crews and Tarzi, *Taliban and the Crisis of Afghanistan*, 277–279.

4. International Crisis Group, "Afghanistan: The Need for International Resolve," *Asia Report*, no. 145 (February 6, 2008), 4, http://www.crisisgroup.org; Maloney, *Enduring the Freedom*, 52–53, 96–100; Hodes and Sedra, *Search for Security*, 11–12; Atiq Sarwari and Robert D. Crews,

"Epilogue," in Crews and Tarzi, *Taliban and the Crisis of Afghanistan*, 319–324; Kathy Gannon, "Afghanistan Unbound," *Foreign Affairs* 83 (May–June 2004); International Crisis Group, "Countering Afghanistan's Insurgency," 3; Abdulkader H. Sinno, *Organizations at War in Afghanistan and Beyond* (Ithaca, N.Y.: Cornell University Press, 2008), 273; Mills, *Karzai*, 188–189.

5. Raymond A. Millen, *Afghanistan: Reconstituting a Collapsed State* (Carlisle, Pa.: Strategic Studies Institute, 2005), 2–3, 11; Jalali, "Rebuilding Afghanistan's National Army," 78; Giustozzi, *Koran, Kalashnikov, and Laptop*, 167–170.

6. Hodes and Sedra, *Search for Security*, 65, 71; Andrew Wilder, "Cops or Robbers? The Struggle to Reform the Afghan National Police," Afghanistan Research and Evaluation Unit, July 2007, 3–4, http://www.areu.org.af; Giustozzi, *Koran, Kalashnikov, and Laptop*, 17–20; International Crisis Group, "Reforming Afghanistan's Police," 5; Chayes, *The Punishment of Virtue*, 292–297, 312; Ali A. Jalali, interview with author, August 26, 2008.

7. International Crisis Group, "Reforming Afghanistan's Police," 6–7.

8. Corine Hegland, "It's Great to Be a Warlord in Afghanistan," *National Journal*, November 5, 2005, 3465.

9. Hodes and Sedra, *Search for Security*, 62–63.

10. International Crisis Group, "Reforming Afghanistan's Police," 8 (quotation); Hodes and Sedra, *Search for Security*, 63–64; Jones, "Rise of Afghanistan's Insurgency," 23.

11. Jalali, "Rebuilding Afghanistan's National Army," 80; Hodes and Sedra, *Search for Security*, 58; Maloney, *Enduring the Freedom*, 143–144.

12. Sarah Lister, "Moving Forward? Assessing Public Administration Reform in Afghanistan," Afghan Research and Evaluation Unit, September 2006, 3–4, 9–10, 14–15 (quotation on p. 10), http://www.areu.org.af.

13. Giustozzi, *Koran, Kalashnikov, and Laptop*, 2–4, 99–100; Jones, "Rise of Afghanistan's Insurgency," 29–33; Rashid, *Descent into Chaos*, 242–250.

14. Daniel Marston, "Lessons in 21st-Century Counterinsurgency: Afghanistan 2001–07," in Daniel Marston and Carter Malkasian, eds., *Counterinsurgency in Modern Warfare* (Oxford: Osprey, 2008), 229–230; Tarzi, "Neo-Taliban," 275–276, 291–310; Sarwari and Crews, "Epilogue," 318–321; Rashid, *Descent into Chaos*, 128; Chayes, *Punishment of Virtue*, 194; Bhatia and Sedra, *Afghanistan, Arms and Conflict*, 199–201, 217–220, 238–241, 258–259, 275, 290–292.

15. Tarzi, "Neo-Taliban," 281–282; Hodes and Sedra, *Search for Security*, 8; Jones, "Rise of Afghanistan's Insurgency," 26, 34; Giustozzi, *Koran, Kalashnikov, and Laptop*, 101–103, 110–113.

16. Bernd Horn, "Full Spectrum Leadership Challenges in Afghanistan," in Bernd Horn, ed., *"The Buck Stops Here": Senior Military Commanders on Operations* (Kingston, Ontario: Canadian Defence Academy Press, 2007), 196.

17. Barno, "Fighting 'The Other War,'" 33–34, 38 (quotation).

18. "Insights from OEF: Commanding in Afghanistan," *Army*, February 2007, 59.

19. See Appendix, question 16. Colonel Dale Alford, a distinguished commander who served in both Iraq and Afghanistan, represented the comments of numerous veterans when he said, "If the commander is weak, the unit will be weak no matter who the other officers and NCOs are." Dale Alford, interviews with author, spring 2008.

20. Kaplan, *Imperial Grunts*, 209–210, 216, 226–229, 254–255. In the Counterinsurgency Leadership Survey, 60 percent of Afghanistan veterans agreed that emphasis from higher headquarters on protecting forces from harm unnecessarily reduced the ability of security forces to accomplish their missions. Appendix, question 27.

21. Michael J. McNerney, "Stabilization and Reconstruction in Afghanistan: Are PRTs a Model or a Muddle?" *Parameters* 35 (Winter 2005–2006), 38; Giustozzi, *Koran, Kalashnikov, and Laptop*, 201; Rashid, *Descent into Chaos*, 252; Barno, "Fighting 'The Other War,'" 34–39; David W. Barno, interview with author, August 26, 2008.

22. Robert M. Perito, "The U.S. Experience with Provincial Reconstruction Teams in Afghanistan: Lessons Identified," U.S. Institute of Peace Special Report no. 152 (October 2005), 2–4, 9, http://www.usip.org; McNerney, "Stabilization and Reconstruction in Afghanistan," 32–33, 38–39, 43–44; Barbara J. Stapleton, "A Means to What End? Why PRTs are Peripheral to the Bigger Political Challenges in Afghanistan," *Journal of Military and Strategic Studies* 10 (Fall 2007), 25–49; Rashid, *Descent into Chaos*, 189–190, 198–201. NATO began forming Provincial Reconstruction

Teams in 2004, but the NATO teams contributed very little to counterinsurgency because they were largely located in areas with no insurgent presence and their personnel often operated under restrictions that severely limited or eliminated the possibility of armed conflict.

23. "Afghan Counterinsurgency: In the Words of the Commanders," *Army*, August 2007, 73.

24. Stapleton, "Means to What End?" 27–49; McNerney, "Stabilization and Reconstruction in Afghanistan," 41–44; Perito, "U.S. Experience with Provincial Reconstruction Teams," 5–7; Jalali, interview with author.

25. Maloney, *Enduring the Freedom*, 304; Rashid, *Descent into Chaos*, 202–203.

26. Rubin, "Saving Afghanistan"; Hodes and Sedra, *Search for Security*, 41–42; Millen, *Afghanistan*, 8–9.

27. Chayes, *Punishment of Virtue*, 320–358.

28. Bhatia and Sedra, *Afghanistan, Arms and Conflict*, 130–136, 143–145; Hegland, "It's Great to Be a Warlord," 3464; Rashid, *Descent into Chaos*, 261; Hodes and Sedra, *Search for Security*, 60; Maloney, *Enduring the Freedom*, 305; Giustozzi, *Koran, Kalashnikov, and Laptop*, 203; Chayes, *Punishment of Virtue*, 359–360; Millen, *Afghanistan*, 3–5.

29. Carl Robichaud, "Remember Afghanistan? A Glass Half Full, On the *Titanic*," *World Policy Journal* 23 (Spring 2006), 20, 23; Ahmed Rashid, "Letter from Afghanistan: Are the Taliban Winning?" *Current History*, January 2007, 17–20; Barno, "Fighting 'The Other War,'" 42; Rubin, "Saving Afghanistan"; Giustozzi, *Koran, Kalashnikov, and Laptop*, 123–129; International Crisis Group, "Countering Afghanistan's Insurgency," 7; Hodes and Sedra, *Search for Security*, 7, 27.

30. Senlis Council, "Countering the Insurgency in Afghanistan: Losing Friends and Making Enemies" (London: MF Publishing, February 2007), 38, http://www.senliscouncil.net; International Crisis Group, "Countering Afghanistan's Insurgency," 8–12; Hodes and Sedra, *Search for Security*, 25–32; Sarwari and Crews, "Epilogue," 345; Giustozzi, *Koran, Kalashnikov, and Laptop*, 60–70, 174–177; Bhatia and Sedra, *Afghanistan, Arms and Conflict*, 25.

31. Rashid, *Descent into Chaos*, 203; Giustozzi, *Koran, Kalashnikov, and Laptop*, 186.

32. Giustozzi, *Koran, Kalashnikov, and Laptop*, 174; "Insights from OEF: Commanding in Afghanistan," *Army*, February 2007, 61.

33. Seema Patel and Steven Ross, "Breaking Point: Measuring Progress in Afghanistan," *A Report of the Post-Conflict Reconstruction Project*, Center for Strategic and International Studies, March 2007, 36–37, http://www.csis.org; Wilder, "Cops or Robbers?" 11–12, 31–33, 52–53; International Crisis Group, "Countering Afghanistan's Insurgency," 16; Rubin, "Saving Afghanistan"; International Crisis Group, "Reforming Afghanistan's Police," 16.

34. International Crisis Group, "Reforming Afghanistan's Police," 12; Hodes and Sedra, *Search for Security*, 69–70; Wilder, "Cops or Robbers?" 40–42.

35. Wilder, "Cops or Robbers?" 54.

36. Patel and Ross, "Breaking Point," 41; Giustozzi, *Koran, Kalashnikov, and Laptop*, 203–206; Hodes and Sedra, *Search for Security*, 78–79; Bureau of International Narcotics and Law Enforcement Affairs, "International Narcotics Control Strategy Report," March 2008, http://www.state.gov/p/inl/rls/nrcrpt/2008/vol1/html/100779.htm.

37. Jason Motlagh, "Reform and Function," *American Prospect*, February 15, 2007; Rubin, "Saving Afghanistan"; Rashid, "Letter from Afghanistan"; Mills, *Karzai*, 210–211; David Rohde, "Overhaul of Afghan Police Is Expensive New Priority," *New York Times*, October 18, 2007.

38. International Crisis Group, "Countering Afghanistan's Insurgency," 21.

39. Stapleton, "Means to What End?" 33.

40. Nick Grono, "How to Beat the Taliban," *The Australian*, April 9, 2007; "There's Marijuana in Their Socks," *The Economist*, November 18, 2006; Rashid, *Descent into Chaos*, 362–363; Giustozzi, *Koran, Kalashnikov, and Laptop*, 39.

41. Robichaud, "Remember Afghanistan?" 19–20; Hodes and Sedra, *Search for Security*, 46; Giustozzi, *Koran, Kalashnikov, and Laptop*, 165; Rashid, *Descent into Chaos*, 354, 371.

42. Marston, "Lessons in 21st-Century Counterinsurgency," 236–239.

43. Ian Hope, "Reflections on Afghanistan: Commanding Task Force Orion," in Horn, *"The Buck Stops Here,"* 211, 217, 226.

44. Ali A. Jalali, "Afghanistan: Regaining Momentum," *Parameters* 37 (Winter 2007-2008), 5–8; U.N. Department of Safety and Security–Afghanistan, "Half-Year Review of the Security Situa-

tion in Afghanistan," August 13, 2007, http://www.un.org; Hodes and Sedra, *Search for Security,* 25–32; International Crisis Group, "Countering Afghanistan's Insurgency," 11; Rashid, *Descent into Chaos,* 383–390; Senlis Council, "Countering the Insurgency in Afghanistan," 52; Bureau of International Narcotics and Law Enforcement Affairs, "International Narcotics Control Strategy Report"; David Rohde, "Afghan Police Suffer Setbacks as Taliban Adapt," *New York Times,* September 2, 2007; Karen DeYoung, "U.S. Notes Limited Progress in Afghan War," *Washington Post,* November 25, 2007.

45. Nasreen Ghufran, "Afghanistan in 2007: A Bleeding Wound," *Asian Survey* 48 (January–February 2008), 157; Hodes and Sedra, *Search for Security,* 57, 66; Bing West, "Securing Afghanistan: The Americans Keep Trying," *National Review,* March 19, 2007, 38–40; Rohde, "Overhaul of Afghan Police"; Jalali, "Afghanistan," 10; Rohde, "Afghan Police Suffer Setbacks"; DeYoung, "U.S. Notes Limited Progress"; Bureau of International Narcotics and Law Enforcement Affairs, "International Narcotics Control Strategy Report"; International Crisis Group, "Reforming Afghanistan's Police," 11; Transparency International, Corruption Perceptions Index, http://www.transparency.org/policy_research/surveys_ndices/cpi/2007.

46. Jason Straziuso, "US Troop Levels Up in Afghanistan," *San Francisco Chronicle,* April 10, 2008; Mark Sedra, "Security Sector Reform and State Building in Afghanistan," in Hayes and Sedra, *Afghanistan,* 193–194; coalition military personnel in Afghanistan, interviews with author, May 2008.

47. Jeffrey M. Haynes, interview with author, May 2008.

48. Coalition military personnel in Afghanistan, interviews with author, May 2008; U.S. Government Accountability Office (GAO), "Afghanistan Security: Further Congressional Action May Be Needed to Ensure Completion of a Detailed Plan to Develop and Sustain Capable Afghan National Security Forces," Report to Congressional Committees, June 2008, 18–21, http://www.gao.gov/new.items/d08661.pdf.

49. Coalition military personnel in Kabul, interviews with author, May 2008; GAO, "Afghanistan Security," 31–43; Ann Marlowe, "The New Strategy for Afghanistan's Cops," *Wall Street Journal,* April 25, 2008.

50. Sedra, "Security Sector Reform," 193.

51. Sarah Chayes, E-mail to author, July 28, 2008. Similarly, a majority of the surveyed American military personnel who had served in Afghanistan believed that many Afghans with the right leadership traits were not serving in the government or its security forces. Appendix, question 9.

52. Sultana Parvanta, E-mail to author, July 30, 2008.

53. Appendix, questions 5–6.

54. Appendix, questions 7–8.

55. Appendix, question 13.

Chapter 10. The Iraq War

1. Ricks, *Fiasco,* 76 (quotation); Tommy Franks with Malcolm McConnell, *American Soldier* (New York: Regan Books, 2004), 330.

2. Packer, *Assassins' Gate,* 121–123.

3. Chandrasekaran, *Imperial Life in the Emerald City,* 35.

4. Packer, *Assassins' Gate,* 128–129; Ricks, *Fiasco,* 104; Gordon and Trainor, *Cobra II,* 152–154, 160–162.

5. Gordon and Trainor, *Cobra II,* 458–460.

6. Ricks, *Fiasco,* 136–137, 150–152, 155–156, 167–169; Bruce Hoffman, "Insurgency and Counterinsurgency in Iraq," *Special Warfare* 17 (December 2004), 13; Packer, *Assassins' Gate,* 136–142; Gordon and Trainor, *Cobra II,* 467–468.

7. Packer, *Assassins' Gate,* 138.

8. Diamond, *Squandered Victory,* 34.

9. Hashim, *Insurgency and Counter-Insurgency in Iraq,* 293–296; Diamond, *Squandered Victory,* 32–36; Peter W. Galbraith, *The End of Iraq: How American Incompetence Created a War Without End* (New York: Simon and Schuster, 2006), 117 (quotation).

10. Wright et al., *On Point II,* 91–92; Nathaniel Fick, *One Bullet Away: The Making of a Marine*

Officer (Boston: Houghton Mifflin, 2005), 315–317; David Rieff, "Blueprint for a Mess," *New York Times Magazine,* November 2, 2003; Galbraith, *End of Iraq,* 111–113.

11. Ricks, *Fiasco,* 155 (first quotation), 167; Chandrasekaran, *Imperial Life in the Emerald City,* 54–55, 67–68; Diamond, *Squandered Victory,* 36–37 (second quotation), 71.

12. Diamond, *Squandered Victory,* 299.

13. Bob Woodward, *State of Denial: Bush at War, Part III* (New York: Simon and Schuster, 2006), 249; Diamond, *Squandered Victory,* 39, 91–94, 115–116, 180–181, 194–196, 289–290, 298–299; Ricks, *Fiasco,* 205–211; Chandrasekaran, *Imperial Life in the Emerald City,* 64–65, 91–94; Peter Foster, "America's Rebuilding of Iraq Is in Chaos, Say British," *Daily Telegraph,* June 17, 2003; Cordesman, *Iraqi Security Forces,* 55–56; Zinsmeister, *Dawn over Baghdad,* 54–55.

14. Packer, *Assassins' Gate,* 190–198; Gordon and Trainor, *Cobra II,* 482–484; Ricks, *Fiasco,* 159–160; West, *Strongest Tribe,* 7.

15. James Fallows, *Blind into Baghdad: America's War in Iraq* (New York: Vintage Books, 2006), 160–161; Packer, *Assassins' Gate,* 193–195, 240; Gordon and Trainor, *Cobra II,* 479–485; Ilene R. Prusher, "US Antiguerrilla Campaign Draws Iraqi Ire," *Christian Science Monitor,* June 16, 2003; Bing West, "American Military Performance in Iraq," *Military Review* 86 (September–October 2006), 3; West, *Strongest Tribe,* 8–9, 13–17; Mansoor, *Baghdad at Sunrise,* 108; Travis Patriquin, "Using Occam's Razor to Connect the Dots: The Ba'ath Party and the Insurgency in Tal Afar," *Military Review* 87 (January–February 2007), 20–24; Cordesman, *Iraqi Security Forces,* 11–14, 61. The Counterinsurgency Leadership Survey, taken in 2008, found that 73 percent of American veterans of Iraq agreed, and only 8 percent disagreed, that the Iraqi security forces would have been much better by that time had the United States not purged the supporters of Saddam Hussein's regime. Appendix, question 11.

16. Allawi, *Occupation of Iraq,* 162 (first quotation), 361–368; Hannah Allam, "Audit: Fraud Drained $1 Billion from Iraq's Defense Efforts," *Knight Ridder Washington Bureau,* August 12, 2005; Packer, *Assassins' Gate,* 141–142; Michael Isikoff and David Corn, *Hubris: The Inside Story of Spin, Scandal, and the Selling of the Iraq War* (New York: Crown, 2006), 224–225; Inspectors General, U.S. Department of State and U.S. Department of Defense, "Interagency Assessment of Iraq Police Training," July 15, 2005, 16 (second quotation), http://oig.state.gov/documents/organi zation/103475.pdf; Hashim, *Insurgency and Counter-Insurgency in Iraq,* 305–307; Fouad Ajami, *The Foreigner's Gift: The Americans, the Arabs, and the Iraqis in Iraq* (New York: Free Press, 2006), 148; Cordesman, *Iraqi Security Forces,* 226.

17. Gordon and Trainor, *Cobra II,* 490–494; West, *No True Glory,* 22; Nora Bensahel, "Mission Not Accomplished," in Mahnken and Keaney, *War in Iraq,* 136; West, *Strongest Tribe,* 12–15; Peter R. Mansoor, "Counterinsurgency in Karbala," in Mahnken and Keaney, *War in Iraq,* 195.

18. Ricks, *Fiasco,* 173–176 (quotations on pp. 173 and 174); John Agresto, *Mugged by Reality: The Liberation of Iraq and the Failure of Good Intentions* (New York: Encounter Books, 2007), 162–163; Yon, *Moment of Truth in Iraq,* 63; West, *Strongest Tribe,* 23.

19. Packer, *Assassins' Gate,* 240–241; Ricks, *Fiasco,* 227.

20. Fick, *One Bullet Away;* Robert D. Kaplan, *Imperial Grunts: The American Military on the Ground* (New York: Random House, 2005), 265–271; M. D. Capstick, "Establishing Security in Afghanistan," in Geoffrey Hayes and Mark Sedra, eds., *Afghanistan: Transition under Threat* (Waterloo, Ontario: Wilfrid Laurier Press, 2008), 264–265; Yon, *Moment of Truth in Iraq,* 95. For this reason, Marines were more likely than soldiers to believe that adaptive leadership could overcome lack of training and education specific to a particular type of conflict. See Appendix, question 42.

21. Matthew Morgan, *A Democracy Is Born* (Westport, Conn.: Praeger, 2007), 90; Appendix, question 17; interviews with U.S. military personnel.

22. James Mattis, interview with author, August 6, 2008.

23. Max Boot, "Reconstructing Iraq," *Weekly Standard,* September 15, 2003; Michael R. Gordon, "Leathernecks Plan to Use a Velvet Glove in Iraq," *New York Times,* December 12, 2003; Carl E. Mundy III, "Spare the Rod, Save the Nation," *New York Times,* December 30, 2003; West, *Strongest Tribe,* 8, 13–17; U.S. military personnel, interviews with author.

24. Linda Robinson, *Masters of Chaos: The Secret History of the Special Forces* (New York: Public Affairs, 2004), 217–223; James A. Gavrilis, "The Mayor of Ar Rutbah," *Foreign Policy,* November–December 2005, 28–35 (quotation on p. 33); Ricks, *Fiasco,* 152–154.

25. Rick Atkinson, *In the Company of Soldiers: A Chronicle of Combat* (New York: Henry Holt, 2004), 35–38 (quotations); Robinson, *Tell Me How This Ends*, 50–67.

26. Isaiah Wilson, "Rediscovering the Way of Lawrence," in Mahnken and Keaney, *War in Iraq*, 236–238; Robinson, *Tell Me How This Ends*, 68–72; Ricks, *Fiasco*, 228–232, 270–271; Ajami, *Foreigner's Gift*, 118–121; West, *Strongest Tribe*, 12–13; Malkasian, "Counterinsurgency in Iraq," 243–244.

27. David Petraeus, interview with author, June 4, 2008.

28. Leonard Wong, "Developing Adaptive Leaders: The Crucible Experience of Operation Iraqi Freedom" (Carlisle, Pa.: Strategic Studies Institute, 2004); Wright et al., *On Point II*, 191–204; Hashim, *Insurgency and Counter-Insurgency in Iraq*, 322; Vernon Loeb, "Instead of Force, Friendly Persuasion; Armor Division in Baghdad Attempts Makeover into Intelligence Gathering Unit," *Washington Post*, November 5, 2003; Ralph O. Baker, "Humint-Centric Operations: Developing Actionable Intelligence in the Urban Counterinsurgency Environment," *Military Review* 87 (March–April 2007), 12–21.

29. Peter W. Chiarelli, "Winning the Peace: The Requirement for Full-Spectrum Operations," *Military Review* 85 (July–August 2005), 16.

30. Petraeus, "Learning Counterinsurgency," 52.

31. Petraeus said of his time at Mosul in 2003, "There were a few commanders that did not get it right off the bat, and were a little uncomfortable with, or were reluctant to carry out, the stability and support operations, nation building. In those cases, you work it with the brigade commander: explain that you'd like a back-brief in a couple of days from those individuals on their nation-building plans and send the assistant division commander for operations down ahead of time. By the time you get down there, they are doing nation building." Petraeus, interview with author.

32. Eliot A. Cohen, "Conclusion," in Mahnken and Keaney, *War in Iraq*, 252.

33. Ricks, *Fiasco*, 274–277; U.S. military personnel, interviews with author.

34. Prusher, "US Antiguerrilla Campaign Draws Iraqi Ire"; Hashim, *Insurgency and Counter-Insurgency in Iraq*, 100–101; Ricks, *Fiasco*, 142–144, 193–195, 261; Packer, *Assassins' Gate*, 303; Allawi, *Occupation of Iraq*, 186; Malkasian, "Counterinsurgency in Iraq," 243.

35. In the Counterinsurgency Leadership Survey, 65 percent of Army respondents and 83 percent of Marine respondents agreed that most mistreatment of indigenous civilians by U.S. military personnel was the result of poor leadership, while only 4 percent from each service disagreed. Appendix, question 21.

36. Sean Herron, *Twice the Citizen: The New Challenges of Serving in the Army Reserve and National Guard* (Bloomington, Ind.: AuthorHouse, 2004), 31; Sean Michael Flynn, *The Fighting 69th: One Remarkable National Guard Unit's Journey from Ground Zero to Baghdad* (New York: Viking, 2007), 201; U.S. military personnel, interviews with author.

37. Huba Wass de Czege, "Of 'Intellectual and Moral' Failures," *Army*, July 2007, 10.

38. Zinsmeister, *Dawn over Baghdad*, 106–107; West, *Strongest Tribe*, 157; "Switching Gears in the Counterinsurgency Fight," *Army*, September 2006, 78–81; "Resilient Leadership," *Army*, May 2007, 75; U.S. military personnel, interviews with author.

39. Mansoor, *Baghdad at Sunrise*, 128–129; Wright et al., *On Point II*, 287–288; Cesar G. Soriano and Steven Komarow, "Poll: Iraqis out of Patience," *USA Today*, April 29, 2004; Appendix, question 26.

40. Rod Nordland, "Iraq's Repairman," *Newsweek*, July 5, 2004; Jim Michaels, "Colonel Walks Baghdad 'To Make People Believe,'" *USA Today*, August 22, 2006; Diamond, *Squandered Victory*, 243–245.

41. Greg Jaffe, "Change of Command," *Wall Street Journal*, February 24, 2005.

42. Julian Barnes, "An Open Mind for a New Army," *U.S. News and World Report*, October 31, 2005. For corroboration of this assessment, see Appendix, question 1.

43. West, *Strongest Tribe*, 46.

44. Wright et al., *On Point II*, 463–464; "Training Iraqi Forces," *Army*, March 2006, 71–73; Tyson F. Belanger, "The Cooperative Will of War," *Marine Corps Gazette* 90 (January 2006), 63.

45. Mark Etherington, *Revolt on the Tigris: The Al-Sadr Uprising and the Governing of Iraq* (Ithaca, N.Y.: Cornell University Press, 2005), 80–81, 137, 155–156, 166–168, 225–227 (quotations on pp. 155 and 227).

46. Malkasian, "Counterinsurgency in Iraq," 248–255; Bing West, "Streetwise," *Atlantic Monthly* 299 (January–February 2007), 70–76; West, *Strongest Tribe*, 44, 51, 79–81; Kalev I. Sepp, interview with author, May 2, 2008; Ricks, *Fiasco*, 392–394; George Packer, "The Lesson of Tal Afar," *New Yorker*, April 10, 2006, 48–65.

47. West, *Strongest Tribe*, 396–397.

48. Allawi, *Occupation of Iraq*, 349–369; Hashim, *Insurgency and Counter-Insurgency in Iraq*, 291, 300–303, 310–311; Cordesman, *Iraqi Security Forces*, 65, 88–90; Tony Karon, "Why Iraq's Not Getting Better," *Time*, September 15, 2004; Aamer Madhani, "Among Iraqi Units, 1 Really Earns Its Stripes," *Chicago Tribune*, December 26, 2005; Bryan Bender, "Report Paints Bleak Picture of Iraqi Forces," *Boston Globe*, January 8, 2005.

49. Kaplan, *Imperial Grunts*, 309–312; West, *No True Glory*, 49–52.

50. West, *No True Glory*, 74–88, 94–111, 124–133, 317–318, 323.

51. Carter Malkasian, "The First Battle for Fallujah," in Mahnken and Keaney, *War in Iraq*, 170–171; West, *No True Glory*, 58–60; L. Paul Bremer, *My Year in Iraq: The Struggle to Build a Future of Hope* (New York: Simon and Schuster, 2006), 317.

52. John F. Sattler and Daniel H. Wilson, "Operation AL FAJR: The Battle of Fallujah—Part II," *Marine Corps Gazette* 89 (July 2005), 12–13; West, *No True Glory*, 208–251; Malkasian, "First Battle for Fallujah," 177–181; John Toolan, interviews with author, 2008 (quotation); Mattis, interview with author; Belanger, "Cooperative Will of War," 63; Rajiv Chandrasekaran and Scott Wilson, "11 Troops Killed in Attacks in Iraq," *Washington Post*, May 3, 2004; Tony Perry, Patrick J. McDonnell, and Alissa J. Rubin, "How Marines Kept Fallujah from Becoming Dresden," *Los Angeles Times*, May 18, 2004; Brian Bennett, "Shooting with the Enemy," *Time*, September 20, 2004; Bremer, *My Year in Iraq*, 353, 381.

53. Zachary J. Iscol, "CAP India," *Marine Corps Gazette* 90 (January 2006), 57–60.

54. Ricks, *Fiasco*, 406.

55. West, *Strongest Tribe*, 71, 82–83, 108–111; Ricks, *Fiasco*, 414–418; Sepp, interview with author.

56. Kalev I. Sepp, "The U.S. Army and Counterinsurgency in Iraq," in Mahnken and Keaney, *War in Iraq*, 220.

57. Malkasian, "Counterinsurgency in Iraq," 248–255; West, *Strongest Tribe*, 77–83, 113; Liz Sly and Aamer Madhani, "Iraqi Forces Better, but GIs to Be Needed for Some Time," *Chicago Tribune*, December 1, 2005; Cordesman, *Iraqi Security Forces*, 151–235; Inspectors General, "Interagency Assessment of Iraq Police Training," 16 (quotation).

58. Agresto, *Mugged by Reality*, 175; Hashim, *Insurgency and Counter-Insurgency in Iraq*, 315; Allawi, *Occupation of Iraq*, 400–401, 419–423; West, *Strongest Tribe*, 104–105, 108, 191 (quotation on p. 104).

59. Babak Dehghanpisheh and Michael Hirsh, "Reckoning in Iraq," *Newsweek*, October 24, 2005 (quotation); Galbraith, *End of Iraq*, 189.

60. Patriquin, "Using Occam's Razor to Connect the Dots," 16–25; H. R. McMaster, E-mail to author, July 23, 2008; Packer, "Lesson of Tal Afar" (quotation); Ricks, *Fiasco*, 422–424; Ricardo A. Herrera, "Brave Rifles at Tall Afar, September 2005," in William G. Robertson, ed., *In Contact! Case Studies from the Long War* (Fort Leavenworth, Kans.: Combat Studies Institute Press, 2006), 125–152; Malkasian, "Counterinsurgency in Iraq," 251–252.

61. Yon, *Moment of Truth in Iraq*, 37–46 (quotation on p. 44).

62. Hannah Allam and Mohammed al Dulaimy, "Marine-Led Campaign Killed Friends and Foes, Iraqi Leaders Say," Knight Ridder Washington Bureau, May 16, 2005; Kirk Semple and Edward Wong, "U.S.-Iraqi Assault Meets Resistance Near Syrian Border," *New York Times*, November 15, 2005; Kurt Wheeler, "Good News in Al Anbar?" *Marine Corps Gazette* 91 (April 2007), 36–40; Charles Crain, "Counterinsurgency Strategy: Staying Put," *Christian Science Monitor*, June 7, 2006; Michael D. Visconage, "Turning the Tide in the West: New Initiative and New Opportunities," *Marine Corps Gazette* 92 (February 2008), 8; West, "Streetwise"; Malkasian, "Counterinsurgency in Iraq," 252; Austin Long, "The Anbar Awakening," *Survival* 50 (April 2008), 78–79; West, *Strongest Tribe*, 98–102 (first quotation on p. 102); George Casey, Jr., interview with author, September 16, 2008; Dale Alford, interviews with author, spring 2008 (second quotation); Brendan

Heatherman, interview with author, August 1, 2008; Robb Sucher, interview with author, August 13, 2008; Stephen W. Davis, interview with author, August 8, 2008.

63. Davis, interview with author.

64. West, *Strongest Tribe*, 104, 108, 220 (quotation).

65. Jonathan Finer, "Threat of Shiite Militias Now Seen as Iraq's Most Critical Challenge," *Washington Post,* April 8, 2006; David Voorhies, "Making MiTT Work: Insights into Advising the Iraqi Army," *Infantry* 96 (May–June 2007), 30–34; Leila Fadel, "Iraqi Security Forces Tied to Kidnappings, Killings," *Fort Worth Star-Telegram,* May 9, 2006; Adrian T. Bogart, *Block by Block: Civic Action in the Battle of Baghdad, January–November 2006* (Hurlburt Field, Fla.: Joint Special Operations University Press, 2007), 26–28.

66. Allawi, *Occupation of Iraq,* 443; Kirk Semple and Richard A. Oppel, Jr., "Shiite Drops Bid to Keep His Post as Iraqi Premier," *New York Times,* April 21, 2006.

67. U.S. Department of Defense, "Measuring Stability and Security in Iraq: Report to Congress in Accordance with the Department of Defense Appropriations Act 2006 (Section 9010)" (Washington, D.C.: U.S. Government Printing Office, 2006), 51; International Crisis Group, "Iraq's Civil War, the Sadrists and the Surge," Middle East Report no. 72, February 7, 2008, 2–6, http://www.crisisgroup.org; West, "American Military Performance in Iraq," 6; West, "Streetwise"; Edward Wong, "Doubts Increase about Strength of Iraq Premier," *New York Times,* September 20, 2006.

68. Julian Barnes, "General Explains Baghdad Buildup," *Los Angeles Times,* July 27, 2006; West, *Strongest Tribe,* 160–165; Casey, interview with author.

69. Cordesman and Mausner, *Iraqi Force Development,* 156–160; West, *Strongest Tribe,* 162–165; U.S. Department of Defense, "Measuring Stability and Security in Iraq," 58; David S. Cloud and Michael R. Gordon, "Attacks in Iraq at Record Level, Pentagon Finds," *New York Times,* December 19, 2006; James Kitfield, "The Thin Iraqi Line," *National Journal,* June 9, 2007 (quotation).

70. Megan K. Stack and Louise Roug, "Fear of Big Battle Panics Iraqi City," *Los Angeles Times,* June 11, 2006; Niel Smith and Sean MacFarland, "Anbar Awakens: The Tipping Point," *Military Review* 88 (March–April 2008), 42; Martin Fletcher, "Fighting Back: The City Determined Not to Become Al-Qaeda's Capital," *Times* (London), November 20, 2006; Andrew Lubin, "Ramadi from the Caliphate to Capitalism," *Proceedings* 134 (April 2008).

71. Lubin, "Ramadi"; Jim Michaels, "An Army Colonel's Gamble Pays Off in Iraq," *USA Today,* April 30, 2007; Robert M. Hancock, "Task Force 1/6 in Ramadi: A Successful Tactical-Level Counterinsurgency Campaign" (M.M.S. paper, U.S. Marine Corps Command and Staff College, 2008); Robert M. Hancock, interview with author, May 2008; Fletcher, "Fighting Back"; Mark Kukis, "Turning Iraq's Tribes against Al-Qaeda," *Time,* December 26, 2006; Wheeler, "Good News in Al Anbar?" 36–39; Bing West and Owen West, "Iraq's Real 'Civil War,'" *Wall Street Journal,* April 5, 2007; John F. Burns, "Showcase and Chimera in the Desert," *New York Times,* July 8, 2007; Greg Jaffe, "Tribal Connections: How Courting Sheiks Slowed Violence in Iraq," *Wall Street Journal,* August 8, 2007; Smith and MacFarland, "Anbar Awakens," 42–52; Martin Fletcher, "How Life Returned to the Streets in a Showpiece City That Drove Out al-Qaeda," *Times* (London), August 31, 2007; Multi National Force–West personnel in Ramadi and Fallujah, interviews with author, May 2008.

72. Appendix, question 27.

73. Field Manual 3-24/Marine Corps Warfighting Publication 3-33.5, *Counterinsurgency,* 1–27.

74. Petraeus, interview with author.

75. Donald E. Vandergriff, "Old Dogs Teaching New Tricks," *Army,* November 2007, 59–66; December 2007, 49–62.

76. Mattis, interview with author.

77. Field Manual 3-24/Marine Corps Warfighting Publication 3-33.5, *Counterinsurgency,* A-3.

78. Ibid., 1-25, 7-6.

79. Ibid., A-8.

80. Todd S. Brown, *Battleground Iraq: Journal of a Company Commander* (Washington, D.C.: U.S. Army Center of Military History, 2007), 247–263.

81. Robinson, *Tell Me How This Ends,* 215–216; Greg Jaffe, "A Camp Divided," *Wall Street Journal,* June 17, 2006; U.S. military personnel, interviews with author.

82. Field Manual 3-24/Marine Corps Warfighting Publication 3-33.5, *Counterinsurgency,* 1–9.

83. Headquarters Multi-National Force–Iraq, "Multi-National Force–Iraq Commander's Counterinsurgency Guidance," June 21, 2008, copy in author's possession (quotation); Petraeus, interview with author; Mattis, interview with author.

84. Field Manual 3-24/Marine Corps Warfighting Publication 3-33.5, *Counterinsurgency,* 5–15, A-6.

85. Packer, "Lesson of Tal Afar."

86. The principle that U.S. forces should be kept to a minimum became popular after the fighting in Vietnam and El Salvador. See, for instance, Ernest Evans, "El Salvador's Lessons for Future U.S. Interventions," *World Affairs* 160 (Summer 1997), 45–46; John T. Fishel and Max G. Manwaring, *Uncomfortable Wars Revisited* (Norman: University of Oklahoma Press, 2006), 272; Max G. Manwaring and Court Prisk, eds., *El Salvador at War: An Oral History of Conflict from the 1979 Insurrection to the Present* (Washington, D.C.: National Defense University Press, 1988), 407, 457, 471; Victor Rosello, "Lessons from El Salvador," *Parameters* 23 (Winter 1993–1994), 102–103; Ricks, *Fiasco,* 192.

87. Petraeus, interview with author.

88. Robinson, *Tell Me How This Ends,* 104–106; West, *Strongest Tribe,* 250–251, 273–274; Babak Dehghanpisheh and Evan Thomas, "Scions of the Surge," *Newsweek,* March 24, 2008; Kimberly Kagan, "How They Did It," *Weekly Standard,* November 19, 2007; Farook Ahmed, "Multi-National Division—Center's Operations during the 2007–2008 Troop Surge," Backgrounder no. 28, Institute for the Study of War, April 10, 2008, http://www.understandingwar.org.

89. Peter Mansoor, E-mail to author, August 21, 2008.

90. Conrad Crane, conversation with author, December 12, 2007, and E-mail to author, August 24, 2007.

91. Appendix, question 35. Although some of the survey respondents had not been to Iraq or Afghanistan since the publication of the counterinsurgency manual, most were in regular contact with those who had been, and thus their responses reflect, by and large, current conditions.

92. Appendix, question 40.

93. Appendix, question 36.

94. Dominic J. Caraccilo and Andrea L. Thompson, *Achieving Victory in Iraq: Countering an Insurgency* (Mechanicsburg, Pa.: Stackpole, 2008), 24–25; U.S. military personnel, interviews with author.

95. Casey, interview with author.

96. Ann Scott Tyson, "Petraeus Helping Pick New Generals," *Washington Post,* November 17, 2007.

97. West, *Strongest Tribe,* 247.

98. Joshua Partlow, "Maliki's Office Is Seen Behind Purge in Forces," *Washington Post,* April 30, 2007; U.S. Department of Defense, "Measuring Stability and Security in Iraq," 18; David S. Cloud and Damien Cave, "Commanders Say Push in Baghdad Is Short of Goal," *New York Times,* June 4, 2007; Robinson, *Tell Me How This Ends,* 157.

99. James Kitfield, "More Art Than Science," *National Journal,* June 9, 2007; Bing West, "Start of the Surge," *National Review,* May 28, 2007; Julian Barnes, "A Trying Test of U.S.-Iraqi Teamwork," *Los Angeles Times,* July 6, 2007; Kitfield, "Thin Iraqi Line" (quotation).

100. Trudy Rubin, "U.S. Envoy's Challenge: The Political Iraq," *Philadelphia Inquirer,* June 17, 2007; Sudarsan Raghavan, "Maliki's Impact Blunted by Own Party's Fears," *Washington Post,* August 3, 2007; Robinson, *Tell Me How This Ends,* 156–157; Cordesman and Mausner, *Iraqi Force Development,* 79–106.

101. Kitfield, "Thin Iraqi Line"; Cordesman and Mausner, *Iraqi Force Development,* 2–9, 115–151.

102. Petraeus, interview with author.

103. U.S. House of Representatives, Committee on Armed Services, Subcommittee on Oversight and Investigations, "Stand Up and Be Counted: The Continuing Challenge of Building the Iraqi Security Forces," 2007, 102–103, http://armedservices.house.gov/pdfs/OI_ISFreport062707/OI_Report_FINAL.pdf.

104. Ibid., 134–136; U.S. Army advisers at Fort Riley, Kans., interviews with author, May 8, 2008; Appendix, question 15; Tyson, "Petraeus Helping Pick New Generals."

105. Cordesman and Mausner, *Iraqi Force Development*, 190.

106. Cloud and Cave, "Commanders Say Push in Baghdad Is Short of Goal"; Ann Scott Tyson, "Military Reports Slow Progress in Securing Baghdad," *Washington Post*, June 5, 2007.

107. Kitfield, "Thin Iraqi Line." In May 2007, Bing West observed that "the local effectiveness of the [Iraqi] army is dependent upon the battalion commander and one or two aggressive company commanders." West, "Start of the Surge."

108. U.S. Government Accountability Office (GAO), "Securing, Stabilizing, and Rebuilding Iraq: Progress Report—Some Gains Made, Updated Strategy Needed," Report to Congressional Subcommittees, June 2008, 29–30, http://www.gao.gov/new.items/d08837.pdf; Cordesman and Mausner, *Iraqi Force Development*, 192–206; West, *Strongest Tribe*, 273–276, 295–308.

109. Colum Lynch and Joshua Partlow, "Civilian Toll in Iraq at 'Higher Levels,'" *Washington Post*, June 12, 2007; Cordesman and Mausner, *Iraqi Force Development*, 192–206; West, *Strongest Tribe*, 273–276, 325–326.

110. GAO, "Securing, Stabilizing, and Rebuilding Iraq," 11–14.

111. Fletcher, "How Life Returned to the Streets in a Showpiece City That Drove Out al-Qaeda"; Ann Scott Tyson, "U.S. Widens Push to Use Armed Iraqi Residents," *Washington Post*, July 28, 2007; Robinson, *Tell Me How This Ends*, 252–261; Burns, "Showcase and Chimera in the Desert"; James Kitfield, "Shifting Strategies," *National Journal*, September 15, 2007; West, *Strongest Tribe*, 294–303; Erik Swabb, "The Lessons of Iraq," *Wall Street Journal*, January 14, 2008; Visconage, "Turning the Tide in the West," 9.

112. International Crisis Group, "Iraq's Civil War, the Sadrists and the Surge," 2–19; Jon Lee Anderson, "Inside the Surge," *New Yorker*, November 19, 2007; Peter Mansoor, "How the Surge Worked," *Washington Post*, August 10, 2008; James Kitfield, "Baghdad, Surged," *National Journal*, July 14, 2007; GAO, "Securing, Stabilizing, and Rebuilding Iraq," 22; Robinson, *Tell Me How This Ends*, 166–168, 285–286; West, *Strongest Tribe*, 318–319, 325–326.

113. Kim Gamel, "Iraqi Prime Minister Vows to Fight Militias in Basra to the End," *San Diego Union-Tribune*, March 27, 2008; Bushra Juhi, "1,300 Iraqi Troops, Police Dismissed," *USA Today*, April 13, 2008; Stephen Farrell and Qais Mizher, "Iraq Fires 1,300 Security Force Members Who Quit Basra Fight," *New York Times*, April 14, 2008.

114. Petraeus, interview with author.

115. Coalition military personnel in Baghdad, interviews with author, May 2008; Stephen Farrell and Richard A. Oppel, Jr., "Big Gains for Iraq Security, but Questions Linger," *New York Times*, June 21, 2008; Michael R. Gordon, "The Last Battle," *New York Times Magazine*, August 3, 2008; Robinson, *Tell Me How This Ends*, 341–342.

116. Solomon Moore, "In Mosul, New Test of Rebuilt Iraqi Army," *New York Times*, March 20, 2008; Andrew Kramer, "Iraqi Military Extends Control in Northern City," *New York Times*, June 1, 2008; coalition military personnel in Iraq, interviews with author, May 2008.

117. Coalition military personnel in Iraq, interviews with author, May 2008; GAO, "Securing, Stabilizing, and Rebuilding Iraq," 27–32. See also Appendix, question 7.

Chapter 11. How to Win

1. Donald Vandergriff, *Raising the Bar: Creating and Nurturing Adaptability to Deal with the Changing Face of War* (Washington, D.C.: Center for Defense Information Press, 2006); John A. Nagl and Paul L. Yingling, "New Rules for New Enemies," *Armed Forces Journal* 144 (October 2006); Hy S. Rothstein, *Afghanistan and the Troubled Future of Unconventional Warfare* (Annapolis, Md.: Naval Institute Press, 2006); Thomas P. M. Barnett, *Blueprint for Action: A Future Worth Creating* (New York: Putnam, 2005).

2. Studies of organizations have continued to show that the principal reason for organizational change is a leader who has the desire and the right personality to effect change. James Q. Wilson, *Bureaucracy: What Government Agencies Do and Why They Do It* (New York: Basic Books, 2000), 227–232; Ann M. Van Eron and W. Warner Burke, "The Transformational/Transactional

Leadership Model: A Study of Critical Components," in Kenneth E. Clark et al., eds., *Impact of Leadership* (Greensboro, N.C.: Center for Creative Leadership, 1992), 149–167.

3. For detailed description of the personality types, see Otto Kroeger et al., *Type Talk at Work: How the 16 Personality Types Determine Your Success on the Job* (New York: Dell, 2002); David Keirsey, *Please Understand Me II: Temperament, Character, Intelligence* (Del Mar, Calif.: Prometheus Nemesis, 1998).

4. Reg Lang, "Type Flexibility in Processes of Strategic Planning and Change," in Catherine Fitzgerald and Linda K. Kirby, eds., *Developing Leaders: Research and Applications in Psychological Type and Leadership Development* (Palo Alto, Calif.: Davies-Black, 1997), 487–511; William Bridges, *The Character of Organizations: Using Personality Type in Organization Development* (Palo Alto, Calif.: Davies-Black, 2000); Lee Barr and Norma Barr, *The Leadership Equation: Leadership, Management, and the Myers-Briggs* (Austin, Tex.: Eakin Press, 1989), 154; Rothstein, *Troubled Future of Unconventional Warfare*, 53–59; Greg A. Stevens and James Burley, "Piloting the Rocket of Radical Innovation," *Research Technology Management* 46 (March–April 2003), 16–25. Leadership analysts have used a variety of other instruments to test personality and creativity, some of which are more consistent with MBTI than others. Most of them, nevertheless, characterize the two main organizational leadership types in terms similar to those describing the NT and SJ types, as do numerous other studies that do not address personality types. See, for instance, Allan H. Church and Janine Waclawski, "The Relationship between Individual Personality Orientation and Executive Leadership Behaviour, *Journal of Occupational and Organizational Psychology* 71 (June 1998), 99–125; Joseph L. Moses and Karen S. Lyness, "Leadership Behavior in Ambiguous Environments," in Kenneth E. Clark and Miriam B. Clark, eds., *Measures of Leadership* (West Orange, N.J.: Leadership Library of America, 1990), 327–335; Christa L. Walck, "Using the MBTI in Management and Leadership: A Review of the Literature," in Fitzgerald and Kirby, *Developing Leaders*, 63–114; W. Scott Sherman et al., "Organizational Morphing: The Challenges of Leading Perpetually Changing Organizations in the Twenty-first Century," in James G. Hunt et al., eds., *Out-of-the-Box Leadership: Transforming the Twenty-First-Century Army and Other Top-Performing Organizations* (Stamford, Conn.: JAI, 1999), 43–62.

5. For data on the distribution of personality types, see Dianna Lea Williams, "Frequencies of Myers-Briggs Type Indicator (MBTI) among Military Leaders," *Journal of Leadership Studies*5 (Summer 1998), 50–56; Mary H. McCaulley, "The Myers-Briggs Type Indicator and Leadership," in Clark and Clark, *Measures of Leadership*, 381–418.

6. Stephen A. Stumpf and Roger L. M. Dunbar, "The Effects of Personality Type on Choices Made in Strategic Decision Situations," *Decision Sciences* 22 (November–December 1991), 1047–1072; Bridges, *Characters of Organizations*; Barr and Barr, *Leadership Equation*, 146–150, 154; Keirsey, *Please Understand Me II*, 104–109; Gordon Sullivan, "Foreword: From Theory to Practice," in Hunt et al., *Out-of-the-Box Leadership*, xviii; Rickey Rife and Rosemary Hansen, "Defense Is from Mars, State Is from Venus," Strategy Research Project (Carlisle Barracks, Pa.: U.S. Army War College, 1998).

7. Appendix, questions 37–38.

8. Keirsey, *Please Understand Me II*, 163.

9. Paul E. Roush, "The Myers-Briggs Type Indicator, Subordinate Feedback, and Perceptions of Leadership Effectiveness," in Kenneth E. Clark et al., *Impact of Leadership*, 544.

10. A study of lieutenant colonels at two of the U.S. military's top-level schools, published in 1999, reached this conclusion. Michael L. McGee et al., "Conceptual Capacity as Competitive Advantage: Developing Leaders for the New Army," in Hunt et al., *Out-of-the-Box Leadership*, 221–237. No comparable study has been done since that time, but the problem clearly has not gone away, as indicated by the sources cited in the remainder of this chapter.

11. David W. Barno, interview with author, August 26, 2008. See also Walter F. Ulmer, "Military Leadership in the 21st Century: Another 'Bridge Too Far'?" *Parameters* 28 (Spring 1998), 18–20.

12. Peter R. Mansoor, *Baghdad at Sunrise: A Brigade Commander's War in Iraq* (New Haven: Yale University Press, 2008), 350.

13. Charles Krulak, interview with author, July 15, 2008.

14. George Casey, Jr., interview with author, September 16, 2008.

15. Appendix, question 30.

16. Appendix, question 33. See also Appendix, questions 17 and 30.

17. Appendix, question 34.

18. Appendix, question 32.

19. Appendix, question 31.

20. This conclusion is based largely upon the written comments of respondents to the Counterinsurgency Leadership Survey.

Select Bibliography

The Civil War

Ash, Stephen V. *When the Yankees Came: Conflict and Chaos in the Occupied South, 1861-1865.* Chapel Hill: University of North Carolina Press, 1995.

Castel, Albert E. *Civil War Kansas: Reaping the Whirlwind.* Lawrence: University Press of Kansas, 1997.

Fellman, Michael. *Inside War: The Guerrilla Conflict in Missouri during the American Civil War.* New York: Oxford University Press, 1989.

Fisher, Noel C. *War at Every Door: Partisan Politics and Guerrilla Violence in East Tennessee, 1860-1869.* Chapel Hill: University of North Carolina Press, 1997.

Goss, Thomas J. *The War Within the Union High Command: Politics and Generalship during the Civil War.* Lawrence: University Press of Kansas, 2003.

Grimsley, Mark. *The Hard Hand of War: Union Military Policy toward Southern Civilians, 1861-1865.* New York: Cambridge University Press, 1995.

Groce, W. Todd. *Mountain Rebels: East Tennessee Confederates and the Civil War, 1860-1870.* Knoxville: University of Tennessee Press, 1999.

Mackey, Robert R. *The Uncivil War: Irregular Warfare in the Upper South, 1861-1865.* Norman: University of Oklahoma Press, 2004.

Marszalek, John F. *Commander of All Lincoln's Armies: A Life of General Henry W. Halleck.* Cambridge: Belknap Press of Harvard University Press, 2004.

Sutherland, Daniel E., ed. *Guerrillas, Unionists, and Violence on the Confederate Home Front.* Fayetteville: University of Arkansas Press, 1999.

Reconstruction in the South

Budiansky, Stephen. *The Bloody Shirt: Terror after Appomattox.* New York: Viking, 2008.

Cimbala, Paul A., and Randall M. Miller, eds. *The Freedmen's Bureau and Reconstruction.* New York: Fordham University Press, 1999.

Dawson, Joseph G. *Army Generals and Reconstruction: Louisiana, 1862-1877.* Baton Rouge: Louisiana State University Press, 1982.

Foner, Eric. *Reconstruction: America's Unfinished Revolution, 1863-1877.* New York: Harper and Row, 1988.

Martinez, J. Michael. *Carpetbaggers, Cavalry, and the Ku Klux Klan: Exposing the Invisible Empire during Reconstruction.* Lanham, Md.: Rowman and Littlefield, 2007.

Rable, George C. *But There Was No Peace: The Role of Violence in the Politics of Reconstruction.* Athens: University of Georgia Press, 1984.

Randall J. G., and David Herbert Donald. *The Civil War and Reconstruction.* 2nd ed. Lexington, Mass.: D. C. Heath, 1969.

Richter, William L. *The Army in Texas during Reconstruction, 1865–1870.* College Station: Texas A & M University Press, 1987.

Sefton, James E. *The United States Army and Reconstruction.* Baton Rouge: Louisiana State University Press, 1967.

Simpson, Brooks D. *The Reconstruction Presidents.* Lawrence: University Press of Kansas, 1998.

Taylor, Joe Gray. *Louisiana Reconstructed, 1863–1877.* Baton Rouge: Louisiana State University Press, 1974.

Thompson, Jerry. *Civil War to the Bloody End: The Life and Times of Major General Samuel P. Heintzelman.* College Station: Texas A & M University Press, 2006.

Trelease, Allen W. *White Terror: The Ku Klux Klan Conspiracy and Southern Reconstruction.* New York: Harper and Row, 1971.

The Philippine Insurrection

Birtle, Andrew J. *U.S. Army Counterinsurgency and Contingency Operations Doctrine, 1860–1941.* Washington, D.C.: U.S. Army Center of Military History, 1998.

———. "The U.S. Army's Pacification of Marinduque, Philippine Islands, April 1900–April 1901." *Journal of Military History* 61 (April 1997): 255–282.

Gates, John Morgan. *Schoolbooks and Krags: The United States Army in the Philippines, 1898–1902.* Westport, Conn.: Greenwood Press, 1973.

Linn, Brian McAllister. "The Philippines: Nationbuilding and Pacification." *Military Review* 85 (March–April 2005): 46–54.

———. *The Philippine War, 1899–1902.* Lawrence: University Press of Kansas, 2000.

———. *The U.S. Army and Counterinsurgency in the Philippine War, 1899–1902.* Lawrence: University Press of Kansas, 1989.

May, Glenn Anthony. *Battle for Batangas: A Philippine Province at War.* New Haven: Yale University Press, 1991.

———. *A Past Recovered.* Quezon City: New Day, 1987.

Miller, Stuart Creighton. *"Benevolent Assimilation": The American Conquest of the Philippines, 1899–1903.* New Haven: Yale University Press, 1982.

Ramsey, Robert D. *A Masterpiece of Counterguerrilla Warfare: BG J. Franklin Bell in the Philippines, 1901–1902.* Fort Leavenworth, Kans.: Combat Studies Institute Press, 2007.

Roth, Russell. *Muddy Glory: America's "Indian Wars" in the Philippines, 1899–1935.* West Hanover, Mass.: Christopher Publishing House, 1981.

Sexton, William Thaddeus. *Soldiers in the Sun: An Adventure in Imperialism.* Harrisburg, Pa.: Military Service Publishing Company, 1939.

Silbey, David J. *A War of Frontier and Empire: The Philippine-American War, 1899–1902.* New York: Hill and Wang, 2007.

Young, Kenneth Ray. *The General's General: The Life and Times of Arthur MacArthur.* Boulder, Colo.: Westview Press, 1994.

The Huk Rebellion

Baclagon, Uldarico S. *Lessons from the Huk Campaign in the Philippines.* Manila: M. Colcol, 1956.

Blitz, Amy. *The Contested State: American Foreign Policy and Regime Change in the Philippines.* Lanham, Md.: Rowman and Littlefield, 2000.

Brands, H. W. *Bound to Empire: The United States and the Philippines.* New York: Oxford University Press, 1992.

Currey, Cecil B. *Edward Lansdale: The Unquiet American.* Boston: Houghton Mifflin, 1988.

Greenberg, Lawrence M. *The Hukbalahap Insurrection: A Case Study of a Successful Counter-*

Insurgency Operation in the Philippines, 1946-1955. Washington, D.C.: U.S. Army Center of Military History, 1986.

Joes, Anthony James. *America and Guerrilla Warfare.* Lexington: University Press of Kentucky, 2000.

Kerkvliet, Benedict. *The Huk Rebellion: A Study of Peasant Revolt in the Philippines.* Lanham, Md.: Rowman and Littlefield, 2002.

Lachica, Eduardo. *The Huks: Philippine Agrarian Society in Revolt.* New York: Praeger, 1971.

Pomeroy, William J. *The Forest: A Personal Record of the Huk Guerrilla Struggle in the Philippines.* New York: International Publishers, 1963.

Romulo, Carlos P. *Crusade in Asia: Philippine Victory.* New York: John Day, 1955.

Romulo, Carlos P., and Marvin M. Gray. *The Magsaysay Story.* New York: John Day, 1956.

Scaff, Alvin H. *The Philippine Answer to Communism.* Stanford, Calif.: Stanford University Press, 1955.

Smith, Robert Aura. *Philippine Freedom, 1946-1958.* New York: Columbia University Press, 1958.

Taruc, Luis. *He Who Rides the Tiger: The Story of an Asian Guerrilla Leader.* New York: Praeger, 1967.

Valeriano, Napoleon D., and Charles T. R. Bohannon. *Counter-Guerrilla Operations: The Philippine Experience.* New York: Praeger, 1962.

The Malayan Emergency

Barber, Noel. *The War of the Running Dogs: The Malayan Emergency, 1948-1960.* New York: Weybright and Talley, 1972.

Chin Peng. *My Side of History.* Singapore: Media Masters, 2003.

Cloake, John. *Templer: Tiger of Malaya.* London: Harrap, 1985.

Clutterbuck, Richard L. *The Long, Long War: Counterinsurgency in Malaya and Vietnam.* New York: Praeger, 1966.

Coates, John. *Suppressing Insurgency: An Analysis of the Malayan Emergency, 1948-1954.* Boulder, Colo.: Westview Press, 1992.

Gregorian, Raffi. "'Jungle Bashing' in Malaya: Towards a Formal Tactical Doctrine." *Small Wars and Insurgencies* 5 (Winter 1994): 338-359.

Henniker, M. C. A. *Red Shadow over Malaya.* Edinburgh: William Blackwood and Sons, 1955.

Marston, Daniel. "Lost and Found in the Jungle: The Indian and British Army Jungle Warfare Doctrines for Burma, 1943-5, and the Malayan Emergency, 1948-60." In Hew Strachan, ed., *Big Wars and Small Wars: The British Army and the Lessons of War in the Twentieth Century,* 84-114. London: Routledge, 2006.

Miller, Harry. *The Communist Menace in Malaya.* New York: Praeger, 1954.

Mockaitis, Thomas R. *British Counterinsurgency, 1919-60.* New York: St. Martin's Press, 1990.

Nagl, John A. *Counterinsurgency Lessons from Malaya and Vietnam: Learning to Eat Soup with a Knife.* Westport, Conn.: Praeger, 2002.

Newsinger, John. *British Counterinsurgency: From Palestine to Northern Ireland.* Houndmills, England: Palgrave, 2002.

Shennan, Margaret. *Out in the Midday Sun: The British in Malaya, 1880-1960.* London: John Murray, 2000.

Short, Anthony. *The Communist Insurrection in Malaya, 1948-1960.* London: Frederick Muller, 1975.

Stubbs, Richard. *Hearts and Minds in Guerrilla Warfare: The Malayan Emergency, 1948-1960.* Singapore: Oxford University Press, 1989.

Sunderland, Riley. *Army Operations in Malaya, 1947-1960.* Santa Monica, Calif.: Rand, 1964.

Thompson, Robert. *Defeating Communist Insurgency: The Lessons of Malaya and Vietnam.* New York: Praeger, 1966.

The Vietnam War

Allnutt, Bruce C. *Marine Combined Action Capabilities: The Vietnam Experience*. Washington, D.C.: Office of Naval Research, 1969.

Birtle, Andrew J. *U.S. Army Counterinsurgency and Contingency Operations Doctrine, 1942–1976*. Washington, D.C.: U.S. Army Center of Military History, 2006.

Davidson, Phillip B. *Vietnam at War: The History, 1946–1975*. Novato, Calif.: Presidio Press, 1988.

Draude, Thomas V. "When Should a Commander Be Relieved: A Study of Combat Reliefs of Commanders of Battalions and Lower Units during the Vietnam Era." M.A. thesis, U.S. Army Command and General Staff College, 1976.

Gole, Henry G. "Gen. William E. DePuy's Relief of Subordinates in Combat." *Army*, August 2008, 35–47.

Hunt, Richard A. *Pacification: The American Struggle for Vietnam's Hearts and Minds*. Boulder, Colo.: Westview Press, 1995.

Lewy, Guenter. *America in Vietnam*. New York: Oxford University Press, 1978.

Moyar, Mark. *Phoenix and the Birds of Prey: Counterinsurgency and Counterterrorism in Vietnam*, new ed. Lincoln: University of Nebraska Press, 2007.

———. *Triumph Forsaken: The Vietnam War, 1954–1965*. New York: Cambridge University Press, 2006.

Sorley, Lewis. *A Better War: The Unexamined Victories and Final Tragedy of America's Last Years in Vietnam*. New York: Harcourt Brace, 1999.

———. *Thunderbolt: General Creighton Abrams and the Army of His Times*. New York: Simon and Schuster, 1992.

———, ed. *Vietnam Chronicles: The Abrams Tapes, 1968–1972*. Lubbock: Texas Tech University Press, 2004.

Zaffiri, Samuel. *Westmoreland: A Biography of William C. Westmoreland*. New York: Morrow, 1994.

The Salvadoran Insurgency

Bacevich, A. J., et al. *American Military Policy in Small Wars: The Case of El Salvador*. Washington, D.C.: Pergamon-Brassey's, 1988.

Bosch, Brian J. *The Salvadoran Officer Corps and the Final Offensive of 1981*. Jefferson, N.C.: McFarland, 1999.

Byrne, Hugh. *El Salvador's Civil War: A Study of Revolution*. Boulder, Colo.: Lynne Rienner, 1996.

Corum, James S., and Wray R. Johnson. *Airpower in Small Wars: Fighting Insurgents and Terrorists*. Lawrence: University Press of Kansas, 2003.

Doyle, Michael W., et al., eds. *Keeping the Peace: Multidimensional UN Operations in Cambodia and El Salvador*. Cambridge: Cambridge University Press, 1997.

Greentree, Todd. *Crossroads of Intervention: Insurgency and Counterinsurgency Lessons from Central America*. Westport, Conn.: Praeger, 2008.

Joes, Anthony James. *America and Guerrilla Warfare*. Lexington: University Press of Kentucky, 2000.

LeoGrande, William M. *Our Own Backyard: The United States in Central America, 1977–1992*. Chapel Hill: University of North Carolina Press, 1998.

Lungo Uclés, Mario. *El Salvador in the Eighties*, trans. Amelia F. Shogan. Philadelphia: Temple University Press, 1996.

Manwaring, Max G., and Court Prisk, eds. *El Salvador at War: An Oral History of Conflict from the 1979 Insurrection to the Present*. Washington, D.C.: National Defense University Press, 1988.

Meara, William R. *Contra Cross: Insurgency and Tyranny in Central America, 1979–1989*. Annapolis, Md.: Naval Institute Press, 2006.

Ramsey, Robert D. *Advising Indigenous Forces: American Advisors in Korea, Vietnam, and El Salvador*. Fort Leavenworth, Kans.: Combat Studies Institute Press, 2006.

Rosello, Victor. "Lessons from El Salvador." *Parameters* 23 (Winter 1993–1994): 100–108.

Schwarz, Benjamin C. *American Counterinsurgency Doctrine and El Salvador.* Santa Monica, Calif.: Rand, 1991.

Sepp, Kalev I. "The Evolution of United States Military Strategy in Central America, 1979–1991." Ph.D. diss., Harvard University, 2002.

Waghelstein, John D. "El Salvador: Observations and Experiences in Counterinsurgency." Research Paper, U.S. Army War College, 1985.

The War in Afghanistan

Barno, David W. "Fighting 'The Other War': Counterinsurgency Strategy in Afghanistan, 2003–2005." *Military Review* 87 (September–October 2007): 32–44.

Bhatia, Michael, and Mark Sedra. *Afghanistan, Arms and Conflict: Armed Groups, Disarmament and Security in a Post-War Society.* London: Routledge, 2008.

Chayes, Sarah. *The Punishment of Virtue: Inside Afghanistan after the Taliban.* New York: Penguin, 2006.

Crews, Robert D., and Amin Tarzi, eds. *The Taliban and the Crisis of Afghanistan.* Cambridge: Harvard University Press, 2008.

Giustozzi, Antonio. *Koran, Kalashnikov, and Laptop: The Neo-Taliban Insurgency in Afghanistan.* New York: Columbia University Press, 2008.

Hayes, Geoffrey, and Mark Sedra, eds. *Afghanistan: Transition under Threat.* Waterloo, Ontario: Wilfrid Laurier Press, 2008.

Hodes, Cyrus, and Mark Sedra. *The Search for Security in Post-Taliban Afghanistan.* New York: Routledge, 2007.

International Crisis Group. "Countering Afghanistan's Insurgency: No Quick Fixes." *Asia Report,* no. 123 (November 2, 2006). http://www.crisisgroup.org.

———. "Reforming Afghanistan's Police." *Asia Report,* no. 138 (August 30, 2007). http://www.crisisgroup.org.

Jalali, Ali A. "Rebuilding Afghanistan's National Army." *Parameters* 32 (Autumn 2002): 72–86.

Jones, Seth G. "The Rise of Afghanistan's Insurgency: State Failure and Jihad." *International Security* 32 (Spring 2008): 7–40.

Kaplan, Robert D. *Imperial Grunts: The American Military on the Ground.* New York: Random House, 2005.

Maloney, Sean M. *Enduring the Freedom: A Rogue Historian in Afghanistan.* Dulles, Va.: Potomac Books, 2005.

Rashid, Ahmed. *Descent into Chaos: The United States and the Failure of Nation Building in Pakistan, Afghanistan, and Central Asia.* New York: Viking, 2008.

Rubin, Barnett R. "Saving Afghanistan." *Foreign Affairs* 86 (January–February 2007): 57–78.

The Iraq War

Allawi, Ali A. *The Occupation of Iraq: Winning the War, Losing the Peace.* New Haven: Yale University Press, 2007.

Chandrasekaran, Rajiv. *Imperial Life in the Emerald City: Inside Iraq's Green Zone.* New York: Knopf, 2006.

Cordesman, Anthony H. *Iraqi Security Forces: A Strategy for Success.* Westport, Conn.: Praeger, 2006.

Cordesman, Anthony H., and Adam Mausner. *Iraqi Force Development: Conditions for Success, Consequences of Failure.* Washington, D.C.: CSIS Press, 2007.

Diamond, Larry. *Squandered Victory: The American Occupation and the Bungled Effort to Bring Democracy to Iraq.* New York: Times Books, 2005.

Gordon, Michael R., and Bernard E. Trainor. *Cobra II: The Inside Story of the Invasion and Occupation of Iraq.* New York: Pantheon Books, 2006.

Hashim, Ahmed S. *Insurgency and Counter-Insurgency in Iraq.* Ithaca, N.Y.: Cornell University Press, 2006.

Mahnken, Thomas G., and Thomas A. Keaney, eds. *War in Iraq: Planning and Execution.* London: Routledge, 2007.

Malkasian, Carter, "Counterinsurgency in Iraq." In Daniel Marston and Carter Malkasian, eds., *Counterinsurgency in Modern Warfare,* 241–259. Oxford, England: Osprey, 2008.

Mansoor, Peter R. *Baghdad at Sunrise: A Brigade Commander's War in Iraq.* New Haven: Yale University Press, 2008.

Packer, George. *The Assassins' Gate: America in Iraq.* New York: Farrar, Straus and Giroux, 2005.

Petraeus, David. "Learning Counterinsurgency: Observations from Soldiering in Iraq." *Military Review* 86 (January–February 2006): 2–12.

Ricks, Tom. *Fiasco: The American Military Adventure in Iraq.* New York: Penguin, 2006.

Robinson, Linda. *Tell Me How This Ends.* New York: Public Affairs, 2008.

West, Bing. *No True Glory: A Frontline Account of the Battle for Fallujah.* New York: Bantam, 2005.

———. *The Strongest Tribe: War, Politics, and the Endgame in Iraq.* New York: Random House, 2008.

Wright, Donald P., et al. *On Point II: Transition to the New Campaign.* Fort Leavenworth, Kans.: Combat Studies Institute Press, 2008.

Yon, Michael. *Moment of Truth in Iraq.* Minneapolis: Richard Vigilante Books, 2008.

Zinsmeister, Karl. *Dawn over Baghdad: How the U.S. Military Is Using Bullets and Ballots to Remake Iraq.* San Francisco: Encounter Books, 2004.

Index

Abizaid, John, 219, 278
Abrams, Creighton, 158–160, 162, 165, 257, 277, 280
Abu Ghraib, 225
Adaptive Leaders Courses (U.S. Army), 243
Adenauer, Konrad, 122
Afghanistan: Al Qaeda in, 192; corruption in, 196, 203–204, 206, 207–208; counterinsurgency in, 1–2, 107, 198–200, 205–206; counterinsurgency leadership in, 198–200, 205, 210–211, 266; ethnic groups in, 196, 197, 201, 207, 210; Germany's role in, 195–196; insurgency in, 196–199, 202, 205; Karzai as leader of, 193–194, 201–204, 208–209, 210–211; NATO forces in, 203, 204–205; network-centric warfare in, 4; opium industry in, 200–201, 202, 206; police forces in, 197, 201, 203, 207, 209–210; private security contractors in, 195–196, 201; reform efforts in, 196, 203–204; security forces in, 267; social programs in, 204; Soviet occupation of, 191; Taliban in, 192–193, 194, 197–198, 206; U.S. civilian involvement in, 279–280; U.S. military involvement in, 194, 198–201, 203, 206, 207, 210–211, 278; warlords in, 191–192, 194, 201–202, 209
Afghan Militia Forces (AMF), 194
Afghan National Army, 197, 200, 203, 210; leadership problems in, 206–207
Aguinaldo, Emilio, 65–67, 68, 79, 89
Akerman, Amos T., 52
Alejandrino, Casto, 93
Alford, Dale, 235–237, 241
Allawi, Ali, 218

Allawi, Iyad, 228
Allen, Henry T., 70
Al Qaeda, 192, 193, 197
Al Qaeda in Iraq (AQI), 239–240, 241–242, 252–253, 256–257
Al Qaim, Iraq, 235–237
An, Pham Xuan. See Pham Xuan An
ARENA party (El Salvador), 178, 183, 185, 187
Arkansas: during the Civil War, 26–28; Ku Klux Klan in, 47–50; during Reconstruction, 37–38, 47–50
Army of Northern Virginia, 36. See also Civil War
ARVN (South Vietnamese army), 161, 162. See also South Vietnam
Askariya Mosque, bombing of, 237
Australian Communist Party, 111
Azimi, Abdul Salam, 204

Baathists, in post-invasion Iraq, 217, 222–223
Balangiga, Philippines, 80–81
Banks, Nathaniel Prentiss, 29–30, 279
Bao Dai, Emperor, 134
Barnes, Julian, 226
Barno, David W., 198, 199–200, 270, 280
Bataan Death March, 91
Batangas, Philippines, 83–86
Bates, John C., 69
Battle of the Bulge, 158–159
Bell, J. Franklin, 68–69, 83–86
Binh Xuyen, 134, 136
bin Laden, Osama, 192
Birkhimer, William E., 71
Birtle, Andrew J., 18

Black Codes, 35, 42

blacks: and racial tensions during Reconstruction, 35–36, 41–54, 55–56, 60; violence
against, 45

Blandon, Adolfo Onecifero, 181

Blazer, Richard: leadership skills of, 16–17, 30

Blunt, James G., 22

Bohannon, Charles, 101

Bolani, Jawad Al, 250

Bourne, Geoffrey, 129

Bowen, William C. H., 76–77

Bremer, L. Paul: as head of the Coalition
Provisional Authority, 215–219, 226, 229,
254–255, 256, 279

Briggs, Harold, 116–119, 120, 131, 261, 272

Brown, Todd S., 245

Brownlow, John, 25

Brownlow, William G., 34, 44–45, 47

Bryan, William Jennings, 75

Buddhist protests: during the Vietnam War,
144, 148–149, 150

Burchett, Wilfred, 143

Burton, J. B., 250

Bush, George H. W., 181, 186

Bush, George W., 192, 194, 214, 246; administration of, 213, 214, 246. *See also* Iraq

Bushwhackers, 23

Bussey, Cyrus, 27

Butler, Benjamin, 28–29

Calley, William, 160

Cao Dai, 136

Captain General Gerardo Barrios Military
School, 170–171, 174

Carpetbaggers, 43, 60

Carter, Jimmy: and human rights as issue in
El Salvador, 169–170; and the Salvadoran
Insurgency, 173; and the Salvadoran junta,
171

Carter, Samuel P., 25

Casey, George W., 227

Casey, George W., Jr., 227–228, 231, 232, 235,
237, 246, 249, 256, 270, 278

Castro, Fidel, 172

Catterson, Robert F., 47–49

Cedar Creek, Battle of, 38

Central Intelligence Agency (CIA): in
Afghanistan, 193; and the Salvadoran
Insurgency, 174, 183; and the Vietnam War,
147–148

Chaffee, Adna R., 79–80, 81, 272

charisma, 10, 234, 281

Chayes, Sarah, 208

Chester, George, 98

Chiarelli, Peter, 223

Chinese Communists: in Malaya, 109, 115

Chin Peng, 110–111, 112

Christian Democratic Party (El Salvador),
183, 184

Churchill, Winston, 120

CIA. *See* Central Intelligence Agency

Civil Operations and Rural Development
Support (CORDS), 156, 161–162, 166

Civil War: in Arkansas, 26–28; civilian elites
in, 282, 283; counterinsurgencies during,
16–18, 20–22, 23–26, 27–28, 30–32; counterinsurgency leadership during, 16–22,
24–25, 29–32, 262, 280; differing strategies
proposed during, 30; insurgencies during,
15–17, 18, 23, 26–27, 30–32; in Louisiana,
28–30; in Missouri, 18–22; in Tennessee,
24–26. *See also* Union army

Clayton, Powell, 47, 49

Coalition Provisional Authority (CPA), 215–
219, 226, 229, 255

Cohen, Eliot, 224

Colby, William, 161

Collins, J. Lawton, 136

Combined Action Program (Vietnam), 154–
155, 165, 277

Comintern, 90, 109

Communist Party: in Afghanistan, 191; in El
Salvador, 172–173; in Malaya, 109–113, 115,
130; in the Philippines, 90, 91–92, 93, 96–
97, 105; in Vietnam, 134, 136–137, 140. *See
also* Chinese Communists; Ho Chi Minh;
North Vietnam; Viet Cong

*Conduct of Anti-Terrorist Operations in
Malaya, The*, 125–126

Confederacy: insurgent activity on behalf of,
15–17, 18, 23, 26–27, 30, 32; post–Civil War
violence in states of, 33–34. *See also* Civil
War

Connell, Thomas W., 80

Conway, James T., 229

Cosgrove, James H., 57

counterinsurgencies: in Afghanistan, 198–
200, 205–206; changing perception of,
1–2; during the Civil War, 16–18, 21, 23–26,
27–28, 30–32; defined, 303*n*3; field manu-
als for, 125–127, 242–249, 257; against the
Huk Rebellion, 94–95, 99–107; in Iraq, 1–2,
107, 222–225, 227–238, 251–254; lessons of,
304–305*n*12; and the Malayan Emergency,
113–130; against the Philippine Insurrection, 68–86; principles of, 5; during Reconstruction, 46–50; and the Salvadoran
Insurgency, 173–178, 187–189; theories of,

2–4; during the Vietnam War, 138–139, 140–144, 145–148, 154, 161, 163–164. *See also* counterinsurgency leadership

counterinsurgency leadership: adaptive, 243–244, 257, 260–261, 270, 305*n*14; in Afghanistan, 198–200, 205, 210–211; attributes of, 7–13, 24, 30–32, 99, 100–101, 107, 116, 124–125, 131–132, 152–153, 157, 162, 166–167, 220, 223–224, 242, 243, 246–247, 255, 257–258, 259–261, 262, 266–267, 305*n*13, 305*n*15; changes in and selection of, 272–273, 275–276, 329*n*2; and charisma, 10, 234, 281; and civilian elites, 282–285; during the Civil War, 16–22, 24–25, 29–32; and creativity, 9, 260–261; and dedication, 10–11, 259–260; and delegation of authority, 280–281; development of, 265–268; dynamics of, 6; and empathy, 10; experience as factor in, 12, 279; failures of, 19–20, 39–41, 48–50, 58–59, 68, 69, 81–83, 92–93, 114–115, 130–131, 140, 166, 173–174, 184, 189, 199, 209, 224–225, 254–256, 262, 265, 272–273; and flexibility, 8–9, 260–261; foreign influence on development of, 267–268, 272, 275–278; hierarchical nature of, 5–6; and the Huk Rebellion, 99–107; importance of, 3–8, 12–13, 87–88, 126–127, 223–224, 244, 268–274, 285–286, 304*n*11; improving, 259–261; and indigenous elites, 282–285; and initiative, 8, 259–260; and integrity, 11, 259–260; and intelligence collection in Vietnam, 157; in Iraq, 219–221, 222, 224, 226–228, 231, 234–237, 239–242, 246–258; and judgment, 9, 260; and lines of authority, 278–280; and the Malayan Emergency, 113–118, 120–130; Marines in positions of, 219–220; methods of, 281–282; and organization, 11, 260; and personality type as indicator of ability, 262–263, 269–271, 330*n*4; persuasion as aspect of, 277–278; and the Philippine Insurrection, 67–79, 87–88; and political considerations, 271; during Reconstruction, 35, 36–37, 47–50, 52–54, 60–61; recruitment of, 261–265; and the Salvadoran Insurgency, 176–178, 180–182, 184, 187–189; seniority as basis for, 68–69; and shared identity, 12; and sociability, 10; turnover of, 273–274; during the Vietnam War, 141–144, 154, 159, 161–162, 166–167, 265–266. *See also* decentralization of command

Counterinsurgency Leadership Survey, 210, 248, 249, 271–272, 273, 287–301, 324*n*15, 325*n*35

Cowen, Myron, 98

Crane, Conrad, 248
creativity, 9, 260–261
Cristiani, Alfredo, 184–185, 186–187
Crocker, Ryan, 250
Crook, George, 18
Cuba, 65, 172

D'Aubuisson, Roberto, 178, 180, 183, 185, 275
Davidson, Phillip B., 159
Davies, Thomas A., 22
Davis, Jefferson, 26
Davis, Stephen W., 236–237
Day, John H. A., 82–83
decentralization of command, 5–6, 261–272, 280–281; in Afghanistan, 199, 206–207; in Iraq, 219, 280–281; and the Philippine Insurrection, 70–71, 87–88; and the Salvadoran Insurgency, 176; in the Union army, 18, 36; and the Vietnam War, 160, 280–281
dedication, 10–11, 259–260
Dehghanpisheh, Babak, 233
Del Tufo, Vincent, 121, 122
Demby, J. H., 47–48
Democratic Alliance (Philippines), 93
Democratic Party, during Reconstruction, 55–56, 57–58, 59
Dempsey, Martin, 224, 251
Denver, James W., 22
deployment, length of, 274
DePuy, William, 152
DeSaussure, Edward H., 152
Dewey, George, 63, 64
Diamond, Larry, 216
Diem, Ngo Dinh. *See* Ngo Dinh Diem
Draude, Thomas V., 152–153
Duarte, José Napoleón, 183–184, 185, 188, 275
Dulles, Allen, 136
Dulles, John Foster, 136
Duong Van Minh, 145
Durbrow, Elbridge, 137, 138, 166, 277
Duryea, Lyman C., 182, 189
DynCorp, 201

Easter Offensive (Vietnam), 163
Economic Development Corps (EDCOR), 103–104
Eisenhower, Dwight D., 136
elections, 284–285
Elements of Military Art and Science (Halleck), 20
El Salvador: CIA operations in, 174, 188, 275; Cuba and Nicaragua as influences in, 172; death squads in, 178, 180, 181, 184, 185–186, 187; elections in, 183–184, 185, 188, 284–285;

El Salvador (continued)
  human rights abuses in, 170, 176, 181, 186–
  187, 267–268; junta in, 170, 171; leadership
  in, 275; reforms in, 171–172, 184; revolutionary fervor in, 169. *See also* Salvadoran
  Insurgency
Emory, William H., 56–57
empathy, 10
enemy-centric school, 3, 4
Estrada, William, 25
Etherington, Mark, 227
Ewing, Thomas, Jr., 22–23
experience as leadership attribute, 12, 279

Fahim, Muhammad, 196, 201
Fallujah Brigade, 230
Farabundo Martí National Liberation Front
  (FMLN), 172, 185, 186–187
Farragut, David Glasgow, 28
Feith, Douglas, 214, 215, 254
Feleo, Juan, 93
Finn, Robert, 195
First Reconstruction Act, 41
flexibility, 8–9
FMLN. *See* Farabundo Martí National Libera-
  tion Front
Focused District Development program
  (Afghanistan), 207, 210
Ford, Gerald, 163
Forrest, Nathan Bedford, 45–46
Fort Benning, Georgia: Salvadoran officer
  training at, 174–175
Franks, Tommy, 214–215, 220, 254
Freedmen's Bureau, 36, 37–38, 39, 44
Frémont, John C.: as Civil War general, 18–20,
  29, 31
Frist, Bill, 222
Fullerton, J. S., 37
Funston, Frederick, 68–69, 78

Galula, David, 3
Galvin, John R., 175
Gambar, Abboud, 251
García, José Guillermo, 177, 178, 180
Garfield, James A., 58
Garner, Jay, 214, 215, 254
Gates, Robert, 249, 251
Gavrilis, Jim, 221
Gent, Edward, 111, 112, 113
Germany: and Afghanistan, 195
Getty, George W., 40
Grant, Ulysses S., 19, 23–24, 30, 36; leadership
  skills of, 24, 37, 262; as president, 50–51, 52,
  54–55, 56, 61
Griffin, Charles, 40

guerrilla warfare: during the Civil War, 15–18,
  21, 25, 26–27; defined, 303n3; and the Huk
  Rebellion, 91, 93; in Malaya, 109–110, 115–
  116; during the Philippine Insurrection, 67,
  75–76, 83; during Reconstruction, 33–34;
  during the Vietnam War, 137–138, 167. *See
  also* insurgencies
Gurney, Henry, 113–114, 115, 119–120, 122, 131,
  281

Hagee, Michael, 220
Halberstam, David, 144–145
Halleck, Henry W., 30, 36; leadership skills of,
  20–22, 31, 36–37
Hancock, Winfield S., 35
Haqqani network, 197
Harkins, Paul, 142–143, 165, 277
Harrison, Marcus La Rue, 27
Hay, John, 23
Hayes, Rutherford, 59
Haynes, Jeffrey M., 207
"hearts and minds" theory. *See* population-
  centric school
Heintzelman, Samuel P., 39, 40
Hezb-e Islami Gulbuddin, 197
Hickey, Chris, 234
Hindman, Thomas C., 26–27
Hirsh, Michael, 233
Hoa Hao, 136
Hobbes, Thomas, 16
Hobbs, Leland, 98, 99
Ho Chi Minh, 109; as leader of North Viet-
  nam, 134, 139
Hope, Ian, 205
Horn, Bernd, 198
Hue massacre, 161
Hukbo ng Bayan Laban so Hapon. *See* Huk
  Rebellion
Huk Rebellion, 91–97; counterinsurgency
  efforts against, 94–95, 99–107; peasant
  support for, 91, 93–96; U.S. efforts in oppo-
  sition to, 91–92, 98–100, 101, 103, 105, 106,
  107, 276
human rights violations: in El Salvador, 170,
  176, 181, 267–268
Hussein, Saddam, 213

initiative, 8, 259–260
insurgencies: in Afghanistan, 196–199, 202,
  205; civic action as response to, 72–73, 75,
  86–87; during the Civil War, 15–17, 18, 23,
  26–27, 30, 32; defined, 303n3; and the Huk
  Rebellion, 91–97; in Iraq, 226, 229–231,
  237–240, 241–242, 256; leaders of, 3–4;
  and the Malayan Emergency, 111–113, 115,

119, 129; and the Philippine Insurrection, 66–67, 73, 74–75, 78–79, 80–81; during Reconstruction, 44–54; reform as response to, 2–3; Salvadoran, 172–173, 178–180, 183, 185–186; against the Soviets in Afghanistan, 191; during the Vietnam War, 139–140, 141. *See also* counterinsurgencies; Ku Klux Klan; Viet Cong

integrity, 11, 259–260

Iraq: civilian elites in, 282, 283–284; "clear and hold" strategy in, 231–232, 233, 256; Coalition Provisional Authority in, 215–216; counterinsurgency efforts in, 1–2, 107, 222–225, 227–238, 244–245, 251–254; counterinsurgency leadership in, 220–221, 222, 226–228, 231, 234–237, 239–242, 246–258, 266, 278; de-Baathification of, 216–218, 254–255, 282, 283–284; and disbanding of security forces in, 216–218; insurgency in, 226, 229–231, 237–240, 241–242, 256; Iraqi leadership in, 249–251, 257–258; leadership vacuum in, 218–219; network-centric warfare in, 4; Petraeus as commander in, 226–227; planning for postwar occupation of, 214–215; police in, 218, 232; police recruitment in, 240; post-invasion chaos in, 215; sectarian violence in, 232–233, 237–239, 252–253; Shiite militias in, 232–233, 252; training of Iraqi military leaders in, 226–227; troop surge in, 246, 252; U.S. advisers to, 226–227, 251; U.S. civilian involvement in, 279–280; U.S. invasion of, 213–215; U.S. military forces in, 218–258, 278

Iraqi Police Service (IPS), 218; leadership of, 232

Iraqi security forces (ISF), 255–256, 267, 276; in Fallujah, 230, 231; problems inherent in, 228, 231–232

Jaafari, Ibrahim Al, 232, 238
Jabar, Bayan, 232–233
Jackson, Stonewall, 15
Jaffe, Greg, 226
Jalali, Ali, 194–195
Japan: invasion of Malaya, 109–110; invasion of the Philippines, 90–91
Jayhawkers, 19, 21
Jennison, Charles, 19
Jewell, Marshall, 43
Jim Crow laws, 42
Johnson, Andrew: as military governor in Tennessee, 24–25; as president, 35, 36, 41
Johnson, Harold K., 151
Johnson, Lyndon, 149, 151, 156, 166
Johore, Malaya, 117–118

Jomini, Baron Henri, 20
judgment, 9, 260
Jung, Carl, 262
Jurney, William, 241

Kaplan, Robert D., 199
Karnow, Stanley, 144–145
Karzai, Ahmed Wali, 204
Karzai, Hamid: corruption under, 203–204; counterinsurgency efforts of, 197; as leader of Afghanistan, 193–194, 201–204, 207–211, 271, 272, 276
Keane, Jack, 222
Kellogg, William P., 54–55, 56, 59
Kelly, James R., 35
Kennedy, Joseph, 122
Khakrezwal, Muhammad Akrem, 201
Khanh, Nguyen, *See* Nguyen Khanh
Kitfield, James, 239
Komer, Robert, 156, 161
Krulak, Charles, 270
Ku Klux Klan: in Arkansas, 47–50; counterinsurgency against, 35, 47–50, 52–54; federal prosecution of, 51–52; as insurgency, 44–54; in South Carolina, 51, 54; in Tennessee, 47
Ku Klux Klan Act, 52
Kurilla, Erik, 234–235
Ky, Nguyen Cao. *See* Nguyen Cao Ky

Lane, James, 19, 22, 23
Lansdale, Edward: as adviser to South Vietnamese government, 136, 165; and the Huk Rebellion, 98, 99–100, 103, 105, 106, 107
Laos, 141
Lapham, Robert, 92
Laurel, José, 96, 105
Lava, Jesus, 95, 104
leader-centric warfare, 3, 285–286. *See also* counterinsurgency leadership
Lee, Robert E., 30, 36
LeMoyne, James, 187
Liberty Place, Battle of, 56
Lincoln, Abraham, 24, 52, 271, 282; and Frémont, 19, 20; policy of conciliation, 16
Linn, Brian, 71, 72
Lodge, Henry Cabot, 145–147, 166, 277
Loudon County, Virginia, 16–17
Louisiana: during the Civil War, 28–30; during Reconstruction, 54–57
Luzon, Philippines: during the Huk Rebellion, 92–93; during the Philippine Insurrection, 69, 72
Lyon, Nathaniel, 18
Lyttelton, Oliver, 120, 123

MacArthur, Arthur, 74–76, 78, 79
MacArthur, Douglas, 74, 90–91; and the Huk
    Rebellion, 92, 98
MacGillivray, Donald, 129
Madoc, Guy C., 123
Magsaysay, Ramon, 97–99; as counterinsur-
    gency leader, 99–107, 260, 272, 276, 279; as
    Philippine president, 105–106; U.S. support
    for, 103, 105, 107
Mahdi Army, 226, 252, 253
Malaya: Communist Party in, 109–113, 115,
    130; Japanese invasion of, 109–110; jungle
    warfare school in, 126
Malayan Emergency: British response to,
    113–130, 277; and the Communist insur-
    gency, 109–113, 115, 119; and counterinsur-
    gency leadership, 113–118, 120–130; guerrilla
    warfare in, 109–110, 115–116, 119; lessons
    of, 130–132; and resettlement of squatters,
    117–118; treatment of Chinese citizens
    during, 114–115
Maliki, Nouri Al, 238, 250, 253–254
Mallory, Samuel F., 47, 48–49
Malvar, Miguel, 85
Manila, Philippines, 65
Mansoor, Peter, 248, 270
Mao Zedong, 103
Marawi, Suleiman Al, 230
Markley, George F., 81
Mattis, James "Mad Dog," 220–221, 228–229,
    242, 243–244, 245, 261
Mazar-i-Sherif, Afghanistan, 201
McClellan, George B., 20, 29
McEnery, John, 54–55, 56
McFarland, Sean, 239–240
McKinley, William, 64–65, 66, 70
McMaster, H. R., 233, 234, 249, 260
McNamara, Robert, 151
media relations: as aspect of counterinsur-
    gency, 10, 282; and the Huk Rebellion, 103
Mena, Fidel Chávez, 185
Merchant, Livingston, 98
Merrill, Lewis, 52–54, 57, 61
military school in El Salvador, 170–171, 174
militias: in Afghanistan, 194, 197; during
    Reconstruction, 43–44, 46–50; in South
    Vietnam, 138, 154, 164
Miller, Frank, 214
Minh, Duong Van. See Duong Van Minh
Minh, Ho Chi. See Ho Chi Minh
Min Yuen (Malaya), 112, 117, 119, 124, 127, 128
Missouri: during the Civil War, 18–22; during
    Reconstruction, 34–35
Mobbs, Michael, 214
Mohammed, Taj, 194

Monterrosa, Domingo, 177–178, 189
Montgomery, Bacon, 34–35
Montgomery, Bernard, 120–121
Mosby, John Singleton, 17, 32
Muggeridge, Malcolm, 122
Muhamdi, Abdullah, 230
Murray, Arthur, 73
Myers-Briggs Type Indicator (MBTI), 262–
    263. See also personality types
My Lai massacre, 160

Nash, Christopher Columbus, 55
National Peasants' Union (Philippines), 93
NATO: in Afghanistan, 203, 204–205
network-centric warfare, 4
Newhall, F. C., 39–40
New Orleans, Louisiana, 28
Ngo Dinh Diem: background of, 133–134;
    enemies of, 144–145; and Khanh's purging
    of loyalists to, 147; as leader of South
    Vietnam, 134–143, 266, 271; overthrow of,
    145, 275;
Ngo Dinh Nhu, 140–141, 142
Nguyen Cao Ky, 150
Nguyen Chanh Thi, 150
Nguyen Khanh, 146–149
Nguyen Van Thieu, 150–151, 161, 162, 163, 166
Nhu, Ngo Dinh. See Ngo Dinh Nhu
Nicaragua: and aid to Salvadoran Insurgency,
    172, 173; Sandinista government in, 173, 186
Nixon, Richard, 163
Northern Alliance (Afghanistan), 192–193,
    194–195
North Vietnam: Ho Chi Minh as leader of,
    134, 139; military successes of, 149–150, 154,
    163; in support of insurgency, 139–140, 141.
    See also Viet Cong; Vietnam War

Ochoa Perez, Sigifredo, 177, 178, 189
Odierno, Raymond, 248
Office of Reconstruction and Humanitarian
    Assistance in Iraq (ORHA), 214, 215
organizational skills, 11, 260
Osmena, Sergio, 92
Otis, Elwell S., 66, 67–68, 72–74

Pakistan: and the Afghan insurgency, 196–
    197; Al Qaeda in, 193, 197
Pampangans (Philippines), 95
Parvanta, Sultana, 208
Pashtuns, 191–192, 196, 197, 210. See also
    Afghanistan
Patriquin, Travis, 239–240
Patton, George S., 159
Penn, David B., 56

personality types: and command selection, 269–271; and leadership attributes, 262–263, 270–271, 330*n*4

Petraeus, David: background of, 221–222; as counterinsurgency leader in Iraq, 222–223, 226–228, 246–251, 253, 254, 257–258, 261, 270, 276, 280–281; and Iraqi leadership, 249–251

Pham Xuan An, 144

Phan Huy Quat, 149, 150

Philippine Constabulary, 94

Philippine Insurrection: civic action as response to, 72–73, 75, 86–87; and civilian elites, 283, 284; counterinsurgency against, 68–86, 279; counterinsurgency leadership in, 67–79; insurgency in, 66–67, 73, 74–75, 78–79, 80–81; role of Filipino elites in, 67, 68, 86–87; and U.S. support for Filipinos, 71–72, 78, 277

Philippines: and American hostilities with the Spanish, 63–65; Communist Party in, 90, 91–92, 93, 96–97, 105; impact of U.S. involvement in, 90; Japanese invasion of, 90–91. *See also* Huk Rebellion; Philippine Insurrection

Phillips, Rufus, 141

Phoenix program (Vietnam), 156–157

Pickett, A. C., 49

Pickett, George, 15

Pomeroy, William J., 95, 102

population-centric school, 2, 4, 285

principalia (Philippines), 67, 87, 89, 90

Provincial Reconnaissance Unit program (Vietnam), 147–148, 165, 276

Provincial Reconstruction Teams (Afghanistan), 200, 279

Qaeda, Al. *See* Al Qaeda

Quat, Phan Huy. *See* Phan Huy Quat

Quezon, Manuel, 91, 92

Quirino, Elpidio, 96, 98–99, 100, 105, 107, 272, 276

racial tensions: during Reconstruction, 35–36, 41–54, 55–56, 60

Radical Reconstruction. *See* Reconstruction

Radical Republicans: during the Civil War, 19, 22; during Reconstruction, 34, 35–36, 40, 44

Ragheef, Ahmed Taha Hashim Mohammed Abu, 250

Rahman, Tunku Abdul, 129–130, 132

Reagan, Ronald, 172; and the Salvadoran Insurgency, 174, 179, 183

Reconstruction: in Arkansas, 37–38; civilian

elites during, 284; counterinsurgency leadership during, 35, 36–37, 47–50, 52–54, 60–61; and exclusion of Southern elites from political activity, 42–43, 60–61, 283; federal legislation during, 41; Ku Klux Klan as insurgency during, 44–54; in Louisiana, 54–59; in Missouri, 34–35; in Tennessee, 33–34; in Texas, 38–41; violence in response to, 33–34, 40–41

Recto, Claro, 105

Rector, Henry M., 26

Republican Party: during Reconstruction, 35–36, 44, 59, 60–61. *See also* Radical Republicans

Republican Youth (South Vietnam), 140–141, 145, 164

Revolutionary Development Cadre program, 155

Ricks, Tom, 219

Ritchie, Neil, 115, 280

Robertson, Brian, 121

Robinson, Charles, 22

Romero, Carlos Humberto, 170

Roosevelt, Franklin, 90

Roosevelt, Theodore, 65

Rosa, John H., 49

Roxas, Manuel, 93, 94, 96, 98

Rumsfeld, Donald, 213, 226, 229

Sabawi, Latif Mahal Hamoud, 230

Sadr, Muqtada Al, 226, 246, 253, 285

Salvadoran Insurgency, 172–173, 178–180, 183, 185–186; counterinsurgency against, 173–178, 179, 187–189; and counterinsurgency leadership, 176–178, 180–182, 184, 187–189, 266; and U.S. involvement in counterinsurgency effort, 174–178, 179, 187–188, 189, 275–276. *See also* El Salvador

Samar, Philippines, 73, 80–82

Sanchez, Ricardo, 219, 227, 229, 254, 281

San Salvador, El Salvador: insurgent attacks in, 185–186

Sattar Abu Risha, Abdul, 240

Scalawags, 43, 60

Schmitt, Gary, 214

Schofield, John M., 22, 42

Scott, Winfield, 20, 29

Sepp, Kalev, 227–228, 231

September 11, 2001, attacks, 192. *See also* Afghanistan

shared identity, 12

Sharkey, Laurence, 111

Sheehan, Neil, 144–145

Sheridan, Philip H., 33, 38–41, 57–59, 61, 262

Sherman, John, 24

Sherman, William T., 23–24, 33, 45; leadership
    skills of, 24, 262
Shiloh, Battle of, 23
Shinwari, Fazel Hady, 204
Shirzai, Gul Agha, 201
Singletary, Otis A., 43
Slim, William, 121
Slocombe, Walter, 217
Small Wars Manual (U.S. Marine Corps), 3,
    126
Smith, Charles H., 37–38, 61
Smith, Edmund Kirby, 38
Smith, Jacob "Hell Roaring Jake," 81–82
"Soccer War," 175
sociability, 10
South Carolina, Ku Klux Klan in, 51, 52
South Vietnam: Buddhist protests against
    government of, 144, 148–149, 150; defeat of,
    163–164; Diem as leader of, 134–143, 145,
    275; Khanh as leader of, 146–149; leader-
    ship challenges in, 164–165, 265–266, 284;
    military setbacks suffered by, 149–150; mili-
    tias of, 138, 164; Thieu as leader of, 150–151,
    161, 162, 163, 166. *See also* Vietnam War
South Vietnamese Civil Guard, 138, 139, 164
South Vietnamese Self-Defense Corps, 138,
    139
Soviet Union: occupation of Afghanistan, 191.
    See also Communist Party
Spain: as U.S. adversary in the Philippines,
    63–64
Spanish-American War, 64–65
Special Branch, 113, 124, 132
Special Forces. *See* U.S. Army Special Forces
Stanton, Edwin M., 22, 36
state militias during Reconstruction, 43–44,
    46–50
Steele, James J., 181–182
Stokes, William B., 25
Sugrue, Dennis, 200

Taft, William Howard, 79
Tajiks, 196, 197, 210. *See also* Afghanistan
Taliban: in Afghanistan, 192–193, 194; as
    insurgency after September 11, 197–198,
    205, 206
Tarbell, John, 37
Taruc, Luis, 91, 93, 104–105
Taruc, Peregrino, 104–105
Templer, Gerald: background of, 121–122, 129;
    as counterinsurgency leader in Malayan
    Emergency, 122–129, 131–132, 260, 261, 265,
    272, 279, 280
Tennessee: during the Civil War, 24–26; Ku

Klux Klan in, 47; during Reconstruction,
    33–34, 47
terrorism, defined, 303*n*3. *See also* insurgen-
    cies
Terry, Alfred Howe, 52
Tet Offensive, 157–158
Texas: during Reconstruction, 38–41
Thayer, Thomas, 162
Thi, Nguyen Chanh. *See* Nguyen Chanh Thi
Thieu, Nguyen Van. *See* Nguyen Van Thieu
Throckmorton, James W., 39, 40
Tilden, Samuel J., 59
Tinio, Manolo, 89–90
Tinio, Manuel, 89
Toolan, John A., 229, 230
Truman, Harry, 107
Tunku Abdul Rahman, 129–130, 132
Turner, Jeremy, 198

Union army: and Confederate insurgents,
    15–17, 18, 23, 26–27, 30–32; as government
    administrators, 17; leadership of, 18–19. *See
    also* Civil War
United States: and Afghanistan, 194, 198–201,
    203, 206, 207, 210–211; and the Huk Rebel-
    lion, 91–92, 98–100, 101, 103, 105, 106, 107;
    and Iraq, 213–258; and the Philippines, 71–
    72, 78, 90; and the Salvadoran Insurgency,
    174–178, 179, 187–188, 189; and the Vietnam
    War, 136–138, 142–143, 145–149, 151–156,
    165–167. *See also* Civil War
Upham, D. P., 47, 49
U.S. Agency for International Development,
    155–156
U.S. Armed Forces Far East (USAFFE), 91–92,
    98
U.S. Army: as adaptive organization, 260–261,
    270; personality types in, 269. *See also*
    Union army
*U.S. Army / Marine Corps Counterinsurgency
    Field Manual*, 2, 125–126, 305*n*14
U.S. Army Special Forces: in Afghanistan,
    193, 199, 266; in El Salvador, 176; in Iraq,
    221, 266
U.S. Marine Corps: as leaders in Iraq, 219–
    220, 266
U.S. Volunteers, 70

Valeriano, Napoleon, 101
Vides Casanova, Carlos Eugenio, 180–181,
    188, 272
Viet Cong, 139, 140–142, 143–144, 146, 147,
    156–158. *See also* Ho Chi Minh; North
    Vietnam

Vietnam: French colonization of, 133–134; leaders of, 133–134. *See also* North Vietnam; South Vietnam; Vietnam War

Vietnam War, 149–150; abuse of civilian population in, 160–161; CIA's involvement in, 147–148; counterinsurgency efforts in, 138–139, 140–144, 145–148, 154, 276, 280–281; counterinsurgency leadership in, 141–144, 154, 159, 161–162; insurgency in, 139–140, 141; U.S. involvement in, 136–138, 142–143, 145–149, 151–156, 165–167, 276, 277–278; U.S. withdrawal from, 163–164, 278; Viet Cong in, 139, 140. *See also* North Vietnam; South Vietnam

Waghelstein, John, 177, 178
Walker, Arthur, 111
Walker, William, 170
Waller, Littleton W. T., 82–83

Wardak, Abdul Rahim, 201, 202–203, 206, 210
Wass de Czege, Huba, 225
Watson, J. L., 50
Wells, Bryan, 116
Wells, G. Wiley, 51
West, Bing, 228
Westmoreland, William, 148–149, 151–153, 155, 158, 162, 280
Wheaton, Loyd, 75
Wheeler, Earle, 151
White League, 55–56, 57, 59
Williams, George H., 54
Williams, Samuel "Hanging Sam," 137–138, 139, 165
Wolff, Terry, 252
Wright, Horatio, 39, 40

Yon, Michael, 234
Young, Samuel B. M., 69

CPSIA information can be obtained
at www.ICGtesting.com
Printed in the USA
JSHW020456270623
43831JS00004B/198